ICSA Study Text

International Finance and Administration Qualifications

International Finance and Administration

ICSA Study Text

International Finance and Administration Qualifications

International Finance and Administration

Carla Channing and Colin Solomon

icsa

The Governance Institute

First published 2015
Published by ICSA Publishing Ltd
Saffron House
6–10 Kirby Street
London EC1N 8TS

Typeset by Paul Barrett Book Production, Cambridge
Printed in Great Britain by Lightning Source, Milton Keynes, Buckinghamshire

British Cataloguing in Publication Data
A catalogue record for this book is available from the British Library.

ISBN 9781 86072 737 5

Contents

How to use this study text

ICSA study texts, developed to support ICSA's Level 4 International Finance and Administration qualifications, follow a standard format and include a range of navigational, self-testing and illustrative features to help you get the most out of the support materials.

Each text is divided into three main sections:

- introductory material
- the text itself
- additional reference information.

The sections below show you how to find your way around the text and make the most of its features.

Introductory material

The introductory section of each text includes a full contents list and the aims and learning outcomes for the modules in question.

Where relevant, the introductory section will also include a list of acronyms and abbreviations or a list of legal cases for reference.

The text itself

Each **part** opens with a list of the chapters to follow, an overview of what will be covered and learning outcomes for the part.

Every **chapter** opens with a list of the topics covered and an introduction specific to that chapter. Chapters are structured to allow students to break the content down into manageable sections for study. Each chapter ends with a summary of key content to reinforce understanding.

Features

The text is enhanced by a range of illustrative and self-testing features to assist understanding and to help you prepare for the examination. Each feature is presented in a standard format, so that you will become familiar with how to use them in your study. These features are identified by a series of icons as shown below. The texts also include tables, figures and other illustrations as relevant.

Reference material

The text ends with a range of additional guidance and reference material, including a glossary of key terms, a directory of web resources and a comprehensive index.

Stop and think

Test yourself

Worked examples

Making it work

Case law

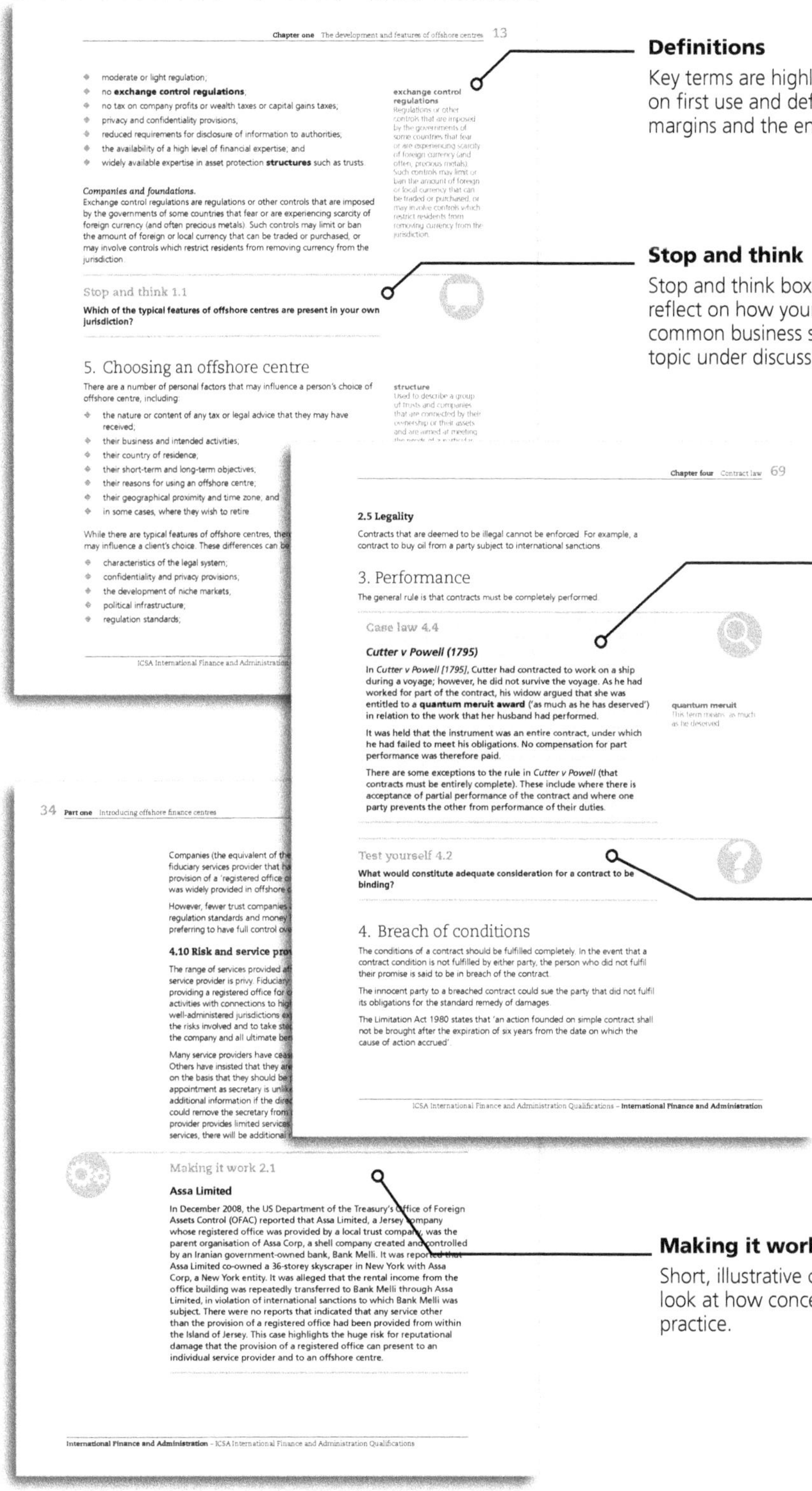
Chapter one The development and features of offshore centres 13

- moderate or light regulation;
- no **exchange control regulations**;
- no tax on company profits or wealth taxes or capital gains taxes;
- privacy and confidentiality provisions;
- reduced requirements for disclosure of information to authorities;
- the availability of a high level of financial expertise; and
- widely available expertise in asset protection **structures** such as trusts.

Companies and foundations.
Exchange control regulations are regulations or other controls that are imposed by the governments of some countries that fear or are experiencing scarcity of foreign currency (and often precious metals). Such controls may limit or ban the amount of foreign or local currency that can be traded or purchased, or may involve controls which restrict residents from removing currency from the jurisdiction.

Stop and think 1.1

Which of the typical features of offshore centres are present in your own jurisdiction?

5. Choosing an offshore centre

There are a number of personal factors that may influence a person's choice of offshore centre, including:

- the nature or content of any tax or legal advice that they may have received;
- their business and intended activities;
- their country of residence;
- their short-term and long-term objectives;
- their reasons for using an offshore centre;
- their geographical proximity and time zone; and
- in some cases, where they wish to retire

Chapter four Contract law 69

2.5 Legality

Contracts that are deemed to be illegal cannot be enforced. For example, a contract to buy oil from a party subject to international sanctions.

3. Performance

The general rule is that contracts must be completely performed.

Case law 4.4

Cutter v Powell (1795)

In *Cutter v Powell [1795]*, Cutter had contracted to work on a ship during a voyage; however, he did not survive the voyage. As he had worked for part of the contract, his widow argued that she was entitled to a **quantum meruit award** ('as much as he has deserved') in relation to the work that her husband had performed.

It was held that the instrument was an entire contract, under which he had failed to meet his obligations. No compensation for part performance was therefore paid.

There are some exceptions to the rule in *Cutter v Powell* (that contracts must be entirely complete). These include where there is acceptance of partial performance of the contract and where one party prevents the other from performance of their duties.

Test yourself 4.2

What would constitute adequate consideration for a contract to be binding?

4. Breach of conditions

The conditions of a contract should be fulfilled completely. In the event that a contract condition is not fulfilled by either party, the person who did not fulfil their promise is said to be in breach of the contract.

The innocent party to a breached contract could sue the party that did not fulfil its obligations for the standard remedy of damages.

The Limitation Act 1980 states that 'an action founded on simple contract shall not be brought after the expiration of six years from the date on which the cause of action accrued'.

ICSA International Finance and Administration Qualifications – **International Finance and Administration**

Making it work 2.1

Assa Limited

In December 2008, the US Department of the Treasury's Office of Foreign Assets Control (OFAC) reported that Assa Limited, a Jersey company whose registered office was provided by a local trust company, was the parent organisation of Assa Corp, a shell company created and controlled by an Iranian government-owned bank, Bank Melli. It was reported that Assa Limited co-owned a 36-storey skyscraper in New York with Assa Corp, a New York entity. It was alleged that the rental income from the office building was repeatedly transferred to Bank Melli through Assa Limited, in violation of international sanctions to which Bank Melli was subject. There were no reports that indicated that any service other than the provision of a registered office had been provided from within the Island of Jersey. This case highlights the huge risk for reputational damage that the provision of a registered office can present to an individual service provider and to an offshore centre.

Definitions

Key terms are highlighted in bold on first use and defined in the page margins and the end of book glossary.

Stop and think

Stop and think boxes encourage you to reflect on how your own experiences or common business scenarios relate to the topic under discussion.

Case law

Case law presents short, illustrative case studies which look at how concepts are applied in practice.

Test yourself

Short, revision-style questions to help you re-cap on key information and core concepts.

Making it work

Short, illustrative case examples which look at how concepts are applied in practice.

The International Finance and Administration modules

Aims

These modules provide an introduction to fundamental topics and issues in offshore finance centres. Subjects covered include the types of products and services offered, the regulation and supervision of offshore financial services providers and anti-money laundering regulations.

Learning outcomes

On successful completion of these modules, you will:

- understand key features of the offshore financial services industry;
- know about products and services offered by offshore financial services providers;
- understand how trust and company services are administered;
- understand the impact of English law in offshore jurisdictions;
- know about statute law and statutory interpretation;
- understand case law and the doctrine of binding precedent;
- understand principles of contract law relating to offshore jurisdictions;
- understand the principles of taxation as applied to offshore jurisdictions;
- understand how to prevent harmful tax practices;
- understand banking services provided by offshore centres;
- know about bank accounts, payment methods and payment systems;
- understand the regulation and supervision of offshore banks;
- understand how the offshore financial services sector is regulated;
- know about data protection issues, insider dealing and market abuse;
- understand money laundering and measures used to prevent it;
- know about trust law;
- understand how to create a valid trust;
- know about the parties to a trust; and
- understand the features of different types of trust available in offshore centres.

- understand the main features of companies and how they are financed;
- know the steps involved in incorporating a company and post incorporation procedures;
- understand the roles, powers and duties of members, directors, the secretary and the auditor of a company;
- understand the requirements surrounding meetings and resolutions of directors and stakeholders;
- know about the ways in which a company is wound up;
- know the range of entities available in offshore centres;
- understand the principles of trust and company administration; and
- understand the role of the trust and company administrator.

Past papers and practice questions

Students can access sample papers for these modules by logging into the MyICSA area of www.icsa.org.uk.

Acronyms and abbreviations

AGM	annual general meeting
AIFM	alternative investment fund manager
AIFMD	Alternative Investment Fund Managers Directive
AIM	Alternative Investment Market
AML	anti-money laundering
APACS	Association for Payment Clearing Services
ATE	After The Event (insurance)
ATED	annual tax on enveloped dwellings
ATM	automated teller machine
Bacs	Bankers' Automated Clearing Services
BCBS	Basel Committee on Banking Supervision
BIC	Bank Identification Code
BIS	Department of Business, Innovation and Skills
CDD	customer due diligence
CFT	combating finance for terrorism
CGT	capital gains tax
CHAPS	Clearing House Automated Payment System
CHF	Swiss francs
CRS	Common Reporting Standard
DOTAS	Disclosure of Tax Avoidance Schemes
DPA	Data Protection Act 1998
EC	European Council
EDD	enhanced due diligence
ESMA	European Union Securities and Markets Authority
EU	European Union
EUSTD	European Union Savings Tax Directive (also referred to as EUSD)
FATCA	Foreign Account Tax Compliance Act
FATF	Financial Action Task Force
FCA	Financial Conduct Authority
FEC	forward exchange contract
FIU	Financial Intelligence Unit
FSA	Financial Services Authority
FSMA	Financial Services and Markets Act 2000
FX	foreign exchange (also referred to as forex)
G10	Group of Ten
G7	Group of Seven

GAAR	General Anti-Avoidance Rule
GBP	British pounds
GDPR	General Data Protection Regulation of the EU
GFCI	Global Financial Centres Index
GIFCS	Group of International Finance Centre Supervisors
GIICS	Group of International Insurance Centre Supervisors
HMRC	HM Revenue and Customs
HNWI	high net worth individual
IAIS	International Association of Insurance Supervisors
IBAN	International bank account number
ICAEW	Institute of Chartered Accountants in England and Wales
ICC	Incorporated Cell Company
ICSA	Institute of Chartered Secretaries and Administrators
IHT	inheritance tax
ILP	incorporated limited partnership
IMF	International Monetary Fund
IOM	Isle of Man
IOSCO	International Organization of Securities Commissions
IRS	Internal Revenue Service
ISA	Individual Savings Account
ISO	International Organization for Standardization
JMLSG	Joint Money Laundering Steering Group
KYC	know your customer
LDF	Liechtenstein Disclosure Facility
LLP	limited liability partnership
LP	limited partnership
LSE	London Stock Exchange
MLRO	Money Laundering Reporting Officer
MMOU	Multilateral Memorandum of Understanding
NASDAQ	National Association of Securities Dealers Automated Quotations
NCCT	Non-cooperating countries and territories
OECD	Organisation for Economic Co-operation and Development
OFAC	Office of Foreign Assets Control
OGIS	Offshore Group of Insurance Supervisors
PCC	protected cell company
PEP	politically exposed person
PET	Potentially Exempt Transfer
PIN	personal identification number
plc	public limited company
PoCA	Proceeds of Crime Act 2002
PRA	Prudential Regulation Authority
PTC	private trust company
RBC	remittance basis charge
RDR	Retail Distribution Review
RPTs	Settlor reserved powers trusts
RTGS	real time, gross settlement
SAR	suspicious activity report
SEPA	Single European Payments Area

SIB	Securities and Investments Board
SLP	Separate limited partnership
SOCA	Serious Organised Crime Agency
SPC	Segregated Portfolio Company
SPV	special purpose vehicle
STAR	Special Trusts (Alternative Regime) Law 1997
STRs	suspicious transaction reports
SWIFT	Society for Worldwide Interbank Financial Telecommunication
SYSC	Senior Management Systems and Controls Sourcebook
TIEA	Tax Information Exchange Agreement
UKLA	UK Listing Authority
UNODC	United Nations Office on Drugs and Crime
VAT	value added tax
VISR	Virgin Islands Shipping Registry
VISTA	Virgin Islands Special Trusts Act 2004

Part one

Chapter 1
The development and features of offshore centres

Chapter 2
Offshore financial services

Introducing offshore finance centres

After studying this part, students will gain an understanding of the meaning of 'offshore' and will be able to identify some of the main uses and users of **offshore centres**. Students will be able to identify factors that may influence an investor's choice of **jurisdiction** and services provider when choosing to use an offshore centre. This part discusses factors such as legal systems, the standard of regulation, the reputation, the confidentiality (or in some cases secrecy) provisions, the political environment and the taxation environment.

Students will gain an understanding of key terms used within the offshore financial services industry and of the various products and services available from within offshore centres (including **trust** company business products and services, insurance services, tax compliance and tax planning services, retail fund management and portfolio management).

Learning outcomes

At the end of this part, you will:

1. understand key features of the offshore financial services industry;
2. know about products and services offered by offshore financial services providers; and
3. understand how trust and company services are administered.

Chapter one

The development and features of offshore centres

List of topics

1. The development of the offshore industry
2. The users and uses of offshore centres
3. Various offshore centres
4. Typical features of offshore centres
5. Choosing an offshore centre
6. Choosing an offshore service provider

Introduction

This chapter explains what is meant by the terms 'offshore centre', 'low tax jurisdiction' and 'tax haven'. It outlines the typical features of an offshore centre, discusses some of the main users and uses of offshore centres, and identifies various offshore centres. The chapter outlines some of the many considerations that may influence a **person's** choice of offshore centre and concludes by discussing some characteristics that many clients may seek when choosing an offshore services provider.

1. The development of the offshore industry

1.1 What is an offshore financial centre?

It is difficult to provide an exact definition for 'offshore financial centre' (referred to as '**offshore centre**' for the remainder of this text). An offshore centre could be described as a **jurisdiction** which provides much of its financial services business to non-residents and which seeks to create a competitive advantage through its laws. However, this could describe many, if not all, of the financial centres in the world, including London.

offshore centre
A jurisdiction which seeks to create a competitive advantage through its laws and which provides financial services primarily to non-residents.

jurisdiction
A territory over which authority is exercised by laws which are under the control of a system of courts different to that of its neighbouring areas.

Offshore centres are frequently referred to as 'tax havens', or are perceived to be locations that facilitate money laundering and illegal tax evasion, notwithstanding that most offshore centres do not have statutory banking secrecy laws and most have adopted modern anti-money laundering frameworks that implement the FATF Recommendation and tax information exchange laws and protocols such as **FATCA** and **CRS** that provide foreign countries with tax information which in turn facilitates the identification of tax evasion and the non-disclosure of financial assets.

FATCA
The US standard for the reciprocal exchange of tax information relating to non-resident customers.

CRS
The international standard for the reciprocal exchange of tax information relating to non-resident customers.

The term 'tax haven' is used loosely to describe offshore centres that offer specific zero tax or low tax advantages to non-residents which can be used to substantially mitigate the effects of domestic tax. Reputable offshore centres take great care to ensure that their financial services are regulated to international standards and provide services only for the legitimate avoidance of tax in relation to international finance and trade deals, and personal wealth management. Offshore zero-tax structures can also support corporate financial planning and risk management and provide some of the complex cross-border SPVs necessary for global trade financing, large-scale mergers and acquisitions, commercial joint ventures, aircraft and shipping finance.

In 2000, the OECD identified a number of jurisdictions as tax havens of which 31 jurisdictions made formal commitments to implement the OECD's standards of transparency and exchange of information by 2002.

Seven jurisdictions did not make such commitments and were named as uncooperative in 2002. However, by 2009, the last three remaining jurisdictions on the list (Andorra, the Principality of Liechtenstein and the Principality of Monaco) were removed in the light of their commitments to implement the OECD standards of transparency and effective exchange of information and the timetable they set for the implementation. As a result, no jurisdiction is currently listed as an uncooperative tax haven by the OECD.

In 2017, the EU issued a list of 17 non-cooperative jurisdictions for tax purposes, which was reduced and amended by March 2018 to nine jurisdictions, including American Samoa, Bahamas, Guam, Namibia, Palau, Samoa, Saint Kitts and Nevis, Trinidad and Tobago and the US Virgin Islands.

While there remains a negative political view in some jurisdictions that the tax arbitrage offered by offshore centres undermines domestic tax revenues and thus drains away resources from both developed and developing countries, the US and UK governments also tacitly recognise that the reputable offshore centres continue to play a legitimate and important role in facilitating international finance and commerce.

It should also be recognised that while offshore centres have tended to exploit a legacy of deficient onshore tax laws, it is only in recent years that governments are acknowledging and seeking to gradually rectify the tax 'loopholes' that have encouraged the use of offshore centres. International initiatives such as automatic tax information exchange using the US Foreign Account Tax Compliance Act (FATCA) and the Common Reporting Standard (CRS) are major achievements in fiscal transparency and will represent key developments in addressing illegal tax evasion.

There remains a keen political and public interest in the activities of offshore financial centres that are still perceived to operate as harmful tax havens. Recent high profile publicity around the Panama Papers and Paradise Papers highlight the reputational vulnerability of the offshore financial centres, bearing in mind that in each case, there were no material findings of criminality among the customers of the offshore law firms who had their confidential financial affairs illegally exposed to the public by investigative journalists.

Whereas an onshore jurisdiction will typically service only domestic financial services clients and a small proportion of non-residents, an offshore centre will focus on providing financial services to non-residents and service only a small proportion of domestic financial services clients (if any), Some onshore jurisdictions have created specialist rules or dedicated International Financial Centres (IFC) that are able to offer a number of the benefits of an offshore centre to non-residents. These are sometimes referred to as 'onshore offshore' financial centres.

The term 'onshore offshore' jurisdiction is used to describe jurisdictions such as the UK, Ireland, Canada, Dubai and the Netherlands. These are major onshore jurisdictions that can be used by offshore residents for 'offshore' purposes due to the preferential fiscal treatment that is applied to non-residents (e.g. they are exempt from **direct taxes**).

direct taxes
Taxes on income (e.g. income tax).

An International Monetary Fund (IMF) background paper on offshore financial centres, prepared in June 2000 (while this is now 18 years ago the criteria remain valid), explains that offshore centres are usually jurisdictions that:

- have relatively large numbers of financial institutions engaged primarily in business with non-residents;
- have financial systems with external assets and liabilities out of proportion to domestic financial intermediation designed to finance domestic economies; and
- provide some or all services such as low or zero taxation, moderate or light regulation, banking secrecy or anonymity.

Since the IMF paper was written, the regulations in many offshore centres have become comparable to that found in onshore jurisdictions, and the banking secrecy and anonymity provisions exist only for legitimate business. Nevertheless, the above descriptions remain useful when describing an offshore centre.

1.2 The development of offshore industries

There are various economic influences that allow offshore centres to continue to develop.

Onshore centres have, over the years, introduced anti-avoidance measures to make it more difficult for their residents to benefit from lower taxes by moving their finances offshore. The most important of these measures is the exchange of tax information with the USA under FATCA and between OECD countries under the CRS initiative. A number of offshore centres are now tax transparent by participating in both FATCA and CRS, but still suffer from a negative perception of facilitating illegal tax evasion, so have needed to respond by continuously adapting, becoming more diverse and seeking new opportunities in product and services innovations in order to remain competitive.

common law
A system of law under which the judges are guided by previous decisions of the courts under the doctrine of judicial precedent.

foundation
A type of legal entity which does not have a share capital or shareholders, and which has a separate legal personality.

Offshore centres continue to be innovative in terms of the products that they offer and their legal environments. For example, in the last few years, **common law** offshore centres have introduced legislation allowing for the formation of **foundations**. These appeal to clients from civil law countries where the concept of trusts is not widely recognised.

It has become far easier for clients to switch their business dealings between jurisdictions as the global financial market has become more accessible. Offshore centres have adapted in order to remain competitive with each other. For example, laws have been passed that enable companies to change easily the country under whose laws they are registered while maintaining the same legal identity (a process known as 'redomiciliation'). Meanwhile, offshore product and service offerings continues to expand.

Many jurisdictions are seeking to distance themselves from being described as offshore as the term has become associated with negative stereotypes. Indeed the States of Jersey are so committed to maintaining the most positive profile for the Island's finance industry as possible that it commits (in 2018) over £1 million pounds to the Island's financial industry promotion body, Jersey Finance.

Instead, many offshore jurisdictions are seeking to position themselves as 'international finance centres'. This is a description in line with London and other major global financial centres, which are seen to be acceptable, cooperative, reputable and transparent, and places to do business.

The international community has recognised that not all offshore centres are the same. International organisations such as Financial Action Task Force (FATF) focus on whether individual centres comply or cooperate with the implementation of international standards, rather than simply focusing on whether a jurisdiction is considered to be 'onshore' or 'offshore'. Other terms that are used to describe offshore centres include 'low tax jurisdictions' and 'tax havens'.

1.3 Low tax jurisdictions

Low tax jurisdictions are those such as the Isle of Man, Jersey or Guernsey. These have direct taxes (e.g. taxes on income) set at a rate that, compared with certain onshore jurisdictions, may be considered to be relatively low. Many low tax jurisdictions are said to be 'tax havens' insofar as non-residents are concerned, as these individuals are usually exempt from direct taxes that are applicable to individuals who are resident.

1.4 Tax havens

The term 'tax havens' is sometimes used to negatively describe offshore centres where there are low or no direct taxes. Tax havens are also referred to as 'no-tax jurisdictions' or 'zero tax jurisdictions'.

Offshore centres where there are no direct taxes are sometimes referred to as 'pure tax havens' (e.g. Anguilla or the Bahamas). In tax havens, it is usual to find that **indirect taxes** (i.e. those that are on expenditure) are higher in order to create sufficient revenue for the local government.

indirect taxes
Taxes on expenditure (e.g. VAT).

In 1998, the Organisation for Economic Co-operation and Development (OECD) used the term 'tax haven' in its report entitled 'Harmful Tax Competition: An Emerging Global Issue'.

The report used a number of factors to decide whether a jurisdiction was a 'tax haven'. The key criteria included:

- no or only nominal taxes;
- lack of effective exchange of information;
- lack of transparency; and
- no substantial activity.

In 2000, the OECD published a list of more than 40 jurisdictions that met the criteria for tax havens set out in the 1998 report. In mid-2002, it published a list of 'uncooperative tax havens' that did not make commitments to transparency and exchange of information.

The term 'tax haven' has taken on an increasingly negative meaning. It conjures images of dishonest individuals or companies hiding their money and illegally evading a tax **liability** in their own jurisdiction. Offshore centres that are described as tax havens attract significant undesirable attention from the international community and the media. Therefore, offshore centres have increasingly sought to avoid being referred to as tax havens and many have taken steps to be tax transparent, develop more sophisticated anti-money laundering frameworks in line with the evolving FATF Recommendations and be cooperative in the fight against the illegal abuse of their lower tax regimes. In May 2009, the last three jurisdictions on the OECD's list of uncooperative tax havens (Andorra, Liechtenstein and Monaco) were removed in light of their commitments to implement the OECD standards. The OECD's work on transparency and effective exchange of information is discussed further later in the text.

liability
A legal obligation to another person.

In 2017/18 the EU have created new lists of uncooperative jurisdictions and you should familiarise yourself with these. You should also note the impact of the unauthorised hack on the law firm Mossack Fonseca and the so-called Paradise Papers, the subject of major reportage in 2018.

Test yourself 1.1

What is an offshore centre?

2. The users and uses of offshore centres

Many users of offshore centres are high net worth individuals (HNWIs), global corporates and sovereign funds as well as wealthy families who now maintain family offices for the management of their wealth. The UK's Financial Services and Markets Act 2000 (Financial Promotion) Order 2005 describes an HNWI as 'someone who had an annual income to the value of £100,000 or more during the financial year or net **assets** of £250,000 or more (excluding primary residence)'. In offshore centres, however, the term is generally used more to describe wealthy individuals who are usually advised by professional intermediaries such as tax advisers, accountants or lawyers. Different offshore **service providers** have their own definition of HNWIs.

asset
Something that is owned or from which a benefit can arise and having an economic value.

service provider
Organisations or individuals who provide financial services business offshore may simply be referred to as service providers.

The users of offshore centres include charities, entrepreneurs, individuals, multinational corporations, small businesses and trading companies. Anyone who wishes to secure an advantage that would not be available in their own jurisdiction – for example, protection from taxes, inheritance planning for wealthy families or to secure certainty by limiting the effects of future taxation policies of their governments – could seek to use an offshore centre.

The reasons for using offshore centres mainly stem from their features (e.g. low taxation) or from the products and services that are available offshore (trusts, companies, including PCC and ICC structures, **partnerships**, foundations, etc.). These are discussed later in this text.

partnership
An agreement whereby two or more people run a business and share any profit and loss that they make.

The uses of offshore centres include but are not restricted to the following:

- captive insurance companies;
- holding and investment companies and other SPVs;
- managing pension funds for employees of multinational corporations;
- offshore investment funds;
- private client wealth structuring;
- protection of personal wealth and estates;
- ship and aircraft registration;
- registration of intellectual property rights; and
- tax-efficient structuring of international trade and investment.

Tax neutrality or mitigation is a common reason for individuals choosing to use offshore centres. Factors such as residence (where a person lives) and domicile (which is distinct from a person's residence and is where they truly feel at 'home') are often relevant in deciding whether or not individuals will be taxed in their country of tax residence and determine the basis of taxation to which an individual is subject.

There are often opportunities for individuals who are domiciled in a different jurisdiction to the one where they reside to use offshore centres to minimise a tax liability. For example, they may only be taxed in their country of residence on funds that they bring into that country and not on their 'worldwide' income.

Additionally, taxes in offshore centres often do not apply to non-residents. A full discussion on tax planning concepts such as residence and domicile are discussed further later in this text.

3. Various offshore centres

There are many offshore centres and international finance centres.

3.1 The Crown Dependencies

The Crown Dependencies consist of the Bailiwick of Guernsey (which includes Alderney, with its own company legislation, and Sark), the Bailiwick of Jersey and the Isle of Man. They are self-governing jurisdictions that are not part of the UK and are not represented in the UK Parliament. They are legislatively independent from the UK and have autonomy in relation to their domestic affairs, including taxation and their own local currencies (which are locked to the value of the British Pound).

The UK government is responsible for the international affairs and defence of the Crown Dependencies, although it will not act on behalf of the Crown Dependencies internationally or legislate for them without prior consultation. While they are separate from the UK, the Crown Dependencies have a close relationship with the UK and this has been a significant attraction for business. Much of the business conducted in the Crown Dependencies is UK-related.

The Crown Dependencies have their own legal systems. These are a mixture of customary law and statute law. They make their own legislation; however, primary legislation passed requires royal assent from the Privy Council. This process ensures that there is no conflict with international obligations. While English law does not apply, the courts draw heavily on English common law in some areas. The statutory provisions are often modelled on English Acts of Parliament and where this is the case, English cases are frequently referenced by their courts. In some areas, the Crown Dependencies have adopted laws to meet their own special circumstances. The Judicial Committee of the Privy Council is the court of final appeal for the Crown Dependencies.

The Crown Dependencies wish to be considered as stable and well-regulated jurisdictions that are transparent and do not have statutory banking secrecy provisions.

Under the terms of Protocol 3 of the UK's 1972 Treaty of Accession to the European Communities – now the European Union (EU) – the Crown Dependencies have a limited relationship with the EU. This allows for free movement of goods and trade within EU member states. The Crown Dependencies are not part of the EU and its directives do not apply. The Crown Dependencies are not required to harmonise their **fiscal policies** and legislative framework with those of EU member states, although the Isle of Man has chosen to become a part of the EU's value added tax (VAT) regime.

fiscal policies
Policies that relate to the public revenues (i.e. income from taxation).

The consequences of Great Britain leaving the EU in March 2019 cannot yet be accurately predicted in terms of the impact on the three Crown Dependencies offshore finance industries.

The British Crown Dependencies are not empowered to sign or ratify international conventions on their own behalf. However, the UK may extend the ratification of any convention to the Crown Dependencies. It has done so in some cases; in others, similar requirements have been put in place in order to implement international regulatory standards anti-money laundering (AML) standards and combating finance for terrorism (CFT) requirements.

The Bailiwick of Jersey

Jersey is an island located approximately 85 miles from the English coast and 14 miles off the north-west coast of France. It has a population of approximately 103,000 people.

The main finance industry sectors in Jersey are the banking, fund administration and trust company business sectors. Insurance business is not conducted on a significant scale from Jersey. There are many legal and accountancy practices that operate from within the island and support its finance industry.

The Bailiwick of Guernsey

The Bailiwick comprises the principal islands of Guernsey, Alderney and Sark together with several other small islands. The Bailiwick of Guernsey is located in the English Channel, in the bay of St Malo off the north-west coast of France (close to Jersey). Guernsey's population is approximately 63,000, Alderney's population is approximately 1,500 and Sark's population is approximately 500.

The financial services industry in Guernsey includes:

- asset management;
- banking;
- fund administration;
- insurance; and
- the trust and fiduciary sectors.

Banking is central to the Bailiwick of Guernsey's finance industry and is a major source of employment in the Bailiwick. Guernsey is the leading captive insurance domicile in Europe in terms of numbers of captives, ranked fourth in the world based on premiums written.

The Isle of Man

The Isle of Man (IOM) is located in the middle of the Irish Sea. While the Isle of Man is a part of the British Isles, it is not a part of the UK. Its population is approximately 85,000. Banking and insurance services represent the most significant financial service businesses in the IOM. Funds business has been a growing sector and the IOM has also licensed some online gambling businesses. The use of **legal persons** and arrangements such as trusts are also prevalent.

legal persons
Those persons that are incorporated by law (e.g. companies).

3.2 The British Overseas Territories

The constitutional relationship of British Overseas Territories is quite different to that of the Crown Dependencies.

Offshore centres such as Anguilla, Bermuda, the British Virgin Islands, the Cayman Islands, Gibraltar, Montserrat and the Turks and Caicos Islands are all British Overseas Territories.

Gibraltar

Gibraltar is a self-governing overseas territory of the UK. It is not an island, but instead is situated on the peninsula at the southern tip of Spain, just opposite the north coast of Africa. Its population is approximately 30,000. Gibraltar has been a constituent of the EU since 1973 under the UK Treaty of Accession, as it is a European territory whose external relations are the responsibility of an EU member state. However, it is excluded from the common external tariff, the common agricultural policy and the requirement to levy VAT. Financial services are a significant part of Gibraltar's economy, including:

- banking;
- fund management including collective investment schemes;
- insurance; and
- trust and company business.

British Virgin Islands

The Territory of the British Virgin Islands is a non-self-governing overseas territory of the UK. The territory is located within the Virgin Islands archipelago a few miles east of the United States Virgin Islands. It consists of approximately 60 islands, islets and cays – 20 of which are inhabited. The capital of the Virgin Islands is Road Town, which is situated on the largest island, Tortola. This island is approximately 13.5 miles long and 3 miles wide, and its population is approximately 29,000.

The financial services sector is important to the British Virgin Islands economy. Services such as accountancy, banking and legal services, captive insurance, company **incorporations**, mutual funds administration and trust formation are all provided from within the British Virgin Islands. The Virgin Islands are regarded as being among the world's leading domiciles for hedge funds and the territory has also sustained substantial growth in the areas of captive insurance companies. In addition, the UK government launched the Virgin Islands Shipping Registry (VISR) in 2006, which enabled the Territory to be upgraded to a Category 1 Shipping Registry. The Virgin Islands have locally enacted legislation and imperial legislation, which is enacted by order of Her Majesty and with the advice of the Privy Council. The common law of England also applies. The Judicial Committee of the Privy Council is the final court of appeal for the British Virgin Islands.

incorporation
The legal process by which a company and other legal bodies are created by law.

3.3 Mainland countries

Offshore centres also include some mainland countries, such as:

- Monaco, which is surrounded on three sides by France and lies on the coast of the Mediterranean Sea;
- Panama, which is the southern-most country of Central America; and
- Liechtenstein, which is a landlocked country in Central Europe (although it is not a part of the EU).

3.4 Other offshore centres

The Bahamas, Barbados, Belize, the Commonwealth of Dominica, St Kitts and Nevis (both parts of this Federation have separate company and trust litigation), St Lucia, St Vincent, the Grenadines, Cyprus, Malta, the Seychelles, Curacao (part of the Netherlands Antilles) and Aruba are all offshore centres, as is the Republic of Mauritius.

The Republic of Mauritius

The Republic of Mauritius consists of the islands of Mauritius (the main island), Rodrigues, Agalega, St Brandon and the Chagos Archipelago. The Republic of Mauritius obtained its independence from the UK in 1968 and became a Republic on 12 March 1992. The population of Mauritius numbers around 1.2 million people. English is the official language but French is also widely used. Mauritius is a member of the Commonwealth, the United Nations and related organisations, the Organisation of African Unity and the Indian Ocean Commission.

The financial sector in Mauritius is growing. It consists of banking business, insurance companies, a stock market and other financial intermediaries. The banking sector is the largest sector in the Republic, and no bank secrecy laws apply to banks there.

The Mauritian legal system is largely based on English and French law. Criminal procedure law is mainly English, while its Criminal Code was influenced by the French Code and civil law is modelled on the Napoleonic Code. The ultimate court of appeal is the Judicial Committee of the Privy Council in England.

Test yourself 1.2

State three uses of offshore centres.

4. Typical features of offshore centres

Features of a typical offshore centre may include:

- low or zero taxation (or exemption) for non-residents or companies with no domestic commercial activities;

- moderate or light regulation;
- no **exchange control regulations**;
- no tax on company profits or wealth taxes or capital gains taxes;
- privacy and confidentiality provisions;
- reduced requirements for disclosure of information to authorities;
- the availability of a high level of financial expertise; and
- widely available expertise in asset protection **structures** such as trusts.

Companies and foundations.
Exchange control regulations are regulations or other controls that are imposed by the governments of some countries that fear or are experiencing scarcity of foreign currency (and often precious metals). Such controls may limit or ban the amount of foreign or local currency that can be traded or purchased, or may involve controls which restrict residents from removing currency from the jurisdiction.

exchange control regulations
Regulations or other controls that are imposed by the governments of some countries that fear or are experiencing scarcity of foreign currency (and often, precious metals). Such controls may limit or ban the amount of foreign or local currency that can be traded or purchased, or may involve controls which restrict residents from removing currency from the jurisdiction.

Stop and think 1.1

Which of the typical features of offshore centres are present in your own jurisdiction?

5. Choosing an offshore centre

There are a number of personal factors that may influence a person's choice of offshore centre, including:

- the nature or content of any tax or legal advice that they may have received;
- their business and intended activities;
- their country of residence;
- their short-term and long-term objectives;
- their reasons for using an offshore centre;
- their geographical proximity and time zone; and
- in some cases, where they wish to retire.

structure
Used to describe a group of trusts and companies that are connected by their ownership or their assets and are aimed at meeting the needs of a particular client or group of clients.

While there are typical features of offshore centres, there are differences that may influence a client's choice. These differences can be due to:

- characteristics of the legal system;
- confidentiality and privacy provisions;
- the development of niche markets;
- political infrastructure;
- regulation standards;

- reputation;
- the physical and human infrastructure; and
- the taxation environment.

5.1 Niche markets

Many offshore centres have developed niche positions in the international markets and the activity with which the client is involved may therefore influence their choice of jurisdiction. Guernsey, for example, has an established captive insurance market.

Specialised services such as compliant Islamic financial services may be offered in the key financial sectors in some offshore centres. For some clients, this will be a relevant consideration when choosing an offshore centre.

Making it work 1.1

Niche markets

In December 2008, the Chancellor of the Exchequer commissioned Michael Foot to undertake a review of the British Crown Dependencies (Guernsey, Isle of Man and Jersey) and six overseas territories (Anguilla, Bermuda, the British Virgin Islands, the Cayman Islands, Gibraltar and Turks and Caicos Islands) in order to identify the opportunities and challenges facing them. The review was published on 29 October 2009 and identified the various niche positions in international markets for some of the jurisdictions under review.

- **The Cayman Islands** are the world's leading centre for hedge funds and also has a significant wholesale banking centre, with high volumes of overnight banking business from the USA.
- **Bermuda** is the third largest reinsurance centre in the world and the second largest captive insurance domicile, with firms based in the jurisdiction writing significant volumes of business in the UK and the USA.
- **The British Virgin Islands** are the leading domicile for international business companies, with significant business coming from the Far East in addition to strong business links with the USA.
- **Gibraltar** offers a gateway to the European single market.
- **The Crown Dependencies** provide a gateway to route funds to other financial centres, including London; they also service the financial needs of many UK nationals living abroad.

5.2 Legal systems

The following are considerations relating to the legal system that may influence a person's choice of offshore centre.

The familiarity of the legislation

Offshore centres that have laws similar to English law may appeal to those who are familiar with that legal system. In some offshore centres, such as Mauritius, the highest court of appeal is the UK Privy Council. This may offer some comfort to users.

Legal flexibility

Company law that is flexible and non-prescriptive enables the provisions of onshore legislation to be incorporated into a company's **articles of association**, thus replicating the onshore law.

articles of association
The internal regulations of a company that set out how the company shall be managed.

A lack of exchange control regulations

The absence of exchange control regulations is desirable to allow freedom of fund movement in and out of the jurisdiction.

The range of entities and products available

Legislation in some offshore centres provides for a range of **entities** that can be used as investment vehicles, in addition to the traditional trusts and limited liability companies. These include:

entities
Used to describe both legal persons (such as companies) and legal arrangements (such as trusts).

- incorporated cell companies;
- incorporated limited partnerships;
- limited liability partnerships;
- protected cell companies;
- separate limited partnerships; and
- unit trusts and foundations.

Responsiveness

An offshore centre's infrastructure, legislation and processes should allow it to respond quickly in order to meet the client's needs and expectations. Jurisdictions such as Jersey offer 'fast track' incorporations allowing company incorporation within two hours. Guernsey offers incorporations within 15 minutes where the purpose of the company is a simple asset holding company and where the standard memorandum and articles of association are used.

Access to stock exchanges

Trading the shares of companies incorporated within the jurisdiction on major stock exchanges could be a benefit for some users. Major exchanges include the London Stock Exchange (LSE), NASDAQ, the Alternative Investment Market (AIM), the Hong Kong Stock Exchange and so on.

The ability to issue uncertified securities that enable electronic trading of shares through systems like CREST can also be useful. For example, Jersey has legislation that facilitates this whereas the Caribbean jurisdictions do not.

Administrative requirements
Administrative requirements vary, and offshore centres with fewer administrative requirements allow costs to be kept to a minimum. For example, some jurisdictions – such as Jersey – allow for the requirement for annual general meetings (AGMs) to be waived. Some offshore centres require financial statements for private companies to be audited whereas others only require them to be filed. The Registrar of Companies in the Isle of Man must be informed whenever there is a change in the officers of the company.

Asset protection legislation
The legislation of some jurisdictions provides that, upon the death of individuals, assets must be distributed in accordance with the provisions set out in those laws. These are known as **'forced heirship'** rules. A centre's legislation should protect users against forced heirship rules.

forced heirship
In some countries, the laws require the assets held in a person's estate to pass to stated heirs (usually the person's spouse and children). This is known as forced heirship and such heirs are known as 'forced heirs' (or sometimes 'fixed heirs').

Independence
The local legislature and judiciary need to be able to operate independently and free of government interference.

5.3 Regulation

The global financial crisis, developments in financial crime and a political focus on abusive tax practices has highlighted the need for high standards of financial sector regulation and supervision. Characteristics of offshore centres that operate such standards may include:

- operating with a depositor compensation scheme;
- operating standards that are in line with international standards such as the third and fourth EU AML directive and the FATF Recommendations. Offshore centres which are able to score comparatively or better than the onshore jurisdictions help to highlight misconceptions about the way in which many offshore centres operate;
- having a track record of operating within the supervisory regime for many years;
- being highly rated by the IMF or members of respected international bodies such as the International Organization of Securities Commissions (IOSCO) and the Group of International Finance Centre Supervisors (formerly the offshore group of banking supervisors);
- participation in international tax information exchange initiatives such as FATCA and CRS; and
- high standards of data protection law.

5.4 Reputation

The reputation of the offshore centre is extremely important. Clients who deal with jurisdictions that appear on any blacklist may find it increasingly difficult to deal outside of this jurisdiction. The following is a non-exhaustive list of factors that could be considered when assessing the reputation of an offshore centre.

- Inclusion on the OECD 'white list', meaning that the jurisdiction has implemented internationally agreed tax standards along with onshore jurisdictions such as the UK, France and the USA.
- Comprehensive and wide-reaching Tax Information Exchange Agreements (TIEAs).
- The jurisdiction's rating in the Global Financial Centres Index (GFCI).
- The level of compliance with the FATF 40+9 recommendations.

The latest EU list is of course the issue for offshore centres and many have rushed to publicise their 'white status'.

5.5 Confidentiality and privacy provisions

An offshore centre should protect the privacy and confidentiality of financial information for legitimate business activities while remaining committed to the international fight against financial crime such as **money laundering** and financing of terrorism.

money laundering
Money laundering occurs whenever there is an arrangement involving the proceeds of crime.

The requirements to report information to the authorities differ from jurisdiction to jurisdiction. For example, it is a requirement in some jurisdictions to disclose the beneficial ownership of companies at the time of incorporation only, whereas in others this requirement is ongoing. In some offshore centres there is a central registry of trusts, whereas in others no public information on trusts is held. This is an area where again international standards will no doubt influence what individual centres choose to do. The EU is key to see a registry of trusts in all centres. Many offshore centres have signed TIEAs with other jurisdictions in order to comply with the OECD's international agreement. These TIEAs, usually based on the OECD's model agreement, mean information may be exchanged in certain circumstances where a person is under investigation for fiscal crime in a jurisdiction. The OECD and tax information exchange agreements are discussed later. Many offshore centres have data protection legislation in line with that of the UK. Some offshore centres have strict banking secrecy laws; however, these have attracted negative publicity and have been subject to increased attention from governments in onshore jurisdictions and the OECD.

Making it work 1.2

The US government and UBS

In 2008, the US government alleged that UBS – Switzerland's largest bank – had defrauded US tax authorities between 2006 and 2007. It had done this by creating complex offshore structures for their clients in which they could hide their assets from the Internal Revenue Service (IRS), which collects taxes for the US government.

Despite Switzerland's strict bank secrecy laws, UBS agreed to pay $780 million (£549 million) to the US government in February 2009 and Switzerland's regulator ordered UBS to hand over the identities of approximately 250 to 300 clients.

Many were shocked by the decision of the Swiss authorities. Swiss President and Finance Minister Hans-Rudolf Merz was widely reported to have indicated that, if UBS had failed to meet the deadlines set by the US authorities, this could have led to the loss of its US operating licence. This would have threatened the very existence of the bank, and by extension the Swiss economy.

Immediately after the above events, the USA filed a new civil lawsuit demanding that UBS hand over information on 52,000 US account holders.

Switzerland recognises tax fraud as a crime (and would have been in a position to release information if a client had committed this offence), but not tax evasion – which was the focus of the allegations. UBS therefore faced breaking US tax laws if it did not disclose the details and breaking Swiss secrecy laws if it did.

In August 2009, the Swiss government negotiated on behalf of the bank. An agreement was signed to end the dispute whereby UBS agreed to give the US tax authorities the details of 4,450 accounts of customers who were highly suspected of tax evasion.

As well as the release of information, international pressure has caused Switzerland to sign up to the OECD international standards to facilitate exchange of information, having previously stated that the rules would compromise its long-standing banking secrecy principles. Several commentators have stated that this is the beginning of the end of bank secrecy legislation.

The impact of the UBS deal was seen when a number of other Swiss banks agreed deals with the USA along comparable lines.

Making it work 1.3

The Panama Papers and the Paradise Papers

In 2015, 11.5 million confidential documents belonging to Panamanian law firm Mossack Fonseca, detailing financial and other sensitive confidential information for over 200,000 offshore entities were leaked to investigative journalists and made public. Some documents dated back to the 1970s, and many purported to show that Panama was facilitating money laundering and illegal tax evasion through the use of shell companies, trusts and other offshore structures. It was discovered that while a wide range of high profile politicians, public officials and celebrities from around the world had connections with the law firm and made use of various Panamanian entities, there were relatively few individuals that had actually acted illegally. However, the discovery of such widespread international use of tax avoidance schemes was the subject of much ongoing discussion and heated debate around the ethics and morality of using offshore centres to facilitate the mitigation of tax using legal means, including the exploitation of loopholes in domestic tax laws.

In 2017, law firm Appleby, corporate services providers Estera and Asiaciti Trust, and business registries in 19 tax jurisdictions were subject to a similar leak of over 13 million electronic documents containing the names of more than 120,000 people and companies, famously including the Queen and Prince Charles. Again, analysis of the leaked documents did not reveal extensive illegal activity and the schemes disclosed in the Paradise Papers were largely lawful and tax transparent. The incident was however used politically to taint the reputation of offshore centres at a time when the EU Finance Ministers were reviewing the EU tax haven blacklist.

5.6 Political infrastructure

The political infrastructure of an offshore centre is of utmost importance. Potential investors in an offshore centre will want to be certain that the offshore centre is politically, socially and economically stable, as well as free from problems such as war and **corruption**. Political control must be clearly in the hands of the governing party. The government should have high moral standards and should not allow organised criminals to operate from within its jurisdiction.

corruption
Transparency International defines corruption as 'the misuse of entrusted power for private gain'. Public sector corruption involves, for example, the diversion of state funds for the benefit of politicians' own families.

A strong local economy is preferable, with a good standard of living and an absence of civil unrest. It is important that the government can operate autonomously and, if it is an overseas territory, the ability of the mother country to intervene should be restricted. The political environment in an offshore centre should not make the costs of operating from within the offshore centre excessive.

5.7 Tax environment

A simplified low tax environment that has been stable for number of years offers certainty to users of the offshore centre that may not be present in onshore jurisdictions. Desirable features of an offshore centre's tax environment include:

- no (or nominal) corporation taxes;
- competitive initial registration and winding-up taxes;
- competitive stamp duties;
- no insurance premium taxes;
- no stamp duty on incorporated holding companies;
- no income taxes;
- no capital gains taxes;
- no VAT;
- no withholding taxes on payment of **dividends** or interest paid on loans;
- no wealth taxes;
- no **inheritance taxes**;

dividend
A share of the after-tax profits of a company distributed to its shareholders after a director's decision to pay a class of shareholders.

inheritance tax (IHT)
A tax charged upon the death of a person, based upon the value of their estate.

- a Double Taxation Agreement network;
- scope for tax deferral; and
- the existence of a network of double taxation agreements.

5.8 Physical infrastructure

Desirable features of the physical infrastructure of an offshore centre include:

- operating in the same time zone as major centres (e.g. Jersey, Guernsey and the Isle of Man all operate within the same time zone as the UK, whereas the Caribbean jurisdictions operate within the same time zone as New York);
- being located close to a major onshore centre and having direct flights to major centres on a frequent basis, as this allows easy access for clients and their advisers;
- having an attractive climate and environment with good accommodation for clients and their advisers. Offshore centres with a high-quality tourist industry may have an advantage;
- the presence of major accountancy firms and legal practices;
- the presence of a large number of international banks; and
- a comprehensive and robust information technology infrastructure.

5.9 Human infrastructure

The presence of a large number of finance industry professionals is desirable, including those with experience and qualifications within banking, fund administration and management, trusts and company administration, accountancy and the legal sector.

A solid network of a range of experienced professionals such as accountants, administrators, Chartered Secretaries, custodians, fund managers, investment advisers, lawyers and stockbrokers also combine to offer experience in a range of products and services for customers of offshore centres.

The spoken language in a jurisdiction could also be an important factor for the client (e.g. Mauritius has a bilingual population (French and English)).

Test yourself 1.3

a) What factors might influence an individual's choice of offshore centre?

b) State two desirable characteristics of a legal system in an offshore centre.

6. Choosing an offshore service provider

The range of service providers offshore is vast. Few clients today simply call a service provider as a result of their own research or via a service provider's website. In fact, service providers would exercise caution in most well-regulated jurisdictions if clients did contact them in this way. Instead, clients are usually introduced to service providers either because they are already a client of a part of the group or through an intermediary such as a lawyer, tax adviser or banker. Often, offshore service providers are asked by intermediaries or introducers to attend a 'beauty parade' where they explain the services that they can provide and compete with other service providers for a client's business.

The choice of service provider will depend to some extent on the aims of the client, the resources available to them and their client service expectations. Different clients seek different qualities in a service provider for a variety of reasons. A client looking to settle a trust may wish for their **trustee** to be provided by a trust company that is entirely independent. In this case, they may seek an independent trust company and avoid those that are bank-owned or offer their own portfolio management services.

trustee
The person who holds the trust property for the benefit of the beneficiaries and who has a fiduciary duty to act in their best interests.

Other clients may prefer to keep their business confined to connected entities – for example, with their existing bankers. It is common for banks to own trust companies and to be able to keep the provision of bank accounts, a trustee, portfolio managers and other advisers in-house. The lack of independence may mean that the bank-owned company is unlikely to choose external parties to provide services to the trust (even if they may offer better rates of interest). However, it can be argued that the ability to provide services in-house outweighs the benefits of independence by securing lower fees for the client, creating operational efficiencies and ensuring the ability to know and understand all aspects of the client's business – thus creating opportunities for the client (and the bank).

Fiduciary services, for example, may be provided by banks, bank-owned trust companies, law firm-owned trust companies, accountancy firms or independently owned trust companies. These range from very small to very large organisations. A client with complicated structures spanning across several jurisdictions may wish for their trustee to be a law firm with a presence in several jurisdictions, while a client whose main aim is to provide for their family after their own death may choose a 'family office' or small provider with whom they may build up a close relationship.

There are certain characteristics, however, that many clients will desire from their service provider. Perhaps the gold standard of characteristics is the reputation of the centre in which the service provider is based and regulated. Other key characteristics include the following.

- Service providers should be regulated. A trustee who is asked to transfer a trust to a new service provider should ensure that they are comfortable that it is in the best interest of the client to do so. Such a provider will be conducting 'unauthorised' business in many jurisdictions and the client will not be afforded the usual protections that arise when dealing with trustees who are regulated and supervised.

- The service provider should be qualified and experienced at providing the services for which they are employed. Any marketing material should be accurate and not misleading in any way. The size of the service provider should be suitable for the client in that it should be such that the client feels that their business is important to the organisation.
- Some clients enjoy the security that being connected with a large institution may afford them, whereas others may prefer to be looked after by a small company where the staff know their business and where they receive a personal service.
- The fees and charges levied by the provider should be reasonable and transparent.
- The provider should be a reputable person; there should be a lack of adverse publicity about the provider and a good regulatory track record. A service provider's reputation is key to its ability to attract and retain good quality clients and intermediary contacts.
- There should be a high level of customer service.
- The availability of talented and experienced professional staff is desirable, particularly those with experience of dealing with the jurisdiction or activity with which the client is connected. Clients favour consistency and the ability to liaise with the same members of staff over time. High levels of staff turnover are usually unwelcome.
- Service providers should be efficient. Some service providers take a risk-based approach to account opening and new client take-on procedures whereby the process is kept as simple and proportionate as possible. Other organisations may be more cautious, insisting on more stringent requirements that increase the level of fees charged to the client and increasing compliance time.
- The compatibility of the investment philosophies of the client and the service provider should be considered (e.g. some clients may seek Sharia compliant structures).

The desirability of service providers to act for any given client will limit the choice of service providers available to them. For example:

- some service providers are willing to provide services to clients who present a higher risk to their business than others;
- some will not provide limited services such as only providing a **registered office**, instead seeking to retain full control over the activities of the entities that they administer;
- some will not provide services to clients located in higher-risk jurisdictions or partaking in higher-risk activities;
- some require a minimum investment;
- the service provider may not be authorised to provide the service under its financial services business licence; and

registered office
The address of a company which has been notified to the authorities (as required by law) as the address to which legal notices can be sent.

- a service provider may not have the experience required in order to manage the business properly.

Less scrupulous clients will seek service providers with the opposite characteristics to those usually desired. They will seek, for example, providers where the staff do not understand the business and will accept whatever business opportunities are presented. Some of the more usual concerns – for example, the fees and charges levied by the provider – may be of minimal importance to these individuals.

Test yourself 1.4

What factors might a potential user of an offshore service provider take into consideration when choosing a service provider?

Chapter summary

- An offshore centre is any jurisdiction (not necessarily an island) which has a relatively large number of financial institutions which are engaged primarily in business with non-residents and which provides other benefits – such as low taxation. Offshore business is simply the provision of financial services to non-residents.
- The terms 'offshore' and 'tax havens' have taken on negative meanings notwithstanding that many offshore centres now operate high standards of regulation and have adopted international tax transparency measures.
- Many offshore centres have therefore sought to position themselves as International Finance Centres.
- The users of offshore centres includes wealthy individuals (HNWIs) as well as multinational incorporations, all of which seek to secure an advantage that would not be available to them from within their own jurisdiction.
- Typical features of offshore centres may include low or zero taxation, no wealth taxes or capital gains taxes, privacy and confidentiality provisions, reduced disclosure requirements to authorities, the availability of a high level of financial expertise and a lack of exchange control regulations.
- The factors that may influence a person's choice of offshore centre could include the characteristics of the legal system, confidentiality provisions, their personal ambitions, the reputation of the centre, the standard of the regulation, taxation environment and the political, physical or human infrastructure of an offshore centre.
- Charges, independence, range of services available, reputation and size may all be relevant considerations when choosing a service provider from the vast range of providers available.

Test yourself answers

Test yourself 1.1

An offshore centre could be described as a jurisdiction that provides much of its financial services business to non-residents and seeks to create a competitive advantage through its laws.

Test yourself 1.2

Three uses of offshore centres include:

- holding and investment companies;
- private client wealth structuring using trusts, offshore companies and other entities; and
- tax-efficient structuring of international trade and investment.

Test yourself 1.3

a) The following factors may influence an individual's, choice of offshore centre:

- the characteristics of the legal system;
- confidentiality and privacy provisions;
- the development of niche markets;
- the offshore centre's physical and human infrastructure;
- the offshore centre's reputation and pool of professional expertise;
- the personal circumstances of the individual;
- political infrastructure;
- regulation standards; and
- the taxation environment.

b) Desirable legal characteristics of a legal system in an offshore centre include:

- the familiarity of the legislation; and
- a lack of exchange control regulations.

Test yourself 1.4

The following factors are all relevant considerations:

- whether the service provider is regulated;
- the service provider's qualifications and experience;
- the size of the service provider compared to the business the client wishes to undertake;
- the fees and charges levied by the provider;
- the service provider's reputation;

- the service provider's level of customer service and efficiency;
- the compatibility of the client's and service provider's investment philosophies; and
- the type of business the service provider is willing to accept.

Chapter two
Offshore financial services

List of topics

1. The offshore financial services sector
2. Key terms
3. Trust and company products available offshore
4. Fiduciary services available offshore
5. Offshore insurance services
6. Legal services available in offshore centres
7. Tax compliance and tax planning
8. Investment management services

Introduction

This chapter discusses the financial services that are typically offered in offshore centres and explains key terms that are often used in the finance industry. It highlights some of the trust and company business products that are available offshore – including trusts, companies, foundations and a variety of partnerships – as well as trust company business services provided in connection with these products.

The chapter also discusses the advantages of captive insurance companies, and describes the legal and taxation services that are available in offshore centres. It concludes with a discussion regarding the types of investment management services that are available offshore and some factors that should be considered when planning an investment portfolio.

1. The offshore financial services sector

The financial services sector in an offshore centre may typically offer the provision of the following services:

- fiduciary services (comprising of services for the creation and administration of trusts, companies, foundations and other legal arrangements);

- insurance services including intermediation, fronting and reinsurance;
- investment management services including discretionary portfolio management, fund management and fund administration and custody services;
- legal services; and
- tax compliance and tax planning services.

The term **financial services business** describes the carrying on of funds service business, general insurance mediation business, investment business, money service business or trust company business. An organisation that provides financial services business is often referred to as a **service provider**. In many offshore jurisdictions, the provision of financial services business is a regulated activity. This means it may not be carried on except by a business that has been issued with the relevant licence and is supervised by its regulator.

financial services business
Used to describe the carrying on of funds services business investment business, general insurance mediation business, money services business or trust company business.

fiduciary relationship
A relationship founded on trust. A person with a fiduciary duty has a duty to act in the best interests of another person.

fiduciary duty
A person with a fiduciary duty has a duty to act in the best interests of another person.

settlor
The person who provides trust property whether during their lifetime or by their will.

beneficiary
A person who is entitled by the terms of a trust to benefit from the trust property or in whose favour a discretion to distribute the trust property may be exercised.

beneficial owner
The individual(s) or company that retains a direct or indirect ownership interest in the assets of an entity.

ultimate beneficial owner
The individual(s) that retains a direct or indirect ownership in the assets of a financial product, service, structure or entity, howsoever the legal title is constructed.

legal arrangements
Legal arrangements include fiduciary arrangements such as trusts.

2. Key terms

2.1 Fiduciary relationship

A **fiduciary relationship** is one that is founded on trust and the protection of financial or other interests of another person. A person with a **fiduciary duty** has a duty to act in the best interests of another person. For example, a trustee has a fiduciary duty to act in the best interests of the beneficiaries of the trust, rather than acting in their own best interests.

2.2 Client

'Client' usually refers to the person who approached the offshore services provider to establish a business relationship. However, this is not always the case. A fiduciary services provider may use the term client to describe the **settlor** of a trust even though that person may not be a **beneficiary**; they could also use the term to describe a principal beneficiary who was not the provider of the funds or involved at the outset of the relationship.

In the case of an offshore company, the client may be the major shareholder, or the beneficial owner or underlying ultimate **beneficial owner** (UBO) who retains an indirect ownership interest in the assets of the company where a nominee shareholder of record is used.

The terms client, beneficial owner or **ultimate beneficial owner** are also used sometimes carelessly which can confuse or blur important issues from the anti-money laundering or tax reporting perspectives.

2.3 Entities

The term 'entities' is used to describe legal persons (such as companies) and **legal arrangements** (such as trusts). Rather than referring to trusts, companies, foundations, partnerships and so on, a fiduciary services provider will simply refer to entities under administration.

2.4 Structures

The entities that are aimed at meeting the needs of a particular client or group of clients, and which are connected by virtue of their ownership or their assets, are referred to collectively as a structure.

A structure may be very simple (e.g. a company owned directly by a trust) or could be very complex (e.g. it could be multi-layered, could span across jurisdictions and could include a range of different types of entities).

2.5 Overlying trusts/underlying companies

It is common for trusts and companies to be used together as a part of a client's tax or wealth planning. For example, a trust may own 100% of the **share capital** of a company.

share capital
The money provided by a company's members in return for shares in the company.

In this case, the trust would be referred to as an 'overlying trust' and the company would be referred to as an 'underlying company'. If the underlying company acquired the entire share capital of another company, it would then become the 'overlying company' of that new entity.

2.6 Fiduciary Services Provider or 'Trust company'

A Fiduciary Services Provider is an organisation that conducts trustee and company administration business. The term usually refers to an organisation which offers the full range of fiduciary services (described in section 4 of this chapter). Organisations such as accountancy firms often provide some limited services, such as company formations or the provision of a registered office.

Fiduciary Services Providers may be small or large organisations owned by accountancy practices, legal practices, major international banks or public companies. Alternatively, they may be owned by experienced individuals.

2.7 Service provider

Organisations or individuals that provide financial services business offshore may simply be referred to as service providers.

Test yourself 2.1

Give one example of a 'fiduciary relationship'.

3. Trust and company products available offshore

The main offshore trust and company products include various types of trusts, companies, foundations and partnerships and trusts.

3.1 Trusts

A trust is a legal arrangement whereby a person (the settlor) properly vests (transfers in the correct manner) the legal ownership of assets (later referred to as the trust fund) to another person (the trustee) for the benefit of another person or persons (the beneficiaries of the trust).

The separation of the legal ownership of the trust fund – which lies with the trustee – and the equitable ownership – which lies with the beneficiaries – has many uses in financial planning.

A trust is not a corporate body and thus has no separate legal personality. The trustee administers the trust and contracts the business of the trust in its name but must also specify its **capacity** as trustee. In the offshore environment, the trustee is usually a limited liability company, which provides stability, certainty and continuity for the trust. The terms of a trust depend on the type of trust and are set out in a private document known as a trust deed or a **declaration of trust**.

Trusts may be discretionary trusts where the trustee is given absolute discretion as to who from the class of beneficiaries described in the trust deed will benefit from the trust and in what proportions, if at all. In these cases, the Settlor may provide the trustee with a non-binding Letter of Wishes indicating how the Settlor would like the trust to be operated.

Life interest trusts, also known as 'interest in possession' trusts, entitles a beneficiary (the **life tenant**) to an absolute right to enjoy the income arising from the **trust property** during their lifetime. Only on their death may the other beneficiaries (the remainder-men) stand to benefit. In essence, the life interest trust reverts to a discretionary trust upon the death of the life tenant.

The different types of trusts are discussed further in Chapter 13.

3.2 Companies

There are many types of companies, including, companies limited by guarantee, incorporated cell companies, limited liability companies, protected cell companies and unlimited companies. Companies can also be incorporated to be a public or private company.

A company is an association of people referred to as the **members**, who come together usually for business or profit-making purposes. A company comes into existence when it is incorporated by law and company shares are issued to the members who become the shareholders and decide upon and appoint the directors. Upon incorporation, a company has a separate legal personality distinct from that of its **shareholders** and **directors** (i.e. it can sue and be sued in its own name). The role of the directors is to manage the affairs of the company, which enters into transactions in its own name and purchases assets in its own name.

The shareholders own the shares of the company which entitle the shareholders to a corresponding proportion of the profits of the company, provide voting rights in relation to important decisions for the company and provide an

capacity
A party to a contract must have legal capacity (the power legally to enter into it) for it to be enforceable. Vulnerable people such as children do not have capacity.

declaration of trust (in relation to a settlement)
A declaration of the trustee which sets out the terms upon which the trust assets are held and to which the settlor of the trust is not a party.

life interest trust
A trust where an individual (known as the life tenant) has an absolute right to enjoy the trust property or income arising from the trust property during their lifetime.

life tenant
A person who is entitled to benefit from the income of a fixed income trust during their lifetime.

trust property
The property which is held by the trustee on trust for the benefit of the beneficiaries.

member
A person who subscribed to the memorandum of association of a company or a person who has been allotted or acquired one or more shares in a company and whose name has been entered on to the register of members or shareholders.

shareholder
A person who holds legal title to one or more shares in a company.

entitlement to any return of capital when the company if or when it is liquidated. Thus, and contrary to popular belief, a company is not owned by its shareholders.

director
A person appointed by the shareholders to be responsible for the management and control of a company, defined by the Companies Act 2006 as 'any person occupying the position of a director, by whatever name called'.

The memorandum and articles of association set out the company's constitution. The memorandum of association set out the name of the company, whether it is a public company and the **authorised share capital**. The articles of association of a company set out the rights and obligations of the shareholders.

authorised share capital
The amount of share capital that the company is authorised by its memorandum to issue.

Companies offer a number of significant benefits for the shareholders. For example, with limited liability companies, the liability of the shareholders is limited to the amount that they have contributed for their fully paid shares or still owe the company in respect of any unpaid shares.

The concept of limited liability facilitates broad share ownership, which has significantly contributed to the ability of businesses to raise capital to fund major infrastructure investments, and business expansion projects, including mergers and acquisitions.

perpetual succession
This refers to the fact that incorporated bodies such as companies remain unaffected by the existence of their owners or controllers and will continue to exist until formally dissolved by law.

Companies also offer **perpetual succession**, meaning that a company will continue to exist in the event of the death of the shareholders or directors.

Most offshore companies are incorporated as limited liability companies.

The uses of companies incorporated in offshore centres include:

- holding assets such as property, yachts and aircrafts;
- holding intellectual property rights;
- holding investment portfolios;
- holding real estate;
- ring-fencing a risk in a particular company; and
- trading purposes.

Companies are discussed further in Part 7.

3.3 Foundations

Foundations have similar features to both trusts and companies. Foundations have a separate legal personality in the same way that companies do and can contract in their own name. Foundations do not have shareholders and are governed by a Foundation Council rather than a Board of Directors.

Foundations have become increasingly prevalent in offshore centres. While they have been used extensively in jurisdictions such as Panama and Liechtenstein for some time, they were only introduced in Jersey in 2009 and in Guernsey and the Isle of Man in 2013.

The benefits and uses of foundations include the following.

- Foundations appeal to clients involved with jurisdictions where the concept of trusts is less well known.
- Foundations do not issue shares and thus offer an enhanced level of confidentiality for ultimate beneficial owners.

- Foundations offer an enhanced level of confidentiality.
- Global charities may use foundations for making donations.
- Clients may wish to use foundations within commercial transactions, especially where an 'orphaned' special purpose vehicle is required.
- Foundations can be used for international structuring.
- Foundations are discussed further in Chapter 18.

3.4 Partnerships

A variety of partnership types are offered in offshore centres. General partnerships are not incorporated bodies and do not have a separate legal personality. Instead, they are a contractual arrangement between the individual partners who work together to make a profit. General partnerships have been available for many years.

Other partnership types, such as incorporated limited partnerships and separate limited partnerships are relatively recent developments. Limited partnerships are used extensively in some offshore centres.

Partnerships are discussed in more detail in Chapter 18.

Test yourself 2.2

State four uses of a company incorporated in an offshore jurisdiction.

4. Fiduciary services available offshore

Fiduciary and company administration business is a term that is used to describe the provision of:

- company incorporation and administration services required to maintain, govern and operate the company;
- establishment and administration services provided to foundations; and
- trustee or fiduciary services provided to various forms of trusts.

There are a number of trust company business services that may be provided by a trust company in an offshore centre.

4.1 Acting as a company, a partnership or a foundation formation agent

In some offshore centres (such as Jersey), companies may only be formed for non-residents by a person who is licensed to form companies under the law (e.g. a trust company).

The fiduciary services provider gives assurances to the Registrar of Companies that customer due diligence checks have been completed and that the companies do not undertake any 'sensitive' activities unless they have been specifically authorised to. Sensitive activities are those which may pose a risk to regulators' need to protect the integrity of the jurisdiction or which may not be in the jurisdiction's best economic interests.

In some offshore centres, such as the British Virgin Islands, service providers make 'shelf' companies available. These are companies that have already been incorporated by the service provider and are instantly available. When approached for a **shelf company**, the service provider simply resigns themselves as directors of the company in favour of the person requesting a company and transfers any shares they hold.

shelf company
A company that has been incorporated by a service provider and therefore is instantly available for use.

reserved companies
A company that is incorporated by service providers and the Registrar of Companies is advised that the company will be transferred to a client within the next six months.

Jersey allows **reserved companies**. These are incorporated in advance, with the service provider advising the registry that the company will be transferred to a client within the next six months. At this point, the service provider must advise the registry of the identity of the **beneficial owner**.

4.2 Acting as, or arranging for another person to act as, a director or an alternate director of the company

Fiduciary service providers often provide individuals (or companies) to act as directors to client entities. The individuals are usually directors or senior members of staff of the service provider. It is common for the service provider or one of its wholly owned subsidiaries to be appointed as corporate directors of client entities. Individuals (or a committee of individuals) who are directors of the corporate director are usually authorised to sign on behalf of the corporate director.

The appointment of a corporate director (as opposed to the appointment of individuals) has some administrative advantages. There is increased flexibility for senior members of staff to sign documentation on behalf of a corporate director. If individuals are appointed as directors, any documentation could not be signed if those members of staff were out of the office on business trips, on leave or had left the employment of the organisation.

4.3 Acting as, or arranging for another person to act as, a secretary

In many jurisdictions, it is a legal requirement that a company has a company secretary. It is not uncommon for the trust company or one of its wholly owned subsidiaries to be appointed in this role. The company secretary often takes responsibility for signing important documentation on behalf of the company, such as its annual return or its tax return.

4.4 Acting as, or arranging for another person to act as, a shareholder or unit holder as nominee for another person

Companies are generally required to notify the Registrar of Companies of the name and address of its shareholders upon incorporation. Some jurisdictions require this information to be provided and updated annually. The identity of the shareholder therefore becomes a matter of public record.

In offshore centres, it is extremely common to issue shares to the service provider, who becomes the legal shareholder on behalf of an underlying beneficial owner. The service provider signs a short private document (a **declaration of trust**) within which they admit and declare that they are holding the shares for a beneficial owner absolutely. The beneficial owner could be the ultimate client or the trustee of an overlying trust with further underlying ultimate beneficial owners. In these circumstances, the trust company is referred to as a **nominee shareholder**.

declaration of trust
(in relation to a nominee shareholding)
A short document within which the trustee admits and declares that the shares are held upon trust absolutely for the beneficial owner and in which the trustee undertakes to deal with the shares as instructed by the beneficial owner.

nominee shareholder
A person who is the legal owner of a share and who holds the share absolutely for and on behalf of the beneficial owner.

4.5 Acting as, or arranging for another person to act as, a trustee

A fiduciary service provider is often appointed as the sole trustee of trusts that are settled by non-residents of the financial centre.

The service provider is usually appointed as trustee, although it is not unusual for other wholly owned subsidiaries of the service provider to be appointed. A service provider will typically have a trustee committee whose terms of reference provide for any two individual directors of the service provider to make decisions in relation to the day-to-day administration of the trusts and companies under administration.

4.6 Acting as, or arranging for another person to act as, a partner of a partnership

The services provided are similar to those described in section 4.2.

4.7 Acting as, or arranging for another person to act as, a member of a foundation council

In some offshore centres, the provision of a member of a foundation council is a regulated activity. This must therefore be provided by a regulated fiduciary service provider.

4.8 Providing accommodation, correspondence or administrative address for a company, a partnership, a foundation or any other person

Historically, a fiduciary services provider would provide an accommodation address from which it would forward mail to clients or keep it for them to collect. However, this has become less common in recent years due to developments in AML legislation and concerns over tax evasion. As a result, service providers in well-regulated offshore centres have either ceased the practice or seek to understand whether the client has a legitimate business reason for an accommodation address before providing the service.

4.9 Providing a registered office or business address for a company, a partnership or foundation

It is a legal requirement that every company has a **registered office** address, which is notified to authorities. The address notified to the Registrar of

registered office
The address of a company that has been notified to the authorities (as required by law) as the address to which legal notices can be sent.

Companies (the equivalent of the UK's Companies House) is usually that of the fiduciary services provider that has incorporated the company. Historically, the provision of a 'registered office only' service was seen as a low-risk service and was widely provided in offshore centres for a small fee.

However, fewer trust companies are willing to provide this service alone as regulation standards and money laundering awareness has increased, instead preferring to have full control over the entities under their administration.

4.10 Risk and service providers

The range of services provided affects the level of information to which the service provider is privy. Fiduciary services providers may find themselves providing a registered office for companies that are involved in undesirable activities with connections to high-risk or disreputable jurisdictions. Regulators in well-administered jurisdictions expect service providers to recognise and manage the risks involved and to take steps to ensure that sufficient information about the company and all ultimate beneficial owners is held.

Many service providers have ceased to provide registered office only services. Others have insisted that they are appointed as the secretary for such entities on the basis that they should be privy to additional information. In reality, the appointment as secretary is unlikely to guarantee that they will receive sufficient additional information if the directors are external. In any case, external directors could remove the secretary from its position at any time. Whenever a service provider provides limited services rather than the full range of administration services, there will be additional risks.

Making it work 2.1

Assa Limited

In December 2008, the US Department of the Treasury's Office of Foreign Assets Control (OFAC) reported that Assa Limited, a Jersey company whose registered office was provided by a local trust company, was the parent organisation of Assa Corp, a shell company created and controlled by an Iranian government-owned bank, Bank Melli. It was reported that Assa Limited co-owned a 36-storey skyscraper in New York with Assa Corp, a New York entity. It was alleged that the rental income from the office building was repeatedly transferred to Bank Melli through Assa Limited, in violation of international sanctions to which Bank Melli was subject. There were no reports that indicated that any service other than the provision of a registered office had been provided from within the Island of Jersey. This case highlights the huge risk for reputational damage that the provision of a registered office can present to an individual service provider and to an offshore centre.

4.11 Unregulated services

While the above services may be regulated in the Crown Dependencies and some other offshore centres, they are not regulated in all jurisdictions. In addition, fiduciary and corporate service providers often provide additional non-regulated services. These may include:

- general administration;
- operating personal bank accounts for beneficiaries or settlors of trusts;
- preparing accounts for entities under administration; and
- providing authorised signatories.

Service providers in well-regulated jurisdictions may find that anti-money laundering regulations still capture such activities even if they are unregulated. Therefore, service providers may need to meet the requirements of those regulations when undertaking such activities.

5. Offshore insurance services

A wide range of insurance services are available from offshore centres. Offshore insurance sectors include:

- domestic insurance;
- international insurance; and
- insurance intermediaries.

International insurance includes:

- captive insurance;
- commercial insurance and insurance fronting arrangements; and
- international life and employee benefits.

Insurance businesses also offer products such as:

- after the event (ATE) insurance;
- captive insurance companies;
- credit insurance;
- professional indemnity insurance; and
- reinsurance and transformer cells.

5.1 Captive insurance companies

A captive insurance company is a subsidiary company (one owned by a parent company) formed to insure or reinsure the risks of its parent and/or associated group companies. In effect, the use of captive insurance allows the group to self-insure its risks.

Large companies will typically be faced with a broad range of significant insurable risks and may spend a great deal of money on insurance premiums and require a special type of cover not generally available from conventional insurers, so may set up one or more offshore captive insurance companies to address their specific portfolio of insurance needs.

A number of offshore centres promote the incorporation of captive insurance companies (e.g. Guernsey Finance, a joint industry and government initiative to promote the island's finance sector, claims that Guernsey is the leading captive domicile in Europe and is ranked fourth in the world). It claims that 40% of the leading 100 LSE companies that have established a captive insurance company have done so in Guernsey.

Captives are usually formed to provide alternative risk management solutions to that of the conventional insurance markets. Captive insurance companies generally retain a portion of the overall risk and reinsure the remainder. For example, a large public limited company (plc) that provides employees with permanent health insurance as a part of their remuneration package may set up an offshore captive insurance company into which it pays 'premiums'. Higher health risks would be underwritten and any claims would be paid out of this offshore subsidiary. The plc may benefit from interest generated on the excess funds invested, which would be taxed at a low or zero rate.

Advantages of offshore captive insurance companies include the following.

- Many offshore centres offer captive insurance companies. They can therefore offer a high level of expertise in dealing with captive insurance.
- Offshore centres offer a less bureaucratic supervisory insurance regime in some cases.
- A captive insurance company can be more cost-effective, as premiums charged by commercial insurers include amounts that cover their profit margin and overheads.
- Captive insurance companies can be used to cover common exclusions from usual insurance policies.
- Captive insurance companies offer flexibility (e.g. the captive insurance company can take advantage of low rates by reinsuring a relatively large proportion of its risks). The low cost of reinsurance allows a captive insurance company to build its reserve base. At other times, the captive insurance company can retain a larger proportion of its risks, maintaining cover for its parent even when commercial insurance is too costly.
- Captive insurance companies can make the claims process less bureaucratic and faster than if a third party insurer was involved.
- Excess net premiums over claims can be retained by the group when it experiences lower claims than expected.
- The captive can arrange the timing of premium payments to dovetail with the group's cash flow plans.
- Captive insurance companies may be able to provide cover that is not otherwise available, such as where a risk is too expensive to cover using a common insurance policy or in the case of unusual risks.

Captive insurance companies present disadvantages as well as potential advantages.

- The establishment of a captive insurance company involves a capital commitment of funds at the outset.
- The captive is exposed to claims arising and may make substantial losses. Risks should only be placed in a captive if a tolerable claims record is contemplated.
- An offshore captive insurance company involves the delegation by the parent company to the directors of the offshore insurance company. The parent company will therefore need to satisfy itself that the offshore company has qualified staff with sufficient expertise and recognition of exposure to risk.

Test yourself 2.3

State three advantages of establishing a captive insurance company.

6. Legal services available in offshore centres

Many offshore centres offer legal services. Law firms can provide independence to commercial transactions. They can also provide or facilitate comprehensive cross-border legal advice and provide a range of fiduciary services to HNWIs and corporate entities undertaking business.

Trustees often seek advice in relation to multi-jurisdictional structures. It is unlikely that a trustee would be familiar with the laws of every jurisdiction: therefore, it is wise for them to take legal advice in order to ensure that entities under their control do not break any foreign laws. It also ensures that any additional requirements are considered, such as exchange controls that may restrict the outflows of money when dealing with certain jurisdictions. The bodies responsible for promoting offshore centres will often state the number of first-tier law firms or multi-jurisdictional law firms that operate from within their location.

Offshore law firms are often licensed to conduct trust company business as a part of the legal services provided. Some do so only for specific reasons: for example, a law firm may deal with the formation of a company in connection with a property purchase, but otherwise it might operate a subsidiary company to provide fiduciary and corporate services or make referrals to a reputable third party fiduciary service provider. Law firms are often involved with estate planning. This involves passing wealth to a client's intended beneficiaries, such as the next generation of a family. A law firm would play a key part in ensuring that any structure is sufficiently robust to ensure that only the intended beneficiaries benefit and that any persons who should not benefit would have difficulty challenging the established arrangements.

It is common for law firms to be consulted by settlors and fiduciary services providers when trusts are established and they are often involved in the preparation of trust deeds. Law firms are also consulted throughout the life of a trust – for example, when a deed of addition of beneficiary (or exclusion) is required, or when varying the terms of a trust.

Some law firms have franchise or licence arrangements with fiduciary services providers whereby they provide the trust company with template documentation on an annual basis, allowing them to use it free of charge or for an annual fee. The trustee is more likely to contact the law firm that provided the documentation should a future legal issue ever arise.

Law firms will also give advice in relation to complex structures and strategies, such as when planning captive insurance companies or when listing a company's shares on a stock exchange or for corporate mergers and acquisitions.

Law firms are often consulted in connection with the registration of assets such as ships, yachts, aircrafts and trademarks or other intellectual property. It has become more common for law firms to provide briefings, free seminars and technical updates to the financial services industry, This helps keep finance professionals informed and promotes the services of the law firm.

7. Tax compliance and tax planning

Offshore trust companies rarely provide tax advice or tax planning services, although some do have in-house advisers. Instead, tax advisers are usually stand-alone businesses or form a part of a legal or accountancy firm. A local tax planning firm with international reach and particular expertise of the onshore jurisdictions that has close links to the offshore centre are particularly useful to offshore service providers.

Offshore taxation services fall into two broad categories: tax planning and tax compliance.

7.1 Tax planning

Tax planning as part of an organisation's overall business strategy involves the avoidance of tax risks while benefitting from legal opportunities to minimise tax liabilities.

Tax planning includes the review of a person's financial affairs and is an essential element of any estate planning. Many of the trust company business products discussed in section 3 of this chapter may be used as a part of a person's tax planning arrangements. Professional tax management involves the monitoring of each major corporate transaction – such as mergers, acquisitions and the purchase of assets – and identification of tax implications from an early stage.

Tax services for investment funds cover a wide range of activities, including:

- advising on the initial structure of funds and managing tax residence and permanent establishment issues;

- advising on interpretation and reaction to tax legislation from all over the world;
- obtaining clearances or ruling from tax authorities on behalf of funds;
- preparing tax reportage for fund investors;
- providing guidance on how to make tax-efficient investments into many different jurisdictions; and
- handling any tax compliance obligations.

7.2 Tax compliance

Tax compliance involves the preparation of tax returns for individuals and entities or the provision of information to tax authorities. Offshore tax compliance services may involve assisting clients of service providers who are the subject of a tax investigation or assisting clients to take advantage of disclosure facilities such as the Liechtenstein disclosure facility.

Many offshore entities have no tax to pay from within the offshore centre as they are exempt or taxed at a zero rate. Therefore, it is not always necessary to involve a tax adviser in the preparation of the local tax return, as this may simply involve confirming that there are no locally resident beneficial owners or local assets or income (usually with the exception of local bank interest) connected with the entity.

While offshore centres typically provide local tax neutrality, the non-resident clients who make use of offshore financial products, entities and structures must disclose their use of these services to the relevant domestic tax authorities because it would be illegal to evade tax deliberately by directing capital or revenue flows to offshore locations. Onshore governments are increasingly focussing on ways to minimise the use of offshore centres to avoid tax and have closed many formerly legitimate loopholes in their tax laws so that they are able to capture more tax revenue domestically.

The USA introduced FATCA to capture international tax information for US citizens wherever they reside globally. There has also been international cooperation in recent years to coordinate the extensive automatic exchange of tax information by introducing CRS across the OECD member countries, including many offshore centres, so that tax authorities are automatically informed of foreign products and services including trusts, offshore companies and other entities and structures used by their residents.

Test yourself 2.4

State two ways in which legal services may be used within the offshore business environment.

8. Investment management services

The offshore investment business sector includes the management, administration and custody of open- and closed-ended collective investment funds, as well as discretionary and non-discretionary asset management.

Stockbroking, the provision of investment advice and performance monitoring may also be provided from within offshore centres.

A collective investment fund is one where investors pool their capital within a single fund for the purposes of investing to meet a defined investment objective. The fund will typically appoint a specialist investment manager, the fund manager, to select the investments of the fund and to apply any investment restrictions required by the fund or the investors. Where there are many investors, there may also be a separate fund administrator engaged to manage the fund legal structure and the process of investing into the fund, and a fund custodian is usually engaged to hold and administer the investment assets of the fund independently of the fund manager and fund administrator.

8.1 Fund management, administration and custody

Fund management involves the professional management of the assets of funds. Offshore centres have been popular locations for collective investment schemes for many years. They are also popular choices for private funds for institutional and professional investors. As a result, there are many fund managers and other investment professionals in offshore centres.

Traditionally, funds have been established as either open-ended or closed-ended investment companies or as unit trusts. Some offshore centres are known for their specialised private investment funds, hedge funds and other alternative investment funds designed for expert investors, and these funds may include the use of PCC, ICC or SPC companies as the basis of their legal structure.

Retail funds including unit trusts or open-ended investment companies start off with a pool of cash from a number of investors. A professional fund manager invests the pool with the intention of providing a better return than the individuals could achieve if they were to make an investment themselves.

The funds are invested in accordance with the fund's particular objectives. Units or shares in the funds are issued to the investors in proportion to the amount invested.

The fund manager's responsibilities include selecting, buying and selling investments, calculating the value of the fund (daily in many cases) and may include issuing units to new investors or buying units back at the unit prices.

In managing the fund, the fund manager must observe the investment objectives and restrictions of the fund, and is expected to carry out due diligence on any investments that are selected for acquisition by the fund.

The fund manager will also issue periodic reports to all unit holders covering the fund's activities and current investments.

Where a fund administrator is appointed, it will establish and maintain the legal entity of the fund, including submitting regulatory and tax reporting. The fund administrator will also control subscriptions into the fund and redemptions from the fund, maintain investor accounts and issuing contract notes and statements and deal with general investor queries. The fund administrator will also be responsible for carrying out customer due diligence on investors and managing the anti-money laundering and sanctions risks of the fund.

The investments of the fund are normally held independently of the fund manager and fund administrator by a separate fund custodian, usually a large or reputable bank who provides security and controls over the investments of the fund and the movement of cash within the fund, ensuring that the interests of the fund and investors are protected.

8.2 Portfolio management services

Private portfolios are managed for the benefit of one individual or entity. Many trusts and companies hold investment portfolios that are professionally managed by an investment (or portfolio) manager.

Portfolio managers often specify a minimum sum that they are willing to manage on behalf of any particular client. Portfolio managers who provide services to clients of trust companies may allow lower minimum investments owing to the relationship that they have with the trust company. Portfolio valuations and reports are typically produced for clients on a quarterly basis. A more personal service may be provided for wealthy clients with reports produced on a more frequent basis.

There are three types of portfolio management services available. These include execution-only, advisory management and discretionary management.

Execution-only

Investors may deal through a broker on an 'execution only' basis if they know which securities they want to purchase or sell. Customers who deal on an execution-only basis are not given any advice by the firm when they make investment decisions. The only responsibility of the firm is one of 'best execution' – implementing the customer's investment decisions at the best price available.

Advisory management

Advisory customers are those to whom the firm provides advice and investment management services. However, the customer always makes the investment decisions.

Discretionary management

This service involves the customer empowering the investment manager to exercise discretion regarding the buying, retaining and selling of investments in order to meet the client's objectives. Offshore trustees or companies most commonly appoint an investment manager on this basis as they may not necessarily have the skills to manage an investment portfolio themselves.

The appointment of an investment manager on a discretionary basis does not absolve trustees or directors of their duties to monitor the investments.

It is common in offshore centres for corporate service providers to appoint independent consultants to review investment portfolio performance upon receipt of portfolio valuations. This offers some additional comfort that the portfolio is being managed properly.

Test yourself 2.5

State three types of portfolio management services available.

Portfolio planning

The following is a non-exhaustive list of factors that should be considered when planning an investment portfolio.

- The accessibility of the investment. Some clients may need to be able to access the funds at relatively short notice or in the case of an emergency.
- The client's attitude to risk.
- Ethical investment requirements.
- Family circumstances – for example, whether there is a dependent child or spouse to provide for.
- Income or capital growth requirements.
- The client's investment time horizon.
- Sufficient protection against inflation (e.g. cash does not usually form a large part of an investment portfolio for significant periods of time).
- The tax efficiency of the investment portfolio.

Asset allocation

Investment portfolios usually include an element of cash, fixed-interest securities and equities to spread the investment risk. The proportion of the split between these elements will reflect economic factors and each client's circumstances and requirements such as attitude to risk. The investments will usually be made across a range of jurisdictions, industries and possibly currencies. Investment managers should aim to achieve the maximum return while taking as little risk as possible.

Cash

Cash forms an important part of any portfolio because it provides:

- funds to meet expected expenditure (such as trustee fees);
- funds to meet extraordinary expenses;
- a fund that can be used to take advantage of market opportunities as they arise; and
- a shelter during times of significant volatility.

Fixed-interest securities
As the name suggests, fixed-interest securities pay a fixed amount of income. When interest rates go up, the capital value of fixed-interest securities falls. Fixed-interest securities usually provide a higher rate of return than cash.

Equities
Equities are usually the most volatile elements of a portfolio. However, they also provide the greatest potential for capital growth over the long term. Equities are usually spread over a range of geographic locations and industries, providing diversification and reducing risk.

Chapter summary

- The offshore financial services sector typically offers: insurance services; investment management services; legal services; tax planning and compliance services; and fiduciary and administration services relating to trusts, companies and other entities.
- Offshore trust company business products include companies, foundations and partnerships and trusts.
- Fiduciary business services include: acting as a company or partnership formation agent; acting as a director, secretary or nominee shareholder; acting as a trustee or partner or a member of a foundation council; and providing a registered office or administrative address to a company, partnership or foundation.
- A fiduciary services provider will face additional risks whenever it provides limited services, such as only providing a registered office.
- Offshore insurance services usually offer a wide range of insurance products such as ATE insurance, reinsurance and captive insurance companies. Captive insurance companies provide self-insurance cover to large commercial Groups and represent an alternative risk management solution to the conventional insurance markets.
- Offshore legal services include the provision of legal advice in connection with: simple and complex structures; as a part of a person's estate planning involving trust company business products; when planning insurance strategies such as captive insurance companies; or when listing a company's shares on a stock exchange.
- Offshore taxation services broadly fall into two categories: tax planning and tax compliance. Tax planning involves the avoidance of tax risks and benefitting as much as possible from legal opportunities to minimise taxation liability.
- Investment management services offshore include fund management – often in relation to collective investment schemes – or private portfolio management services on an execution-only, an advisory or a discretionary basis.

- Portfolio planning involves the consideration of a number of factors about the investor, such as accessibility of the investments, attitude to risk, capital or income requirements, family circumstances and taxation consequences. Portfolios usually contain an element of cash, fixed-interest securities and equities.

Test yourself answers

Test yourself 2.1

The relationship between a trustee and a beneficiary is an example of a fiduciary relationship.

Test yourself 2.2

Four uses of a company incorporated in an offshore jurisdiction are:

- holding assets such as property, yachts and aircrafts;
- holding intellectual property rights;
- holding real estate; and
- trading purposes.

Test yourself 2.3

Three advantages of establishing a captive insurance company are:

- Many offshore centres offer captive insurance companies. They can therefore offer a high level of expertise in dealing with captive insurance.
- In some cases, offshore centres offer a less bureaucratic supervisory insurance regime.
- A captive insurance company can be more cost-effective, as premiums charged by commercial insurers include amounts that cover their profit margin and overheads.

Test yourself 2.4

Ways in which legal services may be used within the offshore business environment are:

- law firms can provide independence to commercial transactions;
- law firms can provide comprehensive cross-border legal advice and fiduciary services to HNWIs and corporate entities undertaking business; and
- offshore law firms are often licensed to conduct trust company business.

Test yourself 2.5

Three types of portfolio management services are:

- advisory management;
- discretionary management; and
- execution-only.

Part two

Chapter 3
The importance of English law

Chapter 4
Contract law

The legal environment

After studying this part, students will gain an understanding of the importance of English law in offshore jurisdictions.

Students will understand the difference between common law jurisdictions, which recognise the distinction between legal and equitable rights, and civil law jurisdictions, which tend not to do so.

This part explains the relationship between common law and **equity**, as well as the development of English law in relation to trusts.

equity
A system of law administered by the Court of Chancery that developed alongside the common law in instances where justice could not be delivered from common law remedies.

doctrine of judicial precedent
Under the doctrine of judicial precedent, a judge is bound to follow decisions that have been reached in earlier court cases.

Students will be able to discuss the advantages and disadvantages of legislation, and the rules and issues surrounding statutory interpretation and will also be able to discuss the advantages and disadvantages of the **doctrine of judicial precedent** under which the courts are obliged to stand by their earlier decisions.

Students will gain an understanding of the essential elements required in order to form a binding contract (agreement constituted by an offer and acceptance, consideration, legal intentions, capacity and legality) and identify when there has been a breach of contract and the consequences of such breach. Students will be able to describe the common law remedy of damages and the equitable remedies that may be awarded by the courts.

Learning outcomes

At the end of this part, you will:

1. understand the impact of English law in offshore jurisdictions;
2. know about statute law and statutory interpretation;
3. understand case law and the doctrine of binding precedent; and
4. understand principles of contract law relating to offshore jurisdictions.

Chapter three
The importance of English law

List of topics

1. The importance of English law in offshore jurisdictions
2. The development of English law
3. The distinction between civil law and common law jurisdictions
4. Trust law
5. Legislation
6. Case law

Introduction

This chapter outlines the reasons why English law is of major significance in many offshore centres. It discusses the two historical sources of law, common law and equity.

The chapter explains how common law is embodied in judicial decisions as, under the system, judges are guided by previous court decisions. The chapter also outlines the system of equity (administered by the Court of Chancery) that developed alongside common law in an effort to introduce fairness where justice was not done under the common law system.

The chapter outlines the relationship between common law and equity, and gives a brief outline of statutory law. The rules of statutory interpretation are discussed, as are the advantages and limitations of both legislation and case law.

1. The importance of English law in offshore jurisdictions

English law is of major significance to a great number of offshore practitioners, depending on where they are operating as the Crown Dependencies and many offshore centres have legal systems based on principles of English law (which applies to England and Wales and is distinct from Scots law).

For example, the Crown Dependencies have their own legal system and jurisprudence; however, their statutory provisions (self-proclaimed laws) are often modelled on English law. Where this is the case, English cases are frequently referenced by their courts (as their model of law can be based on what is referred to as the English common law system. The significance of this will become clear after you are familiar with the concept of judicial **precedent** (discussed in section 5.1 of this chapter).

precedent
A previous court decision, which should guide the court in future cases.

In addition, laws passed in the Crown Dependencies require royal assent from the UK's Privy Council. Although local laws in many offshore centres have been developed to accommodate requirements that are specific to the jurisdiction, these are often based upon similar English laws. This is especially the case where the offshore centre has a close relationship with England. Many laws that are applicable in England are applicable by extension in overseas territories (such as the British Virgin Islands) and in many independent Commonwealth countries, including a number of offshore centres.

1.1 The Judicial Committee of the Privy Council

When the British Empire became the Commonwealth of Nations, many members (i.e. former empire members) chose to retain their legal links with the UK. The Judicial Committee (which serves as the highest authority, representing to all intents and purposes the UK queen's government and judiciary) still hears 'appeals to Her Majesty in Council' from many countries worldwide in respect of every kind of case (including civil and criminal cases).

The Judicial Committee of the Privy Council is the highest (and final) court of appeal for many current and former Commonwealth countries, as well as the UK's overseas territories, Crown Dependencies and military sovereign base areas.

Should the Privy Council choose to do so, it may reverse the decision of the lower court in the country from which the case was referred.

Case law 3.1

Spread Trustee Company Limited v Sarah Ann Acato Hutcheson and others [2011]

On 15 June 2011, the Judicial Committee of the Privy Council delivered its judgement in relation to an appeal following a decision of the Court of Appeal of Guernsey on 26 November 2009 in relation to the case known as *Spread Trustee Company Limited v Sarah Ann Acato Hutcheson and others [2011]*.

The trustee held that the liability of a trustee for gross negligence could lawfully be excluded as a matter of Guernsey customary law and under the Trusts (Guernsey) Law 1989. The issue raised by the appeal was whether it was permissible for a trust deed to exclude a trustee's liability for gross negligence prior to the entry into force of the Trusts (Amendment) (Guernsey) Law 1990 (the Amendment Law), which expressly prohibited such an exclusion.

The trust deed contained a clause which stated:

> 'In the execution of the trusts and powers hereof no trustee shall be liable for any loss to the trust fund arising in consequence of the failure depreciation or loss of any investments made in good faith or by reason of any mistake or omission made in good faith or of any other matter or thing except wilful and individual fraud and wrongdoing on the part of the trustee who is sought to be made liable.'

The Board of the Judicial Committee of the Privy Council allowed the appeal by a majority of three to two. It was stated within the judgement that 'there is no reason to treat Guernsey law as following the Scottish view on this point in preference to the view taken under English law with which the Guernsey law of trusts is more closely associated'.

This case demonstrates the importance of English law to offshore centres and is an example of the Privy Council overturning the decisions of lower courts.

The full judgement can be found on the website of the Privy Council at jcpc.gov.uk.

2. The development of English law

The two historical sources of law are common law and equity.

2.1 The common law

The earliest element of the legal system to develop was the common law applied by royal courts. Under the common law system, English courts were guided by and obliged to follow the decisions that had been made in earlier cases.

The common law is therefore embodied in judicial decisions and over the years has become a comprehensive set of rules. The concept of the court being guided by its own previous decisions is known as the concept of judicial precedent (see section 5.1).

Each time the court applies an established principle to new facts, the common law develops. Similarly, it develops in circumstances where the courts choose not to apply such a principle.

While the common law provided some certainty and consistency in relation to the outcomes of future cases, there were some disadvantages of the system.

Strict adherence to the doctrine of precedent under the common law system resulted in a rigid and inflexible set of rules that did not always amount to justice being done. Much emphasis was placed on procedure. This meant that a claimant might lose their case because of a minor technicality of wording. In addition, only a limited remedy of damages was available under the common law where a case was won. This did not always result in a fair resolution.

2.2 Equity

Equity was developed several hundred years after common law as a system of law applied by the Court of Chancery. Where justice did not appear to be done under common law principles, an otherwise innocent party who could not obtain redress for grievances could apply to the King, who had unfettered, unlimited powers to intervene to determine cases on an ad-hoc basis in order to achieve a fair result. The King later delegated his power to the Chancellor, who became the head of the Court of Chancery.

The Court of Chancery sought to decide cases in accordance with what was right, just and fair rather than adhering to the letter of the law. Unlike common law, the new 'equity' system of law did not focus on procedural technicalities but rather focused on achieving a just result – supplementing common law and introducing the concept of fairness. This system developed into a whole system of law, with a specific set of legal principles and rules.

A system of common law, based on strict rules, and a system of equity, based on fair dealings between parties, developed in parallel.

Test yourself 3.1

How does common law differ from equity?

2.3 The distinction between legal and equitable rights

The concept of the trust is understood to have arisen from the Court of Chancery as a result of the unfairness of the common law systems during the time of the Crusades in the 12th and 13th century in England.

Land owners who had entrusted their property to others to look after while they went to fight in the Crusades often returned to find that they could not insist that their property be conveyed back to them. The Crusaders petitioned the king (and later the Chancellor) to intervene. The Chancellor recognised that each Crusader was the true owner and ordered the legal owner to convey the property back to the Crusader.

Over time the recognition that the legal owner of property was not necessarily the person who was entitled to benefit from it (i.e. that there is a distinction between the legal and equitable rights) developed into the concept of the trust that is widely accepted in the common law jurisdictions today.

A trust can be described as a legal arrangement whereby a person (the settlor) properly vests (transfers in the correct manner) the legal ownership of assets (later referred to as the trust fund or trust property) to another person who is not the owner in their own right (the trustee) for the benefit of another person or persons (the beneficiaries). Be sure to be word perfect on this, so much learning follows on from this definition.

It is widely recognised in common law jurisdictions that, while the legal ownership of the trust property lies with the trustee, the equitable (beneficial) ownership lies with the beneficiaries. The separation of the legal ownership of the trust fund and the equitable ownership has many uses in financial planning.

Test yourself 3.2

What is a trust?

2.4 The relationship between common law and equity

Common law applies automatically. The court, however, has discretion to apply the rules of equity and to grant an equitable remedy if it chooses to do so. Equity and common law often conflict. In a landmark case known as the *Earl of Oxford's Case 1615*, it was decided that where common law and equity conflict, equity must prevail.

In the UK, the Senior Courts Act 1981 also provides that:

> 'every court exercising jurisdiction in England or Wales in any civil case or matter shall continue to administer law and equity on the basis that, wherever there is any conflict or variance between the rules of equity and the rules of the common law with reference to the same matter, the rules of equity shall prevail.'

3. The distinction between civil law and common law jurisdictions

Offshore jurisdictions can be either civil law jurisdictions or common law jurisdictions – or, in some regards (for example, law relating to Foundations), a combination. Former British Commonwealth countries usually have common law systems. Offshore centres such as the Bahamas and Bermuda are considered to be common law jurisdictions.

Civil law jurisdictions generally have a system of law that has been developed from and is based on Roman law. Civil law principles are found in countries such as those in continental Europe. There are many offshore centres that have laws based on civil law principles, including Liechtenstein, Luxembourg and Switzerland.

The civil law system is a codified system in which laws are comprehensively set out in a detailed statutory code. The judges in the courts that implement the law only regard the code: they do not need to regard the outcome of previous cases as the doctrine of judicial precedent does not form a part of the system.

Civil law jurisdictions do not generally recognise the division between legal and equitable ownership and it is not always possible to create a trust in such jurisdictions. The concept of a trust is less understood in civil law jurisdictions and it does not always appeal to clients who have dealings with such jurisdictions.

Trusts are mostly administered in common law jurisdictions where there is certainty about their recognition and the way that they are treated in law. The law in such jurisdictions will allow for their creation and the provisions of the trust will be recognised and enforced by the courts of those jurisdictions.

Some civil law jurisdictions have endeavoured to make it more attractive to administer trusts from within their jurisdiction (e.g. Switzerland is a civil law jurisdiction that does not have its own trusts law). In July 2007, it ratified the Hague Convention on the law applicable to trusts and their recognition, which means that it now recognises their existence.

It also made changes to some of its laws to reduce the uncertainty of the legal environment surrounding the administration of trusts.

Common law jurisdictions have increased their offerings of products such as foundations as an alternative to trusts, as these are better known to clients who are more familiar with civil law. Foundations are discussed further in Chapter 18.

Some jurisdictions – such as Liechtenstein and Panama – have hybrid systems of law in that they follow a mixed law tradition.

Test yourself 3.3

How does the law in common law jurisdictions differ from that of civil law jurisdictions?

4. Trust law

There are various laws governing trusts in England. The relevant statute law includes, but is not limited to, the Trustee Act 2000 and the Trustee Act 1925.

Trust law has also developed as a result of judicial precedent. This means some of the law is found in case law. It can therefore be difficult to access easily all of the relevant rules of law and trust law considerations, although over time the established principles have become well known to trust practitioners. The rules set out the rules regarding the validity of trusts, the duties, powers and right of the parties to a trust are all set out either in the trust laws or in case law.

Test yourself 3.4

What is the main law governing trusts in England?

4.1 Offshore trusts

Trust law in offshore centres is largely based upon English trust law, but there are some differences. The legislation in offshore centres is continually developing as offshore centres seek new opportunities to remain competitive with each other and to protect the attractiveness of their trust industries to non-residents. New trust products have been introduced, such as the non-charitable **purpose trust**, and other welcome legislative changes have been made.

purpose trust
A trust in which the trustee holds the property in order to carry out a specific purpose.

Jersey, for example, has amended its trust law to ensure that a professional trustee is entitled to reasonable remuneration where a **trust instrument** is silent on the matter. This was not previously the case: some trustees who did not carefully check the trust instrument before accepting trusteeship found themselves unable to insist upon being remunerated for their services.

trust instrument
The document which creates a legally binding trust arrangement and which sets out the terms of the trust.

4.2 The rule against perpetuities

The rule against perpetuities restricts the period of time that property can be tied up in trust and therefore unavailable for future generations to sell.

In England, the Perpetuities and Accumulations Act 2009 created a new maximum statutory period of 125 years from the date that the instrument takes effect, whether or not the trust instrument provides for a longer period. This replaced the previous statutory period of 80 years, prescribed by the Perpetuities and Accumulations Act 1964.

A trust may therefore only exist for a certain period of time before an interest in its property must be vested in the beneficiaries. The maximum period that a trust may be in duration for is known as the **perpetuity period**. This will usually be specified within the trust instrument and will be no longer than the maximum period specified in the laws of the jurisdiction.

perpetuity period
The time period within which future interests in the trust property must vest with one or more of the beneficiaries.

However, the rule against perpetuities does not exist in all jurisdictions. Jersey law, for example, was amended in recent years to state that a trust may continue in existence for an unlimited period and that no rule against perpetuities applies unless the trust's terms provide otherwise.

The trust duration is usually set out in the trust deed and may match the maximum prescribed by the law.

Test yourself 3.5

What is the rule against perpetuities in England?

4.3 The proper law of a trust

The proper law of the trust is the law that would be used to determine the answers to questions relating to the validity or interpretation of a trust, the effect of any transfer of property into a trust, the capacity of the settlor, and other important matters such as the powers and duties of trustees.

The proper law of a trust is usually expressed by the terms of the trust. The trustees do not have to be resident in the same jurisdiction as the proper law of the trust, although this is preferable as the trustee should be familiar with the laws of their own jurisdiction.

5. Legislation

Statutory laws are enacted by the government or other authorised bodies (i.e. legislatures) through the process of legislation. In the UK, primary legislation is made by Parliament.

Legislation may also be made by other bodies under authority of primary legislation, such as when secondary legislation is enacted. Secondary legislation may be referred to as regulations. When enacting laws in the UK, Parliament must also have regard to obligations that arise as a result of being a part of the European Union and the requirement to transfer European Union Directives into English law.

One of the major motivations behind the Brexit vote to leave the European Union was the strict obligation to adopt European Laws even where this might be contrary to the will of Parliament or of the people.

5.1 Advantages of legislation

- Any issue can be addressed by statute law at any time by Parliament.
- Statute is carefully constructed and is subject to a process of scrutiny, which should ensure that it achieves the result desired by the law makers.
- Statute law is available to and accessible by the general public. This is an advantage over case law, which is difficult to establish and not located in one place.

5.2 Disadvantages of legislation

- Statutes are numerous and voluminous.
- Statute law cannot anticipate all circumstances or situations that may arise.
- Parliament has limited time to consider draft legislation.
- Statute law is inflexible.
- Governments sometimes lack the resources (including the time and finances) to amend legislation when it becomes out of date and no longer fit for purpose.
- Statute can take a long time to change due to the scrutiny process.

- The public can be apathetic about the legislation process.
- Statute often needs to be interpreted.

5.3 Statutory interpretation

The effectiveness of any statute depends to some extent on the interpretation given to it by the courts, especially where the wording of the statute is ambiguous.

The courts have developed a number of basic principles of statutory interpretation that, although referred to as rules, are instead different approaches to statutory interpretation. These general principles are not found in any statute as they have developed from the decisions of the courts and a combination of the common law and principles of equity. The principles are referred to as the literal rule, the golden rule, the mischief rule and the contextual rule. There is no established order of application where the general principles conflict.

The literal rule

The literal rule places emphasises on the literal (i.e. it relies on the plain and ordinary) meaning of the words contained within statutory provisions. Its advantage is that it respects Parliament as the supreme law maker.

However, the rule has been criticised. In a 1969 report, the Law Commission criticised the literal rule for the following reasons:

- it does not give due weight to the wider context of the law maker;
- where the literal rule is followed, it is possible that legislation writers do not take into account the facts or circumstances that judges later consider;
- law draftsmen do not always choose words to describe the situations intended to be covered by the provision; and
- using the literal rule means allowing no room for difference of opinion.

The golden rule

Where the literal meaning of the statute would lead to an absurd result that is unlikely to have been the intention of the law draftsmen, the judge can depart from the literal meaning under the golden rule – as in *R v Allen (1872)*.

The mischief rule

The mischief rule seeks to ensure that statute should be interpreted with regard to the true intent of its makers. The rule was established in the landmark case known as *Heydon's Case (1584)*. The court set out that for the sure and true interpretation of all statutes, judges should consider three factors:

1. what the law was before the act was passed;
2. what problem, or mischief the act was trying to remedy; and
3. what remedy Parliament was trying to provide.

The judge should then interpret the act in such a way as to deal with the problem that Parliament was trying to address.

The case concluded that having considered those things, the office of the judges is always to make such construction as shall suppress the mischief and advance the remedy.

The mischief rule was considered by the Law Commission to be a more satisfactory approach to statutory interpretation than the literal rule, as it requires a judge to interpret the legislation in a manner that promotes the general aims or purposes of the legislation. This is influenced by the European approach to statutory interpretation which focuses on giving effect to the purpose behind the legislation; in the words of Lord Denning, 'looking to the spirit of the law rather than the letter of the law'.

The contextual rule

The contextual rule is that words should be interpreted in context. This means that the purpose of the statute should be considered when interpreting words within it.

Test yourself 3.6

What is the literal rule of statutory interpretation?

6. Case law

English courts are guided by and obliged to follow the decisions that have been reached in earlier court cases.

These judicial decisions, over the years, have become a comprehensive set of rules referred to as 'case law'. Each time the court applies an established principle to new facts or chooses not to apply an established principle, case law develops.

6.1 The doctrine of judicial precedent

The doctrine of judicial precedent (or binding precedent) means that the judge is bound to apply an existing precedent (a previous court decision) from an earlier case to the facts of the case before them, provided that there are no material differences between the cases and that there are adequate and reliable reports of earlier decisions.

stare decisis
A Latin term for 'let the decision stand'.

The doctrine of judicial precedent is often expressed in the maxim ***stare decisis***, which is Latin for 'let the decision stand', although there are instances where a precedent will not be binding on future courts. For example, if the facts of the case are materially different, the court may distinguish the earlier case on the facts and thereby avoid following it as a precedent. In addition, a statute could be passed at any time and therefore a conflicting precedent would not be followed after its introduction.

Only the ***ratio decidendi*** (the reasoning behind the decision) of a case is binding on future decisions; other precedents may be merely persuasive.

ratio decidendi
The ratio decidendi of a case is any rule of law or legal principle that is treated by the judge as necessary for the basis of the decision made.

Whether a court is bound by a particular precedent depends on its position in the hierarchy of courts. Generally, the decisions of superior courts are binding on lower courts and the decisions of lower courts are not binding on higher courts.

6.2 Ratio decidendi

The *ratio decidendi* of a case is any rule of law or legal principle that is treated by the judge as necessary for the basis of the decision made or is a necessary part of the judge's direction to the jury.

The ***obiter dicta*** of a case are words that are said 'by the way'. The *obiter dicta* do not form a part of the ratio decidendi. Only the *ratio decidendi* is binding on future cases; however, the *obiter dicta* may be treated as having persuasive authority in future cases. Persuasive precedents are those that are not binding in future cases; however, judges in later cases may be influenced by them.

obiter dicta
The obiter dicta of a case are words that are said 'by the way' and do not form a part of the ratio decidendi.

Test yourself 3.7

What is the *ratio decidendi* of a case?

6.3 The advantages of precedent

- Precedents provide consistency, leading to certainty about the way that the law will be decided.
- Precedents should ensure that the law is decided fairly.
- Precedents are tested (based on actual cases) whereas legislation is often untested.
- As precedents can be avoided, they are adaptable to new situations and are therefore more flexible than legislation.
- As precedents are based on facts, they are practical in nature, unlike legislation.

6.4 The disadvantages of precedent

- Judges can be forced to make distinctions that are illogical to avoid an unfair result.
- Judges may distinguish on facts in order to avoid a precedent that leads to uncertainty about the way that the law will be decided.
- The judge's discretion is limited.
- It may take some time for a point of law to be tested, since it will only be tested as and when a case arises.

- Judges may be unable to avoid deciding in line with a precedent which produces an unfair result.
- It can be difficult to establish which facts are the ratio decidendi and therefore the binding elements of a case.
- Unlike legislation, cases are not easily located and they are numerous.

Chapter summary

- English law is of major significance to offshore practitioners as many offshore centres have legal systems based on principles of English law. In addition, the Judicial Committee of the Privy Council is the highest court of appeal in many offshore centres in current and former Commonwealth countries.
- There are two historical sources of law: common law and equity.
- The common law system is embodied in judicial decisions as, under the system, the courts are obliged to follow the decisions that have been made in earlier cases in accordance with the concept of judicial precedent.
- Civil law jurisdictions differ from common law systems as they have developed from and are based on Roman law. Civil law is a codified system. The concept of a trust is less understood in civil law jurisdictions.
- Equity (applied by the Court of Chancery) developed in parallel with common law as a result of justice not being done under the common law. The focus of equity is on fairness and what is right and just, rather than adhering to the letter of the law and focusing on procedural technicalities.
- The concept of the trust is said to have arisen out of equity as the Court of Chancery recognised the distinction between legal and equitable ownership of property. This developed into the concept of the trust that is widely accepted in common law jurisdictions today.
- Common law applies automatically; however, the court has discretion to apply the rules of equity and to grant an equitable remedy (instead of the limited remedy of damages available under common law) if it chooses to do so.
- Where equity and common law conflict, equity must prevail.
- A trust can be described as a legal arrangement whereby a person (the settlor) properly vests (transfers in the correct manner) the legal ownership of assets (later referred to as the trust fund or trust property) to another person who is not the owner in their own right (the trustee) for the benefit of another person or persons (the beneficiaries).
- The rule against perpetuities restricts the period of time that a property can be tied up in trust and therefore unavailable for future generations to sell. In England, the maximum statutory period is 125 years from the date that the instrument takes effect. The maximum period that the trust may be in duration is known as the perpetuity period.

- The proper law of the trust is usually expressed by the terms of the trust and is the law that would be used to determine the answers to questions relating to the validity or interpretation of the trust, the capacity of the settlor, and other important matters such as the powers and duties of trustees.
- Statutory laws are enacted by the government or other authorised bodies through the process of legislation. It often requires interpretation. The main rules of statutory interpretation are the literal rule, the golden rule and the mischief rule.
- The doctrine of judicial precedent is often expressed as the maxim *stare decisis*, which is Latin for 'let the decision stand'. Under the doctrine of judicial precedent, the court is obliged to follow the decisions made in earlier cases. Only the *ratio decidendi* – 'the reason behind the decision' – is binding on future decisions; other precedents may be merely persuasive. Higher courts are not obliged to follow decisions of lower courts.

Test yourself answers

Test yourself 3.1

Under the common law system, English courts were guided by and obliged to follow the decisions that had been made in earlier cases. The common law is therefore embodied in judicial decisions, and over the years it has become a comprehensive set of rules. Each time the court applies an established principle to new facts, the common law develops. Similarly, it develops in circumstances where the courts choose not to apply such a principle.

While the common law provided some certainty and consistency in relation to the outcomes of future cases, there were some disadvantages of the system. Strict adherence to the doctrine of precedent under the common law system resulted in a rigid and inflexible set of rules which, when applied, did not always amount to justice being done.

Equity developed several hundred years after common law as a system of law applied by the Court of Chancery. Where justice did not appear to be done under common law principles, an otherwise innocent party who could not obtain redress for grievances could apply to the King, who had unfettered, unlimited powers to intervene to determine cases on an ad-hoc basis in order to achieve a fair result. Cases were decided in accordance with what was right, just and fair rather than adhering to the letter of the law.

Unlike common law, the new equity system of law did not focus on procedural technicalities but rather focused on achieving a just result – supplementing the common law and introducing the concept of fairness.

Test yourself 3.2

A trust can be described as a legal arrangement whereby a person (the settlor) properly vests (transfers in the correct manner) the legal ownership of assets (later referred to as the trust fund or trust property) to another person who is not the owner in their own right (the trustee) for the benefit of another person or persons (the beneficiaries).

Test yourself 3.3

Civil law jurisdictions generally have a system of law that has been developed from and is based on Roman law. Civil law principles are found in countries such as those in continental Europe. There are many offshore centres that have laws based on civil law principles, including Liechtenstein, Luxembourg and Switzerland. The civil law system is a codified system in which laws are comprehensively set out in a detailed statutory code. The judges in the courts that implement the law only regard the code: they do not need to regard the outcome of previous cases as the doctrine of judicial precedent does not form a part of the system. Civil law jurisdictions do not generally recognise the division between legal and equitable ownership.

Test yourself 3.4

Relevant statute law includes but is not limited to the Trustee Act 2000 and the Trustee Act 1925. As explained in section 2.1 of this chapter, law has also developed as a result of judicial precedent. This means that some of the law is found in case law.

Test yourself 3.5

The rule against perpetuities restricts the period of time that property can be tied up in trust and therefore unavailable for future generations to sell. In England, the Perpetuities and Accumulations Act 2009 has created a new maximum statutory period of 125 years from the date that the instrument takes effect, whether or not the trust instrument provides for a longer period. A trust may therefore only exist for a maximum period of time before an interest in its property must be vested in the beneficiaries. The maximum period that a trust may be in duration for is known as the perpetuity period.

Test yourself 3.6

The literal rule emphasises the literal (the plain and ordinary) meaning of the words contained within statutory provisions. Its advantage is that it respects Parliament as the supreme law maker.

Test yourself 3.7

The ratio decidendi – 'the reasoning behind the decision' – of a case is any rule of law or legal principle that is treated by the judge as necessary for the basis of the decision made or is a necessary part of the judge's direction to the jury.

Chapter four
Contract law

List of topics

1. Contract law
2. The essentials required to form a contract
3. Performance
4. Breach of conditions
5. Remedies for breach of contract

Introduction

This chapter outlines the essentials required in order to form a valid or legally binding contract. It explains the essential elements of agreement (offer and acceptance), **consideration** and intention to create legal relations and capacity.

The chapter discusses what constitutes performance of a contract and outlines what constitutes a breach of contract. It explains the remedies for breach of contract, including the common law remedy of damages and equitable remedies such as **specific performance**, **injunction**, **Mareva injunction** and **rescission**.

consideration
For a contract to exist and be binding, there must be the reciprocal exchange between the parties of a promise in return for a financial or non-financial value or benefit, which is referred to as the 'consideration'. Consideration must be given by both parties to a contract and is defined as 'some right, interest, profit or benefit accruing to one party, or some forbearance, detriment, loss or responsibility given, suffered or undertaken by the other' (*Currie v Misa [1875]*).

specific performance
An equitable remedy that a court may make which orders the parties to the contract to fulfil their obligations under it.

1. Contract law

In order to gain a basic understanding of contract law, this chapter discusses the law of England and Wales.

The contract law of some offshore centres is based on that of England and Wales, although the extent to which they do so varies from jurisdiction to jurisdiction. Jersey follows English law for much of its law. In the case of contract law, it has referred to both Norman Law (French) cases and English cases.

The Jersey Law Commission issued a consultation paper in 2002, entitled *The Jersey Law of Contract*, which sets out some of the difficulties that doing so has

injunction
A judicial order that restrains a person from doing something or orders someone do to something.

Mareva injunction
An order of the court which prevents a defendant to an action from disposing of the assets or transferring them from the jurisdiction.

rescission
The revocation or cancellation of a contract. The effect is to bring the parties to the contract back to the position that they were in before the contract was effected.

presented to the jurisdiction – especially in terms of certainty about the way the law is applied.

2. The essentials required to form a contract

A valid contract is an agreement between parties made with the intention for it to be legally binding and supported by consideration.

A contract can be made in any form – orally, in writing or it may be inferred from the conduct of the parties to it.

The law requires that some contracts must be made in writing, such as those involving the sale of land. In the offshore professional environment, it is unlikely that administrators would deal with oral contracts!

The essential elements of a contract are:

- agreement (evidenced by an offer and an acceptance);
- consideration; and
- intention to create legal relations.

In addition, for the contract to be enforceable, the parties to it must have legal capacity to contract and the contract must not be illegal. Minors and enemy aliens will not have capacity.

This is illustrated in the famous case of *Carlill v Carbolic Smoke Ball Co [1893]*. An advertisement for a medicinal smoke ball advertised the following: '£100 reward will be paid by the Carbolic Smoke Ball Company to any person who contracts the influenza after having used the ball three times daily for two weeks according to the printed directions supplied with each ball.'

Mrs Carlill used the smoke ball in accordance with the instructions and claimed the £100 after contracting influenza. The Smoke Ball Company refused to pay the money arguing that no legally binding contract had come into being.

The case illustrated the following points in relation to contract law.

- All of the essential elements of a contract were present.
- The advertisement constituted an offer. The offer was made to 'anybody who performed the conditions named in the advertisement'. Offers do not therefore need to be made to a named individual and can be made to 'the whole of the world'.
- Acceptance of the offer was performance of the condition (i.e. taking the medication in accordance with the printed directions).
- Acceptance was communicated, albeit after the performance of the condition.
- The taking of the medication as per the printed directions was deemed to be adequate consideration.

It was established by the court, despite the company's efforts to avoid liability, that the wording of the advertisement was a definite legal promise that it intended to be acted upon (an intention to create legal relations was present).

Test yourself 4.1

What are the essential elements of a valid contract?

2.1 The offer

An offer is a definite expression of willingness to be bound on specific terms without further negotiations.

An offer cannot be vague or uncertain. There must also be a clear intention to be bound by the terms of the contract. An offer can be in any form (written, oral or by conduct) and must be communicated to the offeree and must be open at the time when it is accepted. An offer may be made to an individual or open to a number of individuals. The famous case of *Carlill v Carbolic Smoke Ball Co [1893]* (discussed above) illustrates this particular point.

An offer must be distinguished from the mere supply of information that is not intended to be acted upon and instead is intended to enlighten the other party. An **invitation to treat** is not an offer.

invitation to treat
An invitation to another person to make an offer.

Invitation to treat

An invitation to treat is distinct from an offer to be bound. An invitation to treat is an invitation to someone else to make an offer. An invitation to treat cannot therefore be 'accepted' to form a contract. A person who invites another to make an offer is entitled to change their mind.

The general rule is that advertisements are invitations to treat rather than offers. However, in *Carlill v Carbolic Smoke Ball Co [1893]*, the wording of the advertisement was such that it was considered an offer that could be accepted without further negotiation.

The display of goods on a shop shelf is considered an invitation to treat rather than an offer. This is demonstrated by the case of *Pharmaceutical Society of Great Britain v Boots Cash Chemists [1953]*. In this case, the law stated that the sale of certain pharmaceuticals must be dealt with under the supervision of a qualified pharmacist. The pharmaceuticals subject to the law were displayed on the Boots shop shelf with a price tag and the arrangement was that customers paid for the goods at the till where a qualified pharmacist was present.

The Pharmaceutical Society claimed that the display of goods in such a manner was contrary to the law, as the sale took place when the customer placed the goods in the basket, which was not supervised by a pharmacist. The court held that the display of goods in a shop was an invitation to treat and not an offer.

In such situations, it was the customer who made the offer and the shop worker could accept or reject this at the till where the pharmacist was present.

The advertisement of a selling price in response to a request for information is not an offer.

Stop and think 4.1

Is an advertisement that states 'car for sale – good condition – £1,000' an invitation to treat or an offer?

Acceptance of an offer

Acceptance of an offer is an unconditional agreement to all of the terms of the offer, although acceptance in contracts may be 'subject to contract'.

Acceptance may be oral or written. It may also be inferred by conduct unless otherwise specified in the terms of the contract.

The general rule is that acceptance must be communicated to the offeror to be effective; however, *Carlill v Carbolic Smoke Ball Co [1893]* demonstrated that there are situations where the offer dispenses with this requirement. It is possible for acceptance of an offer to be implied from conduct, as illustrated in this case where the use of the smoke ball amounted to acceptance.

If an offer is revoked before it is accepted, the offer is considered to have been terminated.

Termination of an offer

An offer can be terminated by:

revocation
An offer may terminated by revocation. This means that the offeror cancels the offer and it is no longer open for acceptance.

- **revocation**, which must be communicated to the offeree;
- rejection, which could be an outright rejection of the offer or by the making of a counter-offer; or
- because it has lapsed.

An offer could lapse on the death of either party, after the expiry of a period of time specified within the contract or after a reasonable amount of time.

2.2 Consideration

Consideration was defined in *Currie v Misa [1875]* as being 'some right, interest, profit or benefit accruing to one party, or some forbearance, detriment, loss or responsibility given, suffered or undertaken by the other'.

All contracts must be supported by some form of consideration from each party, unless they are made by deed. Consideration is the price paid for the promise.

English law does not enforce a bare promise; it will only enforce a bargain. This means that each party to the contract must promise to give or do something for the other.

In the case of *Carlill v Carbolic Smoke Ball Co [1893]*, the consideration was the taking of the medication as per the printed direction. Consideration could include the making of a payment or the provision of a service.

The following is true of consideration.

- Consideration must be provided by both parties to contract before it is likely to be binding.
- Consideration need not be adequate, but must be sufficient.
- Past consideration is not sufficient consideration and is therefore not valid.
- Performance of existing duties is not sufficient consideration.
- Illegal acts do not amount to sufficient consideration.

Case law 4.1

Chappell & Co Ltd v Nestlé Co Ltd [1960]

The point that consideration need not be adequate but must be sufficient is illustrated in the case *Chappell & Co Ltd v Nestlé Co Ltd [1960]*.

Nestlé had promised to give away a copy of a record to people who sent in three chocolate bar wrappers and a postal order for 1s 6d.

A royalty needed to be paid on the ordinary retail selling price to Chappell & Co, which owned the copyright. Nestlé said 1s 6d was the ordinary retail selling price; however, Chappell & Co disagreed.

As the wrappers were worthless to Nestlé when they received them, it was argued that they could not amount to consideration.

The judge thought this irrelevant and overturned a previous court decision.

The judge added that a contracting party can stipulate for what consideration they choose and argued that 'a peppercorn does not cease to be good consideration if it is established that the promise does not like pepper and will throw away the corn'.

Case law 4.2

Stilk v Myrick [1809]

In the case of *Stilk v Myrick [1809]*, Stilk agreed to be paid wages of £5 a month prior to beginning a voyage from London to the Baltic and back as a seaman. During the voyage, two men deserted.

Myrick, the captain, entered into an agreement with the remaining crew that they should have the wages of those who had deserted if he could not procure two other workers. No other workers joined the crew; however, Myrick later refused to pay the extra wages.

It was held that Myrick's promise was not enforceable due to the consideration Stilk had provided for it – the performance of a duty he already owed to Myrick under contract. Performance of existing duties was not good enough consideration for Myrick's promise to increase his wages.

2.3 Legal intentions

The parties to a contract must have an intention that the arrangement would be legally binding (that they would enter into a legal relationship). Legal intention need not be explicit or in writing, and may be implied from the circumstances.

The following assumptions are generally held by the courts:

- social, domestic and family arrangements are not usually intended to be binding; and
- commercial arrangements are usually intended to be binding.

Case law 4.3

Balfour v Balfour [1919]

In the case of *Balfour v Balfour [1919]*, Mr and Mrs Balfour had visited England when Mrs Balfour became ill. Mr Balfour agreed to pay his wife maintenance each month until she could return home with him; however, he later asked to remain separated from her.

It was held that social relationships are presumed unenforceable, because people do not generally intend social promises to create legal consequences.

Contracts that are signed under duress are considered to be void (not legally binding) from the outset and are not therefore enforceable.

2.4 Capacity

For a contract to be binding, the parties to it must have the legal capacity to enter into it – in other words, they must have the legal power to enter into the contract.

As a matter of public policy, vulnerable individuals are protected by various pieces of legislation. In the UK, contracts made by minors (those who have not reached the age of 18 years) are usually voidable and contracts made with people who are mentally incapacitated are not enforceable.

It is vital that offshore practitioners ensure that third parties have the legal capacity to contract, otherwise the contract may not be enforceable.

2.5 Legality

Contracts that are deemed to be illegal cannot be enforced. For example, a contract to buy oil from a party subject to international sanctions.

3. Performance

The general rule is that contracts must be completely performed.

Case law 4.4

Cutter v Powell (1795)

In *Cutter v Powell [1795]*, Cutter had contracted to work on a ship during a voyage; however, he did not survive the voyage. As he had worked for part of the contract, his widow argued that she was entitled to a **quantum meruit award** ('as much as he has deserved') in relation to the work that her husband had performed.

quantum meruit
This term means 'as much as he deserved'.

It was held that the instrument was an entire contract, under which he had failed to meet his obligations. No compensation for part performance was therefore paid.

There are some exceptions to the rule in *Cutter v Powell* (that contracts must be entirely complete). These include where there is acceptance of partial performance of the contract and where one party prevents the other from performance of their duties.

Test yourself 4.2

What would constitute adequate consideration for a contract to be binding?

4. Breach of conditions

The conditions of a contract should be fulfilled completely. In the event that a contract condition is not fulfilled by either party, the person who did not fulfil their promise is said to be in breach of the contract.

The innocent party to a breached contract could sue the party that did not fulfil its obligations for the standard remedy of damages.

The Limitation Act 1980 states that 'an action founded on simple contract shall not be brought after the expiration of six years from the date on which the cause of action accrued'.

If breaches are absolutely fundamental, it may be possible for the aggrieved party to terminate the contract.

An anticipatory breach is an unequivocal indication that a party will not perform its obligations when performance is due. In such an instance, the party that has fulfilled its promise may treat such a breach as immediate and terminate the contract before the breach actually takes place.

5. Remedies for breach of contract

Damages are the standard common law remedy for breach of contract. However, there are occasions where an award of damages would provide insufficient compensation. In these circumstances, the court can award an equitable remedy.

5.1 Damages

The purpose of damages is to put the innocent party in the position that they would have been in if there had been no breach of the contract.

The aggrieved party to a breached contract is obliged to limit their damages so far as they are able. Only damages that are not too remote may be recovered, and the injured party cannot recover damages for every kind of loss they have suffered. The breach might cause a chain reaction of events, and clearly the contract breaker cannot be held responsible for all of the consequences of their breach.

5.2 Equitable remedies

Equitable remedies include:

- specific performance
- injunction
- a Mareva injunction
- rescission.

An equitable remedy cannot be granted if the claimant has acted unfairly. This is due to the equitable maxim that 'he who comes to equity must come with clean hands'.

Specific performance

The court may make an order for specific performance, ordering the parties to fulfil their obligations under the contract. A circumstance where the court may order specific performance may be where unique or limited edition goods are involved. Specific performance will not be awarded where damages would be an adequate remedy.

Injunction

An injunction is a judicial order that restrains a person from doing something or orders someone to do something.

Mareva injunction

A Mareva injunction is sometimes referred to as an asset freezing order. It is a court order that freezes assets, thereby preventing a defendant from disposing of the assets or transferring them from the jurisdiction.

Rescission

Rescission restores the parties to the position they were in before the contract was entered into. Rescission is not usually an option where there has been substantial performance of the contract.

Test yourself 4.3

Outline two equitable remedies for breach of a contract.

Chapter summary

- A contract is an agreement between parties that is made with the intention for it to be legally binding and supported by consideration. It can be made in any form, although some contracts must be made in writing.
- The essential elements of a contract are agreement (an offer and acceptance), consideration and intention to create legal relations. The parties to the contract must have legal capacity to contract and the contract must not be illegal.
- An offer is a definite expression of willingness to be bound on specific terms without further negotiations. The mere supply of information is not considered an offer, neither is an invitation to treat.
- Acceptance of an offer is an unconditional agreement to all of the terms of the offer. An offer must be accepted before it has been terminated and acceptance must be communicated to the offeror (although there are exceptions to this rule).
- Consideration is defined in *Currie v Misa [1875]* as being 'some right, interest, profit or benefit accruing to one party or some forbearance, detriment, loss or responsibility given, suffered or undertaken by the other'.
- Consideration must be provided by both parties to a contract. It need not be adequate, but must be sufficient. Past consideration is not sufficient consideration, and performance of existing duties is also not sufficient consideration.
- The parties to a contract must have an intention that the arrangement would be legally binding.
- Contracts that are deemed to be illegal cannot be enforced.
- The general rule is that contracts must be performed in their entirety, unless there is acceptance of partial performance of the contract or where one party prevents the other from performance of their duties.

- In the event that conditions of a contract are not fulfilled by either party, the innocent party can sue the other party for the standard remedy of damages, providing they bring an action before the expiration of six years from the date on which the cause of action happened.
- Where damages would not provide sufficient compensation, the court can award equitable remedies such as specific performance, injunction, a Mareva injunction or rescission.

Test yourself answers

Test yourself 4.1

The essential elements of a valid contract are:

- agreement (an offer and acceptance);
- consideration; and
- intention to create legal relations.

In addition, for the contract to be enforceable, the parties to it must have legal capacity to contract and the contract must not be illegal.

Test yourself 4.2

Elements of adequate consideration include the following.

- Consideration must be provided by both parties to contract before it is likely to be binding.
- Consideration need not be adequate, but must be sufficient.
- Past consideration is not sufficient consideration and is not valid.
- Performance of existing duties is not sufficient consideration.
- Illegal acts do not amount to sufficient consideration.

Test yourself 4.3

Two equitable remedies for breach of contract could be:

- **Specific performance:** the court may make an order for specific performance, which orders the parties to fulfil their obligations under the contract. An example of a circumstance where the court may order specific performance may be where unique or limited edition goods are involved. However, specific performance will not be awarded where damages would be an adequate remedy.
- **Injunction:** an injunction is a judicial order that restrains a person from doing something or orders someone to do something.

Part three

Chapter 5
Different taxes and their implications

Chapter 6
Taxation of offshore entities

Taxation

After studying this part, students will have gained an appreciation of the complexity of taxation and the need for expert tax advice. Students will be able to distinguish between direct and indirect taxes. Students will also be able to discuss the principles of the main types of taxes that affect individuals and entities such as companies, trusts, partnerships and foundations and the European Union Savings Tax Directive.

Students will gain an understanding of tax planning concepts and of the general principles of residence and domicile, and what affect these may have, depending on the basis that individuals may be taxed under (e.g. the arising basis or the remittance basis).

Students will be able to discuss the use of offshore entities to reduce taxation. Students will gain an awareness of the important difference between tax avoidance and tax evasion, and will gain an understanding of the OECD's work on harmful tax practices and on the internationally agreed standard of exchange of information on tax matters.

Learning outcomes

At the end of this part, you will:

1. understand the principles of taxation as applied to offshore jurisdictions; and
2. understand how to prevent harmful tax practices.

Chapter five

Different taxes and their implications

List of topics

1. The need for expert advice
2. Types of taxes
3. Income tax
4. Corporation tax
5. Capital gains tax
6. Inheritance tax
7. Other taxes
8. The European Union Savings Tax Directive
9. Tax Information Exchange: The US FATCA and the OECD CRS
10. Tax planning concepts
11. Basis of taxation

Introduction

This chapter outlines the need for expert advice in the complex area of taxation.

Some of the many types of taxation that an offshore administrator may encounter are outlined briefly. The most common main taxes to individuals and entities – income tax, corporation tax, capital gains tax and inheritance tax – are discussed in more detail, mainly in relation to how each tax affects individuals (taxation of entities discussed later).

The chapter outlines the European Union Savings Tax Directive, which has been implemented in some offshore centres despite there being no obligation for the centres to do so.

The chapter concludes with a discussion of basic tax planning concepts, including residence and domicile, and outlines how non-UK-domiciled individuals (or those who are not resident in the UK) may choose to be taxed on the special **remittance basis of taxation** rather than the more usual

remittance basis of taxation
Individuals who are non-domiciled in the UK (or those who are not resident in the UK) pay UK tax only on the amount of their foreign income and gains that they remit to the UK.

arising basis of taxation
Under the arising basis of taxation, a person will pay UK tax on all of their income as it arises and on the gains as they accrue, wherever that income and those gains are in the world.

arising basis of taxation. Please take care to ensure you understand these two bases as they are key to how taxation is currently applied by the UK.

1. The need for expert advice

There are many complex rules surrounding taxation that vary depending on the circumstances of an individual (or entity), including their residence, ordinary residence and their domicile.

There was a lack of clarity about the way that all individuals would be treated for tax purposes. Court cases decided the rules to some extent; however, the circumstances of the cases do not apply to every situation. The statutory residence test (explained further later) was intended to (and should) provide some certainty going forward; however, the concept of domicile is still unclear in some situations.

Offshore professionals must be aware that taxation is a very complex issue, that each client's circumstances will be different. Offshore service providers must therefore appreciate the need for expert advice. It is for this reason that offshore service providers such as trust companies usually do not provide taxation advice.

Tax rules change every year, sometimes more than once a year. Offshore service providers should therefore be conscious that, while a structure may have been appropriate at the time that it was created, it may not be tax-efficient years later. In order to act in the best interests of beneficiaries and beneficial owners of offshore vehicles, taxation consequences of services provided should be considered and reviewed on an ongoing basis.

It is not the role of offshore trust and company professionals to give tax advice and they are entitled to trust that their clients are honest individuals who have declared all relevant income and gains to their tax authorities. That said, service providers and their employees cannot shut their eyes to obvious cases where they suspect tax evasion and must adhere to their own AML/CFT obligations under their jurisdiction's AML legislation. Dealing with the proceeds of tax evasion or suspected tax evasion in almost all jurisdictions is dealing with the proceeds of crime and a criminal offence.

2. Types of taxes

Taxes are charges levied by the government in order to raise revenue to pay for public services to meet the needs of communities, to ensure that people are healthy and secure, and to assist those in need.

Taxes are compulsory. Although tax rules differ significantly from jurisdiction to jurisdiction, the considerations that offshore service providers pay attention to in the UK will be similar to those required in other major onshore centres. In order to help you gain an understanding of taxation principles, UK rules are referred to in this chapter. Natural persons, legal persons and legal arrangements are all subject to tax. The basis of taxation varies depending on the type of person (natural or legal) and the jurisdiction that they are deemed to be resident (or domiciled) in. The types of taxes that an individual or a company may have to pay include:

- capital gains tax (CGT);
- income tax;
- corporation tax;
- inheritance tax (IHT);
- stamp duty;
- value added tax (VAT) and Goods & Services Tax (GST); and
- wealth taxes.

Taxes can be direct taxes, indirect taxes or other taxes such as annual wealth taxes. Taxes on income can be described as direct taxes. Examples of direct taxes include:

- capital gains tax;
- corporation tax;
- income taxes;
- inheritance tax;
- stamp duty land tax; and
- stamp duty reserve tax.

Indirect taxes are those on expenditure, for example:

- customs duties;
- excise duties;
- insurance premium tax; and
- VAT.

While the above taxes are common in onshore jurisdictions, as explained in Chapter 1, it is not common to find taxes such as CGT, IHT, VAT or GST in offshore centres.

Offshore administrators with onshore clients will still need to be familiar with such taxes regardless of whether they exist in offshore centres, as their clients and entities under administration may be impacted by them.

Where taxes do exist in offshore centres, they are usually only charged on the residents of the jurisdiction and exist at a much lower rate than is charged in onshore jurisdictions.

Stop and think 5.1

Which of the taxes described above are levied in your jurisdiction?

Test yourself 5.1

Explain the difference between direct and indirect taxes.

2.1 Types of tax systems

Income tax systems include three types: progressive, proportional and regressive.

Progressive
Progressive tax systems are those with a rate of tax that increases as the individual's earnings increase. There is usually a level of income that is exempt from tax, followed by tax rates that increase when certain income thresholds are met. The UK has a progressive tax system.

Proportional
Tax systems where there is a flat tax regime are sometimes referred to as proportional tax systems. With a proportional tax system, there is usually an exemption for a certain amount of **earned income** and then a single rate is charged on the remainder. Offshore centres such as Jersey and Guernsey often have such a taxation system.

earned income
Income that is earned (e.g. salary or bonuses from employment or income from a trade or profession or from a pension).

Regressive
Regressive tax systems are those where the rate of tax falls as the level of income that is subject to tax rises.

3. Income tax

Income tax is levied on the income that individuals receive in excess of an exempt personal allowance. Other entities such as trusts and non-resident companies may also be subject to income tax.

Individuals and other entities, such as trustees, are usually required to complete an income tax return on an annual basis. This declares the amount of income that has been received during the previous fiscal (tax) year.

The fiscal year in the UK starts on 6 April and ends on 5 April. Fiscal years differ from jurisdiction to jurisdiction. Administrators in offshore centres should be conscious of the fiscal year in their own jurisdiction as well as that of their client's residence.

In the UK, income tax is a progressive tax, meaning that the amount of income tax payable increases with the level of income of the taxpayer. The tax band that an individual's earnings fall into determines the rate of income tax to which they are subject. There is a basic rate, a higher rate and an additional rate.

The amount of income tax charged depends on whether the income is earned or unearned. The two types of income are taxed at different rates and on the level of income received.

3.1 Earned income

Earned income is income that is earned – for example, salary or bonuses from employment or income from a trade or profession or from a pension.

3.2 Unearned income

Unearned income includes income that is received from sources other than from employment (or a trade or profession), such as:

- interest on bank deposits (or building society interest);
- dividends received from shareholdings and equity investments;
- interest on bonds and gilts;
- rental income from investment properties; or
- royalty payments.

unearned income
Unearned income includes income that is received from sources other than from employment (or a trade or profession).

Tax on bank interest and dividends are usually 'taxed at source', which means the tax has already been deducted from the amount received. Where income is taxed at source, basic rate taxpayers will have no further tax to pay. However, those paying tax at higher rates will have more to pay.

Dividends are taxed at three different rates, depending on the level of overall taxable income.

Savings income is taxed at four different rates, depending on the individual's overall taxable income.

4. Corporation tax

Income earned by companies is subject to corporation tax (also known as profits tax in some jurisdictions). Corporation tax is charged on the net profits of the company after relevant allowances and reliefs. This tax is discussed later in Chapter 6.

5. Capital gains tax

Capital gains tax (CGT) is a tax on profits or gain that is made when a **chargeable asset** is disposed of (sold, given away, transferred or exchanged for something else) if it has increased in value and a 'gain' has been made.

chargeable asset
An asset that may be subject to capital gains tax when it is disposed of (i.e. sold or given away).

Chargeable assets are those that may be subject to CGT when they are disposed of.

Current examples of items that attract CGT are:

- buildings (not including an individual's main residence);
- land;
- personal possessions (e.g. artwork or jewellery) worth more than £6,000; and
- shares or securities and other investments.

There are some assets that are not subject to CGT. These include:

- an individual's main residence;
- money that forms a part of an individual's income for income tax purposes;
- personal belongings worth £6,000 or less when they are sold;
- special investments such as Individual Savings Accounts (ISAs);
- UK government bonds (gilts); and
- **wasting assets** such as cars.

wasting asset
An asset that has a limited life and therefore decreases in value over time (e.g. a car or a factory machine).

There are other disposals that are not subject to CGT, such as gifts between spouses. Gains made upon the transfer of an asset due to the owner's death are not subject to CGT, although they may be subject to IHT. Losses made – for example, on the sale of an investment property – can be offset against **chargeable gains** made on other assets.

chargeable gain
A gain made on the sale of an asset that is liable to capital gains tax.

Those who make a chargeable gain (i.e. someone who is liable to CGT) must complete a self-assessment tax return.

5.1 Who pays CGT?

CGT is payable in the UK by:

- individuals who are UK-resident;
- UK-resident trusts;
- non-resident persons in respect of UK land and buildings; and
- non-resident persons trading in the UK through a branch.

Individuals who are UK-resident are liable for CGT on their worldwide capital gains.

Individuals who are UK-resident but are not UK-domiciled are liable for CGT on gains arising from the disposal of UK assets and are liable to CGT on 'foreign gains' if the proceeds are remitted to the UK.

See Table 5.1 for details of how to decide whether an asset is a UK or foreign asset.

Table 5.1: Assets and their locations

Type of asset	Location of asset
Land and buildings	Where the property is physically located
Chattels	Where they are physically located (they can move between countries)
Debts	Where creditor is located
Patents and trademarks	Where they are registered

6. Inheritance tax

Inheritance tax (IHT), also known as estate or death tax, is usually paid on a person's estate when they die.

IHT is payable by the person or persons who inherit a deceased person's assets where the estate is valued over a certain threshold (also known as the 'nil rate band'). The rate of IHT can be high – for example, the UK rate of IHT in 2017/18 was 40%. It is therefore very important for an individual with substantial assets to consider any potential IHT liability when planning to pass on their personal wealth and estate to their heirs.

In the UK, IHT is sometimes payable during a person's lifetime when trusts are settled or gifts are made by a person during their lifetime – for example, when setting up a trust, IHT is payable at half of the death rate.

Other gifts are referred to as potentially exempt transfers (or PETs).

If these are made during the lifetime of an individual, a properly executed PET can reduce the level of tax liability on the estate at the time of death.

6.1 Exempt transfers

Some transfers are exempt from IHT. These include those that are made to:

- a spouse or civil partner;
- qualifying charities;
- some national institutions such as museums, universities or the National Trust; and
- UK political parties (if the party meets certain criteria).

In the UK, each person is allowed to make gifts worth up to a certain value in each tax year. These are exempt from IHT. There are also exemptions up to certain limits for other types of gifts, such as gifts made in consideration of marriage, small gifts and regular gifts (e.g. for birthdays and Christmas).

6.2 Potentially exempt transfers (PETs)

Any gifts that are made to individuals will be exempt from IHT as long as the donor lives for seven years after making the gift (this is known as the seven-year rule). An IHT liability will arise in relation to the assets if the donor's estate is worth more than the 'nil rate band'. Taper relief is applied, meaning the amount of tax payable reduces on a sliding scale. A person's estate therefore includes their assets at the time of their death and any assets given away within the seven years prior to their death.

Taper relief

Taper relief is applied if a person dies between three and seven years of making a gift. This reduces the percentage of IHT payable on a sliding scale based on the time between the date that the gift was made and the date of death. IHT is not payable after seven years.

Test yourself 5.2

When is inheritance tax usually payable?

7. Other taxes

7.1 Wealth taxes

Some jurisdictions impose an annual wealth tax on individuals whose assets are valued above a predetermined level on a specific date. As wealth taxes are determined on 'net worth', they can be referred to as 'net worth' taxes. The percentage level of wealth tax is often low, but this is not always the case. France is an example of a country where a significant level of the government's revenue arises from 'net worth' taxes. Wealth taxes are not usually a feature in offshore centres.

7.2 Stamp duty

Stamp duty or stamp duty land tax or document duty as it is known is some jurisdictions is payable on a range of land and property purchase and transfer transactions above a certain value.

Stamp duty is calculated on an ad valorem basis, and is thus linked to the market value of the transaction. In some jurisdictions, duty may also be payable on the purchase of shares if the transaction is paper-based (or stamp duty reserve tax if it is a paperless transaction).

7.3 Annual tax on enveloped dwellings

In the UK, an annual tax is payable on enveloped dwellings (ATED) since 1 April 2013. The ATED introduced an annual fixed-sum tax for residential properties owned by non-natural persons such as companies valued at (now) more than £500,000 and owned by non-natural persons such as companies, trusts or foundations.

7.4 Value added tax

Value added tax (VAT) also known as Goods and Services Tax (GST) in Jersey and some other jurisdictions, is charged at a flat rate and is added to the price that is paid for certain goods or services. VAT is calculated at each level that value is added to an article or service as it progresses to an end user.

VAT is an indirect tax on consumption that is collected by retailers as part of the purchase transaction and typically it is incorporated in the final price of the goods and services. The retailer must subsequently pay the VAT element to the tax authorities, and there can be severe penalties if this process is not carried out correctly. Over the years, VAT has replaced sales tax in many countries because it is less open to abuse, although there have been various schemes to illegally avoid UK VAT using offshore centres to issue false invoicing to disguise the onshore source of taxable goods and services.

Although VAT exists in the Isle of Man and GST exists in Jersey, such taxes are not a common feature of other offshore centres.

7.5 Withholding taxes

Withholding taxes are deducted at source from interest and dividends paid to residents of foreign countries. The investor's country of residence may give some relief against these deductions when it assesses the individual for taxes due. A double taxation agreement between two countries can also reduce the level of withholding tax suffered by a foreign investor.

In some countries – for example, the USA and the UK – there is no withholding tax on interest-paying investments for non-residents. This is because the jurisdictions want to encourage overseas investors to purchase government debt and to deposit funds with banks and other interest-paying institutions.

8. The European Union Savings Tax Directive

The European Union Savings Tax Directive (EUSTD, sometimes referred to as the EUSD) applies to residents of the EU who have overseas investments.

The ultimate aim of the EUSTD is to enable savings income – usually in the form of interest payments – made in one EU member state to beneficial owners resident in another EU member state to be made subject to effective taxation in the owners' country of residence. Automatic exchange of information has been adopted in most member states, although some states were permitted to adopt a withholding tax for a transitional period.

Non-EU jurisdictions had some choice in respect of how they would implement the EUSTD. In the Crown Dependencies, paying agents (service providers that pay interest savings income to EU residents) initially asked their clients to choose from the following options.

- **Retention tax option:** under this option, the service provider retains tax at a predetermined rate and pays this to the relevant country's authorities without giving details of the resident to whom the payment relates.
- **Voluntary exchange of information**: under this option, the service provider will not retain tax from savings and instead provides its own tax authorities with information about the client to whom the interest relates. This option requires the express authorisation of the individual.
- **Exemption:** the paying agent will not be required to apply the retention tax or exchange of information where a beneficial owner presents to the paying agent a certificate drawn up by the competent authority of their EU member state of residence for tax purposes. Some centres have since moved (following changes in 2015) to fully automatic exchange.

9. Tax Information Exchange: The US FATCA and the OECD CRS

In response to increasing global concerns relating to illegal tax evasion and legal, but aggressive tax avoidance schemes and the use of offshore centres by global corporations, big business and high net worth individuals, governments have collaborated through the OECD to create a framework of automatic tax information exchange which now includes well over 100 jurisdictions.

The USA initially introduced the US Foreign Account Tax Compliance Act (FATCA), which was intended to capture tax information relating to the financial assets of US citizens, wherever the assets are located. This was followed by the introduction of the Common Reporting Standard (CRS) by the OECD countries and now means that most developed countries will now automatically disclose tax information relating to the income and assets of non-residents to the tax authorities of their home jurisdiction, and/or their tax domicile where this is different.

There are also many international tax information exchange agreements in place outside of the FATCA and CRS initiatives.

The US Foreign Account Tax Compliance Act (FATCA) was designed to limit the evasion of tax by US taxpayers holding offshore accounts by placing reporting requirements on foreign financial institutions. The Act was implemented further to the Hiring Incentives to Restore Employment Act. Foreign Financial Institutions (FFIs) are required to report information about financial accounts held by US taxpayers, or held by foreign entities in which US taxpayers hold a substantial beneficial interest.

FFIs report directly to the US Internal Revenue Service (IRS). Some jurisdictions have entered into an intergovernmental agreement with the USA that allows FFIs to report information on US account holders directly to their national tax authorities, who in turn will report to the IRS. FFIs include non-US entities such as banks, brokers, dealers, insurance companies and trust or fiduciary services business.

FATCA provides that a withholding tax will be applied on any US-sourced income and gross proceeds paid to non-participating FFIs. A non-participating FFI is one that has not yet signed an agreement with the IRS to undertake due diligence on the accounts held with its organisation and to report on the relevant US persons each year. FFIs that have entered into an agreement are referred to as participating FFIs: these entities can avoid the withholding tax. In contrast, there are no withholding tax provisions under CRS.

Offshore service providers have invested considerable resources into improving their systems and general administration to comply with FATCA and CRS requirements and report tax information such as the name, address and tax identification number of the client, their account balances and the amount of income paid to them. Service providers must be able to identify entities and the tax domicile of their controlling persons and underlying ultimate beneficial owners, as their tax information must be reported if they are a US citizen or are tax domiciled in a CRS participating jurisdiction.

Offshore centres' privacy legislation will not protect clients from the requirements of FATCA or CRS because tax information exchange laws take precedence over all duties of confidentiality. The UK and other jurisdictions have entered into FATCA intergovernmental agreements with the USA and CRS intergovernmental agreements with CRS participating jurisdictions. Many offshore centres, including Jersey, Guernsey, the Isle of Man and the Cayman Islands have also sought to negotiate other such tax transparency agreements in order to facilitate the reporting of relevant tax and financial information held in their jurisdiction.

9.1 Intergovernmental agreements

The automatic tax information exchange arrangements under FATCA and CRS provide coverage of over 100 developed countries and offshore centres.

There is a growing global intolerance of tax evasion that is resulting in a general trend towards the automatic exchange of tax information and a number of jurisdictions that do not participate in CRS have negotiated individual Intergovernmental Tax Information Exchange Agreements, which closely reflect the FATCA and CRS arrangements.

Some offshore jurisdictions have also negotiated a disclosure facility that allows clients with assets outside of their home jurisdiction to come forward and regularise past tax affairs without incurring severe penalties and fines that would otherwise apply for illegal tax evasion.

10. Tax planning concepts

Tax laws differ between jurisdictions. However, many countries usually consider factors such as residence, domicile or citizenship when deciding whether or not an individual is 'fiscally connected' to a jurisdiction and therefore subject to taxation.

Other factors that may cause an individual to be 'fiscally connected' to a country may include their employment or the location of assets held. A client may be fiscally connected to more than one jurisdiction.

Different tax rules apply to an individual depending on their residence and their domicile. The rules on residence and domicile differ from jurisdiction to jurisdiction.

Tax planning is therefore a complicated area and one for which the clients of offshore service providers will often need to take advice. For the purposes of illustrating taxation concepts, the UK's taxation concepts will be discussed.

10.1 Residence

An individual's residence has a significant bearing on an individual's UK tax liability and determines the basis of taxation to which an individual is subject. UK-resident individuals are normally taxed on an arising basis, meaning that UK tax is paid on all income as it arises and gains as these accrue wherever they arise in the world. UK-resident but non-domiciled individuals have the choice of whether to use the arising basis of taxation or the remittance basis of taxation.

Prior to the implementation of the Finance Act 2013, the terms 'residence' and 'ordinarily resident' were not defined in tax legislation. The understanding of these terms had evolved based on legal cases decided by the courts over a long period of time. The court's decisions did not provide clear principles that are applicable to all taxpayers.

Individuals were treated as UK-resident for tax purposes in the following circumstances:

- where they were physically present in the UK for 183 days or more during any tax year;
- where they came to the UK with the intention of living in the UK permanently;
- where they came to the UK temporarily, and spent 91 days or more each year in the UK on average for three complete tax years, they would be treated as UK-resident from the start of the fourth year;
- Where they came to the UK for a purpose which will meant that they remained in the UK for at least two years, whether or not they spent 183 days or more in a particular year in the UK (e.g. due to their employment); and
- where they usually live in the UK and go abroad for short periods (business trips or holidays).

In addition to the number of days spent in the UK, many other different factors also indicated whether an individual was resident in the UK. This included ownership of UK assets, as well as their family, social and business ties. Clients of offshore centres with UK connections had to take great care to count the number of days they spent in the UK to ensure that they did not become UK-resident. Only days where the individual was present in the UK at midnight are counted.

Losing residence

In order to prove that an individual was no longer resident in the UK, they needed to demonstrate that they had severed most ongoing links with the UK. Many factors would be relevant to HMRC when deciding whether an individual was no longer UK resident.

10.2 The statutory residence test

The UK government acknowledged the complexity of the residence rules that had developed over time. It introduced the statutory residence test in the Finance Act 2013 to provide certainty about the rules and encourage individuals and business looking to invest in the UK. The statutory residence test came into effect for the 2013–14 tax year and supersedes all previous legislation, case law and guidance.

The statutory residence test applies for the purposes of establishing a person's residence status for income tax and CGT, as well as corporation tax and IHT (where relevant). Each tax year is considered separately.

Under this legislation, a person will be resident in the UK for a tax year if they spent 183 days or more in the UK in that year.

If they did not, then they will be subject to a series of tests to assess residence.

These include:

- the automatic overseas tests;
- the automatic UK tests; and
- the sufficient ties test.

Automatic overseas tests

If a person has not spent 183 days in the UK in a tax year, then they are subject to the automatic overseas tests.

The automatic overseas tests ask whether:

- the person was resident in the UK for one or more of the three tax years preceding the tax year, and spent less than 16 days in the UK in the tax year;
- the person was resident in the UK for none of the three tax years preceding the tax year, and spent fewer than 46 days in the UK in the tax year; and
- the person worked full-time overseas over the tax year, without any significant breaks during the tax year, and spent fewer than 91 days in the UK in the tax year. In addition, the number of days in the tax year in which they worked for more than three hours in the UK is less than 31 (this test does not apply in certain circumstances where the person has a relevant job on board an aircraft, ship or vehicle).

If any of the automatic overseas tests for a tax year are met, the person is automatically non-resident for that year and there is no need to consider any of the other parts of the statutory residence test.

The automatic UK tests

If a person does not meet any of the automatic overseas tests, they are UK resident if they meet one of the automatic UK tests. The automatic UK tests are as follows:

- 183 days or more were spent in the UK in the tax year;
- the person had a home in the UK during all or part of the tax year and spent at least 91 consecutive days there (30 of which fall in the tax year in consideration) the person had no overseas home or, if they have one, not more than a permitted amount of time was spent there; and
- the individual worked full time in the UK for a period of 365 days, at least some of which fell into the tax year.

The sufficient ties test

If none of the automatic overseas tests or any of the automatic UK tests are met, the sufficient ties test is used to determine a person's UK residence status for a given tax year. If a person was not UK-resident for any of the three years before the tax year, their sufficient ties are considered. A person's ties are their connections to the UK and include:

- a 90-day tie;
- a country tie (if the person was resident in the UK for one or more of the three tax years before the one in question);
- accommodation ties;
- family ties; and
- work ties.

Of particular relevance is whether the person was tax resident for any of the three years before the tax year in question. The number of days that a person has spent in the UK in the tax year is also important, as this decides the number of UK ties that are needed for a person to be UK-resident. If a person has spent less time in the UK in a tax year, more ties are required to for them to be deemed UK-resident.

10.3 Ordinary residence

The new statutory residence test has abolished the concept of ordinary residence. Ordinary residence for tax purposes was a separate concept from tax residence, but which had a bearing on an individual's tax liability. There was no statutory definition of ordinary residence.

The term applied to people who were deemed resident in the UK for a particular tax year but who were not typically (ordinarily) resident there.

10.4 Dual residence

It is possible to be resident in the UK and at the same time be resident for tax purposes in another country. Individuals with 'dual residence' would be taxed in accordance with any double taxation agreement that exists between the individual and the other country.

Double taxation agreements

Different countries have different tax rules. It is therefore possible that a person could become liable to tax in two countries on the same income. In order to avoid the double taxation that would arise in these circumstances, countries such as the UK have negotiated double taxation agreements with a large number of countries. Individuals who find themselves subject to double taxation need to make a claim under the relevant agreement.

10.5 Domicile

Domicile is not defined in tax law. Domicile is distinct from a person's nationality and place of residence. A person's domicile is typically where they have their permanent home.

Everyone must have a domicile. There are three types of domicile:

- domicile of choice;
- domicile of dependence; and
- domicile of origin.

A person's domicile only affects their position for income tax and CGT purposes if they have foreign income and gains.

A person's domicile is also relevant for determining if a person's estate is subject to IHT.

Deemed domiciled

The concept of being **deemed domiciled** is only relevant for IHT purposes. Becoming deemed domiciled for IHT purposes does not affect a person's income tax or CGT position.

deemed domiciled
A person becomes deemed domiciled for IHT purposes if they have been present in the UK for any part of the last 17 out of 20 years including the tax year in question.

An individual will be deemed domiciled in the UK for a tax year if they have been resident in the UK for any part of the last 17 out of 20 years, including the tax year in question.

Domicile of origin

A person acquires a domicile of origin when they are born. This is acquired from their father, unless their parents were not married, in which case the domicile of origin is acquired from the mother. This domicile is retained until a person acquires a domicile of choice.

Domicile of choice

To acquire a domicile of choice, a person must leave their current country of domicile and settle in another country. It is not sufficient simply to be present in the jurisdiction of the domicile of choice. In order to demonstrate that a person has acquired a new domicile of choice, they would need to provide strong evidence that they intend to leave the UK permanently.

The following factors may be relevant to acquiring a new domicile of choice:

- an individual's business interests;
- an individual's intentions;
- an individual's permanent residence;
- an individual's social and family interests; and
- the property that an individual owns.

Domicile of dependence

Until a person has the legal capacity to change their domicile, their domicile follows that of the person on whom they are legally dependent. Before 1974, a married woman automatically acquired her husband's domicile. This is no longer the case.

Test yourself 5.3

What is the difference between an individual's domicile and their residence?

11. Basis of taxation

11.1 The arising basis of taxation

A person who is resident in the UK is normally taxed on the arising basis of taxation. This means that they will pay UK tax on all of their income as it arises and on the gains as they accrue, wherever that income and those gains are in the world.

11.2 The remittance basis of taxation

The remittance basis of taxation is an alternative tax treatment to the arising basis. It is available to people who are resident in the UK and who are either non-UK domiciled or not UK-resident. Individuals who have the option to use the remittance basis of taxation may still choose to use the arising basis of taxation if they so wish.

Under the remittance basis, non-domiciled individuals (or those who are not UK-resident) pay UK tax only on the amount of their foreign income and gains that they bring (or remit) to the UK. Tax is still paid on income and gains that accrue in the UK. Individuals who are not UK-resident but are domiciled in the UK can use the remittance basis in respect of foreign income, but cannot use it in respect of foreign gains.

If a long-term UK resident (one who has been in the UK for seven out of nine of the previous tax years) decides to claim the remittance basis, they may have to pay the remittance basis charge (RBC). The RBC is an annual tax charge for non-domiciled individuals who have been UK-resident for at least seven years. It is higher for those who have been UK-resident for 12 years or more.

Chapter summary

- Taxes are a charge levied by the government in order to pay for public services and are compulsory.
- There are complex rules surrounding taxation that vary depending on an individual's (or an entity's) circumstances including their residence and their domicile. As the rules change (and new rules are introduced) each year, it is important that offshore administrators appreciate the need for expert advice.
- The types of taxes that an individual or entity may have to pay include income tax, capital gains tax, inheritance tax, wealth taxes, stamp duty and VAT. Many of the types of taxes found onshore will not be present

in offshore centres, although clients of offshore centres may be subject to them. It is therefore important that offshore administrators have an understanding of the taxes and basic tax concepts.

- Taxes on income can be described as direct taxes, while taxes on expenditure can be described as indirect taxes.
- Tax systems can be progressive (where the rate of tax increases as the individual's earnings increase), proportional (where the amount of tax charged is at a single rate) and regressive (where the amount of tax charged falls as the level of taxable income rises). The UK's system is a progressive system. It is more common in offshore centres for the system to be proportional.
- Income tax is levied on the income that individuals receive in excess of a personal allowance. Income is levied at different rates depending on whether the income is considered earned income or unearned income. Corporation tax is charged on the income of companies.
- Capital gains tax is charged on profits or gains that are made when a chargeable asset is disposed of and a gain has been made. Capital gains tax is charged to UK residents and non-resident persons in relation to their UK land and buildings and those who trade in the UK through a branch.
- Inheritance tax is charged on a person's estate when they die if the estate is valued over a certain threshold known as a 'nil rate band'. Inheritance tax can also be payable during a person's lifetime – for example, when an individual settles a trust. Some transfers are exempt from inheritance tax. Others are potentially exempt, meaning that the gift will be free of inheritance tax providing the donor lives for seven years after making the gift and that the gift was not a **gift with reservation**.

gift with reservation
A gift whereby the donor retains an interest in the asset (this could involve retaining a benefit or control of the asset).

- Some offshore centres have implemented the European Union Savings Tax Directive, even though they were not under an obligation to do so. This applies to residents of the EU with overseas investments. The ultimate aim of the directive is to enable savings income in the form of interest in one EU member state to beneficial owners resident in another to be made subject to effective taxation in their country of residence.
- The US Foreign Account Tax Compliance Act and Common Reporting Standard have been designed to limit the evasion of clients holding offshore accounts by placing statutory automatic reporting requirements on offshore financial institutions and service providers that operate such accounts.
- In many jurisdictions, concepts such as a person's residence and domicile are key factors in deciding whether or not they will be subject to taxation in their jurisdiction. In the UK, the term 'residence' is very important although it was not defined in the tax legislation until recently, when the UK government introduced a statutory residence test. The term 'domicile' is not defined in legislation and is typically considered to be where an individual has their permanent home.

- Individuals in the UK are usually subject to tax on the arising basis, which means that they will pay UK tax on all of their income as it arises and on the gains as they accrue, wherever that income and those gains are in the world. Individuals who are not domiciled in the UK or who are not resident there may choose instead to use the special remittance basis of taxation, which means that tax is only paid on income when it is remitted into the UK.

Test yourself answers

Test yourself 5.1

Taxes on income are direct taxes. Examples of direct taxes include:

- capital gains tax;
- corporation tax;
- income taxes;
- inheritance tax;
- stamp duty land tax; and
- stamp duty reserve tax.

Indirect taxes are those on expenditure, such as VAT, GST, customs duties, excise duties and insurance premium tax.

Test yourself 5.2

Inheritance tax (IHT), also known as estate or death tax, is usually paid on a person's estate when they die. IHT is payable by the person or persons who inherit the deceased person's assets when the estate is valued over a certain threshold (also known as the 'nil rate band').

In the UK, IHT is sometimes payable during a person's lifetime when trusts are settled or gifts are made during a person's lifetime – for example, when setting up a trust, tax is payable at half of the death rate. Other gifts are referred to as potentially exempt transfers. If these are made during the lifetime of an individual, this can reduce the level of tax liability on the estate at the time of death.

Test yourself 5.3

Domicile is not defined in tax law. Domicile is distinct from a person's nationality and place of residence. A person's domicile is typically where they have their permanent home, but their residence is just where they happen to be. Everyone must have a domicile. There are three types of domicile:

- domicile of origin;
- domicile of choice; and
- domicile of dependence.

The Finance Act 2013 introduced the statutory residence test. The statutory residence test applies for the purposes of establishing a person's residence status for income tax and CGT, as well as corporation tax and IHT where relevant. Each tax year is considered separately. Under the new legislation, a person will be resident in the UK for a tax year if they spent 183 days or more in the UK in the tax year. If they did not, then they are subject to the automatic overseas tests. If they do not meet one of these, then they are subject to the automatic UK tests. If one of these applies, the person is considered to be UK-resident. If they do not, then they are subject to the sufficient ties test. If this final test is met, the person is UK-resident; if they do not, they are not UK-resident.

Chapter six
Taxation of offshore entities

List of topics

1. The use of offshore entities to reduce taxation
2. Taxation of companies
3. Taxation of trusts
4. Taxation of partnerships and foundations
5. Tax avoidance and tax evasion
6. The OECD
7. Transfer pricing

Introduction

This chapter begins with a discussion of the use of offshore entities to reduce taxation before outlining how a company's residence is determined and discussing the important issues surrounding management and control. Corporation tax, to which companies are subject, is explained.

The chapter discusses the taxation of trusts (i.e. of trustees), which includes the inheritance tax charges that can arise on the creation of the trust and on each ten-year anniversary, and the exit charges that arise when funds are paid out of the trust.

The taxation of partners and partnerships is explained briefly, as is the taxation of foundations.

The chapter outlines the important difference between tax avoidance and tax evasion, and some circumstances in which offshore administrators may find themselves inadvertently assisting clients to evade taxation. The OECD's contribution to the global fight against tax evasion is discussed, including its model agreement on exchange of information and its guidelines to address what is commonly referred to as transfer pricing.

1. The use of offshore entities to reduce taxation

As discussed in Chapter 5, tax planning is a very complex area that requires expert advice from a taxation professional, particularly when it involves the use of offshore entities or structures.

In some circumstances, offshore entities (such as trusts and companies) can be used to retain income or profits offshore, thus deferring a tax liability until distributions are made, which could be at a time when the client's basic rate to tax has fallen.

Tax deferral is a key feature of tax planning.

Chapter 5 also discussed how non-residents of a jurisdiction may be taxed more favourably than its residents. Offshore companies incorporated (and managed and controlled) and trust that are administered in a low-tax jurisdiction provide an opportunity to hold the assets or undertake a specific activity at arm's length from the beneficial owner(s). This allows the client (who may be the ultimate beneficial owner) to benefit from the non-resident status of the company or trustees, although **anti-avoidance legislation** must always be taken into consideration because as we have seen, governments are ever eager to limit the opportunities for the mitigation of taxation.

anti-avoidance legislation
Legislation that has been introduced in order to restrict or eliminate the opportunities to minimise taxation via the use of offshore centres, particularly where the transaction has no purpose other than the minimisation or avoidance of taxation.

You will also be aware that the FATCA and CRS initiatives have already introduced tax information transparency across more than 100 jurisdictions. The common reporting standard (CRS) is part of international efforts in this regard. The FATF have issued a recommendation that every jurisdiction should also ensure there is a register of the beneficial ownership of companies and of the beneficiaries of trusts available for public inspection. At the time of the revision of the text, these issues are a matter of extensive and ongoing debate in the UK parliament, where proponents of such a move claim this will help address difficulties in deterring illegal tax evasion and money laundering.

An example of how offshore trusts and companies have been used together to reduce a taxation liability is where funds are settled into a trust and then loaned on a commercial (on an 'arm's length') basis to an underlying company for the specific purpose of enabling the company to purchase a property to be rented out. When rent is received, the cost of repaying the loan to the trust can be offset as an expense against the rental receipts, thus reducing the taxable income of the company.

Over the years, anti-avoidance legislation has been introduced in onshore jurisdictions. This is designed to reduce the opportunities available to residents (or domiciled individuals) to avoid taxation via the use of offshore entities by preventing certain types of financial activity from receiving favourable tax treatment.

Every time one tax 'loophole' becomes unavailable, tax specialists work hard to identify new opportunities. The UK government, to name just one onshore jurisdiction, has a difficult task in keeping up with the strategies that are devised. It has to balance legislation with rules that encourage wealthy people to live and remain in the UK and incentivise businesses to operate from within the UK. It has made a substantial effort by requiring advisers to pre-register details of schemes that they plan to have their clients use.

2. Taxation of companies

2.1 Residence of companies

Companies that are incorporated in the UK are usually considered resident in the UK. For foreign incorporated companies (those incorporated in offshore centres), a company is considered to be resident wherever the central management and control actually abides (as established by *De Beers Consolidated Mines Ltd v Howe*).

The significance of a company's residence is as follows.

- UK-resident companies are subject to corporation tax (discussed later in this chapter) on the whole of its chargeable profits on a worldwide basis.
- Companies that are not resident in the UK are liable to corporation tax only if they carry on a trade in the UK through a permanent establishment.
- Non-resident companies may also be liable to UK income tax (rather than corporation tax) on non-trading income.

2.2 Management and control

Company law requires that a company is managed and controlled by its directors. The role of directors is subject to extensive legal obligations requiring them to act autonomously and without influence so that their decisions are taken only in the best interests of the company.

For tax purposes the director's actions represent what is referred to as the 'mind and management' of the company and as such the location of both the directors and where their decisions take place is a critical starting point for determining where any tax liabilities might arise.

The directors of companies acting as offshore service providers are often directors of companies that are incorporated, managed and controlled outside of the UK (i.e. from within the offshore centre). A service provided might also incorporate and control a dedicated company that can be appointed as the director of client companies serving as a 'corporate director'.

Such companies are considered non-resident in the UK.

Where it is the case that management and control must be outside of the UK for a structure to be tax-efficient, it is very important that service providers explain this concept to the client (who may be the beneficial owner or beneficiary of a trust that owns the company).

Providers must ensure the client understands that they will not be able to take part in the management or decision making of the company. Often this is easier said than done!

It can be difficult for offshore service providers to keep their client from interfering in the affairs of the company. Offshore directors who simply follow their client's wishes run the risk of allowing their client to become a **shadow director** (one who has not been formally appointed but who is deemed in law to be a director due to the function that they are fulfilling).

shadow director
One who has not been formally appointed but who is deemed in law to be a director due to the function that they are fulfilling.

If such a client is resident in the UK, it could be successfully argued that the company is managed and controlled from within the UK and that the company should therefore be paying corporation tax on the whole of its profits on a worldwide basis. Management and control must therefore be firmly with the offshore directors.

All too often, offshore administrators face the situation where an onshore client decides to become involved in the affairs of the company, sometimes signing documentation on behalf of the company or negotiating major deals on its behalf and failing to keep the offshore directors informed.

In some circumstances, offshore directors have good reason to involve or take advice from the client – for example, they may be an expert on the business that the company is engaged in and the client's opinions, contacts and general involvement is of great assistance to the directors.

It is perfectly acceptable for directors to involve their clients in such circumstances.

However, it is vital that the terms of such an arrangement are documented and respected. Perhaps the client could be engaged as a consultant, with an agreement that makes it clear the scope of their involvement and providing for the client to be properly remunerated for their services.

It should also be well documented that decisions are made by the directors and not the client. There is an ever-increasing body of case law decisions (which many examiners enjoy reading) addressing how well (or not) offshore service providers manage this process.

Offshore directors will have taken some comfort from the decision in the case known as *Wood v Holden [2006]*.

Case law 6.1

Wood v Holden [2006]

In this case, HMRC had decided that Eulalia Holding BV (Eulalia), a company incorporated in the Netherlands, was resident in the UK and a large CGT sum was payable by Mr and Mrs Wood.

The sole director of the Eulalia Holding BV was AA Trust (a part of ABN AMRO in the Netherlands), which took decisions in relation to a transaction in Amsterdam.

HMRC argued that ABN AMRO did not in fact take the decisions but did what it was told to do by Mr Wood. The court of appeal decided that 'the transaction was conducted by AA Trust as the director of Eulalia and in the Netherlands. AA Trust might have had every incentive to carry it out; but it had the right to refuse if it wished, and had the power to do so. In my judgement Eulalia was and remained in the Netherlands, and was not resident in the United Kingdom'.

In essence, the case demonstrates that although offshore directors may make decisions that are ill informed, what is important in determining management and control is that the decision lies with the directors. In light of developments in anti-avoidance legislation, a court faced with the same circumstances may well reach a different conclusion today, and in any event the UK's HMRC would now have the ability to apply tax directly to certain UK situs assets such as land and buildings. As a consequence, non-resident ownership of UK property now provides a lesser protection from the assessment of tax liabilities.

Test yourself 6.1

Where is a company usually considered to be resident?

2.3 Corporation tax

Corporation tax is a tax on the taxable profits of limited companies and some unincorporated organisations (for example, partnerships, some sole traders, depending on the jurisdiction).

Taxable profits for corporation tax include:

- profit from taxable income such as trading profits and investment profits; and
- capital gains (known as chargeable gains for corporation tax purposes).

Offshore service providers often appoint tax advisers to deal with the tax authorities and to complete corporation tax returns on their behalf.

Companies that are resident in the UK are subject to corporation tax on the whole of their worldwide income and gains. Companies that are non-resident in the UK pay corporation tax only if it carries on a trade in the UK through a permanent establishment.

The amount of tax payable is usually a percentage of the taxable profits of the company. The profits that are chargeable to corporation tax will not usually match the amount of profit that is shown in the accounts of the company, as certain expenses charged to the profit and loss account (e.g. entertainment expenses) are not allowed as a deduction for corporation tax purposes.

3. Taxation of trusts

A trust will normally be considered resident wherever the majority of its trustees are resident. If all trustees are resident outside of the UK, the trust will not be considered UK-resident. But do bear in mind if a company can be ruled resident where it is managed (rather than where its directors are resident) then might the same be applied to a case where someone other than the trustees is seen to 'direct' the trustees' activities or usurp them?

If, however, there is a mixture of resident and non-resident trustees, the trust will be resident unless the settlor was non-resident and non-domiciled. Trusts that are resident in the UK are liable to income tax on their worldwide income.

Non-resident trusts are treated differently depending on the type of trust (such as whether they are discretionary trusts or life interest settlements) and depending on the residence status of the settlors or beneficiaries.

In the same way that offshore directors of companies that claim to be non-resident in the UK must ensure that the management and control of the company is firmly with them, offshore trustees must ensure that the assets of the trust (properly referred to as the 'trust fund') are properly vested in them and that they are in control of them (rather than the client).

This ensures the trust cannot be considered to be a sham (that the settlor never really gave their assets away and continues to control them), ensures that gifts with reservation (discussed later in this chapter) are not created, unless this is intended, and avoids unintended taxation consequences.

Trustees will need to consider their dealings with the settlor and any beneficiaries in order to avoid any problems arising.

For example, it may be better to charge the client a market rent for the use of a property owned by the trustees, thereby introducing funds into the trust, rather than create a gift with reservation. In such circumstances, offshore administrators must also ensure that any relevant documentation is also in place (such as an adequate (fully commercial)) tenancy agreement).

When a beneficiary receives distributions from the trust assets, this does not usually result in a liability on the trustees; however, it may result in a tax liability for the beneficiary. Trustees should consider the impact of taxation when deciding whether to make distributions (and whether they should distribute capital or income).

The beneficiary should be informed that they may be subject to tax on the distribution and be advised to take their own tax advice. The type of trust as well as the residence and domicile of the settlor and the beneficiaries may also result in the settlor being liable to tax. It Is not unheard of for beneficiaries to attack trustees for making distributions to them that result in unexpected tax consequences on their part.

It has been said that in general, capital distributions to beneficiaries will be free of liability to income tax while income distributions are likely to result in a liability. That said, the tax authorities can view regular capital distributions as income. It is therefore very important to keep income and capital entirely separate so that it can always be shown whether a distribution is capital or income. This is the reason that separate bank accounts for capital and income are maintained for offshore clients and that capital and income should not be mixed.

As is always the case with taxation, it is important that both the trustee and those who will receive distributions obtain suitable taxation advice. A prudent trustee might choose to ask to see confirmation that advice has been obtained by the beneficiary(ies).

As a trust is not a legal person, any tax liability of a trust is assessed on the trustees (rather than the trust itself) and due to be paid by the trustee.

3.1 UK inheritance tax charges in relation to trusts

Gifts donated to discretionary trusts are chargeable lifetime transfers and immediately subject to an IHT charge of 20% over the nil rate band. IHT at the usual death rate will be payable if the donor does not survive for seven years after settling the trust.

Offshore trusts can therefore be a useful way to reduce the level of IHT that is payable from a person's estate, providing the assets are gifted in a timely manner.

If assets were held by an individual rather than in a trust, IHT would be due on the individual's death in respect of any UK assets. If the individual were deemed domiciled in the UK, IHT would be due in respect of their worldwide assets.

Wealthy individuals can therefore reduce their IHT liability by giving away their assets.

If an asset is given away to an offshore trust but an interest is kept in the asset (e.g. a settlor settles their house into the trust but continues to live in it rent-free), then this gift is known as a gift with reservation and is not a potentially exempt transfer. Such a gift would still form a part of the person's estate upon their death.

The payment of rent at the prevailing market rate by a settlor residing in a gifted property can be expected to address and remove the reservation and this is an important consideration if property transfers into a trust are to be tax efficient.

3.2 Excluded property trusts

Non-UK-domiciled individuals (who have not yet been deemed domiciled in the UK) can create **excluded property trusts**. These are trusts that are created with non-UK situs assets (i.e. assets that are not situated in the UK).

excluded property trust
Excluded property trusts are those created by non-UK domiciled individuals (who have not yet been deemed domiciled in the UK) with non-UK situs assets. Such trusts receive favourable IHT treatment.

Such trusts receive favourable IHT treatment. Non-UK situs assets will be exempt from IHT to the extent that these assets are held within such a trust. In addition, the ten-year anniversary charge to IHT and the exit charges that are charged when property leaves the trust can be avoided, depending on the extent that non-UK assets are held in the trust.

If assets were not held in trust, the IHT would become payable upon the death of the individual on their UK assets. If they had become deemed domiciled in the UK, tax would be due in respect of their worldwide assets.

3.3 Ten-year anniversary charge

The assets of discretionary trusts (and some other trusts) may give rise to IHT charges every 10 years and a charge when the property leaves the trust (known as an exit charge). To the extent that an excluded property holds non-UK situs assets, these charges will not arise.

With careful tax planning, charges on UK situs assets may also be avoided. Offshore administrators should diarise the consideration of what steps may need to be taken prior to the 10-year anniversary of trusts under their administration to reduce the IHT charge that becomes payable. They will also need to remember to take active steps to declare and pay the tax due to HMRC, which may be unaware of the existence of the trust.

Test yourself 6.2

What is meant by the term 'gift with reservation'?

4. Taxation of partnerships and foundations

4.1 Partnerships

Partners of a general partnership are required to pay income tax on their share of the partnership's profits. A nominated partner completes a partnership tax return showing each partner's share of the profit or losses. With limited partnerships, limited partners are taxed on their share of the profits as if they had carried out the activity of the limited partnership alone. Although a limited liability partnership (LLP) is regarded as a corporate body for tax purposes, it is treated in the same way as a general partnership. LLPs are transparent for tax purposes, which means that they are not taxed in their own right. Instead, each member is assessed for tax as if they were members of a general partnership. In other words, they are treated as having carried on the activities of the LLP in proportion to their membership.

For CGT purposes, the partners are charged on the disposal of their interests in chargeable assets of the partnership where gains arise.

4.2 Foundations

Foundations are incorporated bodies, although they differ somewhat from companies.

UK tax law does not specifically deal with entities such as Foundations and it is for HMRC to seek to tax foundations (perhaps as corporate bodies or as trusts) and see if they succeed. This situation is likely to change with firm rules established.

Tax advisers have stated that it is likely that the residence of foundations will be determined as if they were companies (i.e. resident wherever they are managed and controlled).

Those administering offshore foundations should be aware that anti-avoidance legislation applied to offshore trusts and foreign companies may well be applied to foundations.

5. Tax avoidance and tax evasion

5.1 Tax avoidance

Tax avoidance involves the legitimate minimisation (or avoidance) of a taxation liability. In a House of Lords' decision (*Inland Revenue Commissioners v Duke of Westminster [1936]*), Lord Tomlin commented that:

> 'Every man is entitled if he can to arrange his affairs so that the tax attaching under the appropriate Acts is less than it otherwise would be. If he succeeds in ordering them so as to secure that result, then, however unappreciative the Commissioners of Inland Revenue or his fellow taxpayers may be of his ingenuity, he cannot be compelled to pay an increased tax.'

The UK and other onshore jurisdictions have sought to minimise the opportunities for tax avoidance by the implementation of anti-avoidance legislation.

This legislation is designed to remove the potential to use any arrangements that result in the avoidance of taxation and involves using the tax laws to gain an advantage that Parliament did not intend. Attitudes to tax avoidance have changed significantly since the global financial crisis and offshore centres are working in a very different environment than may have been the case in past years.

While tax avoidance is not illegal, it is becoming more socially unacceptable. The former UK Prime Minister, David Cameron named Jimmy Carr (a comedian as someone whose legal tax minimisation was morally unacceptable from the dispatch box in the UK parliament! Mr Carr undid those arrangements!

The shift in global sentiment against permitting the mitigation of tax together with the anti-avoidance initiatives of governments to 'address' loop holes in their tax laws provides a challenge to practitioners in offshore centres that have historically benefitted from providing legal tax avoidance solutions that are now being outlawed as demand for such services may contract.

As a result, successive UK governments are aiming to crack down on tax avoidance.

The so-called Panama papers and the Paradise papers have revealed legitimate planning (as well as perhaps some that was illegal too) and led to an increased focus on what might now be said to be a grey area.

If evasion is black and avoidance white then 'aggressive avoidance' or 'morally unacceptable avoidance, might be legal but grey.

Making it work 6.1

In 2012, a number of large organisations received negative publicity after it was revealed that they had structured their affairs in a manner that resulted in tax avoidance.

Public pressure and media attention resulted in one organisation, Starbucks, writing to its customers to announce changes that resulted in the company paying higher corporation tax in the UK, even though it had complied with all UK tax laws and no corporation tax was actually owed to HMRC.

HMRC published its tax avoidance strategy in March 2011. The foreword to that document states:

> 'Being open for business does not mean being open to tax avoidance. We are committed to creating the right tax environment for business and individuals, which encourages enterprise and minimises red tape. In return we expect everyone to pay their fair share. And where we see tax avoidance, we will crack down on it. That's particularly important at a time when the Government has had to make tough choices elsewhere.'

There are three core elements to HMRC's anti-avoidance strategy. These are as follows:

- preventing avoidance at the outset where possible;
- detecting it early where it persists; and
- countering it effectively through challenge by HMRC.

5.2 Disclosure of Tax Avoidance Schemes (DOTAS)

Disclosure of Tax Avoidance Schemes (DOTAS) is one way that HMRC identifies tax avoidance schemes. The DOTAS regime enables the government to react quickly to close loopholes by changing the law and by allocating resources to conduct investigations whenever a disclosure is made.

Under the DOTAS rules, promoters of tax avoidance schemes are required to give HMRC early information about schemes that bear certain 'hallmarks'.

Promoters must provide HMRC with details of any clients who have used their avoidance scheme. Anyone using a tax avoidance scheme that falls within the DOTAS rules must also disclose this fact to HMRC. Rangers FC (the Scottish club fell foul of such arrangements in court with regard to an 'employee benefit trust' scheme which it used to try to pay sums to players in the most tax effective manner.

5.3 The General Anti-Abuse Rule (GAAR)

The Finance Act 2013 introduced the UK General Anti-Abuse Rule, which was designed to counteract the tax advantages arising from tax arrangements that are deemed to be 'abusive'.

GAAR permits tax adjustments that are just and reasonable in all circumstances in whatever form is appropriate. This could include making or modifying assessments, amending or disallowing claims or other actions.

The UK introduced GAAR in part 5 of the Finance Act 2013. It introduced an important caveat to the approach taken historically by the courts when considering tax disputes to the effect that taxpayers were free to use ingenuity to reduce their tax bills by any lawful means. GAAR imposes an overriding statutory limitation on the nature and extent to which taxpayers can go in their attempts to reduce their tax bills.

That limit is reached when the tax avoidance arrangements go beyond what is judged as a 'reasonable course of action'. GAAR provides HMRC with discretion to decide on what is a 'tax abusive arrangement' and allows HMRC unilaterally to impose a liability to counteract any avoidance benefit by imposing a new tax liability or adjusting an existing one.

The primary objective of GAAR is to deter taxpayers from entering into 'abusive arrangements' and to deter would-be promoters from promoting such arrangements. The exact parameters of what is permitted are decided by HMRC on a case-by-case basis.

GAAR applies to the following taxes:

a) Income Tax;
b) Corporation Tax, including any amount chargeable as if it were corporation tax;
c) Capital Gains Tax;
d) Petroleum Revenue Tax;
e) Inheritance Tax;
f) Stamp Duty Land Tax; and
g) Annual Tax on Enveloped Dwellings.

Test yourself 6.3

What is meant by the term 'tax avoidance'? (Don't skimp on writing out your answer to this test yourself! It will matter.)

5.4 Tax evasion

Tax evasion, in contrast to tax avoidance, involves the illegal activity of evading a tax liability that is otherwise due and payable.

Tax evasion could simply involve an individual failing to declare to the relevant tax authority their income, gains or profits that would be liable to tax, resulting in a lower tax bill than would have otherwise been incurred.

Tax evasion may involve the failure to declare income or gains received in respect of an offshore interest-bearing bank account or the making of a fraudulent return by under-declaring income to the authorities in their country of residence.

Offshore administrators could find themselves inadvertently assisting clients to evade taxation in a number of circumstances and for a number of reasons.

- Aggressive tax avoidance schemes are being actively targeted by tax authorities and can become superseded by anti-avoidance legislation and become tax-inefficient as tax legislation changes.
- Administrators that do not keep up with changes or check the tax efficiency and ongoing legitimacy of the structures under their administration risk facilitating tax evasion.
- Tax advice may be perfectly adequate and outline clear advantages to the client in certain circumstances; however, if the administrator fails to administer the case in accordance with the advice, this can have adverse consequences.
- Credit cards drawn on an offshore trust or company provide clients with access to funds in their home jurisdiction without them needing to receive funds into personal bank accounts in their own jurisdiction. This is obviously open to abuse and offshore administrators should seek to understand any request for a credit card.

The UK government is working with the international community to pursue offshore tax evasion. Agreements such as the Liechtenstein Disclosure Facility, the UK-Swiss Agreement on Tax Cooperation have now been largely superseded by the adoption of CRS, which provides for the automatic reporting of information between more than 100 jurisdictions and represents the current global standard in international tax transparencies. CRS also has replaced the agreements the UK government reached with many offshore centres including Jersey, Guernsey and the Isle of Man and facilitates HMRC in addressing on a more global scale historic tax evasion by UK taxpayers.

As offshore administrators do not necessarily understand the taxation advantages of using an offshore centre, there is a risk that they take a 'tick box' approach when they are in receipt of tax advice, simply filing the advice and taking comfort from the fact that they have received it. This could be the route to committing (no matter how unintentionally) the crime of assistance – as in assisting a criminal retain the proceeds of their crime. Not checking the adequacy of the tax advice is a risk.

Administrators should ensure that they read the tax advice to ensure that it makes sense and is likely to be adequate. If they are unsure, they should refer the matter to a more senior colleague. The risk might be that real. Tax advice that specifically states that it does not cover, for example, the client's country of residence or domicile may not give a full picture of the client's taxation circumstances. The suitability of the tax adviser is a risk factor to consider. A tax adviser who will produce a document that clearly states the adviser is not an expert in the tax laws in the jurisdiction that the document purports to give advice in relation to should be viewed with caution.

Offshore administrators sometimes find themselves with tax advice that outlines advantages to their client on a particular basis (e.g. that the client is resident or domiciled in a certain jurisdiction). If it is clear to the administrator from their dealings with the client that this basis is not correct, this should be questioned.

While it is currently unnecessary in every jurisdiction for offshore administrators to obtain tax advice in relation to every client relationship, it is good practice to consider obtaining tax advice if the client cites tax reasons for the business relationship or informs the administrator that they have already taken tax advice. Using a fiscal excuse to explain away a transaction that should invoke an administrator's suspicion is very convenient, as administrative staff do not always have an understanding of taxation.

The UK government is working with the international community to pursue offshore tax evasion. Agreements such as the Liechtenstein Disclosure Facility, the UK–Swiss Agreement on Tax Co-operation and other agreements providing for the automatic reporting of information set a new standard in international tax transparency. The UK government has reached agreements with many offshore centres including the Isle of Man, Guernsey and Jersey, and is providing disclosure facilities to address historic tax evasion by UK taxpayers. HMRC has set out its offshore evasion strategy for 2013 and beyond in a document entitled *No Safe Havens*.

HMRC explains that the objectives of its new strategy are to ensure that:

- there are no jurisdictions where UK taxpayers feel safe to hide their income and assets from HMRC;
- would-be offshore evaders realise that the balance of risk is against them;
- offshore evaders voluntarily pay the tax due;
- those who do not come forward are detected and face vigorously enforced sanctions; and
- there will be no place for facilitators of offshore evasion.

HMRC has also set out that the way that it will achieve these objectives, including:

- reducing the opportunities to evade offshore;
- increasing the likelihood of evaders, and those who make offshore evasion possible, being caught; and
- strengthening the severity of the punishments for those who are caught.

The publicity following the leaking of the so-called 'Paradise Papers' and those from Panama will have helped HMRC a great deal.

In the UK, those connected with companies also need to be aware of the impact of the Criminal Finances Act 2017 which introduced two new criminal offences. The first applies to all business, wherever located, in respect of the facilitation of UK tax evasion.

The second offence applies to businesses with a UK connection in respect of the facilitation of non-UK tax evasion, meaning that a company (or partnership) can be prosecuted for failing to prevent its employees and other 'associated persons' (such as sub-contractors or agents) from facilitating tax evasion in the UK and abroad. Crucially these offences can expose directors to personal, criminal liability for corporate tax evasion practices allowed to operate unchecked. In 2018, at the time of writing, there have already been such criminal prosecutions in the UK.

Making it work 6.2

Tackling tax evasion

The UK government has made tackling tax evasion (and being seen to be doing so) and recovering funds from secrecy jurisdictions a priority in recent years.

The Liechtenstein Disclosure Facility (LDF)

Under an agreement signed in August 2009 between the UK and Liechtenstein governments, people with unpaid tax linked to investments or assets in Liechtenstein could settle their tax liability under a special arrangement that ran from 1 September 2009 until 31 March 2015. Under the arrangement, tax offences were guaranteed not to be prosecuted, there was a penalty of 10% and tax was only assessed from April 1999 onwards.

The agreement also required 'financial intermediaries' in Liechtenstein to be satisfied that their UK customers would declare their Liechtenstein investments to HMRC in future. HMRC indicated that it expected £3 billion to be recovered via the Liechtenstein Disclosure Facility during its existence.

The Swiss Agreement

On 24 August 2011, HMRC announced that the UK and Switzerland had reached 'an historic agreement' to tackle tax evasion by those who have abused Swiss banking secrecy.

Under the terms of the agreement, UK taxpayers who have not paid their taxes will be subject to a significant one-off deduction of between 19% and 34% to settle past tax liabilities. As a gesture of good faith, Switzerland agreed to make an up-front payment to Britain of CHF (Swiss francs) 500 million. In addition, a new information-sharing provision allows HMRC to find out when Swiss accounts are held by UK residents and a new withholding tax of 48% on investment income and 27% on gains was introduced from 2013. The withholding tax will not apply if the taxpayer authorises a full disclosure of their affairs to HMRC. George Osborne, the then Chancellor of the Exchequer, was reported to have said:

> 'Tax evasion is wrong at the best of times, but in economic circumstances like this (meaning at that time) it means that hard-pressed law-abiding taxpayers are forced to pay even more. That is why this Coalition Government made it a priority to go after those who don't pay their fair share. We will be as tough on the richest who evade tax as on those who cheat on benefits. The days when it was easy to stash the profits of tax evasion in Switzerland are over.'

Many have commented that the deal with Switzerland will encourage tax evaders to move their funds to Liechtenstein to take advantage of the LDF instead. As referred to above the introduction of CRS has largely superseded the LDF and the Swiss Agreement.

6. The OECD

The Organisation for Economic Co-operation and Development (OECD) was formed on 30 September 1961. It is an international organisation with the mission to promote policies that will improve the economic and social well-being of people around the world.

There are more than 30 member states. A representative from each member state, plus a representative from the European Commission, makes up the OECD Council, which has the power to make decisions on behalf of the organisation. The UK is a member of the OECD.

The OECD provides a forum in which governments can work together to share experiences and seek solutions to common problems. Tax evasion and what the OECD deems to be 'harmful tax practices' are a problem that the OECD has been addressing for many years.

6.1 'Harmful Tax Competition'

The OECD published a report (22 years ago but nonetheless still important) in 1998 entitled 'Harmful Tax Competition: An Emerging Global Issue'.

The report identified jurisdictions that it deemed to be tax havens. In deciding whether a jurisdiction was a tax haven, the lack of effective exchange of information was a key criterion.

In 2000, the OECD published a list of over 40 jurisdictions that met the criteria for tax havens set out in the 1998 report.

In mid-2002, it published a list of uncooperative tax havens that did not make commitments to the exchange of information. Each of the jurisdictions on the list made the relevant commitments to implement the OECD standard and as a result, the last three jurisdictions (Andorra, Liechtenstein and Monaco) were removed from the list in May 2009. So in just 13 years, all the 40 jurisdictions were 'encouraged' to improve – and did so!

6.2 Exchange of information

The OECD views transparency and effective information exchange as essential in enabling countries to apply and enforce their tax laws. The OECD's focus on transparency and effective exchange of information is designed to ensure that a legal framework is in place to allow jurisdictions to cooperate with each other without violating their own laws.

The standards of transparency and effective exchange of information that have been developed by the OECD are primarily contained in Article 26 of the OECD Model Tax Convention and the 2002 Model Agreement on Exchange of Information on Tax Matters.

6.3 The OECD's Model Tax Convention

The Model Tax Convention creates an obligation to exchange information that is relevant to the correct application of a tax convention, as well as for the purposes of the administration and enforcement of domestic tax laws of the contracting states.

Article 26 of the OECD Model Tax Convention provides the most widely accepted legal basis for bilateral exchange of information for tax purposes. More than 3,000 bilateral treaties are based on the Model Convention.

The internationally agreed tax standard developed by the OECD in conjunction with non-OECD countries – also endorsed by the UN and G20 – requires exchange of information on request in all tax matters for the administration and enforcement of domestic tax law, without regard to a domestic tax interest requirement or bank secrecy for tax purposes.

Austria, Belgium, Luxembourg and Switzerland, which have all been described as 'secrecy jurisdictions', initially indicated that they had reservations concerning Article 26. However, after succumbing to international pressures in March 2009, each of these countries notified the OECD that they were withdrawing their reservation.

Where information is exchanged, it is subject to strict confidentiality rules. In addition, the information that is exchanged may only be used for the purposes provided for in the convention. Only information that is relevant may be exchanged, and the requesting state should also have pursued all domestic means to access the requested information except those that would give rise to disproportionate difficulties.

6.4 The OECD Model Agreement on Exchange of Information on Tax Matters

The Global Forum is the continuation of a Forum created in the early 2000s and developed the OECD Model Agreement on Exchange of Information on Tax Matters.

It consists of OECD countries and other jurisdictions that agreed to implement both transparency and the automatic exchange of information for tax purposes. It was restructured in September 2009 following a call from the G20 for a strengthening of the implementation of automatic tax information exchange. It was instrumental in developing the OECD Model Agreement, which in turn evolved into the core Common Reporting Standard Agreement of the CRS framework.

7. Transfer pricing

Very large multinational enterprises operate on a global basis. This gives them the opportunity to decide where to 'locate' their business activities.

It also gives them the opportunity to take advantage of different pricing opportunities and to decide how profits and losses might be allocated across the group.

transfer pricing
Agreeing a price between two connected parties for the sale of goods or services.

The OECD refers to **transfer pricing** activity as Base Erosion and Profit Shifting (BEPS), which exploits gaps and mismatches in tax rules to artificially shift profits to low or non-tax locations where there may be little or no actual economic activity. However, it also recognised that while some of the schemes used were illegal most were (and are) not. In order to solve this transfer pricing problem, the OECD has issued so far a package of 15 BEPS measures which adopted by governments equip them with tools to address corporate tax avoidance, ensuring profits are taxed where economic activities generating the profits are performed and where value is created.

Whenever goods are sold or services are provided, a price is charged by the seller (the provider) and a price is paid by the buyer (the receiver of the service). The prices that are agreed upon determine the taxable profits (or losses) of any business.

Where parties to a transaction are connected (e.g. they are both part of the same group of companies or the transaction is between an individual and a company which they own), any price set in relation to the sale or transfer of assets or goods will not be determined by market forces, as would be the case if they were not connected (i.e. if the transaction was an 'arm's length' transaction). This enables the group to allocate some of its global profits to group members in low-tax jurisdictions, even though it may not have actually undertaken the activity from which the profits have arisen from within that jurisdiction.

The price that is agreed between two connected parties is known as the transfer price. When set between connected parties, this does not affect the wealth of the common owner; however, it may, where the two connected parties are located in different jurisdictions, incentivise the owner to structure the business so that profits are earned in the jurisdiction that pays the lowest rate of tax. This causes an unfair division of taxable profit between jurisdictions.

The transfer of goods and services within multinational enterprises is a significant part of world trade and the transfer pricing issue, which can artificially shift a tax liability from one jurisdiction to another, is therefore of interest to the OECD.

The BEPS measures include transfer pricing guidelines which endorse the internationally recognised 'arm's length principle'. This requires the actual terms of a contract to be replaced by the terms that would have been achieved if the transaction had been undertaken at arm's length (between unconnected parties). Profits should be recalculated accordingly when determining the tax liability.

The application of this principle involves hypothetically replacing the actual terms of the transaction (the price) with terms that are considered to be arm's length and recalculating the profits that will be subject to tax on this basis.

The guidelines also address the issue of minimising double taxation that can occur when multinationals operate. The UK has implemented the OECD's 'arm's length' principle.

Test yourself 6.4

What is the 'transfer pricing' problem?

Chapter summary

- Offshore entities can be used to provide opportunities to minimise the amount of taxation payable by offshore clients; however, this is a complex area that requires expert advice from a tax professional.
- The residence of a company is considered to be wherever it is managed and controlled.
- The residence of a company is significant as UK-resident companies are subject to corporation tax on the whole of their chargeable profits on a worldwide basis, whereas non-resident companies are liable to corporation tax only if they carry on a trade in the UK through a permanent establishment. Corporation tax is a tax on the taxable profits of a limited company.
- Where it is essential for the management and control of an offshore company to be outside of the UK in order to achieve tax efficiency, it is vital that management and control is firmly with the offshore directors. Offshore administrators will need to ensure that their clients understand this from the outset of the relationship.

- Trusts are considered resident wherever the majority of its trustees are resident.
- Inheritance tax charges can arise on the creation of certain types of trust, during its existence (e.g. on each ten-year anniversary) and exit charges may arise when funds leave the trust.
- Partners of partnerships, even those that are considered to be corporate bodies, are required to pay income tax on their share of the partnership's profits.
- UK tax legislation does not specifically deal with entities such as foundations and it is not entirely clear whether HMRC will tax them as corporate bodies or as settlements.
- Tax avoidance involves the legitimate minimisation (or avoidance) of a tax liability. In recent years, the UK has introduced anti-avoidance legislation in order to minimise the opportunities for tax avoidance, especially where arrangements are used purely for the avoidance of taxation.
- Tax evasion is the illegal activity of evading a tax liability that is otherwise due and payable. Tax evasion could simply involve the failure by an individual to declare to the relevant tax authority their income, gains or profit that would otherwise be liable to tax.
- The OECD has been addressing the problem of tax evasion for many years, beginning with its 1998 report entitled 'Harmful Tax Competition: An Emerging Global Issue'. The international community has put pressure on jurisdictions (particularly those seen as secrecy jurisdictions) and has sought commitments to an international standard on transparency and effective exchange of information. Much progress has been made and, in 2009, the last three jurisdictions that had previously been classified as uncooperative tax havens committed to the OECD standard.
- The CRS facilitates the automatic exchange of tax information between over 100 jurisdictions.
- In the UK, the HMRC has powers to decide what constitutes abusive tax avoidance and can impose additional tax liabilities or amend existing ones to counteract any benefit gained from such activity.
- In the UK there are corporate criminal offences of facilitating (or preventing the facilitation of) tax evasion in the UK or elsewhere.
- The price agreed for goods or services between two connected parties is known as the transfer price. The transfer price can be manipulated in order to shift profits so that they are earned in a low tax jurisdiction, which causes an unfair division between the jurisdictions. This is known as the transfer pricing problem.

Test yourself answers

Test yourself 6.1

Companies that are incorporated in the UK are usually considered resident in the UK. For foreign incorporated companies (those incorporated in offshore centres), a company is considered to be resident wherever the central management and control actually abides (as established by *De Beers Consolidated Mines Ltd v Howe*).

Test yourself 6.2

If an asset is given away to an offshore trust, but an interest is kept in the asset (e.g. a settlor settles their house into the trust but continues to live in it rent-free), this is known as a gift with reservation and is not a potentially exempt transfer. Such a gift would still form a part of the person's estate upon their death.

Test yourself 6.3

Tax avoidance involves the legitimate minimisation (or avoidance) of a taxation liability.

Test yourself 6.4

A price that is agreed between two connected parties is known as the transfer price. When set between connected parties, this does not affect the wealth of the common owner. However, where the two connected parties are located in different jurisdictions, it may incentivise the owner to structure the business so that profits are earned in the jurisdiction that pays the lowest rate of tax. This causes an unfair division of taxable profit between the jurisdictions. The transfer of goods and services within multinational enterprises is a significant part of world trade and the transfer pricing issue, which can artificially shift a tax liability from one jurisdiction to another, is therefore of interest to the OECD.

Part four

Chapter 7
Accounts and payments

Chapter 8
Offshore banking services

Banking

After studying this part, students will gain an understanding of the banking services provided from within offshore centres. Students will be able to discuss the reasons for using offshore bank accounts, how to choose an offshore bank and explain the main disadvantage of banking offshore – that is, the potential lack of depositor compensation schemes.

Students will be able to discuss the process of choosing, opening and closing a bank account, and will understand various payment methods and the roles of important payments to industry bodies. Students will gain an understanding of the regulation and supervision of offshore banks, as well as the role of the Basel Committee on banking supervision. Students will gain an understanding of the banking secrecy provisions in offshore centres.

Learning outcomes

At the end of this part, you will:

1. understand banking services provided by offshore centres;
2. know about bank accounts, payment methods and payment systems; and
3. understand the regulation and supervision of offshore banks.

Chapter seven
Accounts and payments

List of topics

1. Types of bank accounts
2. Opening a bank account
3. Closing a bank account
4. Payment methods
5. Payment systems
6. Payment industry bodies and other organisations

Introduction

This chapter describes basic bank accounts, current accounts and savings accounts (including fixed-term deposits) and describes their differences and main features. It outlines the steps involved in choosing and opening a bank account and describes various payment methods such as cheques, banker's drafts, the use of bank cards and automated payments such as direct debits and standing orders.

Payment systems including Bacs, Faster Payments and CHAPS are discussed, as is the SWIFT messaging system and the cheque clearing system. Finally, the chapter explains the role of various bodies and organisations that play an important part in the payments industry including the Payments Council, UK Payments Administration Limited and the Cheque and Credit Clearing Company.

1. Types of bank accounts

Banks offer a range of different types of bank accounts with different features. The terms and conditions of similar types of account will vary (but often only by very little) from bank to bank.

1.1 Basic bank accounts

Basic bank accounts offer a convenient place to keep money to meet day-to-day expenditure.

Basic bank accounts offer some of the features that current accounts provide; however, the customer is not usually issued with a cheque book and does not have the ability to go overdrawn if there are insufficient funds available within the account. The inability to go overdrawn is an attraction for some people. Some basic bank accounts also offer debit cards. It is possible to receive funds directly into a basic bank account and they can be used to set up direct debits or standing orders.

1.2 Current accounts

Current accounts (also known as cheque accounts) are very popular. They have more features than basic bank accounts. For example, they usually offer:

- a cheque book (and historically a cheque guarantee card);
- a debit card providing access to automated teller machine (ATM) facilities;
- direct debits and standing orders;
- the facility to receive Bankers' Automated Clearing Services (Bacs) payments directly into the account;
- the facility to make Bacs payments to others from the account;
- an overdraft facility; and
- telephone or internet banking facilities.

Customers may withdraw money on demand by using the above services and may withdraw cash at the counter. Historically, current accounts did not earn interest; however, this is often no longer the case. Interest is usually earned, albeit at a very low rate. The interest rates on current accounts may be tiered so that the higher the balance, the higher the interest rate earned.

The advantages to the bank of having current account holders are as follows.

- The customers are more likely than others to use other bank services, providing an income to the bank (such as overdraft charges).
- The more services the customer uses, the more income they generate for the bank in interest and transaction charges.
- Current account balances provide a cheap **source of funds** for banks, as they can lend these balances and receive more interest than they pay on the current accounts.

source of funds
Activities that generate funds for a relationship.

A new current account switching service was launched in September 2013. The service is designed to make switching between one current account to another simpler for customers. Accounts can be switched within seven working days, with all existing direct debits and standing orders automatically transferred from the old account to the new account. A redirection service also directs any payments to the correct account for 13 months after the switch. Initiatives such as the current account switch service help to increase competition in the banking sector.

1.3 Savings accounts

Savings accounts are suitable for customers who seek a return on their savings while keeping them in a safe, accessible place. Banks offer a range of different types of savings accounts with different features. The following types of savings accounts are available.

Fixed-term deposits

A fixed-term deposit involves the customer agreeing to deposit a sum of money with the bank for a specified period of time. Some banks impose a minimum balance requirement. Fixed terms could range from daily to weekly or monthly, or could even be fixed for one year or more. As the deposit is 'fixed' and no withdrawals or additions are anticipated, the account does not offer the payment facilities that are available on, for example, a current account.

Usually, the interest rates paid on a fixed deposit increase the longer the funds are committed and the interest is applied to the account at the end of the term. The bank can offer a better rate of interest as it knows that it has use of the money for a specified period. Fixed-term deposits do not usually allow for part withdrawals. Penalties for breaking a fixed deposit are usually severe and a customer must therefore ensure that they will not require access to the funds during the term. Trust and company administrators should be conscious of any liquidity requirements (such as the need to have funds available to settle liabilities such as trustee fees) when fixing or re-fixing deposits at their maturity.

Instant access accounts

Instant access accounts may require a large initial investment. The interest rate payable is usually preferable and tiered in accordance with the level of funds in the account. These accounts allow instant access to funds without the loss of interest. The terms of instant access accounts may provide that no interest will be payable if the account falls below a minimum balance – for example, £5,000.

Other savings accounts

The terms and features of savings accounts available differ from bank to bank. Some accounts allow funds to be withdrawn on demand with instant access, while others require the customer to give the bank notice before funds can be withdrawn. The notice period can vary from one week to three months or longer.

Some savings accounts require regular savings of a minimum savings amount each month while others are suitable for those with a large lump sum. Interest at varying frequencies may be applied to savings accounts (e.g. on a monthly or six-monthly basis).

Test yourself 7.1

Distinguish between a fixed-term deposit account and a current account.

1.4 Sharia accounts

Sharia-compliant bank accounts are designed and run in accordance with Islamic laws. They offer features similar to other kinds of accounts but do not pay interest or charge interest on the bank account. In addition, the bank usually undertakes not to invest the customer's money in interest-based activities. They do not usually allow an account to go overdrawn. Such accounts are usually supervised by Islamic scholars who ensure that the account is operated in accordance with Islamic law and finance.

2. Opening a bank account

The following steps are involved in opening a bank account.

1. The customer chooses the type of account required.
2. The customer completes an application form.
3. The customer provides the bank with any due diligence documentation that it may require in order to prove the identity of the customer. This commonly involves providing the bank with a certified copy of a document (e.g. a passport) which verifies the customer's identity, a certified copy of a utility bill which verifies the customer's residential (or registered office) address, providing a Tax Identification Number (TIN) and a recent bank statement that verifies the customer's wealth or earnings.
4. The account is funded.

Corporate applicants will usually be asked to provide due diligence documentation in respect of their controllers (the directors and controlling shareholders) or other account signatories. They may also be requested to provide additional documentation in relation to the legal person (the company) including certified copies of:

- the memorandum and articles of association;
- the Certificate of Incorporation;
- a Certificate of 'Good Standing' issued by the Companies Registry (or a resident agent in some jurisdictions);
- a copy of the board resolution authorising the opening of the bank account documentation to be signed;
- a copy of the latest audited financial statements or similar proof of trading activities;
- a structure chart detailing the major shareholders/controllers of the company (including details of all individuals able or potentially able to exert significant direct or indirect influence on the directors or the management of the company such as ultimate beneficial owners);
- client due diligence evidence in respect of all individuals who represent owners or controllers of the company;
- a copy of the **register of members**;

register of members
A register which is required to be maintained by law and which contains the name and other particulars of a company's members.

- a copy of the **register of directors** and secretaries; and
- a copy of the signatory list of the company.

register of directors
A register which is required to be maintained by law and which contains the name and other particulars of a company's directors.

Trustees who wish to open trust bank accounts may be requested to provide client due diligence documentation containing details of:

- the trust (e.g. the name and type of trust and trustees);
- the settlor;
- the principal beneficiaries; and
- any protector.

Corporate trustees will be asked to provide additional information in line with that of corporate applicants.

In all cases, the rationale for the opening of the bank account, the activity of the entity, the source of funds, **source of wealth** and expected volume and value of transactions are likely to be requested.

source of wealth
Activities which have generated the total net worth of a person.

Banks are required to identify accounts that they consider present higher risks to them and will ask questions such as whether individuals connected to the proposed bank account and the company or trust concerned are or not a politically exposed person, or whether the funds in the account are received as a result of consultancy fees or commissions. The bank will need to understand the economic and geographic trading activities or other sources of revenue involved.

This process looks simple as described above whereas in reality some banks seem increasingly reluctant to operate accounts for the clients of offshore service providers. Their reluctance is based on their assessment that some clients represent too high a risk for them. Both banks and service providers, after all, can choose what degree of risk they wish to accept.

2.1 Bank mandates

When a new account is opened, the customer signs a mandate, which often forms a part of the account opening documentation. The mandate appoints the bank as the customer's banker and authorises it to open the bank account.

The mandate also:

- authorises the bank to honour all cheques drawn on the account;
- authorises the bank to accept and act on all instructions in relation to the account (including payment instructions);
- sets out the signing authorities from whom the bank should accept instructions. Offshore trust and company businesses may have an authorised signatory list that includes their staff members. It is common for them to complete this section of the mandate with a statement which authorises the bank to accept instructions where they are signed 'in accordance with the global signatory list of (e.g. the trust company) as amended from time to time'; and

- sets out that the bank may allow the account to go overdrawn if it acts on the customer's instructions.

2.2 Facsimile indemnity

Where a customer wishes to communicate with a bank by facsimile, the bank may insist upon receiving an indemnity, which absolves the bank of all responsibility and releases it from claims and demands that the bank may incur due to it having acted on faxed instructions. This indemnifies the bank against liability and loss as a result of having honoured a faxed instruction. Increasingly internet facilitated direct processing by service providers of their banking needs is permitted subject to suitable security checks.

2.3 Choosing a bank account

The following considerations may be relevant when choosing a bank account:

- account charges;
- account opening fees or any ongoing monthly fees;
- the account's rate of interest and whether interest is paid gross of tax;
- accessibility of the funds (i.e. any notice requirement and low penalties);
- the choice of currencies;
- compensation arrangements;
- 24-hour banking facilities;
- internet and telephone banking facilities;
- international money transfers;
- minimum balance requirements;
- credit rating, reputation and financial strength of the bank; and
- whether the account is Sharia-compliant.

Some banks aim their accounts at particular types of customers and may therefore refuse to open an account for someone who does not meet the criteria for a particular account (e.g. a requirement for the customer to earn a certain level of salary). Some clients of offshore service providers will be declined by banks on account of what the bank concerned perceives as the client's risk profile.

3. Closing a bank account

It is usually possible to close a bank account at any time without charge or penalty. Some accounts may have conditions upon closing the account – for example, fixed-term deposits – however, any such conditions must be made clear to the customer before the account is opened. The bank or building society may decide to close a bank account. The bank should give 'reasonable notice' to enable its customer to make other arrangements. Reasonable notice will differ from account to account.

Stop and think 7.1

It is good practice to ensure that trust and company administrators properly close the bank accounts of client entities (i.e. trusts or companies under administration) when they are no longer required or at the end of the business relationship. Dormant accounts that are not monitored present risks to the service provider (e.g. unexpected receipts may arrive in the account and remain unnoticed). This leaves the trust company unable to perform the required due diligence in respect of the source of funds – therefore breaching AML/CFT legislation – and exposes the company to the risk of theft by its employees.

4. Payment methods

4.1 Cash

Cash is used for many everyday small transactions and is a very convenient payment method. Cash is a trusted method of payment. Cash is available on demand by customers with access to ATMs. Prior to the introduction of legislation on the proceeds of crime, customers could visit their bankers in offshore centres and deposit or leave with large sums of cash. This practice is no longer acceptable in well-regulated jurisdictions, and indeed the deposit or withdrawal of large sums of cash will now attract suspicions as to the origin of the funds and possible money laundering.

4.2 Cheques

A cheque is a written instruction from an account holder to their bank to pay a specified sum of money to a named beneficiary (a payee). Cheques are usually written on a standard form provided by the bank in a cheque book. The standard form is a slip which contains pre-printed information such as the branch of the bank on which the cheque is drawn, the sort code number of the branch on which the cheque is drawn, the account number and the name of the drawer (the writer) of the cheque.

The cheque number, the sort code and account number is included at the bottom of each pre-printed cheque in ink that can be read electronically when the cheque passes through the general cheque clearing system. The general cheque clearing system is discussed in section 5.7 of this chapter.

The customer completes the cheque by hand when they wish to make an instruction to pay a beneficiary by completing the name of the payee, the amount of the payment in words and numbers, and signs and dates the cheque.

The use of cheques has been in decline for several years as electronic methods of payment have become more popular. It was for this reason, in December 2009, that the Payments Council – that sets the strategy for payments in the UK – set a target date for closing the general cheque clearing system by October

2018. The Payments Council announced that a decision to continue with the closing of the general cheque clearing system would be made in 2016 as long as viable alternatives to cheques had been put in place.

Many stakeholder groups including charities and pensioner lobby groups objected to the closure of the general cheque clearing system. In July 2011, the Payments Council announced that, having listened to stakeholders, it had decided that the cheque would stay and that the 2018 target date had been withdrawn.

In offshore centres, cheques are seen as a convenient and cost-effective way for companies (particularly property holding companies) to settle invoices including property maintenance expenses and they are often used for this purpose.

4.3 Banker's drafts

Banker's drafts are cheques drawn directly on the account of the bank rather than the account of the customer.

Before a person can request their bank to issue a banker's draft, they are required to have cleared funds available in their account in order to cover the amount of the draft. The customer's account is then immediately debited with the amount of the draft and the bank's own account credited. The funds remain on the bank's account until the draft is presented by the payee and cleared.

As banker's drafts are drawn on the account of the bank, they provide additional comfort to the payee that they are unlikely to be returned unpaid due to a lack of funds. Banker's drafts were often used for transactions involving large amounts of money where the payee wished to eliminate the risk of the cheque bouncing. However, they do not provide a guarantee against fraudulent use.

4.4 Bank cards

Debit cards

Debit cards are plastic cards that allow a customer to pay for goods and services and have largely replaced the need for people to write cheques. The card sends an instruction to the cardholder's bank to debit their account and credit the payee's account for the cost of the goods or services.

Debit cards can be used at ATM machines (discussed later in this section) to withdraw cash or access other bank services. They can also be used to purchase goods by telephone and over the internet.

At the point of payment (when used in person), the cardholder hands their card to the salesperson, who will ask the cardholder to key their private personal identification number (PIN) into a machine.

Prior to the introduction of PINs, the retailer would have asked the cardholder to sign a sales voucher. However, from February 2006, cardholders have been required to use their PIN. Without it, their card may be declined.

Since 1 January 2005, if the use of a Chip and PIN device could have prevented a fraud and a retailer does not use one, the retailer may bear the cost of the fraudulent transaction. Prior to this date, the UK card issuers suffered the cost of any fraud. The change in liability to retailers was referred to as 'the liability shift'.

Credit cards

Credit cards can be used in the same way as debit cards to pay for goods and services; however, they differ from debit cards as the cost of the goods or service is not taken directly from the cardholder's bank account. Instead, the card funds up to a personal spending limit which varies from cardholder to cardholder and from bank to bank. The amount of the personal spending limit is made available to the customer by the bank. The cardholder can use the credit card to access these funds directly from the bank when purchasing goods and services. The cardholder can then choose how much to repay the bank each month, subject usually to a minimum amount (which could be as low as £5). The cardholder could repay the balance in full if they chose to do so. The customer can pay their chosen amount each month using a range of payment methods including cash or direct debit.

Any unpaid balance on the credit card incurs interest, usually at a very high rate.

Stop and think 7.2

Some offshore service providers have issued their clients with credit cards that are drawn on the account of the trust or an underlying company. Consider the trustee issues, the management and control issues, and the AML issues that could arise as a result of this practice.

Automated teller machine (ATM) cards

An ATM is a machine that can be located outside a bank (e.g. within a shop or the high street) which enables customers to gain access to some banking services 24 hours a day, seven days a week. While the services differ from bank to bank, they may include:

- cash withdrawals (usually limited to a certain amount per day, such as £250);
- viewing the account balance;
- ordering a bank statement;
- ordering a cheque book;
- paying in cheques; and
- obtaining a mini statement listing the last few transactions on the account.

The customer accesses the services by inserting their ATM card into the machine and entering in their PIN. Debit cards and credit cards can usually be used at an ATM.

Internet and telephone

Internet or telephone transactions are either processed using the faster payments service or by using the Bacs system. The Bacs system is discussed further in section 5 of this chapter.

4.5 Automated payments

Direct debits

A direct debit is an instruction from a customer to their bank authorising an organisation to collect varying amounts from their bank accounts, provided the customer has been given advance notice of the collection amounts and dates. The bank then allows the money to be taken from the account. Direct debits are an extremely convenient way to pay household bills or other regular invoices where the amount varies. There is no need to inform the bank that the amount has changed, as would be required if the bills were settled by standing order. Direct debits are settled via the Bacs system.

Direct credits

A direct credit enables organisations to make payments by electronic transfer directly into bank accounts.

Direct credit is mainly used for paying wages and salaries. Organisations may also use direct credits for supplier payments, pensions, employee expenses, insurance settlements and dividends.

Making direct credits over other methods such as cheques is a more secure and reliable payment method because payments cannot be lost or stolen.

Standing orders

A standing order is an instruction to a bank to make payments for a fixed amount to the same beneficiary at a UK bank or building society account on a regular basis – for example, every month on a particular date during the month. Any person with a current account at a bank in the UK can set up a standing order.

Online banking has made it extremely easy for customers who have access to the online banking facility to set up standing orders online. They can also be set up after the customer has completed a pre-printed form that includes the details that the bank requires. The bank follows the customer's instructions and continues to make the payments until the customer cancels the standing order or a specified final payment date is reached.

The funds will be transferred either through the Bacs system or through the faster payments service. Funds transferred through the Bacs system will be received by the recipient within three working days and funds transferred through the faster payment system will be processed on the same day.

International Bank Account Numbers

International bank account numbers (IBANs) were introduced to help speed up international payments by standardising the identification of bank accounts, thereby reducing errors and delays. To make a European cross-border payment, customers need to quote an IBAN and its associated Bank Identification Code (BIC). The IBAN is comprised of the country code (two digits), a two-digit check number, the first four characters of the BIC, the sort code and the account number.

Test yourself 7.2

State six methods of withdrawing funds from a bank account.

5. Payment systems

5.1 Bacs

Bankers' Automated Clearing Services (Bacs) is a not-for-profit, membership based industry body that is owned by 16 of the leading banks and building societies in Europe, the UK and the US.

Bacs is responsible for the schemes behind the clearing and settlement of automated payments in the UK, including direct debits and Bacs direct credit.

5.2 Faster Payments

The Faster Payments Service was introduced in 2008 and was the first new payment service to be introduced in the UK for more than 20 years. All UK banks and building societies are able to send and receive Faster Payments.

UK Payments Administration Limited started the Faster Payments initiative to improve the speed of lower-value transactions, to be used in parallel with the CHAPS and Bacs systems. The Faster Payments Service enables the movement of telephone, internet and standing order payments. Direct debits are not a part of the service.

The Faster Payments Service can be used to make one-off payments or standing orders in sterling. Payments of up to £100,000 can be made via Faster Payments; individual banks have set their own transaction limits for their customers.

The funds must be in the receiving customer's account within two hours; however, payments may be made within minutes. Payments made via Faster Payments cannot be recalled as it operates in near-real time.

5.3 CHAPS

The Clearing House Automated Payment System (CHAPS) is a British company that was established in 1984. CHAPS offers same-day sterling fund transfers. It used to offer euro fund transfers but this service is now closed.

A CHAPS transfer is initiated by the customer to move money to a recipient's bank account at another bank, where the funds need to be cleared (made available) the same working day. CHAPS is generally used for higher value transactions.

Unlike a bank giro credit, a pre-printed slip specifying the recipient's details is not required. Unlike cheques, the funds transfer is performed in real time and is irrevocable. This removes the potential for payments to be stopped by the sender, or returns due to insufficient funds even after they appear to have arrived in the destination account, a problem that can be experienced with payment methods such as cheques.

CHAPS is a real-time gross settlement (RTGS) system. RTGS is the continuous settlement of funds or securities transfers on an order-by-order basis (without netting).

5.4 SWIFT

The Society for Worldwide Interbank Financial Telecommunication (SWIFT) is a member-owned cooperative society under Belgian law. Twenty-five independent directors govern and oversee its management. From 1998, oversight of SWIFT has been carried out by the central banks of the G10 countries.

In 1973, SWIFT, supported by 239 banks in 15 countries, started the creation of a shared data processing and communications language for international financial transactions. At the time that SWIFT went live in 1977, there were 518 members (who were commercial banks) in 22 countries. As of August 2014, there were 10,717 users in 215 countries.

SWIFT is neither a payment nor a settlement system; however, a number of payment systems depend on it. SWIFT operates a network that facilitates the exchange of messages (including payment messages) between financial institutions. A SWIFT payment message is an instruction to transfer funds. The settlement then takes place via a payment system.

SWIFT users are able to develop internal applications that link into the SWIFT network via computer terminals which meet SWIFT specifications. These terminals are used to process transactions without re-inputting the information manually.

Messages formatted using SWIFT standards can be read and processed by many payment systems. SWIFT cooperates with international organisations such as the ISO (the International Organization for Standardization) in order to define standards for message format and content.

Users of SWIFT include its shareholders (members such as banks, eligible securities broker dealers and regulated investment management institutions), organisations that meet the criteria to be members (but are not members) and sub-members (organisations that are owned and controlled by shareholders).

5.5 Single European Payments Area

The Single European Payments Area (SEPA) programme is an initiative of the European Payments Council that brings together the European payments industry.

SEPA is the area within Europe where participants can make and receive payments in euros under the same basic conditions, regardless of national boundaries (i.e. all euro payments are considered domestic). SEPA aims to achieve faster settlement and simplified processing, improving cash flow while reducing costs.

Rules have been established which set out the requirements for credit transfers and direct debits that effectively mean that existing national euro credit transfer and direct debit schemes are being replaced by SEPA credit transfer and SEPA direct debits. This took place in the euro area on1 February 2014, and will take on 3 October 2016 in non-euro countries.

SEPA *direct debits*

This system was introduced in February 2014 and replaces euro denominated schemes in countries within the euro area.

It does not affect the UK's direct credit and Bacs Direct credit schemes. However, many of the UK's major banks have opted to allow SEPA direct debit collections from accounts held with them.

5.6 PayPal and Paym

PayPal is a worldwide online payments system established in 1998 that facilitates online money transfers and offers an electronic alternative to more traditional payment methods. It acts as a payments processor for online vendors, auction sites and other commercial users to whom it charges a small fee.

Paym is a secure way of making payments of small sums using only a mobile telephone number. It was launched in April 2014.

Account holders who wish to receive funds through Paym must register both their mobile number and the relevant current account with a bank or building society that is participating in the scheme.

The banking payments industry is changing very rapidly and there is regular adoption of new technologies – for instance, contactless payments. With the expected further evolution of crypto currencies we might expect to see further arguably radical changes in money transmission and the way in which payment and receipts are processed.

5.7 The cheque clearing system

As explained above, a cheque is a written order to pay a specified sum from an account (the drawer's account) to that of the beneficiary (the payee). After the cheque is passed to the payee, the process is as follows.

1. The payee sends the cheque to their bank.
2. The payee's bank sends the cheque to central clearing.
3. Central clearing forwards it to the main clearing department of the drawer's bank (not the drawer's own branch).
4. The clearing department of the bank then sends the cheque to the branch at which the bank account is held.
5. If funds are available, the cheque will be cleared for payment by the drawer's branch.

If there are insufficient funds to clear the cheque, the cheque is returned unpaid. Unpaid cheques are usually returned on the same day that the paying banker receives them.

It is possible for cheques to be sent for direct clearance or presentation. In these circumstances, the payee's bank sends the cheque by post to the paying banker.

The next morning, the collecting banker (the payee's banker) telephones the paying banker and receives confirmation over the telephone as to whether or not the cheque has been paid. A fee is charged for this service.

In November 2007, changes to the cheque clearing cycle came into force. Known as the 2-4-6 and the 2-6-6 cheque clearing timescales changes, these gave customers increased clarity and certainty regarding the timescale involved in the clearing of the cheque.

The 2-4-6 timescale for the clearing of the cheques paid into current accounts means that:

- the process starts when the cheque is received by the payee's bank;
- no later than two days after this, the payee starts to receive interest on the money (the second business day after paying in the cheque);
- no later than four days after the cheque was received by the payee's bank, the bank will allow the payee to withdraw the funds (the fourth business day after paying in the cheque); and
- by the end of six days, the payee can be certain that the cheque will not bounce and that the money cannot be reclaimed from their account without their consent (the sixth business day).

For savings accounts, the maximum time limit for withdrawal is longer (six days) and is known as 2-6-6.

The clearing system does not operate on Saturdays, Sundays or bank holidays.

Test yourself 7.3

If a cheque was paid into a savings account on a Monday, on what day would the bank allow the payee to withdraw the funds?

6. Payment industry bodies and other organisations

6.1 The Payments Council

The Payments Council is a voluntary membership organisation funded by its members. It is governed by a set of published rules and a board of directors.

Organisations that are payment service providers with qualifying payment volumes can join the Payments Council.

The Payments Council is the organisation that sets the strategy for UK payments. It has been established to ensure that UK payment systems and services meet the needs of users, payment service providers and the wider economy.

The payments council works to improve the future of payments. A recent development is the launch of Paym in April 2014 (discussed further in section 5.6 above). The board of the Payments Council consults on important issues such as proposals for innovation, any significant policy statements and any proposals to create wind-down payment systems in the UK. The principal UK payment schemes such as Bacs, CHAPS, the Cheque and Credit Clearing Company Limited and the LINK ATM scheme have all entered into a contract with the Payments Council. Each scheme has entered into a contract or other formal arrangement with the Payments Council to set up their respective rights and duties towards each other.

Under the contracts, schemes are required to report to the board of the Payments Council. The board is also able to make decisions that are binding on scheme members in order to implement its strategy.

6.2 The European Payments Council

The European Payments Council is the decision-making body of the European banking industry in relation to payments. It is an international not-for-profit association. Its members represent banks and payment institutions, with the European central bank acting as an observer. The European Payments Council's central purpose is to promote SEPA.

6.3 UK Payments Administration Limited

UK Payments Administration Limited, previously known as APACS (Association for Payment Clearing Services) is a UK trade organisation. It describes itself as a 'service company providing people, facilities and expertise to the UK payments industry'.

The organisation covers most forms of payments within the UK including cash, credit cards, debit cards, cheques and automated payments such as direct debits. UK Payments Administration Limited also provides services to a wide range of companies, including:

- Bacs;
- CHAPS;
- Cheque and Credit Clearing Company;
- Faster Payments;
- Payments Council; and
- SWIFT UK.

UK Payments Administration Limited brings together all payment systems organisations, giving banks, building societies and card issuers a forum where they can work together on non-competitive issues. It was responsible for the creation of rules regarding customer liability in cases of card and cheque fraud, and oversaw the transition of debit cards to Chip and PIN.

Test yourself 7.4

Describe the work of UK Payments Administration Limited within the payments industry.

6.4 The International Organization for Standardization

The International Organization for Standardization (ISO) is the world's largest developer and publisher of international standards. The ISO is a nongovernmental organisation.

The ISO is a network of the national standards institutes of 157 countries – one member per country – with a central secretariat in Geneva that coordinates the system.

Relevant standards to banking include:

- *ISO 3166: Country codes*
- *ISO 4217: Currency codes*
- *ISO 9362: Business Identifier Codes (BIC Codes)*
- *ISO 13616: Structure of the IBAN number.*

6.5 The Cheque and Credit Clearing Company

The Cheque and Credit Clearing Company is a membership-based non-profitmaking industry body that manages the cheque clearing system in the UK. As well as clearing cheques, the system processes banker's drafts, building society cheques, postal orders and traveller's cheques.

The Cheque and Credit Clearing Company also manages the system for the clearing of paperback giro credits (credit clearing), euro cheques (euro clearing) and US dollar cheques (the currency clearing the US dollar cheques drawn on Great Britain accounts).

The Cheque and Credit Clearing Company describes its role as:

- providing consumers, via its members, with the central payment system services for the exchange and settlement of cheques and credits. These services are underpinned by payments infrastructure including the exchange centres, the network for the transfer of electronic cheque data and an automated settlement system; it also includes a courier service for the return of unpaid cheques to the collecting bank;
- managing the operational processes of the central payment system services;
- determining the rules, standards and procedures required to maintain the integrity of the clearings, including the criteria for joining the clearings, and ensuring compliance with those rules;

- engaging with the full range of stakeholders, including consumers and businesses that use cheques, banks that offer cheque clearing services, cheque processors, cheque printers and other suppliers; and
- managing the Cheque Printer Accreditation Scheme (CPAS).

Chapter summary

- There are different types of bank accounts such as basic bank accounts, current accounts and savings accounts which include fixed-term deposit accounts.
- Current accounts allow customers to withdraw funds on demand and pay low rates of interest, whereas savings accounts usually require notice before funds can be withdrawn and usually offer higher rates of interest.
- Banks offer a range of different types of savings accounts with different features. The terms and conditions of similar types of accounts will vary from bank to bank. Some may aim their accounts at particular types of customers and may therefore refuse to open an account for someone who does not meet the criteria for a particular account.
- It is usually possible for the customer to close a bank account at any time without charge although some accounts (e.g. fixed-term deposits) may have conditions upon closing the account. If the bank decides to close a bank account, it should give reasonable notice to the customer.
- Cash, cheques, banker's drafts, the use of bank cards such as credit or debit cards and automated payments such as direct debits or standing orders are all payment methods which are useful in different circumstances.
- Payment systems include Bacs, CHAPS, the cheque clearing system, Faster Payments and Paym. The SWIFT messaging system is also an important system.
- The Payments Council, UK Payments Administration Limited and the Cheque and Credit Clearing Company are all important industry bodies in the UK payments industry.

Test yourself answers

Test yourself 7.1

Current accounts (also known as cheque accounts) are very popular. They have more features than basic bank accounts. For example, they usually offer:

- a cheque book (and historically a cheque guarantee card);
- a debit card allowing access to ATM facilities;
- direct debits and standing orders;
- the facility to receive Bacs payments directly into the account;
- the facility to make Bacs payments to others from the account;

- an overdraft facility; and
- telephone or internet banking facilities.

Customers may withdraw money on demand by using the above services and may withdraw cash at the counter. The interest earned on current accounts is usually low, if any.

A fixed-term deposit account is a savings account that involves the customer agreeing to deposit a sum of money with the bank for a specified period of time. Some banks impose a minimum balance requirement. Fixed terms could range from daily to weekly or monthly, or could even be fixed for one year or more. As the deposit is 'fixed' and no withdrawals or additions are anticipated, the account does not offer the payment facilities that are available on, for example, a current account.

Usually, the interest rates paid on a fixed deposit increase the longer the funds are committed and the interest is applied to the account at the end of the term.

The bank can offer a better rate of interest as it knows that it has use of the money for a specified period.

Fixed-term deposits do not usually allow for part withdrawals. Penalties for breaking a fixed deposit are usually severe and a customer must therefore ensure that they will not require access to the funds during the term. Trust and company administrators should be conscious of any liquidity requirements (such as the need to have funds available to settle liabilities such as trustee fees) when fixing or re-fixing deposits at their maturity.

Test yourself 7.2

Six methods of withdrawing funds from a bank account include:

1. withdrawal of cash at branch;
2. ATM machine withdrawals;
3. banker's drafts;
4. cheques;
5. electronic payments such as CHAPS or Bacs; and
6. internet banking.

Test yourself 7.3

Tuesday the following week.

Test yourself 7.4

UK Payments Administration Limited brings together all payment systems organisations, giving banks, building societies and card issuers a forum where they can work together on non-competitive issues. It was responsible for the creation of rules regarding customer liability in cases of card and cheque fraud, and oversaw the transition of debit cards to Chip and PIN.

Chapter eight
Offshore banking services

List of topics

1. Banking business
2. Banking services provided from offshore centres
3. Regulation and supervision of offshore banking
4. Obtaining a banking licence
5. Managed banks
6. Banking secrecy laws

Introduction

This chapter outlines the main reasons why a customer may wish to open an offshore bank account and the main reasons that a bank may wish to offer services from an offshore location. It discusses various factors that a customer may wish to consider when choosing to use an offshore bank and explains the main downfall of offshore banking: the lack of depositor compensation schemes.

This chapter also outlines banking services provided from offshore centres, including the foreign exchange market and forward exchange contracts. The issue of regulation and supervision of offshore banks is discussed, as are the international standards set by the Basel Committee and the issue of banking secrecy laws present in some offshore centres. The savings directive is also discussed and the advantages of managed banks are outlined.

1. Banking business

Offshore banking is simply having a bank account outside of your country of residence. It is very common for banks in offshore centres to be locally incorporated subsidiaries of large onshore banking groups that wish to provide the offshore banking facility to existing clients. Others are branches of mainland banks.

The banking industry in offshore centres is often complementary to other parts of the international finance sector. It supports the trust and fiduciary sector by providing a range of services, including the taking of deposits, to the structures established within the offshore centre. The banking industry also supports the collective investment fund sector by providing overdraft and liquidity facilities to funds. This enables them to finance the timing differences between the purchase and sale of securities and the flows of subscriptions and redemptions by investors and by taking deposits from the uninvested client money balances of fund administration companies. Insurance sectors may be supported by the provision of guarantees and standby letters of credit to captive insurance companies.

Banks accept deposits from customers, often on a short-term basis, and lend to other customers, sometimes for longer periods – for example, as would be required with a mortgage. Offshore centres are sometimes in the position where the level of deposits they receive outweighs the borrowing needs of local customers. The banks frequently lend the majority of their deposits to parent banks or group companies. Banks in offshore centres are therefore valuable suppliers of funding and liquidity to onshore banks.

1.1 Reasons for using an offshore bank account

The main reasons why a customer may wish to open an offshore bank account include the following.

- Interest is usually paid gross (i.e. it is unlikely that any tax will be deducted at source on interest earned). EU residents will be subject to the EUSTD, discussed in section 8 of Chapter 5.
- Depending on where the client is resident, offshore income may not be subject to tax in their country of residence if the income is not remitted back to that country.
- In some offshore centres, more flexible regulation and supervision could reduce the bank's costs and enable a higher rate of interest to be paid to customers.

A bank may wish to offer services from an offshore location because:

- the tax liability on profits arising may be low;
- there is more flexible regulation and supervision;
- costs for premises and staff may be lower; and
- it wishes to complement the services that it can provide to its client base (i.e. to provide offshore products and services).

Test yourself 8.1

Outline three reasons why a customer may choose to open an offshore bank account.

1.2 Considerations when choosing to use a bank located in an offshore centre

The following are considerations that may be relevant when choosing to use a bank in an offshore centre:

- the quality of the banks operating within the offshore centre;
- the regulatory requirements and the effectiveness of regulatory oversight;
- the relatively very low level of bank failures; and
- the availability of a depositor compensation scheme.

1.3 Depositor compensation schemes

Offshore centres have been 'slower' to introduce depositor compensation schemes than many onshore jurisdictions. For example, until recently, Jersey and Guernsey had no depositor compensation scheme at all.

Reports of bank failures in some jurisdictions during the global financial crisis has caused offshore centres to introduce depositor compensation schemes to give comfort to offshore investors. Jersey, for example, introduced a depositor compensation scheme in November 2009 protecting deposits of up to £50,000 per person in the event of a Jersey bank failing. Guernsey introduced its compensation scheme in November 2008, also guaranteeing deposits of up to £50,000 per person. The Isle of Man scheme is now in line with that of Jersey and Guernsey. Malta also has a depositor compensation scheme that will pay compensation of up to €100,000 in the event of bank failure.

It is common for the benefits of such schemes to be available to private individuals (i.e. retail deposits) and charities only, and to provide protection for deposits of up to a certain amount, for example, £50,000. Depositor protection does not typically extend to corporations, partnerships or trusts. The Isle of Man scheme, however, protects non-individuals (i.e. trusts, charities and businesses) up to a maximum of £20,000. The majority of the cost of the compensation schemes is usually borne by the banking industry.

Making it work 8.1

The collapse of Landsbanki Guernsey Limited

In 2008, Landsbanki Guernsey Limited went into voluntary administration. Its customers were not covered by either the then UK or Icelandic protection schemes because the bank was a Guernsey company. At the time, Guernsey did not have a depositor compensation scheme in place.

Immediately after the collapse of Landsbanki Guernsey Limited, the Guernsey government introduced a depositor compensation scheme, although this excluded the Landsbanki Guernsey customers.

Landsbanki customers in the UK and the Netherlands received 100% of their deposits much sooner than the Guernsey customers, due to the depositor compensation schemes available in their jurisdiction. Customers of Landsbanki Guernsey (a third of whom were expatriates) eventually received approximately 67.5p for every £1 that they had deposited.

It is interesting that prior to its collapse Landsbanki was advertising a rate for depositors of more than 6%. This was far in excess of rates offered by comparable banks and should have served as a 'warning sign' to depositors and perhaps also to the bank's regulator.

2. Banking services provided from offshore centres

Offshore banks typically provide usual common banking services, such as:

- current accounts;
- debit cards, credit cards and cheque books;
- deposit and savings accounts;
- foreign exchange;
- forward exchange contracts;
- lending facilities;
- mortgage facilities;
- overdraft facilities; and
- payments facilities, including online and telephone banking.

The services provided and terms and conditions will vary from bank to bank.

2.1 Foreign exchange markets

Foreign exchange is a service often offered by banks both onshore and offshore. Banks buy currency from and sell foreign currency to customers on the foreign exchange market.

The foreign exchange market is sometimes referred to as the forex market, the FX market or the currency market. The foreign exchange market is a decentralised global marketplace. Some banks offer foreign exchange services by telephone or online banking. The bank may impose transaction limits or require notice of larger foreign exchange transactions or for transactions involving certain currencies, although the terms that banks can offer will vary from bank to bank.

Foreign exchange services offered by banks range from simply informing a customer who has a foreign currency invoice to pay what the cost will be in local currency to more complex transactions such as forward exchange contracts (discussed in section 2.2 of this chapter) or putting in place a portfolio of hedges to manage the foreign currency risk that a business may face.

Currency rates can have an effect on the cost of doing business. For example, a business that needs to pay US$10,000 to import goods to the UK would pay £6,141.38 if the rate was £1 to $1.6283. However, if the rate changed to £1 to $1.5057, the business would have to pay £6,641.38 (an extra £500) in order to pay the $10,000 price.

Banks make a profit by charging a commission on each foreign exchange deal. There is also a spread between the buying rate (the rate at which the bank will buy the currency from the customer) and the selling rate (the rate at which the bank will sell the customer the foreign currency). A spot transaction is a foreign exchange transaction that usually settles within two days. This type of transaction does not involve an ongoing contract (unlike forward exchange deals).

2.2 Forward exchange contracts

A forward exchange contract (FEC) is a binding contract to buy or sell a given quantity of a foreign currency at a future date at a rate of exchange determined when the FEC is made.

Customers may wish to enter into a FEC with a view to using the funds in the future to fulfil a business transaction on a named date. The exact terms of the contract may differ between banks (e.g. some banks may offer flexibility and allow a period of time between two dates to be specified for settlement of the contract).

With an FEC, the customer pays a foreign exchange rate based on the spot rate on the day of the deal. The rate of exchange is guaranteed, enabling a business to determine in advance what its costs will be (or how much income will be received).

FECs offer protection against adverse exchange rate movements in an easy and low-cost way. FECs also assist a business to budget and manage future sales and invoicing.

The risk with an FEC is that if the exchange rate moves against the customer, they are still legally bound to settle at the exchange rate specified in the contract.

Test yourself 8.2

What is a forward exchange contract?

3. Regulation and supervision of offshore banking

3.1 The Group of International Finance Centre Supervisors

The Offshore Group of Banking Supervisors was formed in October 1980 at the instigation of the Basel Committee on Banking Supervision (see section 3.2). It is an association of the authorities concerned with the supervision of banks in offshore finance centres and related financial services. The group changed its name to the Group of International Finance Centre Supervisors (GIFCS) in March 2011 in order to reflect better the wider scope of its activities.

It is a condition of membership that the authorities of the offshore centre must demonstrate a clear commitment to the implementation of the Core Principles set by the Basel Committee. The IMF assesses a jurisdiction's observance of the core principles.

3.2 The Basel Committee on Banking Supervision

The Basel Committee on Banking Supervision (BCBS) was established in 1974 by the Central Bank governors of the Group of 10 (G10) countries. The BCBS is recognised as the primary global standard setter for the prudential regulation of banks. It formulates supervisory standards and guidelines and recommends statements of best practice which it expects member countries to implement in a way that authorities in each country sees fit. The BCBS standards or guidelines do not have legal force and it does not have any formal supervisory authority. That said, offshore centres who wish to be recognised for their standard of regulation will need to comply and GIFCS has made it a condition of membership that offshore centres must demonstrate a clear commitment to the implementation of the standards set out by Basel.

The main functions that BCBS was set up for are as follows:

- enhancing banking stability;
- providing a forum for regular cooperation on banking supervision matters;
- setting global standard for the prudential regulation of banks; and
- strengthening the regulation, supervision and practices of banks worldwide.

The BCBS is best known for its International Standards on Capital Adequacy (the so-called Basel Capital Accord, known as Basel I and its subsequent revisions Basel II and III) and the Core Principles for Effective Banking Supervision (the Core Principles).

3.3 The Basel Capital Accord

Basel I

In 1988, the Basel Committee introduced a capital measurement system referred to as the Basel Capital Accord. The 1988 accord (known as Basel I) primarily focused on the implementation of a credit risk management framework. The Basel I framework was revised on 26 June 2004.

Basel II

The revised capital adequacy framework is known as Basel II. The Basel II framework is documented in a paper entitled *International Convergence of Capital Measurement and Capital Standards – A Revised Framework*. The Basel II framework aimed to:

- further strengthen the soundness and stability of the international banking system;

- establish closer alignment of regulatory capital requirements with economic capital needs; and
- maintain sufficient consistency such that capital adequacy regulation would not be a significant cause of competitive inequality among internationally active banks.

The regulators in Jersey, Guernsey and the Isle of Man worked together as a tri-party group in order to harmonise (wherever possible) their approaches to the implementation of Basel II. By doing so, the regulators hoped to make it easier for those banks that operate in all three jurisdictions and avoid the potential for regulatory arbitrage.

Basel II uses a three-pillar approach. The 'Three Pillars' of Basel II cover:

1. minimum capital requirements, which refined the standardised rules of the 1988 accord;
2. supervisory review of an institution's internal assessment process and capital adequacy; and
3. effective use of disclosure to strengthen market discipline as a complement to supervisory efforts.

On 4 July 2006, the BCBS issued a comprehensive version of the Basel II framework that was a compilation of the June 2004 framework, various amendments that had been made to the 1988 capital accord and a November 2005 guidance paper on the application of Basel II in certain circumstances.

It did not introduce any new elements and was issued purely as a matter of convenience to readers.

Basel III

In response to the financial crisis of 2008, BCBS developed new global standards to address both firm-specific and broader systemic risks. The revised standards have been referred to as Basel III.

This builds on Basel II and is a comprehensive set of reform measures to strengthen regulation, supervision and risk management of the banking sector. The new standards were announced on 12 September 2010.

Basel III aims to:

- improve the banking sector's ability to absorb shocks arising from financial and economic stress;
- improve risk management and governance; and
- strengthen banks' transparency and disclosures.

3.4 The Core Principles for Effective Banking Supervision

In September 1997, BCBS published the Core Principles for Effective Banking Supervision (the Core Principles). The Core Principles address supervisory powers, responsibilities and functions and supervisory expectations of banks including corporate governance and risk management and compliance with the standards. BCBS describes the Core Principles as a comprehensive blueprint for an effective supervisory system. In order to facilitate implementation and assessment, the BCBS developed a 'Core Principles Methodology' in 1999. The documents were revised in October 2006, before a more recent review in 2012. This review merged the separate assessment methodologies into a single document. It also restructured the Core Principles, increasing their number from 25 to 29.

The Core Principles are a voluntary framework of minimum standards for sound and effective banking supervisory practices. They are designed to be applied by all countries in the supervision of the banks in their jurisdiction. While they are considered to be universally applicable, national authorities may put in place supplementary measures in order to achieve effective supervision in their own jurisdictions as they see fit.

Preconditions for effective banking supervision

The Core Principles states that an effective system of banking supervision needs to be based on a number of preconditions. These include:

- an appropriate level of systemic protection (or public safety net);
- a clear framework for crisis management, recovery and resolution;
- effective market discipline;
- sound and sustainable macroeconomic policies;
- a well-established framework for financial stability policy formulation; and
- well-developed public infrastructure.

Test yourself 8.3

State the preconditions that are required for an effective system of banking supervision according to the BCBS Core Principles for Effective Banking Supervision.

4. Obtaining a banking licence

A bank is required to obtain a licence from its regulator before it is permitted to undertake deposit-taking business from within an offshore centre. The regulator may be known as a 'financial services commission'. The requirement to obtain a licence will be set out in the offshore centre's primary legislation. This usually makes it an offence to conduct such business without a licence.

Each offshore centre will have its own licensing policy or set criteria that it uses to determine the eligibility of a bank to operate in its jurisdiction. Jersey, for example, has a strict requirement for the bank to be a member of the top 500 banks in the world, measured by Tier 1 capital size. Other offshore centres impose varying requirements.

Some offshore centres have one all-encompassing category of banking licence, while others impose varying levels of licensing where the banking business that can be undertaken may be restricted.

When issuing a banking licence, the regulator in an offshore centre will undertake a fit and proper assessment of the applicant in order to decide whether or not the applicant should be granted a licence to undertake banking business in their jurisdiction. The regulator may assess the following attributes.

- **The track record of the applicant as a banking business:** whether it has been supervised by a relevant authority, its audit history, the stability of its management team, whether it conducts its business with integrity and has due regard for the interests of its customers. The regulator will also consider the risk profile of the applicant including the nature of activities that it will provide and its intended customer base and target markets.
- **The stature of the applicant**: the regulator will want to ensure that the bank remains well-capitalised, with adequate liquidity levels, and that it is able to meet the financial standards laid down by the regulator. Shell banks may not be permitted.
- **The importance of the bank in its home jurisdiction:** the regulator may seek comfort that the bank is of systematic importance in their home jurisdiction, which in turn should be capable of supporting them financially if ever needed. The home jurisdiction should be considered as an equivalent jurisdiction in terms of the AML/CFT measures that it applies.
- **The competence and experience of the principal persons**: the management and staff of the bank must be suitably qualified by either experience or qualifications to be sufficiently competent in the relevant areas of banking. The regulator will assess the risks involved if there are any dominant controllers.
- **The organisation's systems and controls**: the applicant should be committed to complying with any regulatory requirements (e.g. laws and codes of practice) and should have adequate policies and procedures in place to enable it to do so. This will include having good corporate governance systems in place, including non-executive directors where necessary.
- **The ownership and control of the bank**: an offshore centre may prefer its banks to be public quoted companies or subsidiaries of one. The ownership structure of the bank must be such that it is clear to the regulator who the ultimate owners and controllers are. This enables the regulator to perform 'fit and proper' checks on these principal persons.

As well as the general licence conditions, the regulator may impose specific licence conditions on certain banks to reflect their particular circumstances.

4.1 Ongoing banking supervision

Licensed banks are usually subject to ongoing supervision by the offshore centre's regulator. Ongoing supervision by regulators of banking business may include:

- on-site examinations conducted at the bank's premises and regular meetings with the bank;
- off-site supervision which may include a desk-based analysis of regulatory and statistical returns and other information;
- the requirement for the bank to submit annual audited financial statements;
- a requirement for the principal persons (directors and shareholders) and key persons (the money laundering reporting officer and the compliance officer) to be in receipt of an approval by the regulator, or in some cases a 'no objection' letter, before they may be appointed to act on behalf of the business;
- a requirement to notify the regulator of significant events or changes within the business; and
- a requirement to participate in thematic studies where requested to do so by the regulator.

Regulators in offshore centres are often keen to show that their supervisory approach and performance is compliant with the international standards. In some jurisdictions, the regulation of banks is undertaken by a separate body to that which regulates other financial services. For example, in Mauritius, the financial services sector is regulated and supervised by two independent institutions. These are the Bank of Mauritius for all deposit-taking and foreign exchange matters and the Financial Services Commission for non-bank financial services such as insurance.

4.2 Codes of practice

Regulators often issue codes of practice using powers that are provided in regulatory laws. These establish sound principles and requirements to be upheld by businesses conducting banking business. Codes of practice may include the following requirements.

- The business must be conducted with integrity.
- A business must have due regard for the interests of its customers.
- A business must organise and control its affairs effectively for the proper performance of its business activities, and be able to demonstrate the existence of adequate risk management systems (i.e. uphold customer due diligence and AML and CFT legislation).
- A business must be transparent in its business arrangements.
- A business must maintain and be able to demonstrate the existence of adequate capital resources including minimum capital requirements, risk asset ratio and concentration risk.
- A business must deal with the authorities in an open and cooperative manner.
- A business must not make statements that are misleading, false or deceptive.

5. Managed banks

Some banks cannot meet the criteria to undertake banking business on their own. These banks may be established as managed banks, meaning that the business of the bank is managed by another registered deposit taker (the manager) within the offshore centre.

The manager provides all necessary resources, such as staff, premises and information systems, and operates those resources on behalf of the managed bank. However, the managed bank is a registered person in its own right and must comply with all aspects of the regulatory framework. The managed bank itself remains ultimately accountable to its regulator for the activities that it undertakes.

The fit and proper assessments in respect of the managed bank are undertaken on the manager. In assessing the fitness and properness of a managed bank, the regulator will apply the same standards as a non-managed bank. A managed bank is sometimes known as an administered bank.

5.1 Advantages of being a managed bank

- It allows an organisation that may not otherwise meet the criteria for undertaking business in the jurisdiction to operate with the oversight of a manager to ensure that the laws and codes of practice designed to protect the public are maintained.
- Costs should be reduced (e.g. the costs of employing staff and renting premises).
- It provides administrative efficiencies at the outset by avoiding the need to recruit staff or apply for a licence or permit to employ staff.
- The organisation can avoid much of the learning curve that is experienced by a new organisation, as its manager provides experienced staff, a procedural framework that should allow it to comply with the laws and codes immediately, premises and information technology.
- A managed bank allows a bank to provide offshore services to its existing customer base while taking advantage of the expertise, systems and controls that are already available from the manager.
- A managed bank that has established itself within an offshore centre can apply to become a stand-alone bank when it can meet the criteria for licensing set out by the regulator.

Test yourself 8.4

Explain four reasons why a bank may establish itself as a managed bank.

6. Banking secrecy laws

Banking secrecy is a legal principle in some offshore centres under which banks and others are not allowed to disclose information about their customers.

Switzerland is an example of a jurisdiction where banking secrecy has been a long-standing practice, albeit one which has only recently been formalised in legislation. Article 47 of the Swiss Federal Act on Banks and Savings Banks provides for imprisonment of up to three years or a fine if a person deliberately discloses a secret that is entrusted to them in their capacity as an employee of the bank.

Banking secrecy legislation would not protect criminals responsible for serious crimes; however, in Switzerland, tax evasion, which is deemed unacceptable in most jurisdictions, is not considered to be a crime (although tax fraud is). The OECD has applied pressure to such 'secrecy jurisdictions', and they have suffered reputational damage as a result of their banking secrecy legislation.

Following this pressure, the distinction between tax evasion and tax fraud has been abolished in terms of dealing with foreign residents for the purposes of complying with the OECD information exchange requirements. Importantly, and although only following considerable international pressure (led by the USA) has Switzerland recognised the need to relax its traditional intense bank secrecy provisions. These will remain applicable only in what is considered domestic circumstances. Details of bank accounts will now be automatically disclosed to the tax authorities in respect of bank customers residing outside of Switzerland in a country participating in the CRS regime.

Other bank jurisdictions that are often referred to as secrecy jurisdictions (fairly or not) include Andorra, Austria, Liechtenstein and Luxembourg.

Chapter summary

- Offshore banking is simply having a bank account outside of one's own country of residence.
- Advantages of using an offshore bank for the customer include the receipt of gross interest, and, in some cases, more flexible regulation and supervision that enable cost savings to be passed on to customers by way of higher interest rates.
- There may be a disadvantage regarding offshore banking conducted in a jurisdiction if there is a lack of depositor compensation schemes in some offshore centres.
- Banks may wish to offer services from an offshore location in order to benefit from lower taxation, more flexible regulation and supervision, lower costs for premises and staff, and in order to extend the services that it can offer to its existing client base.
- When choosing an offshore bank, the quality of the banks within the jurisdiction, the regulator requirements and oversight, the low incidence of

bank failures and the availability of a depositor compensation scheme may all be relevant considerations.

- Services provided by offshore banks are similar to those available onshore and include current accounts, deposits and savings accounts, lending facilities, foreign exchange transactions and forward exchange contracts.
- The foreign exchange market is a decentralised global marketplace. Banks facilitate currency exchange and can advise customers with known foreign currency invoices to pay what the cost of settling the invoice may be. Banks may also enter into binding forward exchange contracts with customers that oblige the customer to buy or sell a given quantity of a foreign currency at a future date, at a rate of exchange that is determined when the contract is made.
- The Group of International Finance Centre Supervisors (GIFCS, formerly known as the Offshore Group of Banking Supervisors) has made it a condition of membership that offshore centres must demonstrate a clear commitment to the implementation of the Core Principles set by the Basel Committee on Banking Supervision (BCBS).
- The BCBS is a standard-setting body on all aspects of banking supervision that is best known for its international standards on capital adequacy (the Basel Capital Accord) and its Core Principles for Effective Banking Supervision. These Core Principles are a voluntary framework of minimum standards for sound banking supervisory practices.
- The Core Principles state that an effective system of banking supervision needs to be based upon a number of preconditions including: sound and sustainable macro-economic policies, a well-developed public infrastructure, effective market discipline and mechanisms for providing an appropriate level of systemic protection.
- Banking is usually a regulated activity and banks must therefore obtain a licence from their regulator in order to operate from within their jurisdiction. The regulator usually undertakes a fit and proper assessment of the applicant, which may involve assessing its track record, its stature, the competence and experience of its principal persons, its owners and its risk profile.
- Once licensed, a bank will be subject to ongoing supervision by its regulator, which may include on-site examinations and desk-based analysis of information. In order to facilitate ongoing supervision, the regulator or the jurisdiction's regulations may impose obligations upon licence holders – for example, a requirement for principal persons to be approved by the regulator and for the bank to notify the regulator of significant events or changes within the business.
- Regulators may issue codes of practice that establish sound principles to be upheld by businesses conducting banking business. Such codes include key principles such as a requirement to operate with integrity, with adequate capital resources and to deal with the authorities in an open and cooperative manner.

- Banks that cannot meet the criteria to undertake banking business on their own may be established as managed banks, meaning that the business of the bank is managed by another registered deposit taker within the offshore centre. When a bank is managed, the manager provides all necessary resources such as staff and premises, and operates those on behalf of the managed bank.
- Banking secrecy is a legal principle in some offshore centres under which banks are not allowed to provide authorities with information about their customers. A lot of attention from the international community is attracted to the offshore centres that are known as banking secrecy jurisdictions, not all of which is welcome.

Test yourself answers

Test yourself 8.1

Three reasons why a customer may choose to open an offshore bank account include:

- interest is usually paid gross (i.e. it is unlikely that any tax will be deducted at source on interest earned);
- depending on where the client is resident, offshore income may not be subject to tax in their country of residence if the income is not remitted back to that country; and
- offshore centres often benefit from statutory secrecy or confidentiality provisions that enhance the normal common law principles that apply to the customer/banker relationship.

Test yourself 8.2

A forward exchange contract (FEC) is a binding contract to buy or sell a given quantity of a foreign currency at a future date, at a rate of exchange that is determined when the FEC is made.

Test yourself 8.3

The Core Principles for Effective Banking Supervision paper states that an effective system of banking supervision needs to be based on a number of preconditions. These include:

- an appropriate level of systemic protection (or public safety net);
- a clear framework for crisis management, recovery and resolution;
- effective market discipline;
- sound and sustainable macroeconomic policies;
- a well-established framework for financial stability policy formulation; and
- a well-developed public infrastructure.

Test yourself 8.4

Four reasons why a bank may establish itself as a managed bank include:

- it allows an organisation that may not otherwise meet the criteria for undertaking business in the jurisdiction to operate with the oversight of a manager to ensure that the laws and codes of practice designed to protect the public are maintained;
- costs should be reduced (e.g. the costs of employing staff and renting premises);
- it provides administrative efficiencies at the outset by avoiding the need to recruit staff or apply for a licence or permit to employ staff; and
- the organisation can avoid much of the learning curve that is experienced by a new organisation as its manager provides experienced staff, a procedural framework that should allow it to comply with the laws and codes immediately, premises and information technology.

Part five

Chapter 9
Regulation and supervision of the offshore services sector

Chapter 10
Money laundering

Regulation and supervision of offshore finance centres

After studying this part, students will gain an understanding of a typical framework of regulation in an offshore centre including primary and secondary legislation, codes of practice and guidance notes.

Students will be able to discuss the fit and proper considerations that a regulator may undertake before granting a licence to conduct financial services business and gain an understanding of the ongoing regulation of such entities and the process that the Financial Conduct Authority (FCA) uses in the UK in order to decide upon the level of ongoing supervision that it applies to regulated organisations.

Students will be able to explain the objectives, powers and general functions of the UK financial services regulators, the FCA and the Prudential Regulation Authority (PRA), and will be able to discuss principles-based approach to regulation. Other important UK legislation addressed in this part includes the Data Protection Act 1998, the criminal **insider dealing** legislation and the behaviours that constitute the civil offence of **market**

abuse. Students will gain an understanding of the main aims of the Retail Distribution Review and its impact on offshore centres, and will be able to discuss some of the international bodies and standards that have an impact on offshore regulation.

In addition, students will gain an understanding of money laundering and why it is considered harmful, and will appreciate the impact that international bodies and anti-money laundering (AML) initiatives have had on the offshore environment. Students will be able to explain a typical AML framework in an offshore jurisdiction and will be able to discuss the various money laundering offences and obligations that the AML legislation imposes on offshore professionals. Students will be able to discuss customer due diligence. Finally, students will gain an understanding of how to recognise money laundering.

Learning outcomes

At the end of this part, you will:

1. understand how the offshore financial services sector is regulated;
2. know about data protection issues, insider dealing and market abuse; and
3. understanding money laundering and measures used to prevent it.

Chapter nine

Regulation and supervision of the offshore services sector

List of topics

1. The need for regulation
2. The development of regulation in the UK
3. Regulation of offshore financial services
4. The Alternative Investment Fund Managers Directive
5. Regulation in the UK
6. Data protection
7. Insider dealing
8. Market abuse
9. Retail Distribution Review
10. International bodies

Introduction

This chapter outlines the need for and the development of regulation.

It explains what might make up a typical regulatory framework in an offshore centre and outlines in more detail the regulatory framework in the UK, including the role and powers of the Financial Conduct Authority (FCA), the regulator of financial services providers.

The chapter outlines the principles of the Data Protection Act 1998 (and outlines the changes planned to legislation affecting this area which were due to come into force in the spring of 2018), as well as the offences and associated penalties for non-compliance. It also outlines the insider dealing offences under the Criminal Justice Act 1993 and the behaviours that constitute market abuse under the Financial Services and Markets Act 2000.

The chapter outlines the main elements of the Retail Distribution Review, which raised the standards that the public/investors expect from investment advisers, and concludes with an outline of the more influential international bodies that have had an influence on regulation of the offshore financial services industry (excluding those that set the AML/CFT standards, which are discussed in Chapter 10).

1. The need for regulation

The regulation of organisations providing financial services comprises sets of rules, prohibitions, restrictions and guidelines.

Regulation is necessary in order to maintain efficient, orderly and fair financial markets (both national and international). Regulation protects consumers from abusive practices, fraud and other financial crime, thus maintaining the integrity of the financial markets. It is important that only experienced professionals who are fit and proper are involved in providing financial services.

Regulation prohibits anyone who has not been approved as 'fit and proper' by the regulator from providing financial services and sets out what these organisations can and cannot do. It provides for those who do not meet the desired standard to be sanctioned or prevented from operating where appropriate.

2. The development of regulation in the UK

In May 1997, the supervision of banking and investment services was merged into the Securities and Investments board (SIB). The SIB formally changed its name to the Financial Services Authority (FSA) in October 1997.

Responsibility for banking supervision was transferred to the FSA from the Bank of England.

In May 2000, the FSA took over the role of the UK Listing Authority (UKLA) from the London Stock Exchange.

The Financial Services and Markets Act 2000 (FSMA) transferred responsibility for several other organisations to the FSA, including the Investment Management Regulatory Authority, the Personal Investment Authority and the Securities and Futures Authority (these had all previously had a role in authorising who could be involved in the industry).

In 2005, the FSA took responsibility for the regulation of general insurance business in order to implement the EU Insurance Mediation directive.

In June 2010, the Chancellor of the Exchequer announced the government's intention to restructure the UK's financial regulatory framework. As part of this reform, the FSA was replaced with two new regulatory bodies. The FSA was abolished with effect from 1 April 2013 and two new regulatory bodies, the Financial Conduct Authority (FCA) and the Prudential Regulation Authority (PRA) were created.

The PRA, a subsidiary of the Bank of England, is responsible for regulating deposit-taking businesses, insurers and investment banks. The FCA is responsible for the regulation of conduct in retail and wholesale financial markets, and the infrastructure that supports those markets.

3. Regulation of offshore financial services

Regulatory frameworks in the UK (and many other onshore jurisdictions) have been heavily influenced by international bodies and initiatives.

While many offshore centres are not compelled to incorporate international initiatives into their own regulatory frameworks, many have chosen to do so as they recognise that it is important to embrace the efforts of the international community and conduct their business with equivalent standards. This maintains investor confidence, attracts foreign investment and helps develop or maintain a reputation that allows offshore centres to compete without sanction.

3.1 Primary legislation

Regulatory frameworks for financial services industries offshore typically comprise:

- primary legislation;
- secondary legislation;
- regulatory codes; and
- guidance notes.

The primary legislation is usually a collection of legislation that in aggregate is equivalent to the UK's FSMA and typically provides for the creation of a regulator (equivalent to the FCA), which in offshore centres is often referred to as a financial services commission. The primary legislation usually provides for a general prohibition against the provision of financial services without regulatory authorisation.

The regulator is typically granted powers to:

- authorise organisations to provide financial services business;
- supervise that organisations adhere to the jurisdiction's laws, orders and codes; and
- provide for enforcement and sanctioning powers when they are not.

Sanctions may include the regulator imposing fines, banning individuals from working within the finance industry and/or making a public statement about their conduct.

Stop and think 9.1

What sanctions has the regulator in your jurisdiction imposed recently?

The fit and proper test

Authorisation is usually only granted to 'fit and proper' applicants. A fit and proper test may be set in the law (as they are in the FSMA) or may be influenced by a policy that is set by the regulator. A fit and proper determination by the regulator may include assessment of the following factors.

- **A relevant and satisfactory track record:** The regulator will prefer organisations that have a demonstrable track record. Where an organisation has a track record in another jurisdiction, the regulator may ask the regulator in that jurisdiction whether they hold any adverse information in connection with it. Where the organisation is a new company that cannot demonstrate a track record, the regulator can look instead to that of its proposed controllers (directors and shareholders).
- **The integrity of the applicant:** An assessment of the integrity of the organisation will reflect to some extent the integrity of its senior management team and the individuals employed by it. In assessing the integrity of the organisation or its management, the regulator may look to its past conduct and the proposed governance structure and practices of the entity that is to be licenced.
- **Competence of the staff employed:** An assessment of the level of qualified and experienced staff employed by the organisation will assist the regulator in determining its overall competency.
- **The financial standing of the applicant:** The financial resources available to the applicant and how financial risks will be managed are key to the entity remaining as a going concern. The regulator may require the applicant to have adequate professional indemnity insurance.
- **The resources available to the organisation:** The jurisdiction may require the organisation to be locally managed and controlled (with a majority of the directors being located within the jurisdiction) and to occupy local premises.
- **The structure of the organisation:** An assessment of the structure/organisation of the applicant may include an assessment of the availability of resources to the organisation, the systems and controls, and the transparency of ownership.

The structure of the organisation will need to provide for sufficient oversight by its senior management. The systems and controls of the organisation must be sufficient to manage risk and the affairs of the organisation effectively. Good corporate governance is key to demonstrate a well-run and effective organisation.

Transparency of ownership is very important to an offshore regulator. It is important that it can identify the ultimate controllers. A company that is owned by a structure involving trusts and companies can be a severe hindrance to the transparency of a structure and, for this reason, it is unlikely that the regulator would permit a structure without imposing additional safeguards (such as written undertakings or the involvement of regulated trustees) to ensure that it can always identify and perform due diligence on those who are in control.

3.2 Secondary legislation

Secondary legislation (sometimes referred to as regulations, orders or ordinances) enables a regulator to use powers granted to it in the primary legislation. Regulations typically supplement primary legislation and places additional, often more detailed and targeted requirements on authorised financial services businesses and the principal persons of those firms.

In most jurisdictions, these regulations carry the full authority of law and breaches of them may constitute a criminal offence.

3.3 Codes of practice

Regulators are usually authorised to publish regulatory codes, referred to as codes of practice. These are usually intended to direct the practical application and implementation of the overarching primary law and secondary legislation and contain provisions that are similar to the FCA's principles for business (see below).

In some centres, a failure to follow codes of practice does not of itself render any person liable to proceedings of any kind or invalidate any transaction. However, the codes may be used as evidence in any proceedings if it appears to the court to be relevant to any questions arising in the proceedings, and may be taken into account in determining any such questions.

3.4 Guidance

Guidance may outline the requirements of the jurisdiction's primary and secondary legislation (the statutory requirements) on a particular subject matter and present ways in which authorised organisations may comply with the statutory requirements. Guidance assists service providers through practical interpretation of the requirements of the regulator. Guidance may emphasise or promote a particular approach desired by the regulator and assists authorised organisations to develop their systems and controls accordingly.

The content of guidance is considered a regulatory requirement and failure to follow it may result in a regulatory sanction. Guidance may be taken into account when deciding whether or not a person has committed an offence under the law.

In a well-regulated jurisdiction, a failure to follow guidance is considered to be a serious matter. It may form the basis for a regulator to take action, as a failure on the part of individuals or firms to act with due skill and diligence may form the basis of legal action.

3.5 Regulation of trust and company service providers

Trust company business service providers In the offshore environment are typically regulated in accordance with the principles set out in section 3 of this chapter.

In the UK, the provision of trust and company service providers is not as prevalent as it is offshore. Therefore, the approach to the regulation of organisations that provide such services differs somewhat from that adopted in many of the offshore centres.

UK-based trust and company service providers do not fall within the scope of the FSMA. Instead, there is a requirement under the Money Laundering Regulations 2007 for such service providers to register with HMRC for AML purposes.

Therefore, the HMRC is by default the main supervisory authority for trust and company service providers.

In order to assist you with gaining a further understanding of the regulatory frameworks surrounding financial services business, this chapter will discuss the UK's framework in some detail, comparing it against the framework that exists in the offshore centre in which you are based or with which you closely associate yourself.

Test yourself 9.1

What is a typical regulatory framework in an offshore centre comprised of?

4. The Alternative Investment Fund Managers Directive

Sometimes regulation made outside of offshore centres does affect offshore centres. One such case is the Alternative Investment Fund Managers Directive (AIFMD), which came into effect on 1 July 2011.

Alternative investment funds include hedge funds, private equity funds and other collective funds that principally invest in specialist assets other than securities and bonds listed on the main global stock exchanges.

The directive places conditions on all alternative investment fund managers (AIFMs). It requires them to apply to their home regulator for authorisation to market alternative investment funds across the EU and to manage alternative investment funds domiciled in other EU countries.

AIFMs located in offshore centres are caught by the requirements of the AIFMD if they market or manage alternative investment funds in the EU. However, AIFMs in 'third countries', which include offshore centres such as Jersey and Guernsey, can continue to market to professional investors within the EU until at least 2018 using existing private placement regimes, providing they meet certain conditions.

The governments and regulators in offshore centres are working hard to ensure that jurisdictions remain competitive and can meet the requirements of the AIFMD in due course. Each offshore centre will need to ensure that its laws, orders and codes are compliant with the directive. Offshore centres will also need to sign regulatory cooperation agreements with the home regulator in each EU member state in a form approved by the European Securities and Markets Authority (ESMA).

The FCA (discussed below) is the regulator for the AIFMs in the UK. The rules of the AIFMD should create a level playing field across Europe, making it easier for AIFMs to operate cross border. It will also improve standards and offer more protection for investors.

At the time of writing, the outcome of Brexit negotiations are unclear in terms of what the impact will be on the fund industry generally and alternative funds specifically of the United Kingdom's departure from the European Union after March 2019.

5. Regulation in the UK

5.1 The Prudential Regulation Authority

The PRA is a subsidiary of the Bank of England. It is responsible for regulating deposit-taking businesses such as banks and building societies, insurers and investment firms.

The PRA's general objective is to promote the safe and sound operation of PRA authorised firms. The PRA seeks to advance its objective in two ways:

- ensuring that the business of PRA-authorised firms is carried on in a way which avoids any adverse effect on the stability of the UK financial system; and
- minimising the adverse effect that the failure of a PRA-authorised firm could be expected to have on the stability of the UK financial system.

The PRA also has an insurance objective, namely contributing to securing an appropriate degree of protection for those who are, or may become, policyholders.

In discharging its general functions, the PRA has a duty to have regard to the regulatory principles that are set out in the Financial Services Act 2012. These are discussed further in section 5.4.

The PRA's approach to regulation and supervision

The PRA's approach to regulation and supervision has three main characteristics:

- **A judgement-based approach:** the PRA uses its judgement in determining whether financial firms are safe and sound, whether insurers provide appropriate protection for policyholders and whether firms continue to meet the threshold conditions (see section 4.9).
- **A forward-looking approach:** the PRA assesses firms not just against current risks, but also against those that could plausibly arise in the future. Where the PRA judges it necessary to intervene, it generally aims to do so at an early stage.

- **A focused approach:** the PRA focuses on those issues and those firms that pose the greatest risk to the stability of the UK financial system and policyholders.

5.2 The Financial Conduct Authority

The FCA is the independent regulatory body established as a successor to the FSA, as provided for in the Financial Services Act 2012. The FSA was originally given its statutory powers and objectives by FSMA, which is the primary legislation in the UK. FSMA came into force on 1 December 2001, and was subsequently amended by the Financial Services Act 2012.

The FCA's general duties

The Financial Services Act 2012 provides that the FCA must, so far as is reasonably possible, act in a way which is compatible with its strategic objective, and advances one or more of its operational objectives.

The objectives of the FCA

The FCA's strategic objective is 'ensuring that the relevant markets function well'. Its operational objectives are:

- consumer protection;
- integrity; and
- competition.

The consumer protection objective

The consumer protection objective focuses on securing an appropriate degree of protection for consumers.

In considering what degree of protection for consumers may be appropriate, the FCA must have regard to the following:

- the differing degrees of risk involved in different kinds of investment or other transaction;
- the differing degrees of experience and expertise that different consumers may have;
- the needs that consumers may have for the timely provision of information and advice that is accurate and fit for purpose;
- the general principle that consumers should take responsibility for their decisions;
- the general principle that those providing regulated financial services should be expected to provide consumers with an appropriate level of care, while having regard to the degree of risk involved in relation to the investment or other transaction and the capabilities of the consumers in question;
- the differing expectations that consumers may have in relation to different kinds of investment or other transaction; and
- any information which the consumer financial education body has provided to the FCA in the exercise of the consumer financial education function.

The integrity objective

The integrity objective aims to protect and enhance the integrity of the UK financial system. The integrity of the UK financial system includes:

- its soundness, stability and resilience;
- not being used for a purpose connected with financial crime;
- not being affected by behaviour that amounts to market abuse;
- orderly operation of the financial markets; and
- transparency of the price formation process in those markets.

The competition objective

The competition objective focuses on promoting effective competition in the interests of consumers. This applies to markets for regulated financial services, as well as services provided by a recognised investment exchange when carrying on regulated activities.

The FCA may have regard to the following matters when considering the effectiveness of competition in the market, including:

- the needs of different consumers who use or may use those services, including their need for information that enables them to make informed choices;
- the ease with which consumers who may wish to use those services can access them, including consumers in areas affected by social or economic deprivation;
- the ease with which consumers who obtain those services can change the person from whom they obtain them;
- the ease with which new entrants can enter the market; and
- how far competition is encouraging innovation.

The FCA must discharge its general functions in a way that promotes effective competition in the interests of consumers, as long as it also advances the consumer protection or integrity objectives.

5.3 Powers of the FCA

FSMA and the Financial Services Act 2012 give the FCA a wide range of powers that it may use to achieve its objectives.

The FCA has the power to grant an authorisation to conduct a regulated activity, to vary any granted authorisation and to withdraw an authorisation.

The FCA has rule-making powers, as well as powers to investigate and gather information in order to assess whether an authorised person is abiding by any such rules or regulations.

The FCA has enforcement powers and can appoint a person to hold an inquiry, can issue prohibition orders, holds disciplinary powers and can impose penalties – for example, in cases of market abuse.

The FCA's general functions

The FCA's general functions include:

- making rules;
- preparing and issuing codes;
- the giving of general guidance; and
- determining the general policy and principles by reference to which it performs its functions.

In discharging its general functions, the FCA must have regard to its regulatory principles (see section 5.5). It must also take action to minimise the extent to which a business run by an authorised person or an investment exchange can be used for a purpose connected with financial crime.

5.4 The FCA's ten supervision principles

The FCA's approach to supervision is built on ten principles that form the basis of its interaction with firms. The ten supervision principles are as follows.

1. Ensuring fair outcomes for consumers and markets. This is the dual consideration that runs throughout the FCA's work. It will assess issues according to their impact on both consumers and market integrity.
2. Being forward-looking and pre-emptive, identifying potential risks and taking action before they have a serious impact.
3. Being focused on the big issues and causes of problems. The FCA will concentrate its resources on issues that have a significant impact on its objectives.
4. Taking a judgement-based approach, with the emphasis on achieving the right outcomes.
5. Ensuring firms act in the right spirit, which means they consider the impact of their actions on consumers and markets rather than just complying with the letter of the law.
6. Examining business models and culture, and the impact they have on consumer and market outcomes. The FCA is interested in how a firm makes its money, as this can drive many potential risks.
7. An emphasis on individual accountability, ensuring senior management understand that they are personally responsible for their actions – and that the FCA will hold them to account when things go wrong.
8. Being robust when things go wrong, making sure that problems are fixed, consumers are protected and compensated, and poor behaviour is rectified along with its root causes.
9. Communicating openly with industry, firms and consumers to gain a deeper understanding of the issues they face.
10. Having a joined-up approach, making sure firms get consistent messages from the FCA. It will also engage with the PRA to ensure effective independent supervision of dual-regulated firms, and work with other regulatory and advisory bodies including the Financial Ombudsman Service,

Financial Services Compensation Scheme, Money Advice Service and international regulators.

5.5 The principles of good regulation

The Financial Services Act 2012 provides that the FCA and PRA must follow the regulatory principles outlined in Table 9.1.

Table 9.1: Principles of good regulation

Principle	Description
Efficiency and economy	The need to use the resources of each regulator in the most efficient and economical way.
Proportionality	A burden or restriction which is imposed on a person, or on the carrying on of an activity, should be proportionate to the benefits, considered in general terms, which are expected to result from the imposition of that burden or restriction.
Sustainable growth	The desirability of sustainable growth in the economy of the United Kingdom in the medium or long term.
Consumer responsibility	The general principle that consumers should take responsibility for their decisions.
Senior management responsibility	The responsibilities of the senior management of persons subject to requirements imposed by or under the Financial Services Act in relation to compliance with those requirements, including those affecting consumers.
Recognising the differences in the businesses carried on by different regulated persons	The desirability, where appropriate, of each regulator exercising its functions in a way that recognises differences in the nature and objectives of businesses carried on by different persons subject to requirements imposed by or under the Financial Services Act.
Openness and disclosure	The desirability of each regulator publishing information in appropriate cases relating to persons on whom requirements are imposed by or under the Financial Services Act as a means of contributing to the advancement by each regulator of its objectives, or requiring such persons to publish information.
Transparency	The principle that the regulators should exercise their functions as transparently as possible.

Note: 'Objectives' in relation to the FCA refers to its operational objectives.

5.6 Duties of the regulators

In addition to following the regulatory principles outlined in section 5.4, both the FCA and the PRA have a duty to follow principles of good governance. They also have a duty to ensure coordinated exercise of their respective functions.

This duty requires each regulator to consult with the other on any proposed exercise of a function that may have a material adverse effect on the advancement by the other regulator of any of its objectives. The FCA and the PRA should also obtain information and advice from the other regulator in connection with matters of common regulatory interest, and especially in cases where the other regulator may be expected to have relevant information or expertise.

5.7 The regulatory handbooks

Both the FCA and the PRA have each published Handbooks containing relevant rules and guidance. These are referred to as the FCA Handbook and the PRA Handbook respectively. These Handbooks apply to authorised firms carrying out financial services business in the UK.

5.8 Principles for businesses

The FCA Handbook contains 11 principles for businesses, which are fundamental obligations of all firms under the regulatory system (see Table 9.2).

Firms supervised by the PRA are only subject to principles 1 to 4, 8 and 11. This is reflected in the PRA Handbook.

Table 9.2: The FCA's principles for businesses

Principle	**Description**
1. Integrity	A firm must conduct its business with integrity.
2. Skill, care and diligence	A firm must conduct its business with due skill, care and diligence.
3. Management and control	A firm must take reasonable care to organise and control its affairs responsibly and effectively, with adequate risk management systems.
4. Financial prudence	A firm must maintain adequate financial resources.
5. Market conduct	A firm must observe proper standards of market conduct.
6. Customers' interests	A firm must pay due regard to the interests of its customers and treat them fairly.
7. Communication with clients	A firm must pay due regard to the information needs of its clients and communicate information to them in a way which is clear, fair and not misleading.
8. Conflicts of interest	A firm must manage conflicts of interest fairly, both between itself and its customers, and between a customer and another client.
9. Customers: relationships of trust	A firm must take reasonable care to ensure the suitability of its advice and discretionary decisions for any customer who is entitled to rely upon its judgement.
10. Clients' assets	A firm must arrange adequate protection for clients' assets when it is responsible for them.
11. Relations with regulators	A firm must deal with its regulators in an open and cooperative way, and must disclose to an appropriate regulator appropriately anything to the firm of which the FCA would reasonably expect notice.

Test yourself 9.2

State four of the FCA's principles for business.

5.9 Authorisation to conduct regulated activity

FSMA contains a general prohibition on carrying out a regulated activity in the UK unless the person doing so is a person authorised under the FSMA to do so or is an exempt person.

When an application is made for permission to carry on a regulated activity, the regulators must ensure that the applicant will satisfy (and continue to satisfy) certain 'threshold conditions'. These are set out in schedule 6 to FSMA.

The threshold conditions vary depending on the regulatory activity to which the application relates; however, in general, the conditions that must be met in order for a person to become an authorised person under the FSMA relate to:

- the legal status of the applicant (in some instances the applicant must be a company);
- the location of the offices of the applicant (which should be in the UK);
- any close links with persons that are likely to prevent effective supervision by the regulator;
- the resources of the applicant (resources must be adequate); and
- the suitability of the applicant (the applicant must be a fit and proper person).

5.10 Ongoing supervision by the FCA

Persons who are authorised to conduct a regulated activity by the FCA are subject to ongoing supervision.

The FCA's overall approach to supervision of approved persons is based upon the ten supervision principles explained in section 5.4, as well as the three pillars outlined in Table 9.3).

Table 9.3: The FCA's three supervision pillars

Pillar	Description
Firm-systematic framework	This includes the proactive supervision of firms. The FCA assesses whether the firm is run in the interests of its customers and whether the integrity of the market is at the heart of how the business is run.
Event-driven work	This includes dealing with unforeseen problems that are emerging or have happened. The FCA may seek customer redress or other remedial work where necessary.
Issues and products	Thematic supervision on sectors of the market or products within a sector that may put consumers at risk. This work is driven by the risk assessments of issues and products that are currently driving poor outcomes for consumers.

5.11 Ongoing supervision by the PRA

The PRA divides the firms that it supervises into categories of potential impact. The frequency and intensity of supervision applied to firms varies in line with this. The size of a firm's potential impact depends upon factors such as:

- the firm's size;
- the firm's complexity;
- the firm's interconnectedness with the rest of the financial system;
- the number of policyholders (if an insurance company); and
- the type of business undertaken.

The PRA varies the resources allocated to the supervision of firms based on their proximity to failure and resolvability, as well as the possible adverse effects on the PRA's objectives.

Test yourself 9.3

State three factors that the PRA may take into consideration when deciding on a firm's potential impact.

5.12 Payment Systems Regulator

In April 2015, the FCA created a separate body, the Payment Systems Regulator (PSR), in accordance with section 40 of the Financial Services (Banking) Reform Act 2013. The roll of the PSR is to promote competition and innovation in payment systems, and ensure they work in the interests of the organisations and people that use them.

In June 2017, the PSR published reforms to the infrastructure of the payment systems in the UK in order to encourage better and more innovative services and to update the central infrastructure for the main UK retail payment systems namely Bacs, Faster Payments and LINK, which at that time were considered to not offer effective competition. The PSR are effectively promoting two main changes:

- the introduction of a competitive procurement process for future central infrastructure contracts to ensure fair, open and transparent procurement for central payment systems infrastructure, allowing new technology providers to enter the market; and
- to adopt a common international messaging standard (ISO 20022) for Bacs and Faster Payments. This change aims to reduce or lower barriers and encourage new entrants to this market.

5.13 UK Financial Services Ombudsman

The Financial Services Ombudsman is not a regulator as such. It was established by Parliament to be an official expert to aid customers with resolving problems with financial services providers; as a cost-free alternative to taking complaints and other disputes to regulators or through the court system.

If a complaint cannot be resolved between a financial services provider and a customer, the customer can ask the Ombudsman to give an unbiased answer as to what has happened. If it is decided that a customer has been treated unfairly, the Ombudsman has legal powers to ensure the customer is compensated or to recommend that other action is taken to 'put things right'.

In 2017 alone, more than 2 million people contacted the Ombudsman regarding problems with bank accounts, credit, debit and store cards, payment protection and other insurance, loans including pay day loans, other forms of credit, mortgages, debt collection activity, money transfers and online payments, financial advice regarding savings, investments and pensions.

The UK's crown dependencies have so far each established a comparable Ombudsman, but not all other offshore centres have done so.

6. Data protection

6.1 The Data Protection Act 1998

The Data Protection Act 1998 (DPA) was designed to implement the EU Data Protection Directive. This requires member states to protect the privacy rights and freedoms of individuals in the processing of **personal data**.

personal data
Data that relates to a living individual (the data subject) who can be identified from that data.

The DPA applied to organisations that processed data as 'data controllers' or 'data processors' and provided 20 years of regulation. It has been responsible for embedding a data protection culture across the EU.

The DPA was replaced with effect from 25 May 2018 as a consequence of implementation of the EU General Data Protection Regulation (GDPR) which is the next generation of data protection regulation. It introduces new rights for data subjects (those about whom data is held) and new obligations for data processors and controllers. For the most part GDPR represents an evolution of the previous directive, but importantly it introduces material fines for breaches of its regulation, which will serve to focus further the minds of financial service providers.

The DPA refers to organisations that process data as **data controllers**. The DPA is applicable whenever a data controller processes personal and/or sensitive personal data.

data controller
An organisation that processes personal data.

6.2 The EU General Data Protection Regulation (GDPR)

The EU General Data Protection Regulation (GDPR) replaces the Data Protection Directive 95/46/EC and was designed to harmonise data protection laws across Europe, to protect and empower all EU citizens in relation to data privacy, and to reshape the way organisations approach data protection and data privacy.

The aim of the GDPR is to protect all EU citizens from data protection breaches in an increasingly data-driven world that is radically different from the time in which the 1995 directive was established. Although the key principles of data protection still hold true to the previous directive, many changes and developments have been introduced to EU regulatory policy. The key points of the GDPR are set out in this section.

Increased territorial scope (extra-territorial applicability)

Arguably the biggest change is with the extended jurisdiction of the GDPR, as it applies to all organisations processing the personal data of data subjects residing in the EU, regardless of the location of the organisation. Previously, territorial applicability of the directive was ambiguous and referred to data processing 'in context of an establishment'. This topic has arisen in a number of high profile court cases. GDPR makes its applicability very clear – it will apply to the processing of personal data by controllers and processors in the EU, regardless of whether the processing takes place in the EU or not. The GDPR will also apply to the processing of personal data of data subjects in the EU by a controller or processor not established in the EU, where the activities relate to offering goods or services to EU citizens (irrespective of whether payment is required) and the monitoring of behaviour that takes place within the EU. Non-EU organisations processing the data of EU citizens will also have to appoint a representative in the EU.

Penalties

Under GDPR organisations in breach of GDPR can be fined up to 4% of annual global turnover of €20 Million (whichever is greater). This is the maximum fine that can be imposed for the most serious infringements, e.g. not having sufficient customer consent to process data or violating the core of 'Privacy by Design' concepts. There is a tiered approach to fines, e.g. an organisation can be fined 2% for not having their records in order (article 28), not notifying the supervising authority and data subject about a breach or not conducting impact assessment. It is important to note that these rules apply to both controllers and processors – also meaning 'cloud storage' will be regulated under the GDPR.

Consent

The conditions for consent have been strengthened, and organisations will no longer be able to use long complicated and impenetrable terms and conditions full of legalese, as the request for consent must be given in an intelligible and easily accessible format, with the purpose for data processing clearly attached to that consent. Consent must be clear and distinguishable from other matters and provided in an intelligible and easily accessible form, using clear and plain language. It must be as easy to withdraw consent as it is to give it.

Data subject rights

Breach Notification: Under the GDPR, breach notification to the data protection authority is mandatory where a data breach is likely to 'result in a risk for the rights and freedoms of individuals'. This must be done within 72 hours of first having become aware of the breach. Data processors will also be required to notify their customers, the controllers, 'without undue delay' after first becoming aware of a data breach.

Right to Access: Part of the expanded rights of data subjects outlined by the GDPR is the right for data subjects to obtain from the data controller confirmation as to whether or not personal data concerning them is being processed, where and for what purpose. Further, the controller shall provide a copy of the personal data, free of charge, in an electronic format. This change is a dramatic shift to data transparency and empowerment of data subjects.

Right to Data Erasure: Also known as the 'right to be forgotten', entitles the data subject to have the data controller erase his/her personal data, cease further dissemination of the data, and potentially have third parties halt processing of the data. The conditions for erasure, as outlined in article 17, include the data no longer being relevant to original purposes for processing, or a data subjects withdrawing consent. It should also be noted that this right requires controllers to compare the subjects' rights to 'the public interest in the availability of the data' when considering such requests.

Data Portability: GDPR introduces data portability – the right for a data subject to receive the personal data concerning them, which they have previously provided in a 'commonly used and machine readable format', and have the right to transmit that data to another controller.

Privacy by Design: Privacy by design as a concept has existed for years now, but it has only just become part of a legal requirement with the GDPR. At the core, privacy by design calls for the inclusion of data protection from the onset of the designing of products, services and systems, rather than as an addition or afterthought. More specifically, 'The controller shall... implement appropriate technical and organisational measures... in an effective way... in order to meet the requirements of this Regulation and protect the rights of data subjects'. Article 23 calls for controllers to hold and process only the data absolutely necessary for the completion of its duties (data minimisation), as well as limiting the access to personal data to those needing to carry out the processing.

Data Protection Officers: Currently, controllers are required to notify their data processing activities with local Data Processing Authorities, which, for multinationals, can be a bureaucratic difficulty with most Member States having different notification requirements. Under GDPR, it will not be necessary to submit notifications/registrations to each local authority, nor will it be a requirement to notify/obtain approval for transfers based on the Model Contract Clauses (MCCs). Instead, there are internal record-keeping requirements.

The appointment of a DPO is mandatory but only for those controllers and processors whose core activities consist of processing operations that require regular and systematic monitoring of data subjects on a large scale or of special categories of data or data relating to criminal convictions and offences.

Importantly, the DPO conditions include the following:

- must be appointed on the basis of professional qualities and, in particular, expert knowledge on data protection law and practices;
- may be a staff member or an external service provider;
- contact details must be provided to the relevant DPA;

- must be provided with appropriate resources to carry out their tasks and maintain their expert knowledge;
- must report directly to the highest level of management; and
- must not carry out any other tasks that could result in a conflict of interest.

UK Data Protection Bill

The UK's third generation of data protection law, the Data Protection Bill was published in September 2017 and aims to modernise data protection laws to ensure they are effective in the years to come.

It will update the UK's data protection laws to make them fit-for purpose for the evolving digital economy and implement GDPR standards in preparation for Brexit. Strong data protection laws and appropriate safeguards are necessary for businesses to continue operating across international borders as this ultimately underpins global trade.

Furthermore, modern innovative uses of data must be facilitated while at the same time strengthening the control and protections for individuals over their personal data.

The main elements of the Bill include the following.

General data processing

- Implement GDPR standards across all general data processing.
- Provided clarity on the definitions used in the GDPR in the UK context.
- Ensure that sensitive health, social care and education data can continue to be processed to ensure continued confidentiality in health and safeguarding situations can be maintained.
- Provide appropriate restrictions to rights to access and delete data to allow certain processing currently undertaken to continue where there is a strong public policy justification, including for national security purposes.
- Set the age from which parental consent is not needed to process data online at age 13, supported by a new age-appropriate design code enforced by the Information Commissioner.

Law enforcement processing

- Provide a bespoke regime for the processing of personal data by the police, prosecutors and other criminal justice agencies for law enforcement purposes.
- Allow the unhindered flow of data internationally while providing safeguards to protect personal data.

National security processing

- Ensure that the laws governing the processing of personal data by the intelligence services remain up to date and in line with modernised international standards, including appropriate safeguards with which the intelligence community can continue to tackle existing, new and emerging national security threats.

Regulation and enforcement

- Enact additional powers for the Information Commissioner, who will continue to regulate and enforce data protection laws.
- Allow the Commissioner to levy higher administrative fines on data controllers and processors for the most serious data breaches, up to £17 million (€20 million) or 4% of global turnover for the most serious breaches.
- Empower the Commissioner to bring criminal proceedings against offences where a data controller or processor alters records with intent to prevent disclosure following a subject access request.

It is important to note that the Bill differs from GDPR insofar as it is further reaching and provides a complete data protection system, covers all other general data, law enforcement data and national security data. Furthermore, the Bill exercises a number of agreed modifications to the GDPR to make it work for the benefit of the UK in areas such as academic research, financial services and child protection.

GDPR in Jersey and Guernsey

As they are non-EU jurisdictions, neither Jersey nor Guernsey are directly subject to the GDPR, although some organisations offering goods and services to EU citizens will be covered. Of more importance is the critical requirement to maintain GDPR equivalence so that international transfers of personal data are not unnecessarily interrupted.

In Jersey, the Data Protection (Jersey) Law 2005 was replaced by the Data Protection (Jersey) Law 2018 with effect from 25 May 2018. The new law provides data protection equivalence for Jersey.

In Guernsey, the Data Protection (Bailiwick of Guernsey) Law 2017 replaced Data Protection (Bailiwick of Guernsey) Law 2001 with effect from 25 May 2018. The new law provides data protection equivalence for Guernsey.

inside information
Information that relates to particular securities, is specific or precise, has not been made public and if it were made public, would be likely to have a significant effect on the price of any securities.

Test yourself 9.4

State four data protection rights under the GDPR.

7. Insider dealing

Insider dealing is a criminal offence in the UK under the Criminal Justice Act 1993, which came into force on 1 March 1994. It occurs when an individual with **inside information** (price-sensitive information) uses this information in relation to trading securities on a recognised market (that are price-affected by the inside information) in order to make a profit (or avoid a loss), thus gaining a financial advantage that would not be available to members of the general public.

Preventing, discouraging and (where necessary) detecting acts of insider dealing are vital to market participants having confidence in the UK's various investment markets.

The price-affected securities listed in Schedule 2 of the Act include:

- contracts for differences;
- debt securities including debentures, debenture stock, loan stock and certificates of deposits;
- depository receipts;
- futures;
- options;
- shares and share capital of companies; and
- warrants.

7.1 Insider dealing offences

There are three offences that constitute insider dealing. These are:

1. dealing in securities on the basis of inside information;
2. encouraging another to deal on the basis of inside information; and
3. disclosing inside information otherwise than in the proper performance of the functions of employment or profession.

For an offence to have been committed, the acquisition or disposal must have occurred on a regulated market, or if the person relies on or is acting as a professional intermediary.

For the purposes of insider dealing, inside information is information that relates to particular securities, is specific or precise, has not been made public and if it were made public, would be likely to have a significant effect on the market price of any securities.

No offence is committed if the insider did not know that the information was 'inside information'. The information must have been obtained by virtue of being a director, employee or shareholder of an issuer of securities (or the direct or indirect source of the information is one of these people) or by having access to the information by virtue of their employment, office or profession.

7.2 Insider dealing defences

Under Article 53 of the Criminal Justice Act, an individual will not be guilty of insider dealing if, in relation to the dealing offence or the encouraging another person to deal offence, they can show that they:

- did not expect that a profit attributable to the inside information would be made;

- believed (on reasonable grounds) that the information had been disclosed widely enough that none of those taking part in the dealing would be prejudiced by not having the information; and
- would have dealt in the securities anyway.

In relation to the 'disclosure of information' offence, it is a defence to show that they did not expect:

- any person to deal in the securities as a result of the disclosure; or
- the dealing to make a profit attributable to the inside information.

7.3 Penalties

The maximum penalty for an individual convicted of insider dealing is a fine or imprisonment for a term not exceeding seven years, or both.

Making it work 9.1

Prosecuting insider dealing

In March 2009, the FSA secured its first insider dealing conviction against a solicitor, Mr Christopher McQuoid and his father-in-law, Mr Melbourne.

In the FSA's first insider dealing prosecution (to reach trial), the jury found that Mr McQuoid, who had acted as the legal counsel to TTP Communications (TTP), had passed inside information about a planned takeover of TTP by Motorola to Mr Melbourne. Mr Melbourne profited as a result of a trade that was made based on the information. Two days before the takeover of TTP was made public, Mr Melbourne brought 153,824 TTP shares at 13 pence per share. When the takeover was announced at an agreed share price of 45 pence per share, Mr Melbourne made a profit of £48,919.20, which he later split with Mr McQuoid.

Both were found guilty and were sentenced to eight months' imprisonment (although Mr Melbourne's was suspended). Both also forfeited the profits they had generated.

8. Market abuse

Part VIII of FSMA sets out the behaviour that amounts to market abuse. This involves behaviour in relation to investments which are trading (or have applied to trade) on a UK market. Seven types of behaviour can amount to market abuse (see Table 9.4).

Table 9.4: Types of market abuse

Type of market abuse	Description
1. Insider dealing	Where an insider deals or attempts to deal in a qualifying investment on the basis of inside information relating to the investment.
2. Improper disclosure of inside information	Where an insider discloses information to another person other than in the proper course of exercise of their employment, profession or duties.
3. Misuse of information	Behaviour based on information that is not generally available to those using the market but would, if available to a regular user, be relevant to their decisions about the terms on which to deal.
4. Manipulating transactions	This behaviour includes effecting transactions or orders to trade which may give a false or misleading impression as to the supply of or demand for an investment or to secure the price of an investment at an abnormal or artificial level.
5. Manipulating devices	This involves effecting transactions or orders to trade which employ fictitious devices or any form of deception or contrivance. This could involve spreading misleading information with a view to increasing the price of a shareholding and thereby giving others a false impression of the share price.
6. Dissemination	The dissemination of information that gives a false or misleading impression about an investment by a person who knew (or could reasonably have been expected to have known) that the information was false or misleading.
7. Distortion and misleading behaviour	Behaviour which is likely to give a regular user of the market a false or misleading impression as to the supply of or demand for an investment or that otherwise distorts the market in an investment.

For the purposes of the market abuse offences, an 'insider' is a person who has inside information. Inside information is information of a precise nature which is not generally available and that, if generally available, would be likely to have a significant effect on the price of the investment.

The FSMA describes information as being precise if it indicates circumstances that exist or may reasonably be expected to come into existence, or an event that has or is expected to occur, and is specific enough to enable a conclusion to be drawn as to the possible effect on the price of the investment.

Market abuse is not a criminal offence under the FSMA but civil penalties may be imposed, and these could include unlimited fines. However, criminal insider dealing is an offence under Part V of the Criminal Justice Act 1993 and criminal market manipulation is an offence under Sections 89–91 of the Financial Services Act 2012.

8.1 Market Abuse Regulation (MAR)

The Market Abuse Regulation (MAR), EU Regulation (EU) No 596/2014 replaced the former Market Abuse Directive (MAD) in its entirety and came into effect in July 2016. It aims to increase market integrity and investor protection, enhancing the attractiveness of securities markets for capital raising.

The MAR strengthens the previous UK market abuse framework by extending its scope to new markets, new platforms and new behaviours. It contains prohibitions of insider dealing, unlawful disclosure of inside information and market manipulation, and provisions to prevent and detect these activities.

MAR applies to financial instruments admitted to trading on EU regulated markets, multilateral trading facilities, organised trading facilities and other financial instruments such as credit default swaps or contracts for difference. This means that companies listed on the London Stock Exchange are subject to MAR. In addition, AIM falls within the definition of a multilateral trading facility and therefore, for the first time, AIM companies are subject to the disclosure requirements of MAR.

MAR defines market abuse as encompassing insider dealing, unlawful disclosure of inside information and market manipulation. Because MAR is an EU regulation, rather than a directive, it does not need UK legislation and it is regulated at the EU by the European Securities and Markets Authority (ESMA). The FCA was required to amend the Listing, Prospectus and Disclosure and Transparency Rules to comply with MAR accordingly and implement the requirements at market level.

Test yourself 9.5

State and briefly explain the seven types of market abuse under the FSMA.

9. Retail Distribution Review

In June 2006, the FSA announced the Retail Distribution Review (RDR), which had the specific aim of identifying and addressing the causes of problems in relation to the retail investment market. The RDR intended to raise the standards investors can expect from all investment advisers and aimed to provide the following benefits.

- Consumers would better understand the advice service they are being offered.
- Independent advice would be truly independent and relate to a wider range of products.
- Adviser recommendations would not be influenced by the commission paid by product providers.
- Consumers would know upfront how much advice is costing them and how they would pay for it.

In addition, advisers would be better qualified and will keep their knowledge up to date.

There were three main elements to the RDR:

1. **adviser charging:** this element aimed to ensure that consumers are offered a transparent and fair charging system for the advice they receive;
2. **independent advice:** This element aimed to ensure that consumers are clear about the services that they receive; and
3. **professionalism:** this element aimed to ensure that consumers receive advice from highly respected professionals, thereby inspiring confidence and building trust.

Rules to implement these elements came into effect on 31 December 2012. These apply to all advisers in the retail investment market, regardless of the firm they work for (banks, product providers, independent financial advisers, wealth managers or stockbrokers).

In relation to the 'adviser charging' element, the rules set out that advisers can set their own charges and can separately charge clients for their services, as product providers are now banned from offering commission to advisers.

Charging structures must be based on the level of service that advisers provide, rather than on a particular provider or product that they recommend. Advisers must also be upfront with consumers in disclosing their charges and ongoing charges should only be levied where an ongoing service has been agreed with the client.

In relation to the 'independent advice' element, the rules require advisers to describe their services clearly as either independent or restricted. If they declare themselves to be independent, they must consider a broader range of products beyond packaged products. Independent advisers must be able to provide unbiased, unrestricted advice based on a comprehensive and fair analysis of the relevant market.

In relation to the 'professionalism' element, the rules require that advisers hold a statement of professional standing issued by a body accredited by the FCA, hold an appropriate qualification (completing a 'gap fill' which brings the qualification up to the desired standard where required) and observe a code of ethics that advisers are subject to as an approved person.

9.1 The impact of the RDR on offshore centres

Although the RDR is only applicable in the UK, it is clear that offshore centres have recognised the need to keep pace with the UK initiatives. Regulators in many offshore centres have made public statements informing organisations that conduct investment business about the actions that they will take to bring the legislation in their jurisdiction in line with the new standards imposed by the RDR. However, there are some differences in the standards applied.

Jersey's response to the RDR is known as *The Review of Financial Advice*, with implementing rules taking effect on 1 January 2014. Similarly, the Isle of Man introduced RDR-type competency requirements with effect from 1 January 2014.

In Guernsey, the Guernsey Financial Services Commission launched the Guernsey Financial Advice Standards in 2015. These increased expected professional standards, made adviser charging more transparent and reduced potential conflicts of interest.

Test yourself 9.6

What are the three main elements of the UK's RDR?

10. International bodies

The standards set by international bodies such as the International Organization of Securities Commissions (IOSCO) and the International Association of Insurance Supervisors (IAIS) have had an impact on the regulation of financial services business.

Other bodies such as the Offshore Group of Insurance Supervisors (OGIS) also play a useful role to offshore financial services business providers.

10.1 The International Organization of Securities Commissions

The roots of IOSCO were first established in 1974 as an inter-American regional association. However, its 11 members (securities agencies from North and South America) decided at its 1983 annual conference to develop into a global cooperative body.

In 1984, securities regulators from France, Indonesia, South Korea and the UK were the first to join from outside the Americas. IOSCO now claims that its membership regulates over 95% of the world's securities markets. It is the primary forum for securities market regulatory agencies with its members being drawn from over 100 jurisdictions. The FCA is the IOSCO member for the UK.

IOSCO's role

IOSCO is recognised as the international standard-setter for securities markets. It provides comprehensive technical assistance to its members, including those regulating emerging markets.

IOSCO's objectives

The objectives and principles of securities regulation were last revisited in June 2010. They consist of 38 principles of securities regulation, which are based upon the following three objectives:

1. protecting investors;
2. ensuring that markets are fair, efficient and transparent; and
3. reducing systemic risk.

The principles must be implemented practically under the relevant legal framework in order to achieve these objectives.

The IOSCO Principles

In 1998, the IOSCO adopted a comprehensive set of objectives and principles of securities regulation (the IOSCO Principles). These are now recognised as the international benchmark for all securities markets.

The IOSCO Principles are grouped into the following nine categories:

1. principles relating to the regulator;
2. principles for self-regulation;
3. principles for the enforcement of securities regulation;
4. principles for cooperation in regulation;
5. principles for issuers;
6. principles for auditor, credit rating agencies and other information service providers;
7. principles for collective investment schemes;
8. principles for market intermediaries; and
9. principles for secondary markets.

In 2003, the organisation endorsed a comprehensive methodology designed to enable an objective assessment of the level of implementation of the IOSCO Principles by member jurisdictions.

The Multilateral Memorandum of Understanding

The Multilateral Memorandum of Understanding Concerning Consultation and Cooperation and the Exchange of Information (MMOU) was developed following the terrorist attacks on the USA on 11 September 2001. It facilitates cross-border enforcement and exchange of information between international securities regulators. It sets out how signatories will cooperate and exchange information for securities regulation purposes such as the investigation of insider dealing and market manipulation activities.

IOSCO endorsed the MMOU as the benchmark for international cooperation among securities regulators. In 2005, IOSCO decided that all members with primary responsibility for securities regulation in their jurisdiction should have applied for (and been accepted as) signatories under the MMOU or expressed a commitment to seek legal authority to enable them to become signatories before the target date.

The regulators of offshore centres such as Bermuda, British Virgin Islands, Guernsey, the Isle of Man and Jersey are all signatories to the MMOU.

10.2 The International Association of Insurance Supervisors

IAIS was established in 1994 and represents insurance regulators and supervisors from more than 200 jurisdictions. It has permitted insurance professionals as observers since 1999. Membership of the IAIS is voluntary. Many offshore centres including Jersey, the Isle of Man, Mauritius and Gibraltar are members of the IAIS.

The objectives of the IAIS are:

- to promote effective and globally consistent supervision of the insurance industry in order to develop and maintain fair, safe and stable insurance markets for the benefit and protection of policyholders; and
- contribute to global financial stability.

The IAIS issues global insurance principles, standards and guidance papers. It sets out principles that it deems fundamental to effective insurance supervision. Its Insurance Core Principles serve as a basic benchmark for insurance supervisors in all jurisdictions. The Core Principles were revised on 19 October 2013.

10.3 The Group of International Insurance Centre Supervisors

The Offshore Group of Insurance Supervisors was founded in 1993. The group changed its name in 2012 to the Group of International Insurance Centre Supervisors (GIICS).

The group consists of insurance business regulators and supervisors from offshore jurisdictions. The group has strict criteria, which must be met by members. The Bahamas, the British Virgin Islands and the Cayman Islands, Guernsey, the Isle of Man and Jersey are all members of the GIICS.

The formal objectives of the GIICS are to:

- provide mechanisms and forums whereby insurance supervisors from jurisdictions concerned with offshore insurance business may discuss areas of mutual interest and concern, and formulate appropriate policies;
- provide assistance and encouragement to appropriate non-member jurisdictions to establish regimes for the supervision of offshore insurance business at least to standards equivalent to those of the group;
- represent the interests of the group at international forums; and
- promote the proper supervision of offshore insurance business.

10.4 The Basel Committee on Banking Supervision

The Basel Committee on Banking Supervision was established by the Central Bank Governors of the G10 countries in 1975. It is responsible for issuing guidelines as to standards that the international community expects banks and bank supervisors to meet. In 1988, it introduced a capital measurement system known as the Basel Capital Accord. This established how banking supervisors should measure the amount of capital a bank needs to support its risk and introduced the concept of a minimum risk asset ratio of 8%. A revised framework was issued in 2004.

In 1997, the Committee introduced 25 Core Principles of Effective Banking Supervision followed in 1999 by its Core Principles Methodology which are still in place at the time of writing.

Chapter summary

- Regulation is necessary in order to maintain financial markets that are efficient, orderly and fair. Regulation protects consumers from abusive practices and financial crime, thus maintaining the integrity of the financial markets.
- Regulatory frameworks for financial services industries offshore are often similar to those found onshore and typically comprise primary legislation, secondary legislation, regulatory codes and guidance notes. Many offshore centres incorporate international initiatives into their own regulatory frameworks and conduct their business with equivalent standards.
- The Financial Services and Markets Act 2000 (FSMA) is the UK's primary financial markets legislation. The FSMA provides for a general prohibition against the provision of financial services without authorisation. Such authorisation is not usually granted unless the applicant is fit and proper.
- The UK's financial services regulatory bodies are the Financial Conduct Authority (FCA) and the Prudential Regulation Authority (PRA). These replaced the UK's previous regulatory body, the Financial Services Authority (FSA), from 1 April 2013.
- The PRA is responsible for regulating deposit-taking business, insurers and investment banks. The FCA is responsible for the regulation of conduct in the retail and wholesale financial market.
- The general objective of the PRA is to promote the safety and soundness of PRA authorised persons. There are three characteristics to the PRA's approach to regulation and supervision. These are a judgement-based approach, a forward-looking approach and a focused approach.
- The strategic objective of the FCA is ensuring that relevant markets function well. Its operational objectives are consumer protection, integrity and competition.
- The GDPR aims to protect the privacy rights and freedoms of individuals in respect of the processing of personal data relating to them. Data controllers

and processors must respect the new rights of individuals, referred to as data subjects. Offences under the GDPR are punishable by substantial fines. Non-EU jurisdictions must adopt 'GDPR equivalent' data protection laws in order to maintain free flows of personal data with the EU. Non-EU organisations must in any event comply with the GDPR in respect of the processing of personal data relating to EU citizens if they wish to offer goods and services to individuals in the EU. Data Controllers and Processors responsible for the personal data of EU citizens are therefore subject to a common regulation.

- Insider dealing occurs when an individual with inside information (price-sensitive information) uses this information in relation to securities (that are price-affected) in order to make a profit (or avoid a loss), thus gaining an advantage that would not be available to the general public. Insider dealing is a criminal offence under the Criminal Justice Act 1993.
- Market abuse involves behaviour in relation to investments which are trading (or have applied to trade) on a UK market.
- The three main elements of the Retail Distribution Review (adviser charging, independent advice and professionalism) were intended to raise the standards investors can expect from all investment advisers. Rules implementing these came into effect on 31 December 2012.
- The standards set by international bodies such as the International Organization of Securities Commissions (IOSCO) and the International Association of Insurance Supervisors (IAIS) have had an impact on the regulation of financial services business. Other bodies such as the Group of International Insurance Centre Supervisors (GIICS) also play a useful role for offshore financial services business providers and the Basel Committee on Banking Supervision in relation to the banking sector.

Test yourself answers

Test yourself 9.1

Regulatory frameworks for financial services industries offshore typically comprise primary legislation, secondary legislation, regulatory codes and guidance notes.

Test yourself 9.2

Four of the FCA's principles for business are:

Principle	Description
1. Integrity	A firm must conduct its business with integrity.
2. Skill, care and diligence	A firm must conduct its business with due skill, care and diligence.

3. Management and control	A firm must take reasonable care to organise and control its affairs responsibly and effectively, with adequate risk management systems.
4. Financial prudence	A firm must maintain adequate financial resources.

Test yourself 9.3

Three factors that the PRA may take into consideration when deciding on a firm's potential impact are:

- the firm's size;
- the firm's complexity; and
- the firm's interconnectedness with the rest of the financial system.

Test yourself 9.4

The following are offences under the GDPR:

- processing personal data without notification;
- failure to notify the Information Commissioner of changes to those notified;
- making a false statement in response to an data subject access request;
- obstructing an investigation by a data protection authority; and
- unlawfully obtaining, controlling, processing and/or selling of personal data.

Test yourself 9.5

The seven types of market abuse under the FSMA are:

Type of market abuse	Description
1. Insider dealing	Where an insider deals or attempts to deal in a qualifying investment on the basis of inside information relating to the investment.
2. Improper disclosure of inside information	Where an insider discloses information to another person other than in the proper course of exercise of their employment, profession or duties.
3. Misuse of information	Behaviour that is based on information that is not generally available to those using the market but would, if available to a regular user, be relevant to their decisions about the terms on which to deal.

4. Manipulating transactions	This behaviour includes effecting transactions or orders to trade which may give a false or misleading impression as to the supply of or demand for an investment or to secure the price of an investment at an abnormal or artificial level.
5. Manipulating devices	This involves effecting transactions or orders to trade which employ fictitious devices or any form of deception or contrivance. This could involve spreading misleading information with a view to increasing the price of a shareholding and thereby giving others a false impression of the share price.
6. Dissemination	The dissemination of information that gives a false or misleading impression about an investment by a person who knew (or could reasonably have been expected to have known) that the information was false or misleading.
7. Distortion and misleading behaviour	Behaviour that is likely to give a regular user of the market a false or misleading impression as to the supply of or demand for an investment or that otherwise distorts the market in an investment.

Test yourself 9.6

The three main elements of the UK's RDR are:

1. **adviser charging:** this element aims to ensure that consumers are offered a transparent and fair charging system for the advice they receive;
2. **independent advice:** this element aims to ensure that consumers are clear about the services that they receive; and
3. **professionalism:** this element aims to ensure that consumers receive advice from highly respected professionals, thereby inspiring confidence and building trust.

Chapter ten
Money laundering

List of topics

1. What is money laundering?
2. The traditional model of money laundering
3. The harmful effects of money laundering
4. Terrorist financing
5. International bodies and AML initiatives
6. AML legislation
7. Know your customer and customer due diligence
8. Money laundering in offshore centres
9. Recognising money laundering
10. The impact of AML/CFT legislation on offshore business

Introduction

This chapter explains what is meant by money laundering and outlines the three stages of the traditional model of money laundering: **placement**, **layering** and **integration**. The harmful effects of money laundering that motivate various international bodies such as the FATF to cooperate are discussed, as are some of the more influential anti-money laundering/countering the financing of terrorism (AML/CFT) initiatives.

The chapter outlines what a typical AML/CFT framework in an offshore centre may consist of, using the UK's framework as an example. It explains the UK's substantive offences of money laundering (the concealing offence, the arranging offence and the acquisition offence) and the penalties involved. The offences of 'tipping off' and 'failure to report' are explained, together with the penalties for these offences.

The chapter also discusses customer due diligence requirements and how these differ from those of the 'know your client' approach. Money laundering in offshore centres is discussed, as is the impact of the AML/CFT legislation on the

placement
A stage of the money laundering process which involves placing the proceeds of crime into the financial system (e.g. by depositing the proceeds of crime into a bank account).

layering
A stage of the money laundering process which is designed to hide the source and ownership of criminal property (e.g. by using a complex system of transactions).

tipping off
The committing of an offence under Article 333 of the PoCA.

offshore administrative environment. The chapter concludes with general 'red flags' which can assist a service provider to identify money laundering.

1. What is money laundering?

Money laundering involves the processing ('laundering') of the proceeds of a crime, what might be referred to as criminal property (e.g. by concealing, disguising or converting it) in order to give it the appearance of having arisen from a legitimate source.

Money laundering occurs whenever there is an arrangement involving the proceeds of crime. What constitutes money laundering differs somewhat from jurisdiction to jurisdiction, depending on the laws that create the offences. The term 'money laundering' is slightly misleading as it implies that 'money' is involved. In fact, the proceeds of crime involved could be in the form of any asset – for example, a property or a boat.

Profit from crime may arise as a result of many different types of crime, including but not limited to:

- drug dealing;
- embezzlement;
- illegal arms trades;
- insider dealing;
- organised crime;
- people trafficking;
- tax evasion;
- terrorist financing; and
- theft.

If the money laundering process is successful, the criminals can benefit and control the proceeds while avoiding detection and confiscation.

2. The traditional model of money laundering

Historically, the money laundering process has been described as involving three main stages: placement, layering and **integration**.

integration
A stage of the money laundering process that involves reintroducing the criminal property into the economy so it appears to have originated from a legitimate source.

1. Placement involves placing the proceeds of crime into the financial system. This could be achieved by depositing the proceeds of crime into a bank account.
2. Layering could involve using a complex system of transactions designed to hide the source and ownership of the funds. Trusts and companies located across jurisdictions could be used to achieve this.

3. Integration involves reintroducing the funds into the economy, so they appear to have originated from a legitimate source.

While it is useful to be able to recognise the stages and be familiar with them, there are limitations in describing money laundering in terms of these three stages for a few reasons. It is not necessarily the case that all three stages will always be present. Money laundering instead can take a variety of forms ranging from very simple to very complex arrangements. It is therefore far more useful to be able to recognise the 'red flags' of money laundering, some of which are discussed later in this chapter.

Stop and think 10.1

Would the three stages described by the traditional model of money laundering be useful in assisting you to recognise money laundering where the proceeds of crime arose as a result of insider dealing (discussed in Chapter 9)?

Would the three stages be useful in assisting you to recognise money laundering where the proceeds of crime arose as a result of a customer not declaring the interest earned in respect of an offshore bank account?

3. The harmful effects of money laundering

The following is a non-exhaustive list of examples of the harmful and wide-ranging effects of money laundering on a country.

- The crimes that give rise to the proceeds that are laundered are extremely damaging to the victims and to society as a whole.
- Money laundering undermines democracy by allowing crime to be rewarded and allows organised criminals to expand their enterprise and become entrenched in society.
- Money laundering rewards corruption. Corruption has a devastating effect on developing countries and seriously affects the quality of life and wellbeing of the citizens of those countries.
- Money laundering undermines the legitimate private sector. Organised criminals have access to substantial illegal funds, enabling them to offer products at subsidised rates, and securing a competitive advantage over legitimate business.
- Money laundering makes tax collection more difficult, causing taxes to rise for those that pay and less resource to be available for healthcare or other social support required by people in need of these services.
- The integrity of the banking and financial services marketplace can be undermined if it does not (or is perceived not to) function within a

framework of high legal, professional and ethical standards. Customers, financial intermediaries and regulatory authorities' perception of a jurisdiction will be adversely impacted.

- Legitimate business will not gravitate to jurisdictions that are perceived to be subject to the control and influence of organised crime and it will therefore be more difficult to attract foreign investment.
- Money laundering causes a risk to the soundness of banks and has been linked to the collapse of banks and other financial institutions. Where there is a concentration of criminal funds within an organisation, difficulties can arise if criminals suddenly withdraw their funds in order to avoid detection.
- When criminal funds are invested, the rate of the return that may be obtained is not necessarily the primary reason for investing in any particular jurisdiction or currency. Instead, there may be more concern with keeping the funds undetected. This may lead to increased volatility of international capital flows and exchange rates due to unanticipated cross-border asset transfers and inexplicable changes in money demand affecting interest rates.

For service providers that become involved in money laundering, whether intentionally or not, there are significant consequences.

- The reputation of the organisation would be severely damaged. This damage could also have an effect on the reputation of other organisations in the jurisdiction, the jurisdiction itself, its regulators and any other person who has or was considering dealing with the institution.
- The regulatory risk for an organisation in a well-regulated jurisdiction is likely to be great. A regulator could impose sanctions such as fines or restrictions (e.g. on the firm's ability to take on new business) or require a report relating to the quality of the AML systems and controls within the business to be commissioned at the organisation's expense. Ultimately, a service provider could have its licence to operate within the jurisdiction revoked.
- The risk of criminal prosecution for money laundering exists at both the organisational and individual employee level.
- For the principal or key persons of the financial institution, the consequences could involve an assessment by the regulator of whether or not they are 'fit and proper' persons. This could lead to a variety of sanctions being imposed – for example, the individual may be prevented from obtaining further employment within a financial services business, or a public statement could be made.
- There is great financial risk in becoming involved in money laundering. The organisation may be exposed to the risk of litigation, in addition to the costs of complying with any remediation plan imposed by regulators.

Public statements issued by the Jersey Financial Services Commission and the Guernsey Financial Services Commission in respect of a number of trust and company service providers illustrate the risk to firms of inadvertent involvement with clients who possess the proceeds of crime and for firms who fail to maintain appropriate anti-money laundering measures.

Test yourself 10.1

Describe two of the harmful effects of money laundering.

4. Terrorist financing

The UK's Terrorism Act 2000 describes terrorism as the use of or threat of action which is designed to influence the government or an international government organisation, or to intimidate the public (or a section of the public), and where the use or threat is made for the purpose of advancing a political, religious, racial or ideological cause. Terrorism:

- involves serious violence against a person;
- involves serious damage to property;
- endangers a person's life, other than that of the person committing the action;
- creates a serious risk to the health or safety of the public or a section of the public; or
- is designed seriously to interfere with or seriously to disrupt an electronic system.

The terrorist attacks on the World Trade Centre on 11 September 2001 placed terrorism high on the international agenda. CFT measures are now often discussed synonymously with AML issues.

Terrorist financing differs from money laundering in fundamental ways. For example, the ultimate objective might be to cause intimidation to a population and acts of terrorism can be performed without requiring large amounts of funding. In addition, the funds used to finance terrorism do not necessarily arise from criminal conduct. This can make it very difficult to identify.

Although there are fundamental differences between money laundering and terrorist financing, they do have some features in common, as those involved will usually still wish to conceal or disguise the ownership, movement and ultimate destination of the funds.

4.1 The UN Security Council Resolution 1373

The UN Security Council Resolution 1373 was adopted in September 2001. This imposed a requirement for participating countries to implement measures to combat terrorism. The measures are aimed at freezing the funds of terrorists, prohibiting the financing of terrorists, ensuring that offences are established to punish terrorism and to ensure that terrorists are not provided with a safe haven by participating countries.

4.2 International financial sanctions

The international community attempts to take action in respect of significant breaches of international law, war crimes and what are perceived as terrorist regimes by implementing economic sanctions initiated by the United Nations or the EU, which are then adopted into domestic law by member countries.

The UK implements UN Security Council Resolutions through the Terrorism (United Nations Measures) Orders 2006. Similar orders have been made in many offshore centres, including the Crown Dependencies.

4.3 The Terrorism Act 2000

The offences created by the UK's Terrorism Act 2000 are aimed at criminalising:

- the receipt of funds for, or the provision of funds for, the purposes of terrorism; and
- involvement in an arrangement that may involve an asset being made available for the purposes of terrorism.

Under the Terrorism Act 2000, it is an offence to fail to disclose a suspected offence of terrorism where there are reasonable grounds to know or suspect terrorism. There is also an offence that criminalises the disclosure of information to any person that is likely to prejudice any investigation. This is known as the 'tipping off' offence.

4.4 The FATF's nine special recommendations

The FATF's nine special recommendations (discussed further in section 5 of this chapter) were introduced to set the international standard for combatting terrorist financing. The recommendations require members to:

1. ratify and implement the 1999 UN International Convention for the suppression of the financing of terrorism and to implement the UN resolutions, particularly resolution 1373;
2. criminalise the financing of terrorism and associated money laundering;
3. freeze and confiscate terrorist assets;
4. report suspicious transactions relating to terrorism;
5. cooperate with other countries on an international level (e.g. to exchange information and ensure that they do not provide safe havens for terrorists);
6. ensure that alternate remittance systems are licenced or registered and subject to all the FATF recommendations that apply to banks and nonfinancial institutions;
7. ensure that wire transfers include information about the originator of the funds transfer;
8. ensure that non-profit organisations are not misused; and
9. ensure that cash couriers and the transfer of bearer instruments are disclosed and detected.

Test yourself 10.2

How is 'terrorism' defined under the Terrorism Act 2000?

5. International bodies and AML initiatives

There are compelling social and macro-economic reasons for governments to want to deter people from money laundering. However, there is little incentive for any jurisdiction to place itself at the forefront of AML regulation if the result may be to place its finance industry at a competitive disadvantage, as funds simply flow to an alternative jurisdiction that has weaker AML controls. A global approach is required to combat the problem.

The first international initiatives during the 1980s focused on the prevention of the laundering of funds derived solely from drug-trafficking activity. Since then, the focus has expanded significantly to include all serious crimes in some jurisdictions and all crimes in others.

The following are some of the more influential international bodies and AML initiatives.

5.1 The Financial Action Task Force on Money Laundering

The Financial Action Task Force (FATF) is an inter-governmental, policy-making body that was established in July 1989 by the Group of Seven (G7) summit in Paris in order to coordinate an international response to the problem of money laundering.

FATF acts on the basis of a mandate, set by member jurisdictions at ministerial level. It currently comprises 34 member jurisdictions and two regional organisations, representing most major financial centres in all parts of the globe. There are also associate members and many international bodies and organisations that have observer status.

FATF works to generate political will to bring about national legislative and regulatory reforms in the money laundering and terrorist financing areas.

FATF's mandate explains that the objectives of the FATF are to set standards and to promote effective implementation of legal, regulatory and operational measures for combating money laundering, terrorist financing and other related threats to the integrity of the international financial system. FATF also works to identify national-level vulnerabilities with the aim of protecting the international financial system from misuse.

In order to fulfil its objectives, the FATF carries out a range of tasks, including:

- identifying and analysing money laundering, terrorist financing and other threats to the integrity of the financial system;

- identifying and analysing money laundering, terrorist financing and the methods and trends involved;
- examining the impact of measures designed to combat misuse of the international financial system;
- supporting national, regional and global threat and risk assessments;
- developing and refining the international standards (the FATF Recommendations);
- assessing and monitoring its members, through 'peer reviews' ('mutual evaluations') and follow-up processes, to determine their compliance with the international standards; and
- identifying and engaging with high-risk, non-cooperative jurisdictions and coordinating action to protect the integrity of the financial system against the threat posed by them.

In 1990, the FATF drew up 40 recommendations as an initiative to combat the misuse of financial systems by persons laundering drug money. These have since been revised and a further nine special recommendations have been created, aimed at combating the funding of terrorism. The most recent revision in February 2012 addressed new priority areas such as corruption and tax crimes, as well as dealing with new threats such as the financing and proliferation of weapons of mass destruction, transparency issues and corruption issues. The FATF is recognised as the global standard setter on AML and CFT issues by the United Nations, the IMF and the World Bank. The 49 recommendations (known as the 40+9 recommendations) set the international standards for combating money laundering and terrorist financing.

The 40+9 recommendations set out that countries should take immediate steps to become party to and implement fully the Vienna Convention (see section 5.3), the Palermo Convention (see section 5.4) and the 1999 United Nations International Convention for the Suppression of the Financing of Terrorism. Countries are also encouraged to ratify and implement other relevant international conventions, such as the 1990 Council of Europe Convention on Laundering, Search, Seizure and Confiscation of the Proceeds from Crime and the 2002 Inter-American Convention against Terrorism.

In order to achieve global implementation of its recommendations the FATF relies upon a network of FATF style regional bodies (FSRBs), in addition to its own members. At the time of writing, the 9 FSRBs have an essential role in promoting the effective implementation of the FATF recommendations among their membership and in providing expertise in relation to FATF policy making. In excess of 190 jurisdictions have committed to the FATF recommendations.

The 40+9 recommendations require countries to criminalise money laundering on the basis of the Vienna Convention and the Palermo Convention. The requirements are that countries ensure that intent and knowledge to prove the offence is in line with the standards set out in the conventions, including the concept that the mental state for the money laundering offences may be inferred from objective factual circumstances. In addition, countries must adopt measures to enable their authorities to confiscate property laundered and proceeds from money laundering or predicate offences. The recommendations also cover areas such as politically exposed persons (PEPs), the use of legal persons and arrangements, measures to identify beneficial owners, record keeping, and international cooperation and exchange of information.

There is no legal requirement for countries to follow the FATF's recommendations and it has no legal enforcement or official sanctioning powers. Even so, the FATF is a highly influential organisation, as was demonstrated by the results of its **non-cooperating countries and territories** (NCCT) initiative.

non-cooperating countries and territories (NCCT)
One of the FATF's AML/CFT Initiatives which enabled a classification of centres or jurisdictions so that international pressure could be brought to bear on them to implement changes in their anti-money laundering regimes.

5.2 The FATF's NCCT initiative

One method that FATF employed in order to increase compliance with its recommendations was the 'non-cooperating countries and territories (NCCTs) initiative' of 2000.

Many offshore centres were reviewed during a NCCT identification process. The FATF identified 23 jurisdictions that had not implemented sufficient measures to meet the standards set by its recommendations and published the list of NCCTs. Peer pressure proved to be a very effective way of encouraging the countries on the list to implement the required standard. Each NCCT worked towards improving AML/CFT processes and, in 2006, the last country was removed from the list.

The NCCT initiative attracted criticism for being arbitrary and lacking a consistent methodology. Since 2007, the FATF has instead analysed and published a list of jurisdictions that have strategic AML/CFT deficiencies, have not made sufficient progress in addressing the deficiencies or have not committed to an action plan with the FATF to address the deficiencies. The FATF called upon members to consider the risks arising from the deficiencies associated with each jurisdiction.

It also called on members to apply countermeasures to protect the financial system from the money laundering and terrorist financing risks emanating from Iran and the Democratic People's Republic of Korea.

This process is designed to achieve the same positive results as the NCCT programme, but in a different way. Continued non-compliance by a country for not meeting the standards can lead to sanctions designed to encourage compliance and ultimately could lead to the termination of membership.

Making it work 10.1

The FATF's 40+9 recommendations in action

Offshore centres do not always attract desirable media coverage. They are often portrayed to be secretive tax havens. There have been various BBC *Panorama* episodes where the presenter is located on a beach holding suitcases of cash while discussing offshore centres. In one such documentary, entitled 'How Tax Evasion Works', the presenter stated that 'critics say that tax havens such as Jersey, Guernsey, the Cayman Islands, the Isle of Man and Liechtenstein can help millionaires, tax cheats, dictators or terrorists to hide their money from the tax man or authorities'.

However, a review of the results of the ratings of compliance with the FATF's 40+9 recommendations applied to various jurisdictions following formal assessments reveals that offshore centres such as the Cayman Islands, Cyprus, Guernsey, Jersey, Malta and Panama have all been rated as compliant or largely compliant with more of the recommendations than the UK.

The Moneyval assessment of Jersey published in 2016 went so far as to praise the regime in place in Jersey to combat money laundering and the financing of terrorism.

5.3 The Vienna Convention

The United Nations Convention against Illicit Traffic in Narcotic Drugs and Psychotropic Substances 1988 (also known as the Vienna Convention) came into force on 11 November 1990.

The aim of the Vienna Convention is to promote cooperation among the countries that are a party to it in order to assist them to address more effectively the international aspects of illicit traffic in narcotic drugs and psychotropic substances. Parties to the convention agree to take necessary measures to cooperate (including legislative and administrative methods) in order to combat the trafficking of illegal drugs.

5.4 The Palermo Convention

The United Nations Convention against Transnational Organized Crime 2000 (also known as the Palermo Convention) is the main international instrument in the fight against transnational organised crime. The Palermo Convention entered into force on 29 September 2003. The Palermo Convention signifies the recognition by member countries of the seriousness of the problems posed by organised crime, as well as the need for international cooperation in order to tackle those problems. Countries that ratify this instrument commit themselves to taking a series of measures against transnational organised crime, including the creation of domestic criminal offences (participation in an organised criminal group, money laundering, corruption and obstruction of justice), the adoption of frameworks for extradition, mutual legal assistance and law enforcement cooperation; and the promotion of training and technical assistance.

5.5 The International Monetary Fund

The IMF came into formal existence in 1945 as a specialised agency of the United Nations when a number of countries came together to establish a framework for international economic cooperation after the Second World War.

As of April 2014, the IMF has 188 member countries. The IMF is accountable to the governments of its member countries.

As explained earlier in this chapter, money laundering negatively affects economies and financial stability. This is of concern to the IMF as its fundamental mission is to help to ensure stability in the international monetary system. The IMF provides both technical and financial assistance in the financial sector and exercises surveillance over members' economic systems. Unlike the FATF, the IMF does not seek to set AML/CFT standards; instead, it plays an important role in evaluating jurisdictional compliance with them.

5.6 The Group of International Finance Centre Supervisors

The GIFCS was formerly known as the Offshore Group of Banking Supervisors. It was formed in October 1980 at the instigation of the BCBS as an association of the authorities concerned with the supervision of banks in offshore finance centres and the related financial services. The group changed its name to the Group of International Finance Centre Supervisors in March 2011, in order to reflect better the wider scope of its activities.

The group requires its members to have a clear commitment to the implementation of all relevant standards, including:

- the BCBS Core Principles;
- the FATF Recommendations to combat money laundering, the financing of terrorism and the proliferation of weapons of mass destruction;
- the IOSCO Core Principles;
- the IAIS Core Principles;
- any other standards which members may wish to adopt;
- evidence that the necessary legislation and administrative structure to put these commitments into effect is in place or in early prospect;
- evidence of either a satisfactory track record of translating the commitments into effect or a detailed plan for doing so within a reasonable time frame; and
- evidence that the commitments are entered into with the knowledge and support of the relevant political authority.

Some jurisdictions, such as Gibraltar, Guernsey, the Isle of Man and Jersey, are not members of the FATF. However, they are members of the GIFCS, which is a FATF observer. This means members of the GIFCS are fully committed to the FATF recommendations.

5.7 The European Union

As a prerequisite of membership of the EU, national governments must implement European Council (EC) AML directives. Member states were expected to implement the third European directive by December 2007, and the fourth AML directive by June 2017.

The fourth directive was in line with the FATF recommendations as revised in 2012. However, as FATF international standards continued to involve, the EC has undertaken its own review of the European AML framework and a fifth AML directive was in course of being agreed during 2018 with implementation expected on a phased basis between now and early 2021.

Notwithstanding the impending departure from the European Union of the United Kingdom in March 2019, we should not be surprised to see identical standards in place both within the EU and in offshore financial centres (including London and the rest of the UK) in order that confidence is maintained in the regimes in place outside the EU.

5.8 The Wolfsberg Group

The Wolfsberg Group is an industry association of 11 global banks. The group worked with representatives from Transparency International to draft anti-money laundering principles for private banking (the Wolfsberg Principles).

These were first published in October 2000, then revised in May 2002 and 2012.

The group aims to develop financial services industry standards for 'know your customer' (KYC) and AML/CFT policies, and acts as a mechanism for the banking industry to cooperate in order to achieve this.

The Wolfsberg principles cover:

- anti-money laundering organisation;
- client acceptance (general guidelines and situations requiring additional diligence/attention);
- updating client files;
- practices when identifying unusual or suspicious activities;
- monitoring;
- control responsibilities;
- reporting;
- education, training and information;
- record retention requirements; and
- exceptions and deviations.

The group also published a statement on the financing of terrorism in 2002.

5.9 The Basel Committee on Banking Supervision

The BCBS is made up of a representative from each central bank and a representative from the body with formal responsibility for the prudential supervision of banking business in each country. The BCBS cannot impose legally binding standards; however, it has formulated broad supervisory standards and guidelines known as the Basel Principles, which encourage banks to implement measures to prevent money laundering.

The BCBS published a paper entitled *The Prevention of Criminal Use of the Banking System for the Purpose of Money Laundering* in 1988. The paper is a statement of principles to which financial institutions should be expected to adhere. It outlines some basic policies and procedures that a bank's management should ensure are in place within their institutions, with a view to assisting in the suppression of money laundering through the banking system.

The paper covers areas such as:

- customer identification;
- compliance with laws;
- cooperation with law enforcement authorities; and
- the requirements for banks to formally adopt policies consistent with the principles contained within the statement (e.g. provision of training, implement procedures for customer identification, retention of records of transactions, etc.).

In addition, the BCBS issued a paper entitled *Customer due diligence for banks* in October 2001. This paper states that it strongly supports the adoption and implementation of the FATF recommendations. The Committee's approach to KYC was from a wider perspective than merely AML. The paper addresses four essential elements of KYC standards:

1. customer acceptance policy;
2. customer identification issues (including issues arising from trust and corporate vehicles, introduced business, PEPs and non-face-to-face customers);
3. ongoing monitoring of accounts and transactions; and
4. risk management.

In February 2003, the committee published the *General guide to account opening and customer identification*. This is a guide to good practice and is based on the 2001 paper Customer due diligence for banks. In October 2004, the committee published a paper entitled *Consolidated KYC risk management*, covering establishing KYC processes on a group-wide basis.

5.10 The United Nations Office on Drugs and Crime

The United Nations Office on Drugs and Crime (UNODC) was set up by the United Nations in 1997 to implement the United Nations International Drug Control Program and its Crime Prevention and Criminal Justice Program. The overall aims of the UNODC are to assist UN member states in the struggle against illicit drugs, crime and terrorism. It does this through:

- research and analytical work;
- helping countries to implement treaties, draft domestic legislation; and
- providing other assistance such as the training of judicial officials.

The UNODC has issued model legislation for both common law and civil law legal systems to assist countries to set up legislation that meets the standards set by FATF and other international initiatives.

5.11 The Court of Public Opinion

Public opinion is Increasingly affecting the choices of both firms and individuals in respect of how they choose to avail themselves of opportunities to minimise (i.e. avoid) taxation. We need only look at the choice made by Costa Coffee voluntarily to pay tax that it was not obliged to pay. This followed a public outcry concerning the extent of its commercial activities in the UK, when it was paying no UK corporation tax.

Test yourself 10.3

a) **Why is a global approach crucial in the fight against money laundering and terrorism?**

b) **State two of the more influential international bodies that have encouraged international cooperation in the fight against money laundering and terrorism.**

6. AML legislation

AML legislation criminalises the handling or retention of proceeds of crime, and seeks to prevent criminal funds from entering or passing through the financial system. It ensures that, where they do, they can be detected and restrained, confiscated and returned, where possible.

All national AML frameworks have developed as a result of the influence of international bodies and international initiatives, principally those of the FATF and the EU. As a result, the principles and the wording used within AML legislation are often similar.

It is therefore possible to gain an understanding of the AML frameworks in many offshore jurisdictions by using the UK framework. Many offshore jurisdictions have implemented similar frameworks.

6.1 Primary legislation

The primary legislation contains the criminal offences of money laundering. In the UK, the primary legislation is the Proceeds of Crime Act 2002 (PoCA) which creates three substantive offences of money laundering. These include:

- the concealing offence;
- the arranging offence; and
- the acquisition, use or possession offence.

The concealing offence

Article 327 sets out that a person commits an offence if they:

- conceal criminal property;
- convert criminal property;
- disguise criminal property;
- remove the criminal property from England and Wales or from Scotland or Northern Ireland; or
- transfer criminal property.

Under Article 327, concealing or disguising 'criminal property' includes concealing or disguising its nature, source, location, disposition, movement or ownership or any rights with respect to it. PoCA sets out that property is 'criminal property' if:

- it constitutes a benefit from criminal conduct; and
- the alleged offender knows or suspects that the property is as a result of criminal conduct.

Money laundering as an activity can therefore occur without an offence being committed – for example, the trustee who deals with criminal property is engaged in the activity of money laundering. However, an offence will not be committed unless the trustee knows or suspects that the property is as a result of criminal conduct.

The arranging offence

Article 328 of the PoCA sets out that a person commits an offence if they enter into an arrangement that they know or suspect involves the proceeds of crime. This is a very widely drafted offence and captures the provision of professional services, such as acting as trustee.

The acquisition, use or possession offence

Under Article 329 of PoCA, an offence is committed where a person acquires, uses or has possession of criminal property.

Penalties

The maximum penalty for all of the substantive offences of money laundering in the UK is 14 years' imprisonment or a fine, or both.

Defences

A person does not commit an offence under Articles 327, 328 or 329 if they make an authorised disclosure (i.e. disclosure to a nominated officer) before they carry out the act and they have the appropriate consent (e.g. the consent of the **Serious Organised Crime Agency (SOCA, now part of the UK's National Crime Agency** to act.

Serious Organised Crime Agency (SOCA)
The FIU in the UK.

The nominated officer is often known as a Money Laundering Reporting Officer (MLRO).

The 'failure to report' offence

The primary legislation in many jurisdictions imposes a direct obligation on employees in financial services business to make a suspicious activity report (SAR) to their MLRO if they suspect that money laundering has taken place. Article 330 of the PoCA contains the 'failure to disclose' offence for those in the regulated sector. It sets out that a person commits an offence if three conditions are satisfied.

1. They know, suspect or have reasonable grounds for knowing or suspecting that another person is engaged in money laundering.
2. The information on which their knowledge or suspicion (or reasonable grounds for knowledge or suspicion) is based came to them in the course of a business.
3. They do not make the required disclosure as soon as practicable after the information or other matter comes to them.

Many jurisdictions now apply the 'objective test' to the substantive money laundering offences. This means that actual knowledge or suspicion that a person is dealing with the proceeds of crime is not required. Instead, the test is whether a reasonable person would have formed a suspicion of money laundering. This differs from the historic 'subjective test' where actual knowledge or suspicion was required in order to commit the offence of money laundering.

The maximum penalty for failure to disclose is five years' imprisonment, or a fine, or both.

Suspicious activity reports

The report made to the MLRO is known as a SAR. SARs are sometimes referred to as suspicious transaction reports (STRs). The term SARs is more widely used, as this reflects the fact that a transaction need not necessarily take place for money laundering to be present.

A SAR includes details of the persons involved and the reasons for the suspicion.

The nominated officer analyses the report and, taking all of the circumstances into consideration, decides whether or not in their opinion, the activity does give rise to a suspicion of money laundering. If they decide that it does, they make an external report to the **Financial Intelligence Unit (FIU)**. The UK's FIU is SOCA, which may then give consent to proceed with a transaction, thus providing a defence to the offence of money laundering as explained above.

Financial Intelligence Unit (FIU)
Used to describe the authority in a jurisdiction that has responsibility for receiving and dealing with suspicious activity reports from financial institutions.

The 'tipping off' offence

Under Article 333, a person who knows or suspects that a suspicious activity report has been made commits an offence if they disclose to another person information likely to prejudice any investigation which might be conducted.

PoCA contains a defence to the offence of tipping off where a person did not know or suspect that the disclosure was likely to be prejudicial. The maximum penalty for tipping off is five years' imprisonment, or a fine, or both.

6.2 Secondary legislation

The UK's secondary legislation is in the form of the Money Laundering, Terrorist Financing and Transfer of Funds (Information on the Payer) Regulations 2017 (Money Laundering Regulations 2017), which implements the EU Fourth European Directive. Secondary legislation is often referred to as 'regulations' or 'orders' and usually contains the procedural requirements that financial institutions are required to comply with.

The Money Laundering Regulations 2017 impose a number of requirements on 'relevant persons'. Relevant persons consist of financial institutions, legal professionals and trust company service providers, among other institutions. The Money Laundering Regulations 2017 set out requirements in relation to:

- customer due diligence;
- policies and procedures;
- record keeping (a person must keep records proving the customer identity documents obtained for five years after the business relationship ends to enable a relevant person to demonstrate compliance with the legislation); and
- training.

The policies and procedures that a relevant person must establish and maintain must be appropriate and risk-sensitive. They should relate to:

- customer due diligence measures (including a requirement to identify and verify a customer's identity and identify whether a customer is a PEP);
- improving the transparency of records relating to the beneficial ownership of companies and of those persons connected to trusts;
- seeking to prevent the financing of terrorist activities through new medium such as E Money and Prepaid Cards;
- the effective enforcement of sanctions;
- internal control;
- ongoing monitoring (providing for identification and scrutiny of unusual transactions or activity that may indicate money laundering);
- record keeping;
- reporting knowledge or suspicion that a person is engaged in money laundering or terrorist financing (including a requirement to appoint an MLRO);
- risk assessment and management; and
- the monitoring and management of compliance with and internal communication of such policies and procedures.

The training that a relevant person must provide includes:

- taking appropriate measures so that all relevant employees are made aware of the law relating to money laundering and terrorist financing; and

- regularly giving training in how to recognise and deal with transactions and activities that may be related to money laundering or terrorist financing.

Case law 10.1

The Attorney General v Caversham Fiduciary Services Limited and Caversham Trustees Limited and Nicholas Bell (Caversham) [2006]

In 2002, Caversham, a Jersey trust company, was approached by a solicitor who explained that an attorney who acted for a third party, Mr Lee, wished to set up a trust to hold the proceeds from the sale of a sauna business.

Caversham created the trust (with the attorney as the sole beneficiary) and received documentation in relation to the identity of the attorney, but not the ultimate client. Upon receipt of the trust fund (£850,000) from the solicitor's account, Caversham was asked (and agreed to) pay the funds to four entities that were not connected to the trust.

An order made pursuant to the primary legislation in Jersey required procedures to be 'maintained' by persons carrying on financial services business, for the purpose of forestalling and preventing money laundering. The procedures were to include measures to establish the identity of the person on whose behalf an applicant for business acted.

Caversham and Nicholas Bell (a principal person of Caversham) were charged and convicted with forming a business relationship without 'maintaining' procedures in relation to identification.

On appeal, it was argued that an offence could only be committed by a systemic failure to 'maintain' the procedures required under the law and not by a single instance of failure. The Attorney General submitted that 'maintain' means 'to keep up' in the same way that, in common usage, a boxer who drops his gloves and allows a knockout blow is said to have failed to maintain his guard.

The appeals were dismissed and the convictions upheld in 2006.

6.3 Industry guidance

In the UK, the Senior Management Systems and Controls Sourcebook (SYSC) contains high-level guidance. In addition, however, firms are expected to follow the guidance issued by the Joint Money Laundering Steering Group (JMLSG).

The JMLSG is made up of the leading UK trade associations in the finance industry. It has no regulatory function. Failure to follow the guidance is not considered a breach of the regulations or the FCA Handbook.

The regulatory authorities in many jurisdictions have issued guidance to assist financial institutions to interpret regulations and understand their obligations under primary and secondary legislation.

The words 'guidance' could imply that financial institutions need not follow it, but a failure to follow the guidance is considered a serious matter in well-regulated jurisdictions. Regulations often state that in deciding whether an offence has been committed, the court must consider whether the defendant followed any relevant guidance approved by an appropriate body.

Test yourself 10.4

Under what circumstances will a 'tipping off' offence be committed in the UK?

7. Know your customer and customer due diligence

7.1 Know your customer

When AML/CFT legislation and guidance began to develop, many jurisdictions implemented simple identification requirements. The term KYC became associated with the need for financial institutions to obtain a copy of their client's passports and two utility bills.

Sadly, this tick-box approach was not particularly helpful. While identifying the client plays an important part in the prevention and detection of money laundering, these measures alone are inadequate.

7.2 Customer due diligence

More appropriately the requirements on firms are referred to as customer due diligence (CDD). It is vital that students appreciate CDD is a process which is conducted whereby the firm ensures the proposed client is someone they wish to deal with. The documentary evidence obtained (copy passports, copy proof of address, evidence of source of wealth and source of funds) are merely that, evidence. Firms must be able to evidence the due diligence they have conducted along with the assessment of risk they have undertaken.

This approach that requires the collection of information from financial institutions and the forming of a customer due diligence profile.

This profile enables a financial institution to understand what to expect from the business relationship and to facilitate ongoing monitoring (scrutinising of transactions).

Understanding expectations will enable a financial institution to recognise unusual or suspicious activity and to take any necessary action.

This may involve asking further questions in order to become comfortable with the transaction or may involve making a SAR.

Indeed, the process of conducting CDD is a continuous one in that firms must respond to so-called trigger events (a meeting with a client, a change in the client's circumstances or any event which leads the firm to consider whether the CDD it possesses is adequate) and conduct a formal review as to the adequacy of their client knowledge on a pre-determined frequency.

The Money Laundering Regulations 2017 set out that financial institutions must maintain procedures in relation to customer due diligence measures that include a requirement to:

- identify the customer;
- verify the customer's identity on the basis of documents or information obtained from a reliable independent source; and
- obtain relationship information at the outset of the relationship.

The extent of information and verification undertaken may be determined in accordance with a risk-based approach (discussed later in this section).

Documents such as a copy of the client's passport (which has been certified by an independent and 'suitable certifier' – for example, a professional such as a lawyer) or other government-issued documents and original (or certified copies) utility bills are often collected during this process.

Relationship information includes information such as:

- the source of wealth (commonly referred to as SOW);
- the source of funds (commonly referred to as SOF);
- the purpose and nature of the business relationship (rationale); and
- the expected activity of the client including the volume and value of transactions.

Detailed ways in which a financial institution can meet the requirements of the legislation are set out in industry guidance and firms' performance assessed by their regulators.

Risk-based approaches

International standards set by the FATF and other international bodies advocate a risk-based approach to CDD.

This involves the financial institution undertaking a risk assessment of its clients and deciding the appropriate level of CDD information and verification to collect, as well as the appropriate level of transaction monitoring and reviewing to apply to the customer relationships on an ongoing basis.

A risk-based approach allows a financial institution to focus resources on areas where the risk of money laundering or terrorist financing is higher and therefore allows as far as possible a proportionate and cost-effective approach to managing the risk.

Relationships involving PEPs, for example, are relationships that present a higher risk of money laundering. For these individuals, enhanced due diligence should be undertaken on a risk-sensitive basis.

Enhanced due diligence (EDD) involves:

- obtaining further CDD information;
- taking additional steps to verify the CDD information;
- higher levels of management approval for higher-risk new customers; and
- more frequent reviews of the relationship.

8. Money laundering in offshore centres

The vulnerability to money laundering in any jurisdiction might be considered in light of the effectiveness of the laws, the political will and resource available to enforce them. As discussed in section 6, AML/CFT frameworks in many offshore centres are comparable to those of the onshore jurisdictions.

In fact, we must bear in mind that it is not just the laws, political will or resources that matter. The ability of the management of individual firms to maintain employee awareness and anti-money laundering and financing of terrorism measures is critical. Without the ability and desire of employees to recognise when they possess either knowledge or suspicion relating to a client and his or her assets the efforts of a jurisdiction can be nullified.

That said, the features of offshore centres can prove useful to money laundering, as the following sets out.

8.1 Secrecy laws and confidentiality provisions

Financial service providers in most onshore and offshore jurisdictions are subject to some form of secrecy legislation or more accurately statutory obligations of confidentiality. This can make it difficult to achieve cross-border exchange of information for the purposes of preventing or detecting money laundering.

Laws such as these inevitably hinder cross-border transparency as they may prevent information about suspicions from reaching the relevant FIU. The laws may also be invoked against a foreign FIU, preventing them from investigating reports received. If the FIU cannot access this information, it cannot share it with other jurisdictions.

8.2 Asset protection legislation

Offshore centres often have legislation that ensures that the assets within a structure can only be attacked by action in the local courts. This makes it considerably more costly and complex for authorities outside of the jurisdiction to mount such an attack.

8.3 Products and services

Many products available onshore and offshore can be used to launder money, including insurance products, bank accounts and investment schemes. The products that considerably increase the vulnerability of offshore centres to money laundering include:

- the extensive use of legal persons (those that are incorporated by law) including companies, foundations and the Liechtenstein Anstalt; and
- the extensive use of legal arrangements (such as trusts).

Both legal persons and arrangements are used for legitimate business purposes; however, their features present significant opportunities for those who wish to distance themselves from the proceeds of their crimes and to retain the benefits of those crimes at the same time. Some of the vulnerabilities with these types of products and related services are discussed below.

Legal persons

Legal persons contract and transact business in their own name. The use of directors provided by a service provider or the use of corporate directors (usually a company owned by the service provider) means that transactions are undertaken on behalf of the company by these directors, thus negating the need for the client to be publicly associated with the transaction.

The extent of information available from a company's registry varies significantly from one jurisdiction to another. Some, for example, require information on beneficial ownership at the time of incorporation but do not impose any obligation to update the registry where this changes.

It is often a requirement to inform the authorities of the identity of the shareholders (legal owners). However, this information is not useful in establishing beneficial ownership, as the use of nominee shareholders is routinely provided by trust and company service providers in offshore centres.

With the use of nominee shareholders, a declaration is signed by the service provider admitting and declaring that they hold the shares as nominee for the customer, and that they will do with the shares as they are instructed to do.

A company must usually disclose the address of its registered office to the Companies Registry. This address is, however, usually that of a service provider and the company's physical presence (if it has one) is not necessarily located there.

Bearer shares have been outlawed in most jurisdictions but can still be a feature of companies already in existence and this (the existence of bearer shares) may render any CDD undertaken useless as soon as the shares change hands. At this point, you may well be thinking how difficult it will be to open a bank account for a company with bearer shares in issue. The banker concerned would have no way of knowing who the beneficial owner of the company is or might be and would thus not be willing to open an account.

bearer shares
Shares that are considered to be owned by 'the bearer' (i.e. whoever has them in their possession). Cash is an example of a bearer instrument.

The authorities in a well-regulated jurisdiction should have access to the files of the service provider. However, they may still have difficulty identifying the 'human face' behind a company that retains 'bearer shares', particularly if it is owned by another company, registered in another jurisdiction or if the shares are owned by a legal arrangement or have been issued in bearer form.

Legal arrangements

Most jurisdictions do not require trusts to be registered in the same way as companies. Therefore, the existence of a trust is not a matter of public record.

The benefit of any register would only be as valuable as the information that is contained in the trust deed and this can be minimal.

The FATF recommendations and the fourth EU AML directive will when fully implemented result in the establishment of national registers of the beneficial owners of companies and of persons connected to trusts. In some jurisdictions, there is a demand for these registers to be publicly available. This call is being resisted in some jurisdictions who claim they do not need to be public to fulfil the anti-money laundering aims behind their existence.

In law, a trust is recognised without any written documentation (although it is unlikely that a regulated trust company in an AML-aware jurisdiction would operate in this manner).

dummy settlor
A person whose name is recorded within a trust instrument as the settlor of a trust but who is not the provider of the funds used to create the trust.

In the past, **'dummy settlors'** have been named in trust documentation, disguising the settlor. While this practice is no longer prevalent in well-regulated jurisdictions, it is still acceptable for an instrument referred to as a Declaration of Trust to document the terms of the trust that do not contain the name of the settlor.

For example, a Hong Kong-based individual acted as a 'dummy settlor' in respect of multiple trusts. Her role may have arisen from her employment at a firm of accountants in Hong Kong advising individuals on the creation of trusts prior to their emigration from Hong Kong to Canada. These might be cases where the individual acted as dummy settlor only as a consequence of his/her employment by a fiduciary provider but it was clearly intended to distance any connection between the trust and what may have been the 'true economic settlor'. Arrangements like this could be used to circumvent the public recording of beneficial ownership of companies or connection to trusts under any public register scheme.

Where a settlor's details are recorded on the trust deed, only the first provider of funds is recorded on the documentation. However, trusts are flexible in nature and would usually allow further funds to be added.

A person's ability to benefit can be hidden. It is not uncommon to find that trust documentation has been prepared with only a well-known charity as the named beneficiary. Again, this is an outdated practice.

Beneficiaries can also be included in a 'class' of beneficiaries that does not make it obvious who will receive benefits, or they can be appointed at a later date. All of these features could present significant opportunities for money launderers.

Service providers should be aware of these vulnerabilities.

Test yourself 10.5

How could the features of a company be useful to a person who intends to launder the proceeds of crime?

9. Recognising money laundering

The best way to ensure that unusual or suspicious activity is identified is to understand the purpose of each business relationship and what can be expected from it, and to compare actual activity with what was understood or expected.

However, there are some general 'red flags' that could indicate money laundering. The presence of one red flag alone may not necessarily mean that money laundering has occurred or is occurring; however, its presence should be understood. The following are examples.

- The receipt of unusually large cash deposits.
- The receipt of funds, followed by an immediate request for these to be paid elsewhere.
- The use of multiple transfer requests where a single payment could have been sent. This could indicate an intention to avoid mandatory reporting limits that exist in some jurisdictions. Similarly, the receipt of multiple receipts for no apparent reason could indicate money laundering.
- A reluctance to receive payments directly.
- Requests for third-party receipts or payments without sufficient explanation – particularly where it is known to you that the funds will eventually reach your client.
- Use of multiple bank accounts or corporate entities that do not appear to serve a purpose. These can unnecessarily complicate a structure and could be useful in the layering process.
- The use of dummy settlors.
- The use of 'blind trusts'. There are legitimate uses for these; however, the reason for their use should be understood and be reasonable.
- A reluctance to provide usual due diligence information and a client who is reluctant for you to have direct contact with them.
- A client whose internet profile has adverse public information involving financial or other relevant crime.
- A lack of commercial rationale for the structure.
- A lack of legal or tax advice where the structure appears to be very complex and involves multiple entities or jurisdictions.
- The matching of payment requests to credits received on the same or previous day with no reasonable explanation.
- The use of previously dormant accounts.

- Unexpected early repayment of loans where the customer's means to do so is not apparent.
- The use of safe deposit boxes without reasonable cause.
- Dealings with parties located in known drug-trafficking areas or countries associated with known terrorist organisations.
- The purchase of insurance products together with subsequent early surrender or cancellation with no concern over surrender values.
- A lack of concern on the behalf of the client over the cost of transactions and no interest in minimising cost.
- A lack of a desire to receive reports on the performance of their investments or bank account balances.

Test yourself 10.6

Identify six 'red flags' that indicate that a customer may be using a bank account as a part of the money laundering process.

10. The impact of AML/CFT legislation on offshore business

AML/CFT legislation has had a significant impact on the administrative environment in offshore centres. In general, one can expect:

- to operate in an ever-increasingly regulated environment;
- to maintain numerous policies and procedures, including those surrounding the customer due diligence process both at the acceptance of new business stage and on an ongoing basis;
- an increased standard of documentation and record keeping required in order to demonstrate compliance with the AML/CFT requirements;
- to receive AML training on at least an annual basis;
- to work in an organisation which has an adequately staffed compliance department, including a MLRO whose role it is to receive and deal with SARs. In some jurisdictions, there may also be a money laundering compliance officer whose role it is to monitor compliance specifically with the money laundering regulations of the jurisdiction;
- some resistance from historic client relationships who do not understand why a service provider with whom there is a long-standing relationship is suddenly insisting on receiving a lot of information. There may also be resistance where there are increased costs arising from the work involved in bringing the client files up to today's standards;
- an increased desire to obtain new business via trusted intermediaries and introducers;

- a requirement to undertake regular reviews of client entities (sometimes referred to as periodic or annual reviews) designed in part to facilitate transaction monitoring and to ensure that the customer due diligence documentation on file is still up to date and appropriate;
- a reluctance to accept cash payments into the structure and a reluctance to make cash distributions to beneficiaries or shareholders;
- a reluctance to make payments to or receive funds from third parties who have not been subject to the customer due diligence process; and
- an increased awareness and use of open-source public information to monitor for adverse information in respect of customers.

Chapter summary

- Money laundering has wide-ranging harmful effects on society and on the macro-economy.
- Terrorism involves a threat of harm to a population. Its objectives differ from money laundering and the source of funds is not necessarily illegal.
- The FATF sets the international standards for AML/CFT through their 40+9 recommendations, although there are various other influential bodies that help to facilitate a global approach to money laundering.
- AML frameworks in offshore centres are often similar to those in the UK due to the influence of international initiatives.
- The UK AML framework consists of primary legislation, secondary legislation and industry guidance. The primary legislation creates the principal offence of money laundering.
- The AML/CFT legislation creates obligations for financial institutions such as the requirement to report knowledge or suspicion of money laundering to SOCA, the requirement to maintain AML procedures such as CDD and record keeping.
- Offshore centres can be particularly vulnerable to money laundering due to the products that are widely available and because of the features of offshore centres.
- Money laundering can be recognised by several 'red flags'; their presence in any business relationship should be understood.
- AML legislation has significantly changed the offshore administration environment.

Test yourself answers

Test yourself 10.1

Harmful effects of money laundering include:

- the crimes that give rise to the proceeds that are laundered are extremely damaging to the victims and to society as a whole; and
- money laundering undermines democracy by allowing crime to be rewarded and allows organised criminals to expand their enterprise and become entrenched in society.

Test yourself 10.2

The Terrorism Act 2000 describes terrorism as the use of or threat of action which is designed to influence the government or an international government organisation or to intimidate the public (or a section of the public) and where the use or threat is made for the purpose of advancing a political, religious, racial or ideological cause.

Terrorism:

- involves serious violence against a person;
- involves serious damage to property;
- endangers a person's life, other than that of the person committing the action;
- creates a serious risk to the health or safety of the public or a section of the public; or
- is designed seriously to interfere with or seriously to disrupt an electronic system.

Terrorist financing differs from money laundering in fundamental ways. For example:

- the ultimate objective is to cause intimidation to a population; and
- the funds used to finance terrorism do not necessarily arise from criminal conduct.

Test yourself 10.3

a) There are compelling social and macro-economic reasons for governments to want to deter people from money laundering. However, there is little incentive for any jurisdiction to place itself at the forefront of AML regulation if the result may be to place its finance industry at a competitive disadvantage, as funds simply flow to an alternative jurisdiction that has weaker AML controls. A global approach is required to combat the problem.

b) Two of the more influential international bodies that have encouraged international cooperation in the fight against money laundering and terrorism are:

- the FATF; and
- the Wolfsberg Group.

Test yourself 10.4

The tipping off offence is defined under Article 333 of the PoCA. It is committed when a person who knows or suspects that a SAR has been made discloses to another person information likely to prejudice any investigation which might be conducted.

Test yourself 10.5

There are a number of features of a company that could be useful to a person who intends to launder the proceeds of crime.

Legal persons contract and transact business in their own name. The use of directors provided by a service provider or the use of corporate directors (usually a company owned by the service provider) means that transactions are undertaken on behalf of the company by these directors, thus negating the need for the client to be associated with the transaction.

The extent of information available from a company's registry varies significantly from one jurisdiction to another. Some, for example, require information on beneficial ownership at the time of incorporation but do not impose any obligation to update the registry where this changes.

It is often a requirement to inform the authorities of the identity of the shareholders (legal owners). However, this information is not useful in establishing beneficial ownership, as the use of nominee shareholders is routinely provided by trust and company service providers in offshore centres.

With the use of nominee shareholders, a declaration is signed by the service provider admitting and declaring that they hold the shares as nominee for the customer, and that they will do with the shares as they are instructed to do.

A company must usually disclose the address of its registered office to the Companies Registry. This address is, however, usually that of a service provider and the company's physical presence (if it has one) is not necessarily located there.

Bearer shares are also a feature of some companies that renders any CDD undertaken useless as soon as the shares change hands.

The authorities in a well-regulated jurisdiction should have access to the files of the service provider. However, they may still have difficulty identifying the 'human face' behind a company, particularly if is owned by another company, registered in another jurisdiction or if the shares are owned by a legal arrangement or have been issued in bearer form.

Test yourself 10.6

Red flags include:

- the receipt of unusually large cash deposits;
- the receipt of funds followed by an immediate request for these to be paid elsewhere;
- the use of multiple transfer requests where a single payment could have been sent. This could indicate an intention to avoid mandatory reporting limits that exist in some jurisdictions. Similarly, the receipt of multiple receipts for no apparent reason could indicate money laundering;
- a reluctance to receive payments directly;
- requests for third-party receipts or payments without sufficient explanation – particularly where it is known to you that the funds will eventually reach your client; and
- use of multiple bank accounts or corporate entities that do not appear to serve a purpose. These can complicate a structure unnecessarily and could be useful in the layering process.

Part six

Creating a valid trust

After studying this part, students will have an understanding of the manner in which a trust may come into existence and how trusts may be classified by the method in which they were created. Students will gain an understanding of trust documentation and will be able to describe the role of the settlor, the beneficiaries and the protector, and will be able to explain the different types of trusts.

Students will understand the manner in which a trust may come into existence and how trusts may be classified by the method in which they were created. Students will gain an understanding of trust documentation and will be able to describe the role of the settlor, the beneficiaries and the protector, and will be able to explain the different types of trusts.

Learning outcomes

At the end of this part, you will:

1. know about trust law;
2. understand how to create a valid trust;
3. know about the parties to a trust; and
4. understand the features of different types of trust available in offshore centres.

Chapter eleven
Trust creation

List of topics

1. Trust creation
2. Classification of trusts
3. Validity of a trust
4. The three certainties
5. Users of trusts
6. Advantages and disadvantages of a trust
7. The trust instrument
8. The letter of wishes

Introduction

This chapter explains the manner in which a trust may be created and outlines the four ways in which trusts can be classified by their mode of creation. The factors that may affect the validity of a trust are outlined as the **three certainties** that must be satisfied in order to create a valid trust.

three certainties
The three conditions that are required in order to create a valid trust: certainty of object, certainty of subject and certainty of intent.

The chapter outlines who may wish to use a trust and explains some of the main advantages and disadvantages that may arise in doing so. It also discusses the purpose of the trust deed (and declaration of trust) and outlines the typical content of such documentation, before concluding with an explanation of the purpose of and content of a **letter of wishes** that so many settlors take comfort from providing to the trustee when creating a trust.

letter of wishes
A private document written by the settlor of a trust to the trustee, setting out their wishes in relation to the trust fund.

1. Trust creation

Trusts may come into existence in any manner. They may be created by oral declaration or by an instrument in writing. They may be created ***inter vivos*** by the settlor during their lifetime or they may come into existence upon the death of the settlor as a result of a will. Trusts can also arise by conduct – for example, if a trustee breaches their duty and makes a profit using the trust

inter vivos
A transfer that is made during the lifetime of the settlor.

constructive trust
A trust that arises by operation of the law.

property, a **constructive trust** will arise. Constructive trusts are discussed in section 2.2 of this chapter. In an offshore professional environment, it is unlikely that a trustee would agree to act in relation to a trust that was created by oral declaration. It is likely that there will be an instrument in writing (i.e. a trust deed) in all cases. The legislation of a jurisdiction may specify that certain types of trust can only be created using a particular method. An example of this is the Jersey unit trust, which may only be created by an instrument in writing.

A trust can be described as a legal arrangement whereby a person (the settlor) properly vests (transfers in the correct manner) the legal ownership of assets (later referred to as the trust fund or trust property) to another person who is not the owner in their own right (the trustee) for the benefit of another person or persons (the beneficiaries).

In a trust arrangement, there is an important distinction between the legal ownership of the assets (which lies with the trustee) and equitable or beneficial ownership (which lies with the beneficiaries), which all candidates must feel confident in being able to explain.

2. Classification of trusts

Trusts can be classified by the way in which they are created.

2.1 Express trusts

express trust
A trust created intentionally by the settlor during their lifetime or one that may come into existence upon their death as a result of their will.

deed of settlement
A document that is executed when a settlor creates an express trust. Also referred to as a settlement deed or trust instrument.

Most trusts could be considered **express trusts**. An express trust may be created by the settlor during their lifetime (known as a trust created *inter vivos*) or they may come into existence upon the death of the settlor as a result of their will.

Express trusts are created intentionally by the settlor during their lifetime. They are usually created when a **deed of settlement** made between the settlor and the trustees is executed or when the settlor transfers assets to the trustee, who then executes a declaration of trust. These documents are discussed further in section 7 of this chapter.

2.2 Constructive trusts

Constructive trusts arise by operation of the law (i.e. they are created by an order of the court). A constructive trustee situation arises in circumstances where it would be unfair for the trustee to remain with ownership and control of an asset.

An example would be where a trustee uses trust funds to make a personal profit, gain or advantage. As this is a fundamental breach of their duty as trustee, a constructive trust arises and the trustee is known as a constructive trustee. The constructive trustee is deemed a trustee of that profit, gain or advantage and is required to deliver up the property to the person who is properly entitled to it – that is, the beneficiary of the trust fund which was used to make the profit.

A constructive trust is also an equitable remedy, which is crystallised in circumstances that imply that a trust exists (implied trust). A constructive trust can be imposed by a court to benefit a party that has been wrongfully deprived of its rights either due to a person obtaining or holding money or other assets which they should not possess due to unjust enrichment or interference with an asset, or due to a breach of fiduciary duty, which is the cause of the unjust enrichment and/or interference with the asset(s) in question.

Stop and think 11.1

Consider the constructive trustee issues that may arise if a trustee finds that property that was settled into the trust was actually obtained fraudulently by the settlor. For whose benefit is the trustee really holding the assets in these circumstances?

2.3 Resulting trusts

Resulting trusts arise in circumstances where the trust that was intended has failed. For example, if a trust fails for a lack of **objects** (beneficiaries), a resulting trust occurs as the trustee finds themselves holding the trust fund on trust for the settlor as a result of the failure. Resulting trusts, it can be argued, arise on account of the implications of a party's intentions and can be considered a form of implied trust.

resulting trust
This arises in circumstances where the trust that was intended has failed.

objects (in relation to a trust)
The trust's beneficiaries.

2.4 Implied trusts

Implied trusts are not created intentionally rather they result from a party's actions. Instead, they are implied from the circumstances. Implied trusts are not usually encountered in the offshore environment as the certainty of an express trust is a necessary part of any financial planning involving a trust.

Implied trusts arise through the operation of law and both constructive and resulting trusts can exist. Students must study the references in this text to the Quist close case.

Test yourself 11.1

How is an express trust created?

3. Validity of a trust

In order for a trust to be valid, three conditions known as the three certainties (discussed further in section 4 of this chapter) must be satisfied. In addition:

- the settlor must have the legal capacity to transfer the assets to the trustee;
- the settlor must have owned the assets at the time that they purported to have passed ownership to the trustee; and

completely constituted
For a trust to be completely constituted, the settlor must have properly vested legal ownership of the assets with the trustee.

- the trust must be **completely constituted**. That is, the settlor must have properly vested legal ownership of the assets with the trustee. This means they must have actually transferred legal title and custody of the assets to the trustee and they must have transferred them in the correct manner. Assets must be transferred in accordance with the relevant laws. Some assets, such as chattels (personal property), could simply be physically delivered to the trustee. However, in some circumstances the law requires that a particular procedure be followed. For example, land can only be transferred following a deed of conveyance in some jurisdictions. The trust is said to be incompletely constituted until the legal ownership of the assets properly vests with the trustee.

Case law 11.1

Milroy v Lord [1862]

The settlor had signed a deed that stated he had conveyed certain shares to Mr Lord for the benefit of his niece. Mr Lord had also signed the deed and the scripts for the shares were delivered to him. According to the constitution of the company in which the shares were held, however, the shares were transferable by the proprietor in the books of the company and all certificates of stock were to be surrendered at the time the transfer was made. No transfer was ever made into the name of Mr Lord.

share certificate
A document evidencing a person's title to their shares in the company.

After the death of the settlor, Mr Lord delivered the **share certificates** to Mr Otto, the executor of the settlor's estate. The settlor's niece sought to enforce the settlement.

The court found that the instrument signed **was not sufficient** to constitute a trust. In order to render a voluntary settlement valid and effectual, the settlor must have done everything that according to the nature of the property comprised in the settlement was necessary to be done in order to transfer the property and render the settlement binding upon him. It was held that the shares were never legally vested with Mr Lord.

The intended transaction had left an imperfect gift, which the settlor may have perfected by completing a transfer. The court stated that there is no equity in the court to perfect an imperfect gift. This has become known as a 'maxim' and has been described as 'equity will not perfect an imperfect gift'.

If a settlor purports to settle assets into a trust but fails to transfer the assets properly to the trustee, the potential beneficiary is known as a 'volunteer'.

The equitable maxim 'equity will not assist a volunteer' provides that the donor of the gift will not be forced to transfer the assets and complete the gift.

There are some exceptions to this rule – for example, if the potential beneficiary has provided some consideration for the gift, such as fulfilled their part of a promise.

A trust created under duress or fraudulent purposes is void. A voidable trust is valid, but could be declared void in certain circumstances.

An example of a voidable trust could be a trust created by a minor. The minor could change their mind about the trust's creation and the trust would be declared void.

In addition to the above factors, a transfer to a trust will not be valid if it purports to do anything illegal or if the legislation in a jurisdiction prevents the trust for some reason.

The legislation in Jersey, for example, sets out that a trust is not valid if it purports to apply directly to immovable property in Jersey.

Trusts will not be valid if they are created under duress or by fraud, or if they are immoral or contrary to public policy. Neither will they be valid or enforceable if the terms of the trust are simply too uncertain.

4. The three certainties

It was established in the case known as *Knight v Knight [1840]* that in order to create a valid trust, three conditions must be satisfied.

The conditions are that there must be certainty of:

- intent;
- object; and
- subject.

4.1 Certainty of intent

The settlor must have clearly intended to create a trust. This is known as **certainty of intent**. A trust instrument with unambiguous wording would demonstrate that the intention was present. In offshore centres where professionals are appointed as the trustee, experienced trust lawyers usually prepare the trust instrument.

certainty of intent
The requirement that the settlor must have intended to create a trust.

Where a fiduciary services provider uses a 'template trust deed', which can be common in order to reduce costs, great care must be taken that inappropriate changes are not made to the text which cause unintended affects or outcomes to the trust, the trustees, the settlor, any protector or a beneficiary or beneficiaries.

4.2 Certainty of object

charitable trust
A trust that has been established for charitable purposes.

certainty of object
The requirement to have ascertainable beneficiaries.

With the exception of **charitable trusts** or purpose trusts, there must be certainty about the persons who are the beneficiaries of the trust. This is known as **certainty of object**. The object is the person for whose benefit the trust fund is held. Broad uncertain statements such as 'for the benefit of the people that I like' would not be sufficiently certain. The involvement of a legal professional in the drafting of the trust instrument should ensure that the intended beneficiaries are certain from the trust documentation.

Very often, the objects (beneficiaries) of the trust are not obvious from the trust instrument, despite having been established with certainty. Difficulty in identifying the identity of the beneficiary from the trust documentation will not in itself invalidate a trust. What is important is that there is certainty about who they are (i.e. they can be established). Again, the involvement of a legal professional in the drafting of the trust documentation should ensure that the intended beneficiaries are certain.

Certainty of object must be present throughout the trust period for the trust to remain in existence. If a once-valid trust should find itself without any beneficiaries (e.g. if the sole beneficiary became deceased), the trust will fail for lack of objects. This is one historical reason for the inclusion of a charity such as the Red Cross to be included in the class of beneficiaries, despite there being no real intention on the part of the settlor that they will benefit.

cy-près doctrine
This provides that if a charitable trust finds itself without beneficiaries, the court can make an order that the trust property be applied for similar charitable purposes.

Trusts that are established for charitable purposes are subject to the **cy-près doctrine**. This doctrine provides that if a charitable trust finds itself without beneficiaries (e.g. the charity named within the trust instrument ceases to exist), the court can make an order that the trust property be applied for similar charitable purposes. Charitable trusts were historically the only type of trust that would not fail for a lack of objects.

Similarly, non-charitable purpose trusts do not usually have identifiable beneficiaries but do not fail for lack of objects. Where a non-charitable purpose trust finds itself without a purpose, the court can provide that the trust property be applied for a similar purpose. Both charitable trusts and non-charitable purpose trusts are discussed further in sections 8 and 9 of Chapter 13.

4.3 Certainty of subject

certainty of subject
The requirement to have identifiable trust property.

There must be certainty about the property that will be held upon trust. This is referred to as **certainty of subject**. A broad statement such as 'I settle most of my assets upon trust' would be too uncertain. Dispute could arise over which of the 51% of the settlor's assets were intended for the trust.

initial settled funds
The assets that are used to create the trust.

The trust instrument usually describes the assets that will be held upon trust for the beneficiaries. The instrument usually records a nominal amount (e.g. £100) which constitutes the trust fund. This nominal amount is referred to as the **initial settled funds**. This practice means that the assets are clearly identifiable and certain from the trust documentation.

The practice of recording only the initial settled funds within the trust instrument also enhances confidentiality. While the trust instrument is usually a private document, there are occasions where parties with whom which the trustee wishes to contract with (e.g. bankers) do insist upon sight of a copy of the trust deed. Those who view the trust instrument would not learn the true value of the trust fund as it is very common for **additional settled funds** to be accepted into the trust after its creation. Funds settled into the trust after the initial creation are referred to as additional settled funds or property.

additional settled funds
The funds that are settled into the trust after its creation.

Certainty of subject must remain throughout the trust period. A trust that has no assets no longer exists, and administrators must understand this. It would not, for example, be acceptable to empty a trust's bank account (where there are no other assets) and then allow the settlor to settle funds into the dormant account some time later as if the trust had existed throughout the dormant period.

Stop and think 11.2

At times, the creation of a trust prior to a specific date (such as the end of a tax year) will become urgent in order for the settlor to take advantage of beneficial taxation circumstances that are about to change.

Administrators may mistakenly believe that obtaining a signature on a signed and dated instrument of trust means that the trust has been created.

What if the initial settled funds have not yet been received? What date would the trustee instinctively pass to the taxation authorities if they are later asked for the date of creation of the trust in this instance?

The trust property

The trust property consists of the initial settled funds (or assets) and any additional funds (or assets) settled after the initial creation of the trust. The trustee may usually accept additional property throughout the trust period, although this is dependent upon the terms of the trust.

The trust property (or trust fund) may consist of any property including cash, chattels and property. The duties of the trustees (discussed in Chapter 12) may mean it is likely that the trust property will not contain wasting assets or those considered overly speculative investments.

5. Users of trusts

Individuals who seek to settle offshore trusts are usually wealthy individuals or entrepreneurs who have taken advice from tax advisers, accountants and/or lawyers.

While creating a trust is simple in theory, the costs involved in doing so and in remunerating the trustee mean that a trust may not be the best option for everyone. Some offshore professional trustees will only agree to act as the trustee for settlements of a minimum size to ensure that the trust is worthwhile and that they are likely to receive their remuneration.

Individuals from civil law jurisdictions where the division between the legal and equitable ownership is not recognised may not be as familiar with the concept of a trust and therefore are less inclined to use one. These individuals may choose to use vehicles such as a foundation as an alternative.

Trusts are far more attractive to individuals who are from common law jurisdictions where the concept of a trust is well established. Trusts created in offshore centres that have laws that are similar to those found in the UK, may appeal to those who are familiar with that law. In some offshore centres, such as Mauritius, the highest court of appeal is the Privy Council in the UK and this will offer some comfort.

6. Advantages and disadvantages of a trust

6.1 Advantages of a trust

Trusts are generally used in order for the settlor or the beneficiaries to enjoy an advantage that they would not achieve if the trust property were held in their own name. Despite giving away legal ownership of the property, the settlor may (if they are also a beneficiary) still be able to benefit from it. Some of the main reasons for creating an offshore trust can be consolidated into a mnemonic, STEPFC, as set out below.

- Stability and wealth preservation
- Taxation mitigation
- Estate planning
- Probate avoidance
- Forced heirship avoidance
- Confidentiality

These and other headings under which advantages can be described are discussed below.

Tax mitigation or minimisation

Trusts can be used to avoid a tax liability legitimately. Assets gifted (settled) into a trust legally belong to the trustee and would not usually therefore form a part of the settlor's estate upon their death. For a UK-resident individual this would have the effect of reducing the IHT charge otherwise payable on the value of the individual's UK assets. If the individual was also deemed domiciled in the UK, it would also reduce the IHT payable in respect of their worldwide assets. It is important that gifts into trusts are made in a timely manner, however, as IHT at the usual death rate will be payable if the donor does not survive for seven years after settling the trust.

Trusts may also be used by people when emigrating or temporarily working abroad. An individual migrating to a high-tax country can benefit from the set-up of a pre-migration trust prior to taking up residence in the new country. Trusts need to be managed carefully in order to achieve the taxation advantages.

Preserving confidentiality

A trust is a legal arrangement rather than a legal person. Trusts are extremely confidential arrangements that protect the privacy and confidentiality of legitimate clients. Most jurisdictions do not require trusts to be registered in the same way as companies and therefore the existence of a trust is not a matter of public record. This is at the time of writing very much a moveable feast and a political issue in the UK and its Crown Dependent Territories and Overseas Dependencies.

The benefit of any register would only be as valuable as the information that is contained in the trust deed, and dependant on the quality of effort expanded by those responsible for populating the register. The benefit can be minimal, as shown by the following examples.

- In law, a trust is recognised without any written documentation (although it is unlikely that a regulated trust company in an AML-aware jurisdiction would operate in this manner).
- It is acceptable for an instrument referred to as a declaration of trust to be used instead of a settlement deed to document the terms of the trust. A declaration of trust need not and often does not contain the name of the settlor.
- Where a settlor's details are recorded on the trust deed, only the first provider of funds is recorded on the documentation. However, trusts are flexible in nature and would usually allow further funds to be added. The trustee could therefore accept funds from persons other than the original settlor. This is not a common occurrence where the trust is set up for taxation purposes, as the success of such trusts in reaching its objectives of tax minimisation requires careful planning and particular circumstances.
- A person's ability to benefit can be hidden. It is not uncommon to find that trust documentation has been prepared with only a well-known charity as the named beneficiary. Other beneficiaries are then added after the creation of the trust. It should be noted that this is an outdated practice and far less common than it once was in today's AML-aware environment.
- Beneficiaries can be included in a 'class' of beneficiaries that does not make it obvious who in fact will receive any benefit.

Placing of assets in a safe jurisdiction

Offshore trusts in particular may be used where an individual's own country is not deemed a safe jurisdiction, perhaps due to corruption or political instability. Some wealthy people would not feel safe if their wealth was a matter of public record in their country of residence; feeling they may become kidnap victims.

Estate planning

This involves assisting with an individual's estate planning prior to their death. The assets are administered by a professional trustee until they are distributed to the beneficiaries of the trust on the death of the settlor. This avoids delays often experienced where executors are involved in disposing of assets.

Avoidance of forced heirship rules

Upon the death of individuals in some jurisdictions, the legislation of the jurisdiction provides that their assets must be distributed in accordance with the provisions set out in those laws. The rules are referred to as forced heirship rules. A trust can provide that the assets are held for the benefit of individuals chosen by the settlor, rather than those who would benefit under such rules. Certain jurisdictions restrict the rights of female relatives to inherit.

Provision for minors

Minors cannot hold property and cannot look after their own finances. Therefore, a trust with a professional trustee is an excellent way to provide for them and secure their future.

Protection of family property from dissipation

A trustee can prevent family members from wasting family wealth or giving it away. A trustee can ensure that the property remains within the family for use by future generations, holding it safely until the beneficiaries have gained the life experience that they need in order to preserve it themselves. Such trusts are sometimes referred to as guarding against wastrels.

Asset protection

Trusts can be used to protect capital in the event of a beneficiary's financial difficulty or bankruptcy, because creditors have legal recourse only to those assets held in the name of the debtor. Special types of trusts known as asset protection trusts are especially useful for this purpose. Asset protection trusts are discussed further in Chapter 13. Some professions (for example, plastic surgeons who may face claims for negligence) frequently make use of trusts for this purpose.

Provision for those who are incapable of looking after their financial affairs

A trustee can be appointed in order to protect and preserve the assets on behalf of a person who cannot do so for themselves, for whatever reason. A trust is often used to provide for the future needs of those who are severely, physically or mentally impaired. This can include holding and distributing any funds received from insurance company pay-outs or successful claims for negligence brought against others – for instance, the victims of medical malpractice.

Employee benefits

Trusts are often used to hold shares for employees, or provide for their pensions in a tax-efficient manner and in a way that is independent of the employer.

Charitable purposes
Trusts can be used to hold funds for charitable purposes. They may be set up by an individual for philanthropic purposes or they may be set up to receive donations from the general public for a charitable cause.

Test yourself 11.2

Identify three uses of an offshore trust.

6.2 Disadvantages of a trust

Disadvantages of a trust include the following.

- The cost of the creation and ongoing administration of a trust, including the legal fees and trust service provider fees. Trustees will very often charge a fee in relation to the creation of a trust in order to cover the cost of undertaking due diligence on the parties to the trust. There will also be ongoing charges for the provision of the trustee.
- The concept of the separation of equitable and legal ownership is not recognised in all jurisdictions.
- The settlor no longer owns the trust property and cannot therefore do exactly as they choose with it. Though they may share their wishes with the trustee by writing a letter of wishes (see section 8 of this chapter), they cannot insist that the trustee act upon these wishes.
- Trustees may be unwilling to take the same investment risks that the settlor would like them to take when investing the trust property. The trustees' and settlor's attitude to risk and transactions may not be in alignment.
- The settlor's circumstances may change and the trust instrument may leave the trustees unable to assist. An example may be a settlor who had irrevocably excluded themselves from benefiting from a trust, only to become bankrupt some years later. Any attempt to assist the settlor to benefit to the detriment of the existing beneficiaries would be a breach of the duties owned to the beneficiaries.
- Tax authorities are increasingly adopting a 'look through' approach and challenging some trusts and the actions of trustees seeking to establish them as tax abusive.

7. The trust instrument

The trust instrument creates a legally binding arrangement. It is sometimes referred to as either a settlement deed or a declaration of trust. The difference between these documents is outlined below.

7.1 The trust deed

A trust deed (also referred to as a trust instrument, settlement deed or settlement) is the document that creates the trust. The settlor executes a settlement deed when they create an express trust during their lifetime or when they create a trust by the terms of their will.

The trust deed provides that the trustees must hold the trust property on trust for the beneficiaries upon the terms set out within the deed. The deed may provide that some trustee powers may only be exercised with the consent of a protector. The role of the protector is looked at in more detail in Chapter 12. A sample trust instrument showing typical clauses is included as Appendix 1.

In general, a trust instrument is structured as follows.

Interpretation clause

The interpretation clause provides definitions for the terms used in the trust deed. This provides certainty about the meaning of the terms. This section of the trust deed should always be referred to when interpreting the clauses in the deed. The interpretation clauses will usually define terms such as beneficiary and settlor, **excluded persons**, what is meant by the word minor, the proper law of the settlement and the trust period if the period is limited.

excluded persons
Persons who are specifically named as being excluded from benefit in a trust deed or a person who has been excluded following the exercise of a power by the trustee.

Proper law clause

The proper law sets out the law that will govern the settlement. The significance of proper law was discussed in Chapter 3.

Dispositive provisions

The provisions within a trust deed set out the terms upon which the trustees hold the trust property and the terms upon which they may distribute it to the beneficiaries. These are known as the **dispositive provisions**. These set out either the wide discretionary powers or the fixed interest of the beneficiaries.

dispositive provisions
The provisions within a trust deed that set out the terms upon which the trustees hold and may distribute the trust property.

Administrative provisions

Administrative provisions relate to administrative matters such as how trustees may be appointed and removed.

administrative provisions
Provisions within a trust instrument relating to administrative matters such as the manner in which trustees may be appointed.

Protector

A protector is appointed who can exercise powers of protection. The protector acts as an overseer of the trustee, and will typically have rights of access to information and a power of veto over trust transactions

Schedules

It is very common for schedules to be attached to the trust deed that include:

- general powers;
- details of the initial settled funds;
- details of the beneficiaries at the time of the creation of the trust;
- details of excluded persons at the time of the creation of the trust; and
- details of the first protector, if there is one.

Signature and witness

The trust deed is usually signed by the settlor before an independent witness. It is also signed by the trustee, who does so under a corporate seal if the trustee is a corporate trustee.

7.2 Declaration of trust

A declaration of trust differs from a trust deed as the settlor is not a party to the document. Instead, the settlor transfers assets to the trustee who then signs a declaration. The trustee acknowledges in this declaration that the trust assets are held for the beneficiaries subject to the terms stated within the document. The clauses are otherwise not dissimilar to those found within a settlement deed.

Making it work 11.1

Declaration of trust

At this point take a moment to look at the sample trust deed contained at Appendix 1. They may be set out as follows: THIS DECLARATION OF TRUST known or referred to as the 'NAME OF TRUST' is made on the ... day of MONTH AND YEAR BY NAME OF TRUSTEE of ADDRESS OF TRUSTEE (hereinafter called 'the Original Trustee'). WHEREAS: the property specified in the Second Schedule hereto has been transferred to the Original Trustee to the intent that the Original Trustee should make an irrevocable settlement thereof in the manner hereinafter appearing. A declaration of trust may be used where there is a strong desire for confidentiality or in circumstances where time and logistics do not make it practical for the settlor to be a party to the trust instrument. But do remember that an apparent desperate desire for speed on the part of a client may represent a red flag moment.

8. The letter of wishes

A letter of wishes is a private document written and signed by the settlor of a trust to the trustee. It is not legally binding because a trustee or trustees must at all times exercise independent judgement with regard to the interests of the beneficiaries. A letter of wishes is not binding on a trustee or any court. The purpose of a letter of wishes is to give guidance to the trustee on the manner in which they may decide to execute their discretionary powers. While the trustee may find it helpful to be guided by the letter of wishes, they are under no obligation to follow any request or guidance set out therein. The letter may include:

- reference to the trust created;
- a statement that the letter is not intended to fetter the trustee's discretionary powers in any way;

- guidance as to how the settlor would like the trustee to manage the assets of the trust fund both during their life and after their death; or
- a statement that the settlor would like the trustee to seek their guidance throughout their lifetime.

In order to avoid any suggestion that the letter forms a part of the terms of the trust, the letter should be written after the creation of the trust and not before. On occasion, trust administrators will find that the letter of wishes is inconsistent with the terms of the trust. A trustee who makes a distribution of trust assets at the settlor's request and in accordance with the letter of wishes will be liable for a breach of trust if the recipient is not included as a beneficiary within the terms of the trust instrument. Where a dummy settlor (see Chapter 12) writes a letter of wishes, it is common for the letter to set out that it is the dummy settlor's wish that the trustee be guided by the actual provider of the funds throughout the duration of the trust and to state that they do not wish to be contacted again in relation to the trust. Instances where one individual created multiple trusts stating her reasons for doing so related to fears about the fate of Hong Kong after its return to the rule of China and then disowned any involvement with the trust instead directing the trustees to look to unrelated parties for guidance. This is an example of how third party influence can arise through use of a dummy settlor to a great number of trusts.

Making it work 11.2

A letter of wishes

A letter of wishes may contain wording such as the following.

Dear Sirs

Re: The ... 2018 settlement

I refer to the discretionary settlement created by me on ... 2018, and of which you are the trustee. I appreciate that the under the settlement, you were granted wide discretionary powers over the investment of the trust fund and the making of advances of capital and income from it. This letter is not intended to fetter your discretionary powers in any way; however, I feel it would be helpful to you to know my wishes in respect of the trust fund.

During my lifetime, I should be grateful if you would be guided by me in relation to the investment of the trust fund and if you would give consideration to any requests I might make to you with regard to distributions.

Upon my death, if my husband survives me, I should be grateful if you would be guided by him and if you would give consideration to any requests which he may make to you with regard to the distributions of capital or income from it.

On the death of the survivor of my husband and myself, I would like you to be guided by my two daughters, if they have both reached the age of 30, and to give considerations to their requests for distributions, subject to the trustee having due regard to any taxation consequences. It is my wish that they should benefit equally from the trust fund. Until such time as they do reach the age of 30, I should be grateful if you would be guided by the elder sister in dealing with the trust fund for the benefit of both of my two children.

Yours faithfully

The Settlor

Chapter summary

- Trusts may come into existence in any manner. They may be created by oral declaration or by instrument in writing.
- Trusts may be classified by the way in which they were created. Classes of trusts include express trusts, resulting trusts, implied trusts or constructive trusts. It is important to understand fully those types of trust most commonly encountered, i.e. discretionary trusts and life interest trust.
- Express trusts are those created intentionally by the settlor during their lifetime.
- Constructive trusts arise by operation of the law to protect the interests of a person or persons who a court feels have been unjustly or illegally deprived of some or all of their assets. The courts power is of course limited by the prevailing legislation.
- Resulting trusts arise when the trust intended by the settlor fails.
- Implied trusts are those that are not created intentionally by the settlor and instead are 'implied' from the circumstances.
- Valid trusts are those that satisfy the three conditions known as the three certainties, where the settlor has legal capacity to transfer the assets that are owned by them to the trustee. Valid trusts must be completely constituted (the trust assets must be properly vested in the trustee).
- The 'three certainties' are certainty of intent to create a trust, certainty of subject (trust property) and certainty of object (beneficiaries).
- Users of trusts are usually wealthy individuals who have taken advice from tax advisers, accountants and/or lawyers.
- Reasons for creating a trust include legitimate tax avoidance, the preservation of confidentiality, placing of assets in a safe jurisdiction, estate planning including the avoidance of forced heirship rules, provision for minors, protection of family property from dissipation, provision for those who are incapable of looking after their own financial affairs, provision for employees and for charitable purposes.

- The main disadvantages of creating a trust include the set-up and running costs, their lack of recognition in civil law jurisdictions and the loss of ability by the settlor to control the trust assets and the potential 'look through' and challenge by tax authorities.
- A trustee who blindly follows a settlor's instructions risks:
  - the trust being set aside as a 'sham';
  - mistakenly committing a breach of trust; and
  - causing adverse consequences for the trust and those connected with it.
- The trust instrument may be in the form of a settlement deed or a declaration of trust.
- The trust instrument sets out the terms of the trust and includes dispositive provisions and administrative provisions.
- The letter of wishes is a private letter from the settlor to the trustee in which they provide guidance as to how the trustee may execute their discretionary powers. The letter of wishes is not a legally binding document.

Test yourself answers

Test yourself 11.1

Express trusts are created intentionally by the settlor during their lifetime. They are usually created when a deed of settlement made between the settlor and the trustees is executed or when the settlor transfers assets to the trustee who then executes a declaration of trust.

Test yourself 11.2

Three uses of offshore trusts include:

- for tax avoidance purposes;
- to avoid forced heirship provisions; and
- for confidentiality reasons.

Chapter twelve
The parties to a trust

List of topics

1. The settlor
2. The trustee
3. The beneficiaries
4. The protector
5. The enforcer

Introduction

This chapter outlines the role of the provider of the trust property (the settlor) in creating the trust and explains how they may continue to be involved with the trust after its creation. It also explains the historic and outdated practice of naming a dummy settlor within the trust documentation. The role, duties and powers of the trustee are discussed, as are the use of offshore trustees and some considerations that potential settlors may take into account when choosing a trustee.

The chapter explains how beneficiaries are identified within the trust documentation (or not, in the case of a **blind trust**) and explains their rights. The role and powers of the protector are discussed. The chapter concludes with an outline of the role of an **enforcer** of a non-charitable purpose trust.

blind trust
This may refer to trusts where a charity is the only named beneficiary. The term is also used to describe trusts where the settlor is not aware of the investments that are held by the trustee or where the contributor of funds is not known to the beneficiary.

enforcer
A person appointed to a non-charitable purpose trust whose duty it is to enforce the trust.

1. The settlor

A settlor is a person who provides trust property (whether during their lifetime or by their will) to the trustee to hold on trust for the benefit of the beneficiaries.

The settlor may have included themselves in the class of beneficiaries of the trust. If this is the case, they will have all of the same rights as the other beneficiaries, assuming there is no fixed interest created in the trust. A settlor may also be a trustee, although this is uncommon in offshore centres. However, such arrangements are clearly intended to be abusive of trust law and principles. It is also undesirable where the motivation for the trust is to minimise a taxation liability.

It is important to remember that the settlor is the provider of the funds that are subject to trust, regardless of whose name may appear within the trust instrument or other documentation. All trusts have a settlor, or settlors, whether or not they are named in the trust instrument. The trustee owes a fiduciary duty to the beneficiaries of the trust, but owes no such duty to the settlor (at least in that capacity). This is a concept that some trustees can struggle with, as it is usually the settlor who instigates the business relationship by approaching the trustee.

The trustee (which in an offshore trust is usually a limited liability company) may view the settlor as their 'client'. While it is very often the case that the settlor is also the principal beneficiary, this is not always the case. The trustee must always consider the capacity that their client may be acting in whenever they deal with them.

A trustee who blindly follows a settlor's instructions risks:

- the trust being set aside as a sham (arrangements which purport to be a trust but which are in fact not a trust are often referred to as 'sham trusts' – this is of course a misnomer in that a trust is a trust while a sham is just that, a sham (so-called **'sham trusts'** are discussed further in section 1.1);
- mistakenly committing a breach of trust (e.g. by paying funds to a person who is not a beneficiary at the request of the settlor); and
- adverse consequences for the trust (e.g. taxation consequences) if the trustee accepts additional settled funds from any person who is not the settlor.

sham trust
An arrangement that purports to be something that it is not. Such trusts may be set aside as invalid.

Stop and think 12.1

If a trustee were to accept additional settled funds from a joint account belonging to the UK resident but non-domiciled settlor and his UK resident and domiciled wife, what consequences could this have for the trust?

The relationship between the settlor and the trustee can be a difficult one if the settlor does not fully understand the concept of a trust and if their expectations are not managed. A settlor must understand that the trust fund cannot be treated as another of their personal bank accounts.

There must be strict adherence to the terms of the trust at all times for it to be legally effective.

1.1 'Sham' trusts

A trust may be set aside as being a 'sham trust' in certain circumstances – for example, if the intended settlor had sought to restrict the trustee's powers significantly and continues to operate as if the trust fund still belonged to the settlor. This was the case in *Rahman v Chase Bank (C.I.) Trust Company Limited and five others [1991]*, outlined in Case Law 12.1.

Case law 12.1

Abdel Rahman v Chase Bank (CI) Trust Company Limited and five others [1991]

In 1977, Kamel Abdel Rahman (KAR) settled a trust of which Chase Bank (C.I.) Trust Company Limited was the trustee. After the death of KAR, his widow (surprised by how little funds were left in the trust) and other parties brought an action challenging the validity of the settlement on two grounds. The first ground was that the provisions of the trust deed (discussed further below) breached the Jersey maxim '*donner et retenir ne vaut*' (literally 'to give and retain is worthless') which applied to trusts before the introduction of the Trusts (Jersey) Law 1984.

The maxim applied whenever the settlor failed to dispose themselves of the trust assets and vest ownership with the trustee (i.e. if the settlor retains the power to destroy the gift or exercises dominion and control over the assets, this renders the trust invalid).

The second ground was that the trust was not a trust at all but was a 'sham'.

The court noted the following.

- The trust deed provided that the trust fund and income be held upon trust as KAR should appoint in his lifetime, with the trustee's consent.
- KAR could appoint one-third of the capital of the trust fund in any 12-month period without the trustee's consent.
- The trustee was directed to have regard exclusively to KAR's interests in determining whether or not to exercise their power to pay or apply the capital or income of the fund for his benefit.
- Many administrative powers required KAR's prior written consent prior to their exercise.
- KAR referred to the fund as 'my assets'.
- The trustee made no independent investment decisions and invariably complied with KAR's instructions.

- KAR obtained money and made distributions from the trust fund with the trustee being informed after the event.
- KAR gave direct instructions to banks holding the trust property concerning its investment.

The court ordered that the settlement and the gifts to the trustee were wholly invalid and of no effect under the law of Jersey.

Firstly, it breached the maxim '*donner et retenir ne vaut*' (in the sense that KAR had retained dominion and control over the trust fund throughout his lifetime).

Secondly, if the court had not made its decision on the basis of the Jersey maxim, it would have been set aside anyway as the settlement was a sham (in the sense that it was made to appear what it was not), which KAR did not intend to have legal effect.

1.2 Dummy settlors

In the past, dummy settlors have been named in trust documentation, disguising the settlor. This practice is no longer prevalent in well-regulated jurisdictions. Where dummy settlors were used, either the person named as the settlor in the trust deed was not the originator of the funds or they contributed only the initial settled funds with the bulk of the assets being provided by someone else at a later date. It was common for the dummy settlor to write a letter of wishes to the trustee immediately upon creation of the trust explaining that the trustee should deal with another individual in future (the real provider of the funds) and that they no longer wished to be contacted in connection with the trust. It is not uncommon for trusts that were created prior to the introduction of proceeds of crime legislation to be documented in this way, as this was historically viewed as a way of enhancing confidentiality. In the AML-aware environment that trustees now operate within, this practice and any other practice that leads to the creation of documentation that does not reflect the reality of a situation is no longer common nor acceptable. It is also unnecessary, as the use of a more acceptable 'declaration of trust' would achieve the same level of confidentiality.

Test yourself 12.1

What is a dummy settlor?

2. The trustee

A trustee is a person who holds legal title to the trust property and administers the trust fund for the benefit of the beneficiaries of a trust. The relationship between the trustee and the beneficiaries is a fiduciary relationship – that is, one founded on trust. The trustee has a fiduciary duty to act in the best interests of the beneficiaries, not in their own self-interest. The settlor usually chooses the first trustee (referred to as the original trustee). The trustee usually has the power to appoint a new trustee, although such an appointment may require the consent of the protector if there is one.

There must always be a trustee. However, trust law provides that a trust will not fail for lack of trustee. The law also prevents a sole trustee from resigning from their position. The trustee must therefore find a replacement if they wish to resign, depending on the reason for resignation. It can be difficult to find a replacement. If the trustee dies or ceases to exist trusteeship of the trust will be passed into the control of the court to appoint a new trustee or trustees or in some jurisdictions a public trustee will be appointed as trustee.

Unlike a company, a trust is a legal arrangement and not a legal person. It therefore has no separate legal personality and cannot contract in its own name.

It is the trustee, or trustees, who transacts business in their own name. The trustee also legally owns the trust assets, not the trust itself. In the offshore environment, the trustee is usually a limited liability company that is regulated.

2.1 Duties of a trustee

Trustees have a general duty of care and are expected to exercise such care and skill as is reasonable given the circumstances. When considering what may be considered to be 'reasonable', courts will have regard to:

- any special knowledge or experience that the trustee has (or holds themselves out as having); and
- any special knowledge or experience that one would reasonably expect the person to have (if they are acting as trustee in the course of a business or profession).

A higher standard of care is therefore expected of professional trustees than those who find themselves otherwise acting as a trustee.

Trustees must, in executing their duties or powers and discretions, act with due diligence as a prudent person of business would act, act to the best of their ability and skill, and they must observe good faith. Offshore courts expect higher standards of trustees because they are subject to specific regulation and thus higher standards of skill, care and diligence.

Case law 12.2

Bartlett v Barclays Bank Trust Co Ltd [1980]

Barclays Bank Trust Company Ltd (the trustee) owned almost the entire share capital of a company. The trustee did not interfere with the management of the company and sought little information in relation to the company, although it did attend the annual general meeting (AGM). Following unsuccessful speculative property development carried out by the directors the company made large losses.

The court held that the trustee was bound to act in relation to their position as the controlling shareholder in the same manner as an ordinary prudent person of business would act – that is, it was required to act in such a manner as necessary to safeguard the investment, including obtaining information about the company's management and its performance. As the trustee had manifestly not done so, the court found it was therefore liable for breach of trust, and was required to make good some of the losses suffered.

Following this case, it has become common for trust deeds to contain a clause allowing the trustees not to interfere in the business of such companies. Such provisions would not exonerate a trustee from liability, for example, if the trustee had knowledge that the investments were not being managed properly.

Such clauses are often referred to as anti-Bartlett clauses. An example of such a clause can be seen in Making it work 12.1.

Making it work 12.1

Sample anti-Bartlett clause

TRUSTEES NOT BOUND TO INTERFERE IN BUSINESS OF COMPANY IN WHICH TRUST INTERESTED

The Trustees shall not be bound or required to interfere in the management or conduct of the business of any company, wherever resident or incorporated, in which the Settlement shall be interested although holding the whole or a majority of the shares carrying the control of the company but so long as the Trustees shall have no actual notice of any act of dishonesty or misappropriation of moneys on the part of the directors having the management of such company the Trustees shall be at liberty to leave the conduct of its business (including the payment or non-payment of dividends) wholly to such directors without requiring to be supplied with any information concerning the company or its affairs beyond that to which every shareholder would be entitled.

No Beneficiary hereunder shall be entitled to require the distribution of any dividend by any company wherever incorporated or resident in which the Settlement may be interested or require the Trustees to exercise any powers they may have of compelling any such distribution.

Although trustees' duties will differ from case to case depending upon the terms of the trust, general duties of the trustee in administering the trust property typically include:

- to administer the trust in accordance with the terms of the instrument of trust;
- to protect and preserve the value of the trust property;
- to enhance the value of the trust property;
- not to profit directly or indirectly from their position as trusteeship or enter into a transaction that would result in a personal profit;
- not to allow any other person to profit from their trusteeship;
- to keep accurate accounts and records of the trusteeship;
- to keep trust property separate from the trustee's own personal property and separately identifiable from any other property of which they are a trustee;
- to act together with any co-trustees; and
- to act with impartiality where there is more than one beneficiary or purpose. This means not administering the trust for the advantage of one beneficiary over another.

Trust laws may include other general duties relating to specific types of trust – for example, if a trustee of a trust for non-charitable purposes finds itself without an enforcer, it must take the steps that are necessary to appoint a new enforcer.

Settlor-directed trusts (permitted in some jurisdictions such as Jersey) allow for more effective exoneration for trustees. There is however a school of thought that if the duties of trustees are eroded too far then a court might find an arrangement is a simple contract rather than a trust.

Case law 12.3

Keech v Sandford [1726]

The trustee held a lease of a market for the benefit of a minor (infant) beneficiary. The trustee applied for the lease's renewal prior to its expiry. The lessor refused to renew the lease for the benefit of the infant; however, he was prepared to grant a renewal to the trustee himself and the trustee therefore took up the lease in his personal capacity (i.e. not as trustee).

The judge commented as follows:

> 'I do not say there is a fraud in this case, yet he should rather have let it run out, than to have had the lease to himself. This may seem hard, that the trustee is the only person of all mankind who might not have the lease: but it is very proper that rule should be strictly pursued, and not in the least relaxed; for it is very obvious what

> would be the consequence of letting trustees have the lease, on refusal to renew to *cestui que use.*'

The court required the trustee to account to the trust for the profits made in respect of the lease since its renewal. This case established the strict rule that a trustee may not benefit from trust property, even if the profit would not have been made if it were not for the trustee's actions.

2.2 Trustee records

As explained in section 2.1, a trustee has a duty to keep accurate accounts and records of the trusteeship. This will involve keeping minutes of trustee meetings that accurately record the key activities relating to the trust fund and any key decisions made by the trustee.

Where a decision is made, it is good practice to record the relevant clause of the trust deed to demonstrate that the trustee has considered the scope of their powers. If there is a protector, it is good practice to note within the minutes that the protector's consent to an action has been received, if required. If the decision involves a dispositive power, the minutes should clearly identify whether the distribution is to be made from capital or income. Trust administrators who consider these matters routinely are likely to avoid potential beaches of trust and mistakes being made.

Trustee accounting or book keeping records should be kept up to date in order that the trustee can be certain that they are indeed making a distribution from income or capital as stated. The trustee's records should be reconciled with those of the bank (e.g. upon receipt of bank statements).

Test yourself 12.2

Identify three general duties of a trustee.

2.3 Trustees' liability for breach of trust

Breaches of trust occur whenever a trustee does not fulfil or fails to meet any duty imposed upon them by the law or by the terms of the trust.

Trustees are liable for any breach of trust committed. This means they are liable for the loss or depreciation in value of the trust property resulting from the breach and are liable to pay the profit, if any, which would have accrued to the trust property if there had been no such breach of the trust.

Beneficiaries who have legal capacity and a full knowledge of all material facts may relieve a trustee of liability for a breach of trust or may indemnify a trustee against liability for a breach of trust.

A trustee who pays funds to a person who is not a beneficiary of the trust would be liable for the breach of trust, whether or not their 'client' (the settlor, or even a beneficiary) requested them to do so.

Exculpation clauses

In some jurisdictions, exculpatory clauses can be validly included within trust instruments. Such clauses may provide that the trustee shall not be liable for any loss to the trust fund arising as a consequence of any act or omission.

The legislation of a jurisdiction usually prohibits exclusion of liability for breach of trust arising from the trustee's own fraud, wilful misconduct or gross negligence. Any exculpation clauses should be drafted with this legislation in mind. Think of these paragraphs in the context of the earlier section referring to *Bartlett v Barclays Bank Trust Co Ltd [1980]*.

Case law 12.4

Spread Trustee Company Limited v Sarah Ann Acato Hutcheson and others [2011]

On 15 June 2011, the Judicial Committee of the Privy Council delivered its judgment in relation to an appeal following a decision of the Court of Appeal of Guernsey on 26 November 2009 in relation to the case known as *Spread Trustee Company Limited v Sarah Ann Acato Hutcheson and others [2011]*.

The Trustee held that the liability of a trustee for gross negligence could lawfully be excluded as a matter of Guernsey customary law and under the 1989 law. The trustee sought to rely upon an exculpation clause within the trust deed which stated:

> 'In the execution of the trusts and powers hereof no trustee shall be liable for any loss to the Trust Fund arising in consequence of the failure, depreciation or loss of any investments made in good faith or by reason of any mistake or omission made in good faith or of any other matter or thing except wilful and individual fraud and wrongdoing on the part of the trustee who is sought to be made liable.'

The issue raised by the appeal was whether it was permissible for a trust deed to exclude a trustee's liability for gross negligence prior to the entry into force of the Trusts (Amendment) (Guernsey) Law 1990 (the Amendment Law), which expressly prohibited such an exclusion.

The Board of the Judicial Committee of the Privy Council allowed the appeal by the trustee by a majority of three to two. With the passage of time it may be that when any similar instances are heard a court might choose not to follow this decision.

2.4 Trustees' powers

The fiduciary obligations of a trustee mean that the powers of a trustee must only be exercised in the interests of the beneficiaries and in accordance with the terms of the trust.

With a discretionary trust, a trustee is generally granted all of the same powers as a natural person acting as the beneficial owner of property when dealing with the trust property (although subject to the terms of the trust and the trustee's duties under the law).

A discretionary trust is one where the trustee is granted absolute powers of discretion to decide which of the beneficiaries will benefit from the trust fund and in what proportions they may benefit, if at all. They are discussed further in Chapter 13.

The trustee's powers may be said to comprise both administrative powers and dispositive powers. Administrative powers are those powers that relate to the way that the trustee administers the trust (e.g. the way in which they manage and invest the trust fund). Dispositive powers are those powers that relate to the distribution of the trust property.

The following are examples of the types of clauses that typically grant power to the trustees.

Trusts of original and additional property

The trust deed confirms that the trustee is able to receive the original trust property as well as additional property upon the same trust after and/or throughout the trust period. Funds added to the trust property are known as additional settled funds or assets.

Trusts of income and capital

The trustees of a discretionary trust are usually given wide powers to distribute the trust property. The 'trusts of income and capital' clause may give the trustee discretionary power to pay income or capital to any of the beneficiaries or to hold some or all of the trust fund upon a separate trust for any of the beneficiaries.

Trustees may be given powers of accumulation, which allows them to retain income and add it to the capital of the trust fund.

The trusts of income and capital clause may also set out how the trust fund will be distributed at the end of the trust duration if the trust has a set duration.

Making it work 12.2

Trusts of income and capital

Tax is principally assessed on income received while capital assets may be taxed on a separate basis – for example, in relation to capital gains (UK CGT) or on the total value of an estate either during the lifetime of the deceased (the wealth tax regime in France) or on the value of a person's estate on their demise.

Therefore, it is often important to segregate the income of a trust from the capital transactions carried out by the trustees. Incorrect record keeping or the inadvertent intermingling of income with capital can result in the incorrect calculation of a tax liability for which a trustee may be liable including any penalties due to the tax authorities.

A trust of income or capital clause may be written as follows.

TRUSTS OF INCOME AND CAPITAL

The Trustees shall stand possessed of the Trust Fund and the income thereof upon the trusts following, that is to say:

a) Upon trust during the Trust Period at their discretion to pay appropriate or apply the whole or such part of the income or capital of the Trust Fund as the Trustees may in their absolute discretion think fit to or for the maintenance education advancement or otherwise for the benefit of all or such one or more exclusive of the other or others of the Beneficiaries for the time being in existence in such shares and proportions if more than one and generally in such manner as the Trustees shall in their absolute discretion think fit.

b) To hold any income or capital of the Trust Fund appropriated or applied to a Beneficiary under the provisions of the preceding sub-clause to pay or apply the same to or for the benefit of such Beneficiary with power to declare such other trusts in respect of the same (without infringing any rule against perpetuities applicable hereto) for the benefit of such Beneficiary as the Trustees may in their absolute discretion determine including, but without prejudice to the generality of the foregoing, provisions for maintenance education or advancement or for accumulation of income whether during minority or otherwise, and with such discretionary trusts and powers exercisable by such persons as the Trustees shall in their like discretion determine.

c) Subject to the foregoing powers the Trustees shall during the Trust Period accumulate the income of the Trust Fund and add the accumulations to the capital of the Trust Fund.

d) At the expiration of the Trust Period upon trust as to both capital and income of the Trust Fund for all or such one or more exclusive of the other or others of the Beneficiaries in such shares and proportions if more than one and generally in such manner as the Trustees shall prior to or on the date of such expiration in their absolute discretion determine and in default of and subject to such determination upon trust for such of the Beneficiaries as shall then be living in equal shares absolutely.

Powers of appointment and advancement

Trustees may have very wide powers to appoint new trusts or to transfer trust property to a new trust (if there is a beneficiary in common) or to a company formed by the trustee.

Powers to ignore interests

The trust deed may set out that the trustee may ignore the interests of a beneficiary when considering whether to apply the trust property for the benefit of another.

Payment to persons not of full capacity

The trustees may be able to transfer trust property to the carer of a minor or interdict.

Powers of addition and exclusion

Trustees usually have the power to add additional beneficiaries to the class of beneficiaries or to remove a person from the class of beneficiaries or exclude a person from benefit from the trust property. Exclusions can usually be revocable (capable of being undone) or irrevocable.

Exercise of trustees' powers and discretions

The trust deed may set out that the powers of the trustee can be exercised at their absolute discretion and as they think fit.

Powers of delegation

The trustee may have the power to delegate their power to others, providing the delegation is done in good faith.

Retirement and appointment of new trustees

The trust deed may set out the provisions regarding the retirement of the existing trustees and the appointment of a new trustee. The trustee is often granted the power to appoint a new trustee. The trust deed may also provide a release from liability for the retiring trustee.

Remuneration of a trustee

The trust deed may provide for the remuneration of the trustee. In some jurisdictions, the trustee may not otherwise have a right to be remunerated under the law.

Disclosure

The trust deed may set out that the trustee need not disclose information about how they reached their decisions when exercising their powers.

Power to vary the settlement

It may be the case that the terms of a settlement may be varied.

Other general powers

Other general powers may include:

- power to deal with the trust property as if they were the beneficial owner;
- powers of investment;
- power to form companies – it is usual for the trust deed to state that the trustee is not bound to be involved in the affairs of an underlying company;
- power to make loans or to borrow; and
- power to employ agents or professionals.

Some trust instruments provide that the powers may only be exercised with the consent of a protector.

Test yourself 12.3

Explain three general powers of a trustee.

2.5 Number of trustees

The number of trustees that must be appointed is usually set out as a requirement in the trust deed.

However, the laws of the jurisdiction may also require that there are a minimum number of trustees. It is usual for legislation to provide that there must be at least one trustee, although there may be circumstances where more than one is required.

Trust law provides that trusts shall not fail for a lack of trustee.

This means that the trust will continue to exist even if it has fewer trustees than required by the law or the terms of the trust.

There are special provisions in the law that affect the administration of the trust, should this be the case.

2.6 Remuneration and expenses of trustee

The UK's Trustee Act 2000 provides for reasonable remuneration to be paid to professional trustees. Jersey has recently amended its legislation to allow remuneration to be paid to professional trustees. However, not all offshore jurisdictions have incorporated this provision into legislation.

Historically, the trustee was not entitled to remuneration for their services unless the terms of the trust specifically provided for the trustee to be remunerated or the trustee obtained the consent of all of the beneficiaries in writing.

Trustees who did not carefully inspect the trust deed upon their appointment found themselves unable to charge for their services and unable to resign as trustee. Trustees are entitled to reimburse themselves from the trust property all expenses and liabilities reasonably incurred in connection with the administration of the trust.

2.7 Offshore trustees, trusteeship and trust administration

Trust companies in offshore jurisdictions are often appointed as the sole trustee of trusts settled by non-residents. The trust company itself is usually appointed as trustee, although it is not uncommon for other wholly owned subsidiaries of the trust company to be appointed as co-trustees.

The trustee itself is usually a limited liability company (or companies) (known as a corporate trustee). It is common for a trust company to have a trust administration committee whose terms of reference provide for, for example, any two individual directors of the trust company to make decisions in relation to the day-to-day administration of trusts and companies under administration.

Employees of trust companies who deal with settlors and beneficiaries are referred to as trust administrators or trust officers. These are usually qualified and experienced individuals.

In many offshore jurisdictions, the provision of professional trustee services is a regulated activity that may not be carried on except by a business that has been issued with the relevant license and is supervised by its regulator.

The approach to the regulation of trustees in the UK differs somewhat from that of the offshore centres. There is a requirement in the UK for trustee service providers to register with HMRC for AML purposes; HMRC is the main supervisory authority for trust and company service providers.

2.8 Choosing a professional service provider to act as trustee

The choice of trustee will depend to some extent on the aims of the settlor, the resources available to them, their client service expectations and their adviser's recommendations. Different settlors seek different qualities in a trust service provider (e.g. an offshore trust company) for a variety of reasons.

A potential settlor may wish for the trustee to be provided by an entirely independent trust service provider. In this case, the settlor may avoid service providers that are bank-owned or offer their own portfolio management services. Other potential settlors may prefer to keep their business confined to connected organisations – such as with their existing bankers. It is common for banks to own trust companies to be able to keep the provision of bank accounts, a trustee, portfolio managers and other advisers in-house.

The lack of independence may mean that the bank-owned company is unlikely to choose external parties to provide services to the trust (e.g. even if they may offer better rates of interest).

However, it can be argued that the ability to provide services in-house outweighs the benefit of having such independence, as it may secure lower fees for the client, create operational efficiencies and enables the bank to know and understand all aspects of the client's business, thus creating opportunities for clients (as well as the bank).

Trustee services may be provided by accountancy firms, banks, bank-owned trust companies, law firm-owned trust companies or independently owned trust companies. These range in size from very small to very large organisations. A potential settlor with complicated structures spanning across jurisdictions may wish for their trustee to be a law firm with a presence in several jurisdictions while a client whose main aim is to provide for their family after their death may choose a 'family office' or small provider with whom they may build up a close relationship.

There are certain characteristics that many potential settlors will desire from their trustee.

These include the following.

- The trustee should be regulated and supervised.
- The trustee should be qualified and experienced at providing the services for which they are employed.
- The size of the trustee organisation should be suitable for the client in that it should be such that they feel that their business is important to the organisation.
- Some clients enjoy the security that being connected with a large institution may afford them, whereas others may prefer to be looked after by a small company where the staff know their business and where they receive a personal service.
- The fees and charges levied by the provider should be reasonable and transparent.
- The trustee should be a reputable person and there should be a lack of adverse publicity and a good regulatory track record. A service provider's reputation is key to its ability to attract and retain good-quality clients and intermediary contacts.
- There should be a good level of customer service.
- The availability of talented and experienced professional staff (particularly those with experience of dealing with the jurisdiction or activity with which the client is connected) is desirable. Clients favour consistency and the ability to liaise with the same members of staff over time. High levels of staff turnover are therefore undesirable.

3. The beneficiaries

A beneficiary of a trust is a person who is entitled by the terms of the trust to benefit from the trust property or in whose favour a discretion to distribute the property held on trust may be exercised. The terms of a trust may impose an obligation upon a beneficiary as a condition of benefit. It is very common for the settlor to include themselves as a beneficiary of the trust.

3.1 Identification of beneficiaries

As explained in Chapter 11, there must be certainty about who the beneficiaries are for a trust to be valid.

Beneficiaries can be specifically identified in the trust deed by name. If not, they should be ascertainable by reference to a class of beneficiaries or by reference to a relationship to a person, such as the settlor. For example, the trust deed may specify that the beneficiaries are 'the issue and remoter issue of the settlor'.

The beneficiaries in this case would include the settlor's children (issue) and grandchildren (remoter issue).

3.2 Blind trusts

Blind trusts were historically very commonly created in offshore centres. While it is no longer common for trusts to be created in this manner today, there are still many trusts in existence, the instruments of trust for which were created in this manner.

With a blind trust, the trust instrument is created with only a well-known charity identified as a beneficiary. Often the Red Cross is the named charity and blind trusts are very often referred to as 'Red Cross trusts'. It is not usually anticipated that the named charity would, in fact, benefit.

This practice carries risks and is potentially fatally flawed – if such a trust is established and the settlor dies prior to the trustees appointing any beneficiaries other than the named charity, then clearly the true intentions of the settlor will not be satisfied. Furthermore, overt measures that obscure the true beneficiaries of a trust may be viewed as tax abusive or subject to suspicions of money laundering.

After the trust had been established with a charity as the beneficiary, the trustee would exercise a power under the trust instrument to add the person who the settlor intended would benefit as a beneficiary. This could be done many years after the creation of the trust. The identity of the beneficiaries was therefore concealed and not connected to the trust in any paperwork. Trustees and administrators might expect that a trust they administrator today might just have been created 'blind' and bear in mind any consequences that arise as a result.

HMRC also uses the phrase 'blind trusts' to describe two other circumstances, both of which could be used by politicians as follows.

- With the first type, the politician would fund the trust; however, the terms of the trust would provide that they would not be informed of the investment choices. The politician would not then be required to declare an interest in assets of which they are not aware. US President Donald Trump was required to have placed his extensive business assets in such a trust prior to his confirmation as President.
- With the second type, anonymous individuals would fund the trust without the politician becoming aware of (and influenced by) the donors.

Caution must be exercised by trust administrators who are asked to prepare documentation that does not reflect the reality of a situation. A request from a settlor to back-date the creation of a trust would surely be resisted by any reputable trust company.

Test yourself 12.4

What is a beneficiary?

3.3 The addition and exclusion of beneficiaries

The terms of a trust may provide that the trustee can exercise a power to add a person as a beneficiary. Similarly, the terms of a trust may provide that the trustee can exercise a power to exclude a beneficiary from the trust. Such appointments and exclusions may be revocable or irrevocable. Individuals who are excluded from benefitting (excluded persons) are usually identified within a schedule attached to the settlement deed, unless they are excluded at a later date.

It is usually the case that the trustee is an excluded person; while the trustee need not necessarily be excluded, it is very likely that this will be the case where the trustee is a professional service provider. On occasion, where there are tax-planning considerations, a settlor may wish to irrevocably exclude themselves from benefiting from the trust.

In an interesting Jersey law case known as *In the matter of DDD Settlements [2011]*, the settlor had irrevocably excluded herself from being able to benefit from three trusts in order to avoid a substantial tax liability that would have otherwise arisen upon her death. The tax concerned was then abolished and the adult beneficiaries and the trustee sought to vary the trust in order that the settlor would no longer be excluded.

The proposal was also supported by an advocate appointed to represent the interests of the unborn beneficiaries. The court found that, if the settlor were to give its approval, the trustee may be able to consider mechanisms by which savings to capital gains tax otherwise payable could be made.

This it determined would be for the benefit of the unborn beneficiaries as well as the adult beneficiaries. Accordingly, the court ordered that the exclusion of the settlor from the class of beneficiaries be revoked.

Here we see the court demonstrating its inherent jurisdiction (over a trust) and a modern practical approach.

3.4 The rights of beneficiaries

The benefit that a beneficiary is entitled to depends on the type of trust.

- With a discretionary trust, the trustee has discretionary powers to decide whether or not a beneficiary will benefit and if so, in what proportion.
- Where the beneficiary has a fixed interest (e.g. they are a life tenant of a life interest trust), the trustee may **not** have power to vary the beneficiary's interest.
- Where the beneficiary has an interest that they are absolutely entitled to, this is referred to as a vested interest.

Different types of trust are discussed further in Chapter 13.

A beneficiary's interest could be a contingent interest, meaning that it is dependent upon a specified event occurring, such as the beneficiary reaching a specific age.

While there is a presumption that beneficiaries are entitled to some information, such as information relating to the accounts of the trust, the trustee must be cautious when considering what information should be disclosed and to whom, especially when there are many beneficiaries.

A beneficiary's right to information is not absolute.

Trustees will have to consider a number of factors, such as:

- the nature of the beneficiary's interest;
- the information that is the subject of the request;
- the reason why the information is being sought by the beneficiary; and
- their intentions upon receipt of the information. In short, the trustee must ensure that the interests of the beneficiaries as a whole are considered.

Stop and think 12.2

Consider the position of a trustee who has received a request from a beneficiary for information about distributions made to another beneficiary. The trustee is on notice that there is an unsettled family feud and suspects that the beneficiary may use the information to support a claim to have the trust set aside as a sham or that they have been treated unfairly. Would it be in the best interests of the beneficiaries as a whole if the trustee complied with the request for information?

Trustees are not usually required to disclose to beneficiaries (or anyone else) their deliberations as to the manner in which they have exercised a power or discretion, or the reason for their decisions.

Beneficiaries should be treated fairly and with impartiality. Trustees who take risks with the trust fund at the request of one beneficiary may find themselves open to attack from other beneficiaries or even future beneficiaries.

suis juris
Of legal capacity and in agreement.

If all beneficiaries are ***suis juris*** (i.e. if they are of legal capacity and agree) they may terminate the trust.

Beneficiaries have the right to disclaim their interest in a trust either permanently or for such period as they may specify in whole or in part if they do so in writing. As might be expected, this is quite a rare occurrence.

4. The protector

Trustees are afforded a wide range of discretionary powers with discretionary trusts. Settlors may wish to appoint a protector (of their choosing) who the trustees must liaise with or seek consent from when exercising some of their powers. This may be a family friend or a trusted professional such as a lawyer.

The settlor may appoint themselves as the protector of the trust. However, if the settlor needs to demonstrate independence from the trust for taxation or asset protection reasons, it may be more appropriate for them to appoint an independent third party.

Reasons for appointing a protector include:

- to offer comfort to the settlor that there is someone protecting the trust to some extent (the protector's consent is required before certain powers are exercised);
- the protector may be in a position to pass valuable information to the trustees regarding the beneficiaries and their personal circumstances; and
- the protector can ensure that the settlor's wishes are adhered to, which means that they are an indirect way of the settlor retaining some control without appearing to interfere too much with the running of the trust.

If there is a protector, they are usually appointed by the settlor and named within the trust instrument. The protector may resign in writing. It is usual for either the settlor or the existing protector to have the power to appoint a replacement protector.

4.1 Powers of the protector

The extent of the role and powers of the protector will depend upon the content of the instrument of trust. The powers of the protector may include (but are not necessarily limited to) the power to:

- remove the trustee;
- appoint a new trustee;
- obtain information about the trust fund; and
- consent to the remuneration of the trustee.

The protector's consent may be required before the trustee exercises its dispositive powers, usually in writing. This may include making a distribution of capital to a beneficiary or approving the addition or removal of a beneficiary.

Making it work 12.3

Powers of the protector

The clause that creates the requirement for a trustee to obtain the prior consent of the protector before exercising certain powers may be worded as follows.

POWERS OF PROTECTOR

Notwithstanding anything herein contained and in particular anything conferring an absolute or uncontrolled discretion on the Trustees hereof all and every power and discretion vested in the Trustees as are specified (whether by reference to a provision of this Settlement or otherwise) in the Schedule numbered ...... hereto shall only be exercisable by them with the prior or simultaneous written consent of the Protector.

It is important to note that the protector's powers usually only involve the protector consenting to an action (such as a capital distribution) proposed by the trustee. Protectors do not usually instruct the trustee to make distributions and they do not otherwise become involved in the day-to-day running of the trust.

Protectors can be a valuable source of information for the trustees and can offer guidance due to their knowledge of the beneficiaries' circumstances. They can make administering the trust a little more difficult at times, particularly if they believe that the trustee should always follow the wishes of the settlor or if their demanding conduct increases the cost of administering the trust fund. These are all issues that trustees must manage.

They can also make it much more difficult if they fail to understand their role and its fiduciary nature and that duties are owed to the beneficiaries and not the settlor (unless they are a beneficiary).

Test yourself 12.5

Identify three typical powers of a protector of a discretionary trust.

5. The enforcer

The enforcer is a person appointed to a non-charitable purpose trust. It is the duty of the enforcer to enforce the trust in relation to its non-charitable purpose. All non-charitable purpose trusts must have an enforcer at all times. In certain jurisdictions, such as the Cayman Islands, non-charitable purpose trusts may have beneficiaries as well as a purpose. The beneficiaries have a right – albeit not a duty – to enforce the trust. The law does, however, provide that at least one enforcer must have a duty to enforce the trust.

Enforcers may resign in writing to the trustee. The trustee has a duty to appoint a new enforcer immediately upon the resignation of the enforcer and in any other circumstance where the trust should find itself without one. An enforcer may not be a trustee.

Chapter summary

- The settlor is the person who provides the trust property, regardless of whether or not their name (or anyone else's name) is stated within the trust documentation. The settlor may also be a trustee, a beneficiary or the protector, although there may be taxation consequences.
- The trustee must always consider the capacity within which the settlor is acting when dealing with them.
- The use of dummy settlors is an outdated practice that is no longer commonly used in well-regulated jurisdictions.
- The trustee is the person who holds the trust property for the benefit of the beneficiaries. The trustee has a fiduciary duty to act in the best interests of the beneficiaries and not in their own self-interest.
- Trustees have a general duty of care and are expected to exercise such care and skill as is reasonable given the circumstances. What may be considered 'reasonable' depends on whether the trustee purports to have any special knowledge or experience that one would reasonably expect the person to have if they are a professional trustee. Trustees must act with due diligence as a prudent person would act.
- Trustees are required to administer the trust in accordance with the terms of the trust instrument, to protect, preserve and enhance the value of the trust fund, not to profit from their position, to keep accurate records and accounts, to keep trust assets separate from their own, to act together if they are co-trustees and to act with impartiality where there is more than one beneficiary or purpose.
- Trustees are liable for the loss or depreciation in value of the trust property resulting from a breach of any duty (breach of trust).
- Trustees' powers are said to be administrative or dispositive powers. Administrative powers are those that relate to the way in which the trustee administers the trust fund. Dispositive powers are those that relate to the distribution of the trust property. The trustees' powers may only be exercised in the interests of the beneficiaries and in accordance with the terms of the trust.
- In offshore centres, trust companies are usually appointed as the sole trustee of trusts that are settled by non-residents. The trust company itself is usually appointed as trustee. Employees of trust companies who deal with the trust fund are referred to as trust administrators or trust officers.
- A beneficiary is a person who is entitled by the terms of the trust to benefit from the trust property or whose favour or discretion to distribute the property held on trust must be exercised. The settlor may or may not be a beneficiary.
- The rights of beneficiaries are dependent upon the type of trust (to some extent). General rights of beneficiaries include the right to information such

as information relating to the accounts of the trust, the right to terminate the trust (if all are suis juris) and the right to disclaim their interest.

- The protector is usually appointed by the settlor. The protector's powers depend upon the instrument of trust. The protector's consent is usually required in writing before certain powers of the trustee are executed.
- Non-charitable purpose trusts are required to have an enforcer, whose duty is to enforce the non-charitable purpose.

Test yourself answers

Test yourself 12.1

A dummy settlor is used to describe an individual who is named within trust documentation as being the settlor where that person was not also the provider of the bulk of the trust assets. The dumb settlor may have contributed the initial settled funds (usually a nominal sum, for example, £100). The bulk of the assets being provided by someone else at a later date.

Test yourself 12.2

With discretionary trusts, trustees' duties will differ from case to case depending upon the terms of the trust. Some general duties of the trustee in administering the trust property are:

- to administer the trust in accordance with the terms of the instrument of trust;
- to protect and preserve the value of the trust property; and
- to enhance the value of the trust property.

Test yourself 12.3

General trustee powers include:

Powers of appointment and advancement
Trustees may have very wide powers to appoint new trusts or to transfer trust property to a new trust (if there is a beneficiary in common) or to a company formed by the trustee.

Powers to ignore interests
The trust deed may set out that the trustee may ignore the interests of a beneficiary when considering whether to apply the trust property for the benefit of another.

Powers of addition and exclusion
Trustees usually have the power to add additional beneficiaries to the class of beneficiaries or to remove a person from the class of beneficiaries or exclude a person from benefit from the trust property. Exclusions can usually be revocable (capable of being undone) or irrevocable.

Test yourself 12.4

A beneficiary of a trust is a person who is entitled by the terms of the trust to benefit from the trust property or in whose favour a discretion to distribute the property held on trust may be exercised.

Test yourself 12.5

Typical powers of a protector of a discretionary trust may include:

- the power to remove the existing trustee and appoint a new trustee;
- the power to obtain information about the trust fund; and
- the power to consent to the remuneration of the trustee.

Chapter thirteen
Types of trusts

List of topics

1. Revocable and irrevocable trusts
2. Discretionary trusts
3. Settlor reserved powers trusts
4. Fixed interest trusts
5. Bare trusts
6. Spendthrift or protective trusts
7. Accumulation and maintenance trusts
8. Charitable trusts
9. Non-charitable purpose trusts
10. VISTA trusts
11. Unit trusts
12. Employee trusts

Introduction

This chapter explains the terms revocable and irrevocable in terms of trusts and provides an overview of the various types of trust that can be established, including those with wide discretionary powers and those where the beneficiary has a fixed interest.

The chapter outlines some of the powers that are reserved by the settlor with the use of settlor reserved powers trust. It also explains what is meant by a bare trust and outlines a common example of where such a trust is extensively used in the offshore environment.

Protective trusts that alter a person's right to benefit or terminate upon their bankruptcy are explained, as are trusts which are accumulation and maintenance trusts (usually set up to provide for minors), charitable trusts and non-charitable purpose trusts.

1. Revocable and irrevocable trusts

A trust, and any exercise of a power under a trust, may be expressed to be revocable in whole or in part, or irrevocable.

If a trust is revocable, the settlor may 'revoke' the trust and reclaim the assets if they change their mind after settling the trust or if their circumstances change in the future. The trustee would then hold the trust property for the settlor absolutely. Where the creation of the trust is motivated by tax-planning considerations, it is likely that the trust will need to be irrevocable. In order to be effective, most asset protection trusts would also need to be irrevocable.

An irrevocable action is usually considered to be just that (unable to be changed or undone). However, the courts may have power to vary the terms of the trust to address this if it is in the best interest of the beneficiaries (born and unborn) to do so.

2. Discretionary trusts

Discretionary trusts are very popular. They are the most common type of trust used in offshore centres. With these trusts, the settlor specifies who may benefit from the trust either by naming the beneficiaries or by stating a class of beneficiaries who could benefit from the trust. The trustees are usually given wide powers to accumulate income or to distribute the income or capital of the trust as they see fit.

The trustee may exercise their powers at their absolute discretion to decide who will benefit, when they will benefit and in what proportions if at all.

The beneficiaries of discretionary trusts do not therefore have an automatic right to benefit from the trust fund. The trustee only needs to consider whether they should benefit.

It is usual for the settlor of a discretionary trust to write a non-legally binding letter of wishes to the trustee in which the settlor offers some guidance as to how the trustee may deal with the trust property both during their lifetime and after their death. While the trustee is under no obligation to follow the letter of wishes, it is quite unusual that they would not do so in practice unless to do so would result in a breach of trust.

The flexibility of discretionary trusts makes them an attractive option. Trustees who are informed of the settlor's motivations for setting up the trust can change the way they can apply the trust fund at their absolute discretion as and when required. In addition, they may usually add or remove beneficiaries.

Given the wide range of discretionary powers afforded to a trustee of a discretionary trust, it can be daunting for a settlor of a trust to give away their assets and relinquish all control. The settlor may seek to retain an element of control by including a provision within the terms of the trust deed that certain powers may only be exercised with the consent of a protector. The settlor themselves may be the protector (see Chapter 12, section 4), although this is uncommon where the trust is created for tax planning reasons.

Test yourself 13.1

What is a discretionary trust?

3. Settlor reserved powers trusts

Settlor reserved powers trusts (sometimes referred to as RPTs) are a type of trust which provides for settlors to retain some control by reserving certain powers. This type of trust reduces the risk that the trust will be set aside as a sham. The legislation in many offshore jurisdictions now provides for the settlor to reserve certain powers without this affecting the validity of the trust. Examples of the types of powers the settlor may reserve include:

- acting as, or giving binding directions as to the appointment or removal of, a director or officer of any corporation wholly or partly owned by the trust;
- advancing, appointing, paying or applying income or capital of the trust property or giving directions for the making of such advancement, appointment, payment or application;
- appointing or removing any trustee, enforcer, protector or beneficiary;
- appointing or removing an investment manager or investment adviser;
- changing the proper law of the trust;
- giving binding directions to the trustee in connection with the purchase, retention, sale, management, lending, pledging or charging of the trust property or the exercise of any powers or rights arising from such property;
- restricting the exercise of any powers or discretions of a trustee by requiring that they shall only be exercisable with the consent of the settlor or any other person specified in the terms of the trust; and
- revoking, varying or amending the terms of a trust or any trusts or powers arising wholly or partly under it.

Settlor reserved powers trusts have typically been used in offshore centres where the settlor wishes to have some input into the investments that are held within the trust. The settlor may reserve the power to appoint or remove the investment manager or take decisions regarding the investments.

The legislation typically provides that, where powers such as those mentioned above have been reserved or granted by the settlor, a trustee who acts in accordance with the exercise of the power is not acting in breach of trust. While the reservation of powers will not invalidate the trust, tax and legal advisers should be consulted regarding the extent of any powers that a settlor should retain in order to achieve their objectives.

Test yourself 13.2

Identify three powers that may typically be reserved by the settlor when using a settlor reserved powers trust.

4. Fixed interest trusts

Fixed interest trusts are quite unlike discretionary trusts. The trustee does not need to exercise discretion to decide how to distribute the trust property, as the beneficiary is absolutely entitled to a fixed interest. A well-known example of a fixed interest trust is the life interest trust.

4.1 Life interest trusts

With a life interest trust (also known as an interest in possession trust), a beneficiary referred to as the 'life tenant' has an absolute right (an interest in possession) to enjoy the trust property or income arising from the trust property during their lifetime. The beneficiary entitled to the income is usually referred to as the life tenant. A person with an absolute right to benefit from a trust is said to have a vested interest. Only on the death of the life tenant may the other beneficiaries (referred to as the remainder-men) stand to benefit.

Upon the death of the life tenant, the terms of the trust may provide for the trust property to be held on trust for the remainder-men, with the trustee having discretionary powers, or they may provide for the capital to be paid in fixed proportions to the beneficiaries and the trust wound up. Fixed interest trusts are a way of providing for more than one generation.

Trustees must manage the trust fund of fixed interest trusts in a manner that does not unduly affect the interest of either the income or capital beneficiaries.

For example, it would be unfair to tie up the capital of a fixed interest trust in a non-income-earning asset, as this would seriously affect the income due to the life tenant.

Test yourself 13.3

What is an interest in possession trust?

5. Bare trusts

In a bare trust, the trustee holds the trust property upon trust absolutely for the owner (the beneficiary). The trustee has no discretionary powers and must simply hold the property and deal with it or transfer it when instructed.

The main use of bare trust arrangements is for confidentiality reasons. While nominee shareholders (see below) are common, bare trusts involving professional trustees are not otherwise common in offshore jurisdictions.

5.1 Nominee shareholders

It is often the case in offshore jurisdictions that nominee shareholders (usually a service provider) own shares in private companies upon trust for the owner absolutely.

A simple one-page document referred to as a declaration of trust – not to be confused with the document described in section 7.2 of Chapter 11, also referred to as a declaration of trust – sets out that:

- the nominee (the trustee) holds the shares upon trust absolutely for the owner (the beneficial owner);
- they will pay any dividends arising to the owner; and
- the shares will be returned to the owner at the request of the owner.

The use of a nominee shareholder means that where the authorities keep a public record of its shareholders, only the name of the nominee shareholder (the legal owner) will be available to the public.

A sample of a declaration of trust wording is included in Making it work 15.1 (see pages 299–300).

Case law 13.1

In the matter of the representation of Publicis Graphics Group Holdings SA

In this Jersey case of April 2011, 0.02% of the shares in a Jersey company known as Publicis Graphics Holdings Limited (Publicis Graphics) were owned by Mr Assad (the nominee shareholder) as nominee for Publicis Graphics Group SA (the owner).

A dispute arose between the nominee shareholder and the owner. The owner requested that the nominee shareholder sign resolutions on their behalf; however, he did not. The owners then asked the nominee shareholder to return the declaration of trust and a signed stock transfer to the owner; however, he failed to do so.

The court had received judicial notice of the widespread use of nominee shareholders and the reliance placed upon them. In the court's view, it was important to maintain confidence in the use of nominee shareholders by requiring strict and immediate compliance with the terms of the declaration of trust.

The court held that the nominee shareholder was required to exercise his powers as bare trustee only in the interest of the owner and in accordance with the terms of the declaration of trust.

The nominee shareholder was therefore ordered to execute the documents in favour of the owner within seven days.

6. Spendthrift or protective trusts

Article 33 of England's Trustee Act 1925 provides for protective trusts. The terms of a protective trust may make the interest of a beneficiary liable to termination upon a specified event, such as upon them being declared bankrupt or attempting to sell or otherwise dispose of their right to benefit from the assets. The terms of a trust alter or terminate the rights of the beneficiary at the time of the specified event, thereby ensuring that the assets are not available for creditors.

These types of trust can also attempt to guard against beneficiaries who might be termed wastrels or vulnerable, such as those with addictions to drugs or gambling.

7. Accumulation and maintenance trusts

This type of trust is now less commonly established as advisers and trustees now more frequently recommend the creation of discretionary trusts. In an accumulation and maintenance trust, the beneficiaries only become entitled to benefit from the capital of the trust property upon, for example, reaching a specific age (not usually exceeding the age of 25). Until such time, no beneficiary has a fixed entitlement to the income.

The trustees accumulate income arising from the trust property throughout the trust period. The terms of the trust instrument may provide for the trustee to have discretionary powers to make distributions to the beneficiaries for the purposes of their maintenance, education and benefit.

Upon the beneficiary reaching the age specified within the trust instrument, the trustees may distribute the trust property to the beneficiary.

Accumulation and maintenance trusts are typically created by parents or grandparents for the benefit of their children or grandchildren. Trustees would be wise to guard against 'automatically' agreeing to requests for maintenance when the funds provided are to be used for some purposes. For example, what benefit does an 18-month-old child derive from accompanying its parents on a three-month holiday to a five-star resort in the Bahamas?

8. Charitable trusts

A charitable trust is one that has been established for charitable purposes. What constitutes a charitable purpose will differ in the legislation between jurisdictions. However, they typically include the relief of poverty, for the advancement of education and for the advancement of religion.

Charitable trusts are an exception to the rule that a trust must have identifiable beneficiaries in order to be valid. The laws provide that the court can order that the property can be applied to another purpose that is similar to that originally intended if the charitable purpose cannot be carried out within the spirit of the settlor's wishes.

9. Non-charitable purpose trusts

The legislation in many offshore centres (including the British Virgin Islands, the Cayman Islands, Guernsey and Jersey) allows the establishment of trusts for non-charitable purposes. Non-charitable purpose trusts (often simply referred to as purpose trusts) are trusts in which the trustee holds the property in order to carry out specific purposes which are not charitable.

The legislation provides that the trust deed must set out the non-charitable purposes for which the trust property is to be applied. Non-charitable purpose trusts must provide for the appointment of enforcer to enforce the trust. Enforcers are discussed further in Chapter 12.

A non-charitable purpose trust is another exception to the rule that a trust must have identifiable beneficiaries. Instead, it must have an identifiable purpose. The laws provide that the court can order that the property can be applied to another purpose that is similar to that originally intended if the non-charitable purpose trust cannot be carried out within the spirit of the settlor's wishes.

Test yourself 13.4

What is a non-charitable purpose trust?

9.1 The Cayman Islands 'STAR' Trust

The Cayman Islands has a form of non-charitable purpose trust known as the STAR trust. These are trusts that are formed under the Special Trusts (Alternative Regime) Law 1997. The trust instrument must state that this legislation is to apply to the trust.

The STAR trust allows a mix of both purposes and beneficiaries within the same trust. The beneficiaries of a STAR trust do not have enforceable rights in relation to the trust property.

Like non-charitable purpose trusts in other jurisdictions, the trust must have at least one enforcer with a duty to enforce the trust. The beneficiaries of the trust may be entitled to enforce the trust but are not under a duty to do so.

At least one trustee of a STAR trust must be a licensed trust corporation in the Cayman Islands.

10. VISTA trusts

10.1 The Virgin Islands Special Trusts Act 2004

The Virgin Islands Special Trusts Act 2004 enables the creation of a type of trust known as a VISTA trust. VISTA trusts must include a provision within the trust deed that specifically states that the act is to apply.

It is well established that trustees have a duty to preserve and enhance the value of trust investments. The trustee must therefore monitor their investments and consider taking action (such as disposing of the asset if it is not profitable). This places the trustee in a difficult position if the underlying investment is a family business or the settlor wants the trustee to retain the assets regardless of their performance. This can be the case, for example, where the settlor has wealth outside of the trust and it is of no consequence to them whether the investment is profitable or not. The settlor may not wish the trustees to interfere with the running of their family business. For these reasons, such arrangements have not typically been held through trust structures.

VISTA trusts may have the following features, which address the above issues.

- VISTA trusts allow a shareholder of a company to create a trust that does not require the trustee to become involved with its management.
- Designated shares can be held 'on trust to retain', meaning that the trustee's duty is to retain the trust rather than to preserve or enhance their value.
- The trustee cannot generally interfere with the management of the company.
- The trustee's duty to monitor and intervene in the running of the company can be removed or restricted.
- The trustee may require the consent of the settlor to dispose of the shares.

VISTA trusts may be useful where the settlor wishes to retain control over the underlying company or where they wish shares to be retained regardless of their performance. The VISTA trust is also useful where the settlor would like the trustee to make investments that usually would be inappropriate for a trustee due to the risk involved, or where the trustee would have no desire or a lack of skill or expertise to become involved with the running of the company. In Jersey, Settlor Directed Trusts could be said to be comparable.

11. Unit trusts

A unit trust is used as a collective investment fund vehicle for a number of investors. Investors' funds are pooled in a unit trust, enabling them to achieve exposure to a wider range of investments than they could achieve on their own as well as spreading investment risk. It is still a trust and therefore subject to the laws governing trusts and subject to the terms of its trust deed.

The trust deed divides the beneficial investment interests into units, each of which represents the right to receive a proportion of the profits (or losses) of the trust property being the underlying investments. The trust deed sets out the rights and obligations of the trustee and the unit holders, and details the terms of the redemption and the valuation rules. The units are usually freely transferable and redeemable.

As with any trust, legal title of the assets of the unit trust is vested with the trustee. The trustee usually must be regulated and supervised in their jurisdiction, and the contractual provisions between the trustee and the unit holders are usually set out in the subscription agreement. The trustee will ordinarily appoint a professional regulated fund manager to manage the portfolio of underlying investments, a fund administrator to service investors and a regulated custodian usually acts as custodian of all of the investments held within the unit trust. The fund administrator will typically act as registrar and maintain the appropriate registers of the unit trust.

The unit trust fund is divided into a number of units, each representing a proportion of the assets held by the trustee. Unit trusts may be open-ended or closed ended. Most are open-ended. If this is the case, units may, in accordance with the provisions contained within the trust deed and other documentation, be issued or redeemed at their net asset value. Closed-ended unit trusts have a fixed number of units that does not change throughout the trust period. The unit prices are therefore determined by supply and demand. The units may be issued at a premium or a discount to the net asset value.

12. Employee trusts

Employers who may wish to provide for their employees and their families may create trusts for their benefit. Such trusts are usually discretionary trusts related to the provision of employee benefits such as long-term bonus schemes and pension funds where it is important to hold the assets independently of the employer.

However, while the majority of employee trusts are established for entirely legitimate purposes, the last five years (2013–2018) have also seen an exponential increase in the number of professional firms offering such trusts (often referred to as Employee Benefit Trusts (or EBTs)) that are overtly intended to aggressively avoid tax. Some firms and the advisers of the settlors have consequently found HMRC and the Courts less than enthusiastic about some 'schemes'. The background of the limited companies that have owned Glasgow Rangers FC is a relevant case in point.

Chapter summary

- Trusts may be revocable, meaning that the settlor may change their mind and reclaim the assets, or irrevocable, where they may not.
- The trustee of a discretionary trust has absolute discretionary powers to decide if, when and how the beneficiaries of the trust will benefit.
- If the settlor continues to operate as if the trust fund belongs to them by exercising control and restricting the powers of the trustee, the trust could be set aside as a sham trust.
- With settlor reserved powers trusts (RPTs), the law provides that the settlor may reserve certain powers without the validity of the trust being affected.
- With fixed interest trusts such as life interest trusts, the beneficiaries' right to benefit is fixed. There is no need for the trustee to exercise their discretion.
- With a life interest trust, the life tenant is entitled to receive the income from the trust during their lifetime and only upon their death may the remainder-men benefit.
- In a bare trust arrangement, the trustee holds the property upon trust absolutely for the beneficiary and he must therefore deal with the property exactly as instructed by the beneficial owner. A nominee shareholder is a bare trustee.
- Spendthrift or protective trusts are those with provisions that make the interest of a beneficiary liable to terminate upon a specified event (e.g. upon their bankruptcy).
- Accumulation and maintenance trusts are those where the beneficiary becomes entitled to benefit from the capital of the trust property upon reaching a specific age. Until such time, the trustees accumulate the income. The trustees may have the power to make distributions to the beneficiaries for the purposes of their maintenance, education and benefit.
- Charitable trusts are those that have been established for a charitable purpose.
- Non-charitable purpose trusts are those where the trustee holds the property to carry out a purpose that is non-charitable.
- The Cayman Islands STAR trust is a non-charitable purpose trust formed under the Special Trusts Alternative Regime 1997; it allows a mix of purposes and beneficiaries within the same trust.
- The VISTA trust is formed under the Virgin Islands Special Trusts Act 2004, which may replace the trustees' duty to enhance and preserve the trust fund with a duty to hold shares in an underlying company 'on trust to retain'. The trustee is not required to interfere with the management of the company.

- Unit trusts are a type of trust that is used as an investment vehicle. A number of units are issued to investors. The number of units issued may be fixed (if the fund is closed-ended) or new units may be issued and redeemed throughout the trust period (if the fund is open-ended).

Test yourself answers

Test yourself 13.1

A discretionary trust requires the settlor to specify who may benefit from the trust either by naming the beneficiaries or by stating a class of beneficiaries who could benefit from the trust. The trustees are usually given wide powers to distribute the income or capital of the trust as they see fit or to accumulate income. The trustee may exercise their powers at their absolute discretion to decide who will benefit, when they will benefit and in what proportions if at all.

The beneficiaries of discretionary trusts do not therefore have an automatic right to benefit from the trust fund. The trustee only needs to consider whether they should benefit.

Test yourself 13.2

Examples of the types of powers the settlor may reserve include the power to:

- act as, or give binding directions as to the appointment or removal of, a director or officer of any corporation wholly or partly owned by the trust;
- advance, appoint, pay or apply income or capital of the trust property or to give directions for the making of such advancement, appointment, payment or application; and
- revoke, vary or amend the terms of a trust or any trusts or powers arising wholly or partly under it.

Test yourself 13.3

An interest in possession trust gives a beneficiary referred to as the 'life tenant' an absolute right (an interest in possession) to enjoy the trust property or income arising from the trust property during their lifetime.

Test yourself 13.4

Non-charitable purpose trusts (often simply referred to as purpose trusts) are trusts in which the trustee holds the property in order to carry out specific purposes which are not charitable.

Part seven

Chapter 14
Introduction to companies

Chapter 15
Company incorporation

Chapter 16
Company meetings and resolutions

Chapter 17
Winding up

Companies and company law

After studying this part, students will have an understanding of the main features of a company, including the concept of separate legal personality and the **veil of incorporation**.

This chapter explains what a member of a company is and outlines some of their rights. It discusses the different types of directors including ***de jure* directors**, ***de facto* directors**, shadow directors and **alternate directors**. The appointment and termination of a director's appointment is discussed, as are the powers and duties of the directors. The role, powers and duties of the company secretary are outlined.

Students will be able to discuss the advantages and disadvantages of using a company and will be able to describe various types of companies. They will gain an understanding of the share capital of a company and will be able to describe different classes of shares. Students will be able to describe typical incorporation procedures and will be able to describe the purpose and content of the memorandum and articles of association of a company, and their role as contractual documents.

veil of incorporation
See 'corporate veil'.

de jure director
A director who has formally been appointed as a director and whose name should be included on the register of directors of the company.

de facto director
A director who has not formally been appointed as a director but nevertheless fulfils the role of a director.

alternate director
A person who has been appointed to attend and vote at a meeting of the directors on someone's behalf.

They will also understand the purpose of the registered office and be able to explain the statutory registers that must be kept at this address. Students will gain an understanding of the roles, powers and duties of the members, directors, the secretary and the auditor. Students will gain an understanding of the requirements surrounding meetings and resolutions of the directors and of the shareholders. Finally, students will be able to explain the ways in which a company can be wound up.

Learning outcomes

At the end of this part, you will:

1. understand the main features of companies and how they are financed;
2. know the steps involved in incorporating a company and post-incorporation procedures;
3. understand the roles, powers and duties of members, directors, the secretary and the auditor of a company;
4. understand the requirements surrounding meetings and resolutions of directors and shareholders; and
5. know about the ways in which a company is wound up.

Chapter fourteen
Introduction to companies

List of topics

1. Features of a company
2. Members, directors, the company secretary and auditors
3. Advantages and disadvantages of using a company
4. Types of companies

Introduction

This chapter explains what a company is and explains the main features of a company. It discusses the main advantages and disadvantages of a company, along with different types of company. These include public and private companies, limited and unlimited companies, and some of the newer types of company such as the protected cell company and the incorporated cell company. The chapter also discusses how companies can be limited by shares and by guarantee.

1. Features of a company

Company administrators in offshore centres are likely to incorporate and administer companies from various jurisdictions, not just those incorporated within their own centres. It is therefore unlikely that they would be familiar with the legislation of all of the jurisdictions of the companies that are under their administration. The local laws in many offshore centres have been developed in order to accommodate requirements that are specific to the jurisdiction. However, the laws in offshore centres are often very similar to English laws, particularly where the offshore centre has a close relationship with England. It is therefore possible to gain an understanding of the basics of company principles by studying the Companies Act 2006, which will be the focus of the content of the following chapters.

A company comes into existence when it is incorporated by law by an association of people for business or profit-making purposes. The owners of a company are its members (also known as its shareholders) and it is managed and controlled by its directors. The law which allows companies to be created and which governs their existence in the UK is the Companies Act 2006.

Companies are also subject to their own articles of association, which set out the way in which the company will operate. Companies may adopt **model articles** provided within the Companies Act 2006.

model articles
Articles of association created by the Companies Act 2006; these apply unless a company excludes them in place of other articles.

The features of a company make undertaking business through a company more advantageous than undertaking it as an individual (as a **sole trader**) or by way of a partnership. Partnerships are discussed further in Chapter 18.

sole trader
An individual who is the sole owner of their business.

1.1 Separate legal personality

A company is created by a legal process known as incorporation. Once incorporated, the law considers the company to be a separate and distinct legal person. As a legal person, it therefore has its own separate legal personality from that of its owners and directors, meaning that the company itself may be sued (and may sue others) in its own right.

A company can, in the same way that a natural person can, hold assets and incur liabilities. The legal personality of the company is separated from that of its owners and directors. The concept of separate legal personality was established in the well-known case of *Salomon v Salomon & Co Limited [1897]*, discussed below.

In the same way as any legal person, a company cannot be 'owned' in the normal sense and whereas shareholders are often considered to be the owners of a company, in reality this is not the case because it is only the shares of the company that are owned by shareholders. Company shares are the contract with the company that entitles shareholders to:

- a proportionate share of future company profits;
- voting rights and other rights in accordance with the articles of association and company law;
- a proportionate share in the net proceeds of liquidation of the company upon winding up; and
- in the case of a limited company, protection from creditors of the company under the principle of limited liability.

In this way, shareholders have no right of ownership in relation to the individual assets or capital of a company.

Case law 14.1

Salomon v Salomon & Co Ltd [1897]

Mr Salomon ran a business as a sole trader and decided to incorporate a limited liability company and sell his business to the company. Instead of paying Mr Salomon in cash for the business, the company issued a debenture (an instrument acknowledging the debt). The debenture was secured by a floating charge over the company's assets, meaning that if the company did not honour its debt, Mr Salomon could recover the money owed to him from the sale of the assets. Mr Salomon was appointed as a director to the company and therefore continued to run the business.

The company eventually could not pay its debts and went into liquidation owing trade creditors and owing Mr Salomon due to the debenture. As secured creditors take priority over non-secured creditors in the course of the winding up, Mr Salomon was entitled to be paid before the other creditors.

The business did not have sufficient assets to pay all of its creditors. The unsecured creditors argued that Mr Salomon should not have priority over the company's assets as the business really belonged to him; in effect, Mr Salomon and the company were the same thing.

The court held that the legal personality of a limited liability company is separate from that of its owners and directors. Salomon, as a secured creditor, was therefore entitled to the assets of the company.

1.2 The veil of incorporation

The separation of the legal personality of the company from its shareholders and directors is referred to as the veil of incorporation (the **corporate veil**).

corporate veil
This refers to the separation of the legal personality of the company from that of its owners and controllers.

There are instances where the court will lift the veil of incorporation. The court will do so, for example, if the company is judged to be a sham or a party to a fraud. There are also occasions where the court will make the directors liable for the company's debts – for example, if the directors are guilty of fraudulent trading (carrying on a business with the intent to defraud creditors) or wrongful trading (where the director should have known the company would go into insolvent liquidation, yet failed to take reasonable steps to minimise the potential losses of its creditors).

In general, however, the court is extremely reluctant to lift the veil of incorporation, instead upholding the concept of the separate legal personality.

Case law 14.2

Adams v Cape Industries plc [1991]

In this case, which also dealt with the concept of the separate legal personality, a claim was brought against a South African subsidiary of Cape Industries plc for negligence. The claim was successful and as a result, the South African company went into insolvent liquidation.

The court held that the corporate veil could not be lifted to allow the South African litigants to recover the funds from the parent company, Cape Industries plc, whether or not it was desirable to do so. This case established the fact that a company that operates through a group including subsidiaries is entitled to organise its affairs in this manner for its own protection if it chooses to do so.

Increasingly matrimonial courts in the UK have been ordering defendants in divorce cases to arrange 'voluntarily' the lifting of the corporate veil.

1.3 Limited liability of shareholders

As explained in section 1.1, the legal personality of a company is separate from that of the shareholders. The shareholders of a limited liability company are therefore not liable to pay for the company's debts.

A limited liability company is one where the shareholders' liability is limited in that in the event of the company going into insolvent liquidation (i.e. it is unable to pay its debts), their risk is limited to the capital contributed or committed to the company to buy shares. They can only be asked to pay any additional amount where they still owe the company for payment of unpaid shares that are allotted to them, but not yet fully paid for.

1.4 The shares in the company are easily transferable

In some circumstances, it may be time-consuming to go through the process of disposing of an asset in the manner prescribed by the law. For example, the sale of land may have to go through the process of conveyancing. If the land is owned by a company, the owner of the company could simply transfer their shares in the company to the new owner. There would be deemed to be no change of ownership of the underlying asset, which would continue to be owned by the company.

1.5 Perpetual succession

dissolution
The legal process by which a company or a firm ceases to exist.

Companies continue to exist until they are wound up by a legal process such as **dissolution** or are struck from the companies register for an offence such as non-payment of annual fees. Their existence is not dependent on that of their shareholders or controllers (the directors). This is referred to as perpetual succession.

1.6 Confidentiality

If the owner of a business or asset wishes to keep their ownership confidential, the use of a company can achieve this. The information that is disclosed about a company depends on the type of company. This can be minimal, particularly in offshore centres.

For example, it is usual that only the shareholders of a private company are a matter of public knowledge in an offshore centre as reported in the company's annual return. As discussed in section 5 of Chapter 13, the use of a nominee shareholder means the beneficial ownership can remain confidential. The registered office can also be that of a service provider.

Making it work 14.1

Offshore service providers and confidentiality

Onshore clients who appoint an offshore service provider to act as directors, nominee shareholders, registered office and secretary can achieve complete confidentiality. This is because in some jurisdictions, there are currently no public record connecting them to the company or its assets.

2. Members, directors, the company secretary and auditors

2.1 Members

The members of a company are its subscribers and shareholders.

The people who subscribe to the company's memorandum are deemed to have agreed to become the first members of the company. On registration of the company, they become the first members. The first members are referred to as the **subscribers** and they will be issued with the first shares of the company. The name of the subscribers must be recorded in the register of members.

subscribers
The persons who subscribe to the memorandum of a company and who are deemed to be the first members of the company.

After incorporation, membership of a company is evidenced by ownership of shares in that company and in practice, the term 'member' is often used interchangeably with the term 'shareholder'.

Any other person who agrees to become a member of a company, and whose name is entered in its register of members, is also a member of the company.

The Companies Act 2006 provides that the company's constitution binds the company and its shareholding members as though they had individually covenanted to obey their provisions. The articles of association therefore constitute a contract between the company and its members and between the members themselves.

The rights and obligations of the members depend upon the type of share that they hold in the company.

The members do not owe a fiduciary duty to the company and they may therefore act in their own interests.

Rights of members

The rights of members include the right to:

- attend and vote at general meetings (unless the shares are non-voting shares);
- inspect the minutes of general meetings and copies of financial statements;
- inspect the register of members and receive a copy free of charge;
- receive a dividend (if one is declared by the company);
- receive their share in the surplus of any assets at the time the company is wound up; and
- transfer their shares to others subject to the terms of the articles of association.

2.2 Directors

The Companies Act 2006 describes a director as 'any person occupying the position of director, by whatever name called'. As a company is not a natural person, it requires someone to act as its mind and management. The directors are responsible for the management of the company's business. They owe a fiduciary duty only to the company, meaning they must act in its best interest rather than in their own interest or the interests of members.

Requirement to have directors

The Companies Act 2006 requires that a private company must have at least one director and that a public company must have at least two directors.

Test yourself 14.1

How many directors must be appointed in relation to a private company under the Companies Act 2006?

2.3 Appointment of directors

The first directors are usually appointed by the subscribers during the process of incorporating the company. The Companies Act 2006 requires the names of the first directors to be stated on the application form submitted to the Registrar of Companies requesting the incorporation of a company.

ordinary resolution
A resolution that must be passed by a simple majority of members.

The model articles state that any person who is willing to act as a director, and who is permitted by law to do so, may be appointed to be a director by **ordinary resolution** of the shareholders, or by a decision of the directors.

The Companies Act 2006 provides that a person may not be appointed a director of a company unless they have attained the age of 16 years. Directors who are properly appointed to a company may be referred to as *de jure* directors. The particulars of de jure directors will be recorded in the register of directors.

Where a person has not been formally appointed as a director but nevertheless fulfils the role, they may be referred to as *de facto* directors. Individuals who make and implement significant decisions on behalf of the company, and act as if they are directors, may be deemed *de facto* directors. As such, they will owe the same duties to the company as a formally appointed director. A *de facto* director should not be confused with the shadow director, another type of director that is not formally appointed (see section 2.4). The key difference is that while a *de facto* director fulfils the function of a director, the board is not necessarily accustomed to act in accordance with their directions or instructions.

Both *de jure* directors and *de facto* directors would fall into the Companies Act 2006 definition that a director is any person occupying the position of director, by whatever name called. Shadow directors are defined separately.

2.4 Shadow directors

The Companies Act 2006 defines a shadow director as a person in accordance with whose directions or instructions the directors of the company are accustomed to act. Helpfully, the Companies Act 2006 sets out that a person is not to be regarded as a shadow director by reason only that the directors act on advice given by the shadow director in a professional capacity (e.g. taxation or legal advice).

The general duties of directors (discussed in section 2.10) apply to shadow directors.

Shareholders with large shareholdings or the ultimate beneficial owners of the shares can become shadow directors if they exert significant influence over the directors to the extent that the directors become accustomed to act in accordance with their instructions.

The existence of an onshore shadow director may bring into question which jurisdiction the company is managed and controlled in, as well as its residence for taxation purposes. It is very important that directors are not 'instructed' and that they use their own judgement to decide upon a course of action. The records of the company should also reflect this.

2.5 Alternate directors

The articles of a company may provide for the directors to appoint an alternate director to attend directors' meetings on their behalf when they are unable to attend. The alternate director has the power to vote at the meeting in place of the elected director. Alternate directors are responsible for their own acts and are not deemed to act on behalf of the director who appointed them.

The use of alternate directors used to be very popular in offshore centres; however, it has become far less common to use them in recent years. The reason for the decline in use of alternate directors is partly due to the increase in use of corporate directors, which make it far easier to ensure that a quorate meeting can be held at all times. Alternate directors were also used where individual directors may have been absent from the office.

The model articles created under the Companies Act 2006 for private companies do not contain provisions for alternate directors.

Test yourself 14.2

a) **What is the difference between a *de facto* director and a shadow director?**

b) **What is an alternate director?**

2.6 Executive and non-executive directors

non-executive director
A director who is not involved with the day-to-day activities of the company and who can bring an independent view to the board of directors.

Executive directors are those with executive responsibilities. They are involved with the day-to-day running of the company. **Non-executive directors** are not involved with the day-to-day activities of the company and can therefore bring an independent, or if you like objective, view to matters arising within the company. Both executive and non-executive directors owe the same legal responsibilities to the company so it is critical that any prospective non-executive director fully understands the extent of their potential personal liability on appointment to the Board.

2.7 Corporate directors

Companies can also act as directors of other companies. The Companies Act 2006 specifies that companies are required to have at least one director who is a natural person.

In offshore centres, it has become increasingly common for company service providers to appoint corporate directors in place of individuals. Individual directors of the corporate body (or other senior members of staff) attend meetings as representatives of the corporate directors.

The requirement for at least one director to be a natural person is not present in all offshore jurisdictions. Jersey, for example, has no such restriction, although companies that undertake the regulated activity of providing corporate director services must be natural persons.

2.8 Termination of a director's appointment

The office of a director may be terminated by:

- retirement;
- removal – the Companies Act 2006 provides that the shareholders may remove a director by ordinary resolution at a meeting (see Chapter 16, section 5);

- resignation – directors can resign in accordance with the provisions of the articles;
- death; or
- disqualification – directors can be disqualified under the Company Directors' Disqualification Act 1986 (e.g. where a person is convicted of an indictable offence or because they have been deemed unfit to be directors).

In addition, the model articles provide that a person ceases to be a director in the following circumstances:

- that person ceases to be a director by virtue of any provision of the Companies Act 2006 or is prohibited from being a director by law;
- a bankruptcy order is made against that person;
- a composition is made with that person's creditors generally in satisfaction of that person's debts;
- a registered medical practitioner who is treating that person gives a written opinion to the company stating that that person has become physically or mentally incapable of acting as a director and may remain so for more than three months;
- by reason of that person's mental health, a court makes an order which wholly or partly prevents that person from personally exercising any powers or rights which that person would otherwise have; or
- notification is received by the company from the director that the director is resigning from office, and such resignation has taken effect in accordance with its terms.

2.9 Powers of directors

The directors derive their powers from the company's articles of association. The model articles, for example, give the directors a general authority to exercise 'all the powers of the company' for the purposes of fulfilling their responsibility to manage the company's business.

In addition, the Companies Act 2006 states that the power of the directors to bind the company, or authorise others to do so, is deemed free of any limitation under the company's constitution.

Liability

Directors do not usually incur personal liability while acting in their capacity as a director. There are circumstances, however, where a director will become personally liable. These could include where the director acts outside of their authority or acts negligently or fraudulently. While there have been relatively few successful claims made against directors by members this may change in the future notwithstanding there is no statutory requirement that directors be competent in the management of the company on whose Board they serve.

There is a higher risk of personal liability where the company is a regulated financial services business as a consequence of the applicable regulatory laws that typically set higher standards of behaviour for directors than is expected under company law.

2.10 Directors' duties

Directors occupy a position of trust and owe a fiduciary duty to the company. A director must therefore act in good faith and should not seek to secretly profit personally from their position as a director. The Companies Act 2006 sets out the general duties that are owed by a director of a company to the company.

The general duties are based upon certain common law rules and equitable principles, and are stated to have effect in place of those rules and principles.

The Companies Act 2006 states that the general duties shall be interpreted and applied in the same way as common law rules or equitable principles, and regard shall be had to the corresponding common law rules and equitable principles in interpreting them.

Duty to act within powers

A director of a company must act in accordance with the company's constitution, and only exercise powers for the purposes for which they are conferred. In other words, the powers must be exercised for the benefit of the company and not in the director's own self-interest.

Duty to promote the success of the company

A director of a company must act in the way they consider, in good faith, would be most likely to promote the success of the company for the benefit of its members as a whole, and in doing so have regard (among other matters) to:

- the likely consequences of any decision in the long term;
- the interests of the company's employees;
- the need to foster the company's business relationships with suppliers, customers and others;
- the impact of the company's operations on the community and the environment;
- the desirability of the company maintaining a reputation for high standards of business conduct; and
- the need to act fairly as between members of the company.

Duty to exercise independent judgement

A director of a company must exercise independent judgement when fulfilling their duties.

Case law 14.3

Weavering Macro Fixed Income Fund Limited (in liquidation) v Peterson and Ekstrom [2011]

In this landmark case in the Grand Court of the Cayman Islands, the official liquidator of Weavering Macro Fixed Income Fund Limited (the fund) sought damages against its former directors. The fund was put into liquidation after it was discovered that a high proportion of the assets reflected on its balance sheet were fictitious.

The investment adviser to the fund was indirectly owned and controlled by Mr Peterson. The fund was required to have two independent directors. The two directors were in fact close family relatives of Mr Peterson. It was alleged that the directors acted in breach of their duty to exercise independent judgement, to exercise reasonable care, skill and diligence, and to act in the best interests of the fund.

It was said that the directors signed documents whenever they were asked to do so by Mr Peterson without making any enquiry or attempt to understand their content. The court commented that the directors must apply their minds and exercise an independent judgement in the ordinary course of business in all matters falling within the scope of their supervisory responsibilities. The court added: 'they are not entitled to assume the posture of automatons as these directors did, by signing whatever documents are put in front of them by the investment manager without making enquiry or applying their minds to the matter in issue'. Had they applied their minds, the directors might have realised that a high proportion of the assets reflected on its balance sheet were fictitious.

The court gave judgement against each of the directors in the sum of $111 million plus costs. Since this text was first published, this ruling has been overturned and the two non-executives now are no longer required to reimburse this amount. Directors, both executive and non-executive, should nonetheless pay great regard to the failings displayed by the close family members of Mr Peterson.

Duty to exercise reasonable care, skill and diligence

A director of a company must exercise reasonable care, skill and diligence. 'Reasonable' care, skill and diligence is considered to be that which would be exercised by a reasonably diligent person with the general knowledge, skill and experience that may reasonably be expected of a person carrying out the functions carried out by the director in relation to the company.

Duty to avoid conflicts of interest
A director has a duty to avoid a situation in which they have a direct or indirect interest that conflicts with the interests of the company.

Duty not to accept benefits from third parties
A director of a company must not accept a benefit from a third party because of their position as a director unless the benefit could not reasonably be regarded as likely to give rise to a conflict of interest.

Duty to declare interest in proposed transaction or arrangement
If a director of a company is directly or indirectly interested in a proposed transaction or arrangement with the company in any way, they must declare the nature and extent of that interest to the other directors.

Test yourself 14.3

State three general duties of a director.

2.11 The company secretary

The Companies Act 2006 specifies that a private company is not required to have a company secretary. A public company must have a company secretary. In offshore centres, it is usual for the service provider or one of its subsidiary companies to act as a corporate secretary in situations where a professional service provider administers a company on behalf of a client.

2.12 Qualifications of secretaries of public companies

The directors of a public company have a duty to take all reasonable steps to ensure that the secretary of the company is a person who appears to them to have the requisite knowledge and experience to discharge the functions of secretary of the company, and has one or more of the following qualifications:

- they have held the office of secretary of a public company for at least three of the five years immediately preceding their appointment as secretary;
- they are a member of a professional body, such as ICSA or the Institute of Chartered Accountants in England and Wales (ICAEW);
- they are a barrister, advocate or solicitor called or admitted in any part of the United Kingdom; or
- they are a person who, by virtue of their holding or having held any other position or their being a member of any other body, appears to the directors to be capable of discharging the functions of secretary of the company.

2.13 Duty to keep register of secretaries

Companies are required to keep a register of their secretaries. The register must contain the name (and any former name) of the secretary, together with their address. The address that is included within the register may be stated as the company's registered office. If it is the case that the secretary is a corporate secretary, the register of secretaries must contain the name of the company and its registered office.

Inspection of the register of secretaries

The register of secretaries must be kept at the company's registered office. It can be kept at another place, but if so, the company must give notice of the place to the registrar. The register must be open to the inspection by any member of the company without charge, and by any other person on payment of such fee as may be prescribed.

2.14 Liability of the secretary

The company secretary may be liable with the company director for penalties arising as a result of non-compliance with the Companies Act 2006.

2.15 Duties of the secretary

The company secretary's duties may include:

- registrar functions, including the maintenance of the statutory registers of the company and the issuance of share certificates;
- filing certain documents with the Registrar of Companies (e.g. the company's annual return);
- coordinating and attending meetings of the directors and of the company;
- preparation of meeting agendas and notices for meetings, the recording of draft minutes during meetings and preparation of the final version of the minutes for consideration after a meeting;
- ensuring that the meetings of the company are quorate and conducted in accordance with the Companies Act 2006 and the articles of association; and
- ensuring the company meets the requirements of the Companies Act 2006 and any other relevant requirements (e.g. those of the stock exchange).

Test yourself 14.4

State three duties of a company secretary.

2.16 Powers of the secretary

The secretary's signature is, on occasion, a valid alternative to a director's signature. They may therefore sign documentation such as the annual return of the company on behalf of the company. In addition, the secretary may sign as an alternative to a second director when new share certificates are issued.

The company secretary has apparent (ostensible) authority to sign a wide range of documentation on behalf of the company. The secretary may sign bank documentation such as bank account opening forms.

2.17 Auditors

The role of the auditor is to report to the members of the company. The report usually expresses an opinion as to whether the financial statements of the company have been prepared in accordance with the requirements of the Companies Act 2006 and other relevant legislation. The report must also state that the company's financial statements give a true and fair view of the company's finances (if this is the case).

All companies, except those that are exempt or dormant (as defined under the Companies Act 2006) must appoint an auditor. Private companies may resolve not to appoint an auditor if they reasonably resolve that audited accounts are unlikely to be required.

In offshore centres, most private companies will not require the appointment of an auditor.

2.18 Appointment of an auditor

The directors may appoint an auditor of the company:

- at any time before the company's first period for appointing auditors;
- following a period which the company did not have an auditor any time before the company's next period for appointing auditors; and
- to fill a casual vacancy in the office of auditor.

The members may appoint an auditor by ordinary resolution:

- during a period for appointing auditors; and
- if the directors should have appointed an auditor but failed to do so.

2.19 Duties of the auditor

The main duty of the auditor is to report to the members on the financial statements of the company. The auditor should perform their duties with due skill and care.

In order to prepare their report, the auditor has a duty to carry out such investigations that will enable them to give their opinion. If they are unable to do this, they must state in their report that this is the case.

2.20 Auditor's rights

The auditor has a general right to access the company's books, accounts and vouchers at all times. They may also require certain officers of the company to provide them with information or explanation as they think necessary for the performance of their duties. The auditor is entitled to receive all notices of and other communications relating to any general meeting, which a member of a company is entitled to receive. The auditor is also entitled to attend any general meeting of the company and to speak in their capacity as the auditor at any general meeting.

The duties of the auditor are owed to the company, not to its directors, members or creditors. For the auditors to be in a position to fulfil their duties to the company and members as a body, they must be independent and not otherwise involved with the company or its directors, although they may also be engaged by a private company to provide advice and/or consultancy services.

In some jurisdictions, notably Jersey, auditors may only audit regulated businesses such as trust companies if they themselves meet certain specified criteria.

Test yourself 14.5

State the ways in which an auditor may be appointed to a company.

3. Advantages and disadvantages of using a company

When considering the advantages and disadvantages of a company, it is useful to bear in mind the position of an individual who is operating a business in their own right (referred to as a sole trader). The following summarises the position of a sole trader.

- A sole trader carries all of the risks and responsibilities of the business and is entitled to all of the profits and rewards.
- A sole trader has complete control of the business.
- A sole trader has minimum information disclosure requirements.
- If a sole trader were to die, their business would be affected by their death and his assets would be distributed in accordance with their will or the rules of intestacy.

3.1 Advantages of using a company

The advantages of a company stem from its features and include the following.

- The shareholders' liability is limited, offering protection from creditors to all shareholders.
- Perpetual succession means that the business would carry on as usual regardless of the circumstances of its owners and directors.
- Raising finance may be easier as the company may have an increased borrowing ability.

- Shares are easily transferable, enabling ultimate control of the underlying assets to change without having to go through formalities such as those required if the underlying asset is land.
- Zero or low tax rates where an offshore company is concerned.

In addition, companies may facilitate arrangements that would otherwise not be possible. For example, if the laws of a jurisdiction do not allow local property to be owned by a trust, the trust could instead purchase shares in a company and the company in turn could acquire the property.

3.2 Disadvantages of a company

The main disadvantage of a company is the cost involved, arising from the additional administration and record keeping requirements as well as the need to appoint and remunerate one or more directors. There is a cost payable to the government to set up the company; if a company service provider is involved, they will charge for the provision of their services in creating the company and on an ongoing basis (e.g. for the formation of the company, their appointment as directors, secretary and nominee shareholders, and for the provision of general administration).

The requirement to disclose information about the company may be another disadvantage. The extent of disclosure of information depends upon the type of company and the jurisdiction in which it is incorporated.

Companies are subject to regulation and must comply with the requirements of the Companies Act 2006 and any other applicable requirements, such as those of the London Stock Exchange if the company is listed.

4. Types of companies

Companies may be private or public. The shares of a public company may also be (but are not necessarily) quoted on a recognised stock exchange, in which case it is known as a quoted public company.

4.1 Private companies

The Companies Act 2006 defines a private company as 'a company that is not a public company'. Private limited companies can be identified as such because they are required to have the word 'limited' or the abbreviation 'ltd' included at the end of their name. Private companies are not permitted to offer their shares for sale to the public.

The legal requirements relating to private companies are less onerous than those of public companies. For example, private companies may operate with a sole director, whereas public companies must have at least two directors.

Private companies are not required to have a company secretary whereas a public company must have one. Most of the companies administered in offshore centres are private companies.

4.2 Public companies

A company is a public company if its **certificate of incorporation** states that it is. Public companies can be identified as such because they are required to have the words 'public limited company' or the abbreviation 'Plc' included at the end of their name.

certificate of incorporation
A document issued by the Registrar of Companies that is conclusive evidence that a company is duly registered.

There are two major differences between public and private companies.

1. Unlike a private company, a public company may issue its shares to the public.
2. A public company must have an **issued share capital** of £50,000, at least 25% of which must be fully paid up. The meaning of the term 'paid up' share capital is discussed further in section 9.1 of Chapter 15.

issued share capital
The nominal value of shares that have actually been issued to members of the company.

The laws applicable to public companies are more onerous than those governing private companies, as public companies have the ability to offer their shares to the public. Public companies must have at least two directors, at least one of whom must be a natural person (i.e. not a corporate director). The company secretary must also be suitably qualified – for example, they may be a member of ICSA.

Test yourself 14.6

State the two main differences between a public company and a private company.

4.3 Listed and quoted companies

Public companies may choose to list their shares for trading on the London Stock Exchange (the shares of such companies may then be referred to as listed companies) or they may choose to have their shares quoted on any other recognised investment exchange (the shares of such companies are referred to as quoted shares).

The Companies Act 2006 defines a 'quoted company' as a company whose equity share capital:

- has been included in the official list;
- is officially listed in an EU member state; and
- is admitted to dealing on either the New York Stock Exchange or the exchange known as NASDAQ (National Association of Securities Dealers Automated Quotations).

The FCA, in its capacity as the United Kingdom's Listing Authority or UKLA, maintains 'the official list'. Companies that choose to be listed must meet the strict requirements of the relevant stock exchange in addition to those of the company law.

4.4 Limited liability companies

memorandum of association
A short document that evidences the subscribers' intention to form a company under the legislation and that they agree to become members of the company.

A company is a 'limited company' if the liability of its members is limited by its constitution (its **memorandum of association** and articles of association). Companies may be limited by shares or limited by guarantee.

As explained in section 1.3, the maximum amount that a shareholder can be called upon to pay in the event that a limited liability company goes into insolvent liquidation is the amount that the shareholder owed to the company by way of their unpaid shares.

Companies that are limited by guarantee are discussed in section 4.6. The shareholders of a limited liability company cannot otherwise be liable to pay for its debts.

Test yourself 14.7

What is meant by a company being described as having 'limited liability'?

4.5 Unlimited companies

If the constitution of the company does not limit the liability of its members, the company is an 'unlimited company'.

Unlimited companies differ from limited liability companies as the liability of the shareholders is unlimited. These companies are not nearly as common as those that offer limited liability. However, the disclosure requirements are lower than those of limited liability companies in certain jurisdictions, and this is attractive to some individuals.

4.6 Companies limited by guarantee

The liability of the members of companies limited by guarantee is limited to the amount that the members undertake by guarantee to contribute to the assets of the company in the event that it is wound up.

A company that is formed as a company limited by guarantee does not usually have share capital. Instead, the constitution of the company provides that the members of the company undertake to contribute a fixed amount to the capital of the company in the event of its winding up.

Companies limited by guarantee are usually used by charitable or not-for-profit organisations. They are not commonly used in offshore centres.

Test yourself 14.8

What is a company that is limited by guarantee?

4.7 Protected cell companies

Guernsey was at the forefront of the development of protected cell companies (PCCs) in the late 1990s. The motivation behind this was to bring captive insurance work to Guernsey. The Isle of Man and the Cayman Islands both introduced PCC legislation, based on the Guernsey product, while the Jersey model slightly differs.

The key principle behind PCCs is that the assets and liabilities of a cell can be segregated, ring-fencing them. This means that the assets of a cell should only be available to creditors and shareholders of that particular cell.

Each cell has its own constitution and members. A person is not a member of a PCC by virtue of being a member of a cell. The legislation could require that the directors, secretary and registered office of the cells are the same as those of the PCC. Guernsey, for example, imposes this requirement whereas Jersey allows the directors of the PCC to differ from those of the cell. The constitution ensures that the PCC retains ultimate control of the cells.

Protected cells do not have their own legal personality. When a PCC wishes to contract, it does so by the PCC acting on its behalf. In some jurisdictions, such as Jersey, cells are treated as though they are a company for all other aspects of company law; for example, each cell must file an annual return as if it were a legal person. The PCC is responsible for the upkeep of each of its cells.

Many offshore centres limit the use of PCCs. Typically, they may only be used in collective investment funds, insurance and securitisation structures. Jersey does not limit the use of PCCs.

PCCs are a popular vehicle in the captive insurance industry as they enable different insurers and classes of investors to benefit from shared overhead costs without losing protection from insolvency of the other cells.

PCCs are attractive vehicles for use in 'umbrella fund' investment schemes and collective investment funds. Using a PCC, a framework can be established that includes all of the participants (manager, administrators and custodians). The documentation, once in place, can then easily be replicated upon the creation of a new cell. In addition, for those PCCs that require regulatory consent, this can be obtained in respect of one arrangement; obtaining regulatory approval for further cells is a simplified matter. This ability to replicate a structure creates a clear commercial advantage.

4.8 Incorporated cell companies

Incorporated cells are a newer type of cell company whereby each 'incorporated cell' has its own separate legal identity. This makes it simpler for each cell to enter into contracts. It also gives investors in jurisdictions unfamiliar with the concept of protected cells the comfort that their assets are ring-fenced adequately.

Test yourself 14.9

What is a protected cell company?

Chapter summary

- A company comes into existence when it is incorporated by law.
- A company is a separate legal person that is not owned by its shareholders. The shareholders own the shares of the company and possess contractual rights to a proportionate share of company profits and enjoy voting rights as set out in the company's articles of association.
- A company is managed and controlled by its directors.
- The main features of a company include a separate legal personality, limited liability of the shareholders, perpetual succession and confidentiality.
- The liability of the shareholder of a company is limited to the amount that the shareholder owes by way of unpaid shares (if the company has a share capital) or to the amount that the member undertook to contribute to the company in the event that it is wound up (if the company is limited by guarantee).
- A company has a separate legal personality to that of its shareholders and controllers (directors). The separation of the legal personality is known as the veil of incorporation.
- The company will continue to exist until it is dissolved by law. Its existence is not dependent upon its members or controllers whose death or incapacity does not affect the perpetual succession of the company.
- Any person who agrees to become a member of a company and whose name is entered into its register of members is a member of the company. The first members are referred to as the subscribers. The members do not owe a fiduciary duty to the company.
- Members have the right to attend and vote at general meetings (unless the shares are non-voting shares), the right to transfer their shares to others (although there may be **pre-emption rights**), the right to inspect the register of members and the minutes of the general meetings, the right to receive copies of the financial statements and the right to receive their share in the surplus of any assets at the time the company is wound up.

pre-emption right
The right of existing members to be offered the shares in the company for sale whenever a member wishes to sell their shares, before they are offered to non-members.

- The Companies Act 2006 describes a director as 'any person occupying the position of a director, by whatever name called'. The directors act as the mind and management of the business. The directors owe a fiduciary duty to the company.

- *De jure* directors are those who have been properly appointed to the company. *De facto* directors are persons who have not been properly appointed; however, they act as if they are directors and therefore fall within the Companies Act 2006 definition. A shadow director is defined separately within the Companies Act 2006 and is a person in accordance with whose directions or instructions the directors of the company are accustomed to act.
- The articles of a company may provide for the directors to appoint an alternate director to attend directors' meetings on their behalf when they are unable to attend.
- Executive directors are those who are involved with the day-to-day running of the company. Non-executive directors are those who are not involved with the day-to-day running of the company and as such are able to bring an independent view on matters arising within the company. The statutory duties and obligations of a director apply equally to both executive and non-executive directors.
- In some jurisdictions, companies may also be appointed to act as a director. If this is the case, they are referred to as corporate directors.
- The office of a director may be terminated by retirement, removal, resignation, death, disqualification or any provision contained within the company's articles of association.
- Directors' powers are derived from the articles of association of the company and from the company's legislation. The Companies Act 2006 sets out general duties of a director and includes a duty to: act within their powers; promote the success of the company; exercise independent judgement; act with reasonable care, skill and diligence; avoid conflicts of interest; not accept benefits from third parties; and declare an interest in a proposed transaction or arrangement.
- Public companies must have a company secretary who is suitably qualified and experienced to discharge their functions. Private companies need not have a secretary. The duties of a company secretary may include registrar functions, the filing of statutory returns, attendance at meetings of the company and ensuring that any such meetings are quorate and conducted in accordance with the articles of association.
- The role of the auditor is to report to the members of the company, expressing an opinion as to whether the financial statements of the company represent a true and fair view of the company's finance.
- The advantages of a company include limited liability, perpetual succession, increased ability to raise finance and transferability.
- Disadvantages of using a company include the cost, administration and record keeping obligations as well as disclosure requirements.
- Companies may be private or public. Public companies may offer their shares for sale to the public, while private companies may not.

- The liability of the shareholders of limited companies is limited while the shareholders of unlimited liability companies do not benefit from limited liability.
- Protected cell companies (PCCs) offer segregation of assets and liabilities by ring-fencing them in cells, making them available only to the creditors of that cell. Cells do not have a separate legal personality, and it is therefore the PCC that enters into contracts on behalf of the company.
- Incorporated Cell Companies are a newer type of cell company whereby each cell has its own separate legal personality.

Test yourself answers

Test yourself 14.1

The Companies Act 2006 requires that a private company must have at least one director.

Test yourself 14.2

a) A person may be referred to as a *de facto* director in situations where they have not been formally appointed as a director but nevertheless fulfil that role. The Companies Act 2006 defines a shadow director as a person in accordance with whose directions or instructions the directors of the company are accustomed to act.

b) The articles of a company may provide for the directors to appoint an alternate director to attend directors' meetings on their behalf when they are unable to attend. The alternate director has the power to vote at the meeting in place of the elected director. Alternate directors are responsible for their own acts and are not deemed to act on behalf of the director who appointed them.

Test yourself 14.3

Three general duties of a director include:

- the duty to act within powers;
- the duty to promote the success of the company; and
- the duty to exercise independent judgement.

Test yourself 14.4

Three duties of the company secretary include:

- registrar functions including the maintenance of the statutory registers of the company and the issuance of share certificates;
- filing certain documents with the Registrar of Companies (e.g. the company's annual return); and
- coordinating and attending meetings of the directors and of the company.

Test yourself 14.5

The directors may appoint an auditor of the company at any time before the company's first period for appointing auditors, following a period which the company did not have an auditor any time before the company's next period for appointing auditors; and to fill a casual vacancy in the office of auditor.

The members may appoint an auditor by ordinary resolution during a period for appointing auditors and if the directors should have appointed an auditor but failed to do so.

Test yourself 14.6

There are two major differences between public and private companies.

1. Unlike a private company, a public company may issue its shares to the public.
2. A public company must have an issued share capital of £50,000, at least 25% of which must be fully paid up.

Test yourself 14.7

A company is a 'limited company' if the liability of its members is limited by its constitution (i.e. its memorandum of association and articles of association). Companies may be limited by shares or limited by guarantee.

Where a company is a limited liability company, the maximum amount that a shareholder can be called upon to pay in the event that a limited liability company goes into insolvent liquidation due to their shareholding is the amount that the shareholder owed to the company by way of any unpaid shares. The shareholders of a limited liability company cannot otherwise be liable to pay for its debts.

Test yourself 14.8

The liability of the members of companies that are limited by guarantee is limited to the amount that the members undertake to contribute to the assets of the company in the event that it is wound up.

A company that is formed as a company limited by guarantee does not usually have share capital. Instead, the constitution of the company provides that the members of the company undertake to contribute a fixed amount to the capital of the company in the event of its winding up.

Test yourself 14.9

The key principle behind PCCs is that the assets and liabilities of a cell can be segregated, ring-fencing them. This means that the assets of a cell should only be available to creditors and members of that cell. Each cell has its own constitution and members. A person is not a member of a PCC by virtue of being a member of a cell.

Cells of a PCC do not have their own legal personality. When a protected cell wishes to contract, it does so by the PCC acting on its behalf. In some jurisdictions, such as Jersey, cells are treated as though they are a company for all other aspects of company law (e.g. each cell must file an annual return as if it were a legal person). The PCC is responsible for the upkeep of each of its cells.

Chapter fifteen
Company incorporation

List of topics

1. Company incorporation procedures
2. The company name
3. Memorandum of association
4. Articles of association
5. Application for registration
6. Statement of compliance
7. Trading certificate
8. Post-incorporation procedures
9. Shares and share capital
10. Registered office
11. The common seal of the company

Introduction

This chapter outlines the main steps involved when forming a company under the Companies Act 2006 and explains alternative methods of incorporating a company such as the use of shelf companies.

The chapter explains the requirement for a company name, describes the purpose of the memorandum and articles of association, and outlines some of the main clauses found in model articles. It then explains some of the post incorporation documents, such as the receipt of the certificate of incorporation, the holding of the **inaugural meeting** and the updating of the statutory registers.

Share capital and what is meant by terms such as authorised share capital and issued share capital are explained, as is the difference between **par value companies** and no par value companies. Finally, the chapter outlines various types of shares such as **ordinary shares** and **preference shares**, as well as bearer shares.

inaugural meeting
The first meeting of the directors.

par value company
A company registered with a share capital and shares that are expressed as having a nominal value.

ordinary shares
A share of equity ownership in a company that entitles the holder to vote and receive a dividend (if one is paid), after a dividend has been paid to preference shareholders.

preference shares
A share that does not usually have value rights and receives a dividend prioritised over ordinary shareholders and usually at a fixed percentage.

1. Company incorporation procedures

A company is formed under the Companies Act 2006 by one or more persons subscribing their names to a memorandum of association and complying with the requirements of the Companies Act 2006 as to registration.

The first step towards incorporating a company is to check the availability and acceptability of the company name with Companies House. The main functions of Companies House include:

- incorporating and dissolving limited companies;
- examining and storing company information delivered under the Companies Act 2006 and related legislation; and
- making this information available to the public.

The process of forming (incorporating) a company then involves delivering the following documentation to Companies House:

- the application form for the incorporation of a company;
- the registration of the memorandum of association;
- a copy of the articles of association, if the company has not accepted the model articles;
- a statement of compliance; and
- the relevant fee.

If the documentation is deemed acceptable, the registrar will proceed to incorporate the company and will issue a certificate of incorporation. These steps are described in more detail later in this chapter. A company may not be formed for an illegal purpose.

Test yourself 15.1

Identify the main steps when incorporating a company.

1.1 Fast incorporations

Companies House provides a same-day incorporation service for a higher fee than would be charged for an ordinary incorporation. Similar services are available in offshore centres.

Jurisdictions such as Jersey now offer 'fast track' incorporations, which means that a company could be incorporated within two hours. Guernsey can offer incorporations within 15 minutes where the purpose of the company is a simple asset-holding company and where the standard memorandum and articles are used.

1.2 Shelf companies

Service providers make shelf companies available in some offshore centres, such as the British Virgin Islands. These are companies that have already been incorporated by the service provider and are therefore instantly available. The service provider, when approached for a shelf company, simply resigns as a director of the company in favour of the person requesting a company and transfers any shares held.

1.3 Reserved companies

Jersey allows the creation of reserved companies. These are incorporated by service providers and the Registrar of Companies is advised that the company will be transferred to a client within the next six months. At this point, the service provider must advise the registry of the identity of the beneficial owner.

2. The company name

The availability of the desired company name should be checked against the register of names held by the Registrar of Companies before applying to incorporate a company. The Registrar of Companies is appointed by the Secretary of State for Business, Innovation and Skills (BIS) and performs all of the functions conferred upon the Registrar by the Companies Act 2006. The registrar for England and Wales is based at Companies House in Cardiff.

The registrar will refuse to register a company with a name in certain circumstances, for example:

- there is an existing company with the same name or a very similar name;
- the name does not contain the words limited, public limited company or unlimited at the end of the name;
- the name is offensive; or
- the use of the name would be a criminal offence.

In the UK, the Secretary for State has designated certain words as 'sensitive' and these may only be used within a company name if the prior consent of the Secretary for State has been obtained. The Companies House guidance on 'Incorporation and Names', available via their website (see Directory of web resources on page 413 for a list of sensitive words and expressions to avoid.

It is not possible to reserve a company name prior to the incorporation of the company for future use in the UK. However, most offshore jurisdictions do allow company names to be reserved for a maximum period. There is usually no charge for doing so, although some jurisdictions may charge if a company name is reserved again after the maximum reservation period.

3. Memorandum of association

A memorandum of association is a short document (usually only a page) that proves the subscribers' intention to form a company under the Companies Act 2006, as well as stating that they agree to become members of the company. In the case of a company that will have a share capital, the memorandum records their agreement to take at least one share each.

The memorandum for many companies formed prior to the Companies Act 2006 in the UK and companies formed today in offshore jurisdictions whose legislation is largely based upon the UK's previous legislation (the Companies Act 1985) is likely to contain:

- the name of the company;
- the location of the company's registered office;
- the objects of the company;
- a statement that the liability of the members is limited (if this is the case);
- the amount of the company's authorised share capital and a statement that the capital is divided into shares of a stated amount; and
- a statement that the company is a public company (if this is the case).

objects clause
A clause within the memorandum of a company that, prior to the introduction of the Companies Act 2006, restricted the activities of a company to those contained within the clause.

ultra vires
The doctrine of *ultra vires* meant that the activity of a company would be void if the company was not authorised to undertake the activity if it was not specified within the objects clause.

Prior to the introduction of the Companies Act 2006, all companies were required to have 'objects' which were to be specified in the memorandum of association. Companies were limited to acting within the objects of the company. The **objects clause** could run into several pages and listed many potential activities in order to ensure that the company could undertake a wide range of activities. If a company undertook an activity that was not included within its objects clause the act would be ***ultra vires*** (i.e. outside of the company's powers) and void. The Companies Act 2006 provides that unless a company's articles specifically restrict the objects of the company, its objects are unrestricted.

The doctrine of *ultra vires* in its application to companies has been abolished in many offshore centres. Accordingly, the capacity of a company is not usually limited by anything in its memorandum or articles, although the memorandum of many older companies will still contain such a clause.

Test yourself 15.2

Under the Companies Act 2006, what is the purpose of the memorandum of association?

4. Articles of association

A company must have articles of association, which are sometimes referred to as the internal regulations of the company. They are concerned with how the company should be managed by its directors and set out the voting and other rights of members.

If the company does not adopt the model articles discussed in section 4.1, it must register articles of association. The articles must be contained in a single document and be divided into paragraphs numbered consecutively.

Section 33 of the Companies Act 2006 states that the company's constitution binds the company and its members as though they had individually covenanted to obey their provisions. The articles of association therefore constitute a contract between the company and its members, as well as between the members themselves.

4.1 Model articles

A company may create its own articles of association and submit those at the time of incorporation, or it may choose to adopt the model articles created by the Companies Act 2006. Separate sets of model articles are available for private and public companies limited by shares and companies limited by guarantee. The model articles may be adapted entirely or partly, or may be excluded entirely.

The model articles created under the previous companies legislation in the UK (e.g. the Companies Act 1985) were referred to as the 'Table A' articles. Many offshore centres have their own model articles (e.g. Jersey's are referred to as 'the Standard Table').

The 2006 model articles for a private company limited by shares contain clauses covering:

- administrative arrangements;
- appointment of directors;
- capitalisation of profits;
- decision making by directors;
- directors' indemnity and insurance;
- directors' powers and responsibilities;
- dividends and other distributions;
- the liability of members;
- organisation of general meetings;
- shares; and
- voting at general meetings.

Test yourself 15.3

State five clauses that are found within the model articles under the Companies Act 2006.

The 2006 model articles for a private company limited by shares are reproduced in Appendix 2.

5. Application for registration

The application form contains information required by the registrar in order to form the company. It must state information such as:

- the company's proposed name;
- the address of the registered office;
- whether the liability of the members of the company is to be limited and, if so, whether it is to be limited by shares or by guarantee;
- whether the company is to be a private or a public company;
- names and particulars of the directors;
- names and particulars of the secretary;
- details of the extent that the model articles were adopted;
- details of the share capital; and
- details of the subscribers (the first members and shareholders).

6. Statement of compliance

A statement of compliance confirming that the requirements of the Companies Act 2006 have been complied with must accompany the application for the incorporation of a company.

7. Trading certificate

If the company is a public company, an application must be made for (and the company in receipt of) a trading certificate from the registrar before it may commence business or exercise any borrowing powers.

nominal value
This is the amount shown on a share certificate and is also the par value of the shares.

The registrar will usually issue a trading certificate following such an application if they are satisfied that the **nominal value** of the company's allotted share capital is not less than the authorised minimum share capital requirement.

Test yourself 15.4

State three pieces of information that must be included on the application for the registration of a company.

8. Post-incorporation procedures

Upon incorporation, the directors of a company will need to:

- hold an inaugural meeting;
- issue the share certificates;
- update the register of members; and
- update the register of directors.

In the offshore environment, company administrators may need to:

- prepare declarations of trust in respect of nominee shareholdings;
- prepare share certificates;
- order a company seal (if one is required); and
- prepare letters of acceptance for signature by the directors and the secretary accepting their positions.

8.1 Certificate of incorporation

If the registrar is satisfied that the documents are acceptable, they will issue a certificate of incorporation. The certificate of incorporation includes:

- the name and registered number of the company;
- the date of its incorporation;
- whether it is a limited or unlimited company and, if it is limited whether it is limited by shares or by guarantee;
- whether it is a private or a public company; and
- whether the company's registered office is situated in England and Wales (or just in Wales), in Scotland or in Northern Ireland.

The certificate must be signed by the registrar or authenticated by the registrar's official seal. Once issued, the certificate is conclusive evidence that company is duly registered.

8.2 Inaugural meeting

The directors of the company will then proceed to hold their inaugural meeting at which a number of important matters are discussed. These matters may include, but are not limited to:

- appointment of first directors;
- appointment of the chairman of the board (if there is one);
- appointment of the company's auditors;
- appointment of the company's bankers;
- appointment of the company's solicitors;
- appointment of the secretary (if there is one);
- the adoption of the company seal (if there is one);
- adoption of an authorised signatory list;
- allotment or transfer of shares;
- the certificate of incorporation;
- change of the accounting reference dates; and
- noting or changing of the registered office.

There may be a requirement to inform the taxation authorities of the incorporation of the company.

8.3 The register of members

The Companies Act 2006 requires every company to maintain a register of members. This should be kept at the registered office of the company although the Companies Act 2006 does provide for it to be held elsewhere as long as the Registrar of Companies is informed of its location. The register of members must contain:

- the names and addresses of the members;
- the date on which each person was registered as a member;
- the date at which any person ceased to be a member; and
- the shares held by each member, distinguishing each share by its number (if it has one) and by its class if the company has more than one class of issued shares.

The register must also record the amount paid or agreed to be considered as paid on the shares of each member.

In the case of joint holders of shares, the company's register of members must state the names of each joint holder, although they are otherwise regarded as single members.

In the case of a limited liability company with only one member, a statement must be included on the register of members that the company only has one member.

The Companies Act 2006 states that no notice of any trust – expressed, implied or constructive – shall be entered on the register of members of a company.

Inspection of the register of members

Under the Companies Act 2006, a company's register of members must be available for inspection at the registered office or another place that has been notified to the registrar. The register must be open to inspection by any member of the company without charge and by any other person on payment of a fee. Any person may require a copy.

Nominee shareholders

The requirement for the register of members to be available for inspection is a key reason that the use of nominee shareholders to participate as members of the company has become common practice. The current clamour for registers of beneficial ownership of companies to be available for public inspection may bring pressure to bear on exposing or revealing for whom a nominee shareholder is acting as a nominee.

8.4 Register of directors

The Companies Act 2006 states that every company must keep a register of its directors. The register must contain the following information in respect of each person who is a director of the company:

- name and any former name;
- a service address;
- the country or state (or part of the United Kingdom) in which they are usually resident;
- nationality;
- business occupation (if any); and
- date of birth.

Where the director is a corporate director, the register of members must contain the name of the company and the address of its registered office.

Test yourself 15.5

State five pieces of information that a register of directors must contain.

Inspection of the register of directors

The register of directors must be kept at the company's registered office. It may be kept at another location; if so the Registrar of Companies must be informed of the location of the register.

Making it work 15.1

Declaration of trust

The following is an example of the types of wording that is commonly used within a declaration of trust in connection with a nominee shareholding.

DECLARATION OF TRUST

We, ...[Name of trustee]..................of ....[address of trustee] HEREBY ACKNOWLEDGE and declare that we hold the share shown in the schedule hereto registered in our name as Nominee of and Trustee for ......[Name of beneficial owner]......... (hereinafter called 'the owner') and we undertake and agree not to transfer, deal with or dispose of the said share or any of them except as the owner may from time to time direct.

We further undertake and agree to account to the owner for all dividends and profits which may be paid to us from time to time in connection with the share shown in the schedule and for all other money or profit which may be payable to us in respect thereof.

We further undertake and agree to exercise our voting power as holder of the share in such a manner and for such purposes as the owner may from time to time direct or determine.

The schedule 1 Ordinary share of GBP1 each (share certificate number 1) in the limited liability company known as ......[Name of Company] Limited...

Signed for and on behalf of [Name of nominee shareholder]

9. Shares and share capital

9.1 Share capital

The share capital of a company is the money provided to it by its members in return for shares in the company. Membership of the company is signified by the ownership of shares in the company and evidenced by the recording of the shareholder's name on the register of shareholders maintained on behalf of the company.

It is a common misconception that the members (or shareholders) are the owners of the company. A person who owns shares in a company does not own a part of the assets or capital of the company, but only owns his/her shares.

The shares provide their owner with a contractual entitlement to a proportional share of the future profits of the company, and voting and other rights as set out in the articles of association and a proportionate share of any net proceeds following liquidation of the company.

A person who is the registered holder of shares in a company may also be referred to as a member or a shareholder of the company as these terms are used interchangeably.

Authorised share capital

par value
The nominal value of a share.

The authorised share capital is the amount of share capital that the company is authorised to issue by its memorandum. The authorised share capital is usually expressed in terms of the nominal value. The nominal value (also referred to as the **par value**) represents the face value of each share and is the amount of funds that the shareholder is required to contribute to the assets of the company. The nominal value does not give an accurate indication of how much a shareholder actually paid for the shares, as shares may be issued at a premium to their nominal value. Neither does the nominal value of a company's share capital give an accurate indication of what the company shares are actually worth (i.e. their market value). The nominal value of shares does not therefore fluctuate in the same way that the market value of the shares could.

In offshore centres, it is very common for the authorised share capital to be £10,000, divided into 10,000 shares of £1 each. The £1 is said to be the nominal or par value of each share.

Issued share capital

The issued share capital is the nominal value of shares that actually have been issued to the members of the company. For example, if 10,000 shares of £1 each have been issued, the issued share capital is £10,000. The shareholder may not have paid up the £10,000 in full.

Called-up share capital

The Companies Act 2006 states that the **called-up share capital** is:

- the aggregate amount of the calls made on its shares (whether or not those calls have been paid);
- any share capital that has been paid up without being called; and
- any share capital to be paid up on a specified date in the articles.

called-up share capital
The value of the issued shares that remain unpaid and whose holders have been called upon to pay for the shares.

Paid-up share capital

Paid-up share capital is the part of the issued share capital of a company that has actually been paid for. In the example given above, if a shareholder had only paid the sum of 50p in respect of each £1 share, the paid-up capital would be £5,000. The members would owe the company the remaining 50p per share. If the company were wound up, the member would be required to pay this unpaid amount to the company.

paid-up share capital
The amount of the issued share capital of a company that has actually been paid for.

The amount of share capital that the member has not yet been paid for is the uncalled capital. This is the maximum amount that the shareholder may be asked to contribute if the company should go into liquidation.

Test yourself 15.6

What is the difference between issued and authorised share capital?

Par value companies

Par value companies are registered with a share capital and have shares that are expressed as having a nominal value.

No par value companies

In some jurisdictions, including Jersey, it is possible to form 'no par value companies'. Such companies are formed with 'no par value' shares. The characteristics of companies with no par value shares are as follows.

- The memorandum states that it is a no par value company.
- The company is registered with shares that are not expressed as having a nominal or par value.
- The shares are not denominated in any currency.
- The number of authorised no par value shares may be unlimited.
- They may also have a guarantor.

Whereas sums paid up on par value shares are paid to the nominal share capital account and a share premium account, with a no par value, shares are credited to a company's 'stated capital account' instead.

A key advantage of no par value shares is that the procedure for redeeming or repurchasing shares is simplified.

Test yourself 15.7

What is a par value company?

9.2 Types of shares

A company may, subject to its articles, issue different types of shares, with differing rights and obligations.

The model articles, for example, permit different types of shares to be issued following an ordinary resolution. The types of shares are referred to as classes of shares. Different classes of shares have different rights in relation to voting, rights to return of capital and rights to receive dividends, to name just a few.

Ordinary shares

Where a company has only one class of share, the shares will be ordinary shares. Ordinary shareholders have the right to vote at the general meetings of the company and the right to receive a dividend (if one is paid) out of distributable profits.

Shareholders with preference shares will be paid a dividend as a priority over the ordinary shareholders. The ordinary shareholders are also paid after preference shareholders in the event of winding up the company.

Preference shares

Preference shares do not usually have the right to vote at the general meetings of the company. Preference shares usually have the right to a dividend of a fixed percentage of distributable profits.

Redeemable shares

redeemable shares
A type of share that may be repurchased by the company at a future date

A limited liability company may issue **redeemable shares** if its articles permit it. This means that the shares can be redeemed by the company at a specified date in the future.

UK companies that have adopted the model articles may issue shares which are to be redeemed, or are liable to be redeemed at the option of the company or the holder. The directors may determine the terms, conditions and manner of redemption of any such shares.

A company must also have non-redeemable shares if it issues redeemable shares. This provision is to ensure that there is always at least one member of the company.

Bearer shares

Bearer shares are considered to be owned by 'the bearer' (i.e. whoever has them in their possession). Cash is an example of a bearer instrument. Such shares are no longer common in offshore jurisdictions as they present a high level of risk to offshore service providers. This is because any customer due diligence undertaken is rendered useless the moment the shares change hands.

9.3 Transferability of shares

Members are usually able to transfer their shares freely although pre-emption rights may be granted to existing members. A pre-emption right is the right to be offered the shares in the company for sale whenever a member wishes to sell or otherwise transfer their shares before they are offered to non-members for sale.

The Companies Act 2006 model articles provide that shares may be transferred by means of an instrument of transfer in any usual form or any other form approved by the directors. This is executed by or on behalf of the transferor and the transferor remains the holder of a share until the transferee's name is entered in the register of members as holder of it.

Test yourself 15.8

What is a bearer share?

9.4 Share certificates

The Companies Act 2006 states that a share certificate, issued under the common seal of the company, specifying any shares held by a member is **prima facie evidence** of their title to the shares stated on the certificate.

prima facie evidence
'On the face of it' evidence.

The model articles provide that a company must issue each shareholder with one or more certificates free of charge in respect of the shares which that shareholder holds. Each share certificate must specify:

- in respect of how many shares, of what class, it is issued;
- the nominal value of those shares;
- that the shares are fully paid; and
- any distinguishing numbers assigned to them.

No certificate may be issued in respect of shares of more than one class. If more than one person holds a share, only one certificate may be issued in respect of it.

Paper share certificates are becoming much less common, being largely replaced in favour of 'dematerialised' shares. These are an entry on an electronic register of members maintained by the person or body charged with maintaining the register.

9.5 Dividends

One of the main reasons why members invest in a company is for the opportunity to receive dividends and to participate in the profits of the company. Where a company has sufficient distributable profits, it may make a dividend to its shareholders, providing them with an income. The rule surrounding what constitutes distributable profits will not be covered in depth in this textbook.

However, it should be noted that the companies can only distribute from profits that have actually been realised, not just anticipated profits.

Test yourself 15.9

State three pieces of information that must be specified on a share certificate.

9.6 Share allotments

The first shares are usually issued to the subscribers to the company's memorandum.

Shares may be issued at their nominal value, or they may be issued at a higher cost. If this is the case, the difference in the share price paid and the nominal value of the shares is known as the share premium and is credited to a share premium account.

10. Registered office

A company must have a registered office at all times, to which all communications and legal notices may be addressed.

In some jurisdictions, it is a requirement of companies legislation that the address of the registered office be shown on all correspondence and stationery issued by the company.

10.1 Documentation to be kept at the registered office

The Companies Act 2006 states that certain registers should be maintained and kept available for inspection at the registered office. There are, however, exceptions to this requirement, as the registers may be kept available for inspection at a place that is situated in the part of the UK in which the company is registered, as long as the Registrar of Companies is notified of the address of the alternative inspection location.

It is usual for the following documents to be kept at the registered office:

- certificate of incorporation;
- common seal;
- memorandum and articles of association;
- minute book;
- register of charges;
- register of members;
- register of directors;

- register of secretary; and
- register of sealing.

11. The common seal of the company

The Companies Act 2006 states that a company may have a common seal, but it does not need to have one. If a company does have a common seal, the company must have its name engraved in legible characters on the seal.

While common seals are not required for companies incorporated under the Companies Act 2006 nor under the acts of many offshore jurisdictions, they are still regularly used in offshore jurisdictions. This is partly for cases where the company may enter into business dealings with other jurisdictions that do still require a company seal. It can be simpler to produce a seal than to debate the matter.

The model articles provide that a common seal may only be used on the authority of the directors. Unless otherwise decided by the directors, a company seal that is affixed to a document must also be signed by at least one authorised person in the presence of a witness who attests the signature.

The articles provide that the authorised person may be any director of the company, the company secretary or any person authorised to sign documents to which the common seal is applied.

11.1 The sealing register

Where a seal is in use the company will need to maintain a register of sealing where a company seal is in use.

This sets out the documentation to which the company seal has been applied.

The use of the sealing register has declined to the extent that even where a corporate seal has been adopted, a sealing register is not always maintained.

Chapter summary

- The steps involved in creating a company include checking the availability of the company name, completing and submitting an application for incorporation, registering the memorandum and articles (if the model articles are not to be adopted), submitting a statement of compliance and submitting the documentation with the relevant fee.
- There are alternative ways to form a company that may be useful, particularly if the company is required urgently. These include shelf companies and reserved companies.
- Companies House may refuse to register a company in certain circumstances – for example, when there is an existing company with the same name.

- The memorandum of association proves the subscribers' intent to form a company and that they agree to become the first members.
- The articles of association are the internal regulations of the company. Companies may adopt the model articles created under the Companies Act 2006.
- Upon receipt of the necessary documentation, the registrar will, if it is acceptable, issue a certificate of incorporation.
- A company is required to keep certain statutory registers including a register of members and a register of directors.
- The share capital of a company is the money provided by its members in return for shares in the company.
- Authorised share capital is the amount of share capital that the company is authorised by its memorandum to issue. Issued share capital is the nominal value of shares that have actually been issued to the members of the company.
- Par value companies are registered with a share capital and have shares that are expressed as having a nominal value. No par value companies are formed with shares that are not expressed as having a nominal or par value.
- Different types of shares have different rights and obligations attached to them.
- Ordinary shares have the right to vote at general meetings of the company and a right to receive a dividend (if one is paid). Preference shareholders do not usually have the right to vote at meetings and usually have the right to receive a dividend at a fixed percentage of distributable profits as a priority over ordinary shareholders.
- Shares may be redeemable or irredeemable. Redeemable shares may be redeemed by the company at a specified date in the future.
- Bearer shares are owned by the bearer (i.e. whoever has them in their possession).
- Members are usually able to transfer their shares freely, although pre-emption rights may be granted to existing members.
- A share certificate issued under the common seal of the company is prima facie (on the face of it) evidence of their title to the shares.
- When a company has sufficient distributable profits, the company may pay these to the members by way of a dividend.
- Shares may be issued at their nominal value or they may be issued at a premium.
- A company is required to have a registered office and to maintain certain documentation at the registered office.
- A company may or may not adopt a company seal.

Test yourself answers

Test yourself 15.1

The process of forming (incorporating) a company involves delivering the following documentation to Companies House:

- the application form for the incorporation of a company;
- the registration of the memorandum of association;
- a copy of the articles of association, if the company has not accepted the model articles;
- a statement of compliance; and
- the relevant fee.

If the documentation is deemed acceptable, the registrar will proceed to incorporate the company and will issue a certificate of incorporation.

Test yourself 15.2

A memorandum of association is a short document (usually only a page) that evidences the subscribers' intention to form a company under the Companies Act 2006 and that they agree to become members of the company. In the case of a company that will have a share capital, the memorandum records their agreement to take at least one share each.

Test yourself 15.3

Five clauses that are found within the 2006 model articles for a private company limited by shares cover:

1. appointment of directors;
2. decision making by directors;
3. directors' powers and responsibilities;
4. the liability of members; and
5. organisation of general meetings.

Test yourself 15.4

Three pieces of information that must be included on the application form for the registration of a company are:

1. the company's proposed name;
2. the address of the registered office; and
3. whether the liability of the members of the company is to be limited, and if so, whether it is to be limited by shares or by guarantee.

Test yourself 15.5

Five pieces of information that a register of directors must contain include:

1. the director's name and any former name;
2. a service address;
3. the country or state (or part of the United Kingdom) in which they are usually resident;
4. nationality; and
5. date of birth.

Test yourself 15.6

The issued share capital is the nominal value of shares that have actually been issued to the members of the company. For example, if 10,000 shares of £1 each have been issued, the issued share capital is £10,000.

The authorised share capital is the amount of share capital that the company is authorised by its memorandum to issue. The authorised share capital is usually expressed in terms of the nominal value. The nominal value (also referred to as the par value) represents the face value of each share and is the amount of funds that the shareholder is required to contribute to the assets of the company.

Test yourself 15.7

Par value companies are registered with a share capital and have shares that are expressed as having a nominal value.

Test yourself 15.8

Bearer shares are considered to be owned by 'the bearer' (i.e. whoever has them in their possession). Cash is an example of a bearer instrument.

Test yourself 15.9

Each share certificate must specify:

- in respect of how many shares, of what class, it is issued;
- the nominal value of those shares;
- that the shares are fully paid; and
- any distinguishing numbers assigned to them.

(Only three pieces of information are required by the question.)

Chapter sixteen
Company meetings and resolutions

List of topics

1. Directors' meetings
2. Record keeping
3. General meetings
4. Voting
5. Resolutions
6. Written resolutions of the members

Introduction

This chapter explains the requirements surrounding directors' meetings (board meetings), including the requirement for notice, a **quorum** of directors to be present and the agenda. It discusses the role of the chairman and the requirement for a company to keep minutes and other record keeping.

quorum
The number of members that must be present in order for a meeting to be validly constituted.

The chapter then explains similar matters in respect of general meetings (meetings of the members) and looks at the business conducted at the annual general meeting and the special requirements surrounding these meetings. Finally, the chapter discusses voting and explains the requirements in order to pass ordinary resolutions, including those that require special notice and **special resolutions**.

special resolution
A resolution of the members that must be passed by a majority of not less than 75% of members who are entitled to vote.

1. Directors' meetings

The articles of association usually set out how the board of directors will conduct its meetings. At directors' meetings, each director usually has one vote and decisions are made by the vote of the majority. If the votes of the directors are evenly split, article 13 of the United Kingdom's company law, model articles provides that the chairman has a casting vote in addition to their own vote.

There is no requirement in the legislation for board meetings to be held at any particular frequency. An appropriate frequency of meetings will depend upon the company and the type of business that it conducts – for example, a company that holds a property let on a long-term lease to a reliable tenant is unlikely to require board meetings to be held as frequently as a company that is trading or running a business.

In the offshore environment, it is usual for private companies to conduct board meetings on an ad-hoc basis as and when they are required. Companies undertaking a regulated activity will usually meet on a quarterly basis at the very least.

In large operating companies, the chairman will usually instruct the company secretary to call a board meeting, although any director is entitled to call a board meeting should they wish to do so.

Directors are entitled to reasonable notice of board meetings. What determines reasonable notice will depend upon the business of the company and its activities.

In practice, for private companies administered by professional service providers, the directors will be informed by administrative staff that a business transaction or matter requires a directors' meeting to be held.

1.1 Notice of a directors' meeting

Provisions for notice to be given to the directors of a meeting are set out in the articles of association. The model articles set out that notice of any directors' meeting must:

- indicate its proposed date and time, where it is to take place and, if it is anticipated that directors participating in the meeting will not be in the same place, how it is proposed that they should communicate with each other during the meeting; and
- be given to each director, but need not be in writing.

1.2 The chairman

The duty of the chairman is to manage the meeting, ensure that all participants are able to contribute to the meeting, to ensure that the meeting is focused and that all items on the agenda are discussed in the time allocated for the meeting. It is usual for the chairman of the board (if there is one) to chair meetings of the company. The articles of association usually cover the appointment of the chairman.

For private companies administered by professional service providers In the offshore environment, it is usual to appoint a chairman of the meeting rather than a chairman of the board. The person does not necessarily act as the chairman of each meeting of the company. The minutes of each board meeting should record who was appointed to the position of the chairman.

As noted above, if the votes of the directors are evenly split, article 13 of the model articles provides that the chairman has a casting vote in addition to their own vote.

1.3 The agenda

It is unusual for an agenda to be prepared in offshore centres, where all of the directors for a company administered on behalf of a client are typically provided by a service provider. However, discussions are usually held prior to the meeting about the business that is to be discussed or decided upon.

For all other company board meetings, an agenda will usually be required. The agenda sets out the items to be discussed at the meeting to which it relates (in order of importance). The agenda is usually circulated with any relevant papers prior to the meeting so that all attendees are fully aware of what they can expect to discuss and consider at the meeting.

Items that are regularly included on meeting agendas include:

- apologies for absence;
- approval of the minutes of the last meeting;
- matters arising from the last minutes;
- review of action points arising from the last minutes;
- the business or transaction to be discussed;
- any other business; and
- agreement of the date of the next meeting.

Higher-priority items are usually placed high up on the agenda so that they are discussed and given due consideration, rather than rushed. The chairman will need to ensure that the meeting remains focused on the agenda.

Test yourself 16.1

Identify three items that are typically included on a board meeting agenda.

1.4 Quorum

The quorum is the minimum number of persons necessary to be present at a meeting for the business of the meeting to be transacted. The quorum required in order to hold a board meeting is usually set out in the company's articles of association.

The model articles state that the quorum for a board meeting shall be two, unless otherwise fixed by the directors. Directors with conflicts of interest should not form a part of the quorum of the meeting.

1.5 Resolutions and voting

The procedure in relation to voting at directors' meetings is usually set out in the articles of association. The model articles provide that the general rule about decision making by directors is that decisions must be taken:

- by a majority decision at a meeting or when all eligible directors indicate to each other by any means that they share a common view on a matter;
- when they take the form of a resolution in writing, copies of which have been signed by each director who would have been entitled to vote on the matter if it had been proposed as a resolution at a directors' meeting; or
- where each eligible director has indicated agreement in writing.

Articles of association very often provide for directors to make decisions without holding a meeting if they are unanimous. The model articles provide that a resolution in writing, signed by all of the directors entitled to vote at a meeting, shall be as valid and effective as if it had been duly passed at a meeting.

A resolution may be proposed as a written resolution by the directors or the members of a private company. Under the Companies Act 2006, a written resolution means a resolution of a private company (not a public company) that is proposed and passed in accordance with the requirements of the legislation.

A meeting does not need to be held to pass a written resolution. Instead, the resolution is circulated to those entitled to vote on it for signature. Written resolutions are discussed further in section 6 of this chapter.

Under the model articles, decisions not made in a meeting can only be taken if the eligible directors making the decisions would have formed a quorum at such a meeting.

Directors' decisions are usually reached following a discussion and do not usually involve voting. This is often the case for companies for which a professional service provider is providing directors. Where a director opposes a resolution, they have a right to have this recorded in the minutes of the meeting. The articles set out certain circumstances in which a director may not vote – for example, if a conflict of interest arises in relation to the matter to be discussed.

Minutes of directors' meetings

Under the Companies Act 2006, every company must keep minutes of all proceedings of its directors' meetings. Minutes are the official record of the company's activities and a record of key decisions made.

The Companies Act 2006 provides that minutes are evidence of the proceedings at the meeting where are purported to be authenticated by the chairman of the meeting (or of the next meeting). All proceedings at the meeting are therefore deemed to have taken place and all appointments at the meeting deemed valid.

Stop and think 16.1

Given that minutes signed by the chairman of a directors' meeting are considered by law to be evidence of the proceedings at the meeting, it is extremely bad practice for offshore company administrators to record directors as being present at a meeting if they were not, or if a meeting of the directors did not, in fact, take place.

In instances where decisions need to be recorded, however, and a meeting was not held, a written resolution should be used rather than minutes of a meeting which do not reflect the true circumstances. Written resolutions are discussed in section 6 of this chapter.

The minutes of directors' meetings are usually kept in a minute book. In some companies, the board minutes will be kept separate from those of the members' meetings. This is primarily because the members may inspect the minutes of the members; however, they may not inspect the minutes of directors' meetings.

In offshore centres, where it is very rare that a shareholder would request sight of the shareholders' minutes, it is common to find that both the directors' minutes and shareholders' minutes are kept in a single minute book. As electronic filing has become increasingly common, it is usual for minutes to be scanned and stored electronically.

Typical content of minutes include:

- the name of the company;
- the date of the meeting;
- the place of the meeting;
- the names of those who were present at the meeting;
- the name of the person who was appointed as the chairman of the meeting;
- the names of those who had sent their apologies for non-attendance of the meeting;
- a statement that the meeting had been duly convened in accordance with the articles;
- a statement that a quorum was present;
- approval of previous minutes;
- a record of the proceedings and any decisions made; and
- the chairman's signature.

The use of pro-forma minutes has been common in offshore centres. The content of the minutes has generally been kept fairly minimal, with much of the discussion omitted and only the decisions taken at the meeting being recorded.

In practice, company administrators in offshore centres often prepare draft minutes in advance of the directors' meeting in anticipation of the proceedings (where the business of the meeting is not complex or high risk). At the end of the meeting, either the minutes would be signed or any changes required to the minutes would then be made.

However, it is becoming increasingly important that the minutes reflect and record the fact that discussions are held and matters raised if directors wish to rely on them in order to demonstrate that they have discharged their duties to the company. The significance of the content of minutes can be illustrated in the case known as *Weavering Macro Fixed Income Fund Limited (in liquidation) v Peterson and Ekstrom [2011]*.

Case law 16.1

Weavering Macro Fixed Income Fund Limited (in liquidation) v Peterson and Ekstrom [2011]

The background to this case was given in Case law 14.3 (page 277). The board meetings were relied upon as being the most important way in which the directors claimed to have discharged their functions. The court made some interesting observations in relation to the minutes of those meetings. It found that:

- the directors went through the motions of appearing to hold regular board meetings, but in reality the meetings served no purpose other than the recording of information that was largely apparent from the monthly statements sent to the directors;
- there was a lack of agendas prepared and circulated, reflecting input from the investment manager or specifying matters for discussion;
- the minutes 'noted' that the investment manager had been acting within guidelines and the investment restrictions set out by the board; however, there was no evidence of any discussion or the making of any enquiry as to whether or not this was in fact the case;
- directors have a duty to arrange for the minutes to be taken of the meeting which fairly and accurately record the matters which were considered and decisions which were made; however, the minutes appeared to be pro-forma documents, produced by making amendments to a template;
- the form and content of the minutes were such that they could have been (and probably were) produced in advance of the meetings and were signed in the standard form irrespective of the discussion which actually took place – most of the paragraphs contained within the minutes remained the same; and
- there was no reference to any actual discussion that may have taken place and there was no documentary evidence reflecting that these directors ever ought to discuss or enquire about any subject at all throughout the period of almost six years that they held in office.

It was admitted that certain meetings recorded as having taken place did not take place at all.

The minutes of a meeting usually record:

- items that are of particular note;
- discussion points;
- reference to particular documentation such as relevant agreements or documentation that has been presented to the meeting; and
- decisions.

Such information is often recorded using phrases such as 'It was noted that…', 'It was proposed that…' and 'It was resolved that…'. This makes it easier to identify quickly the key events of the meeting. In the past, discussions have not been clearly documented and instead, a broad statement such as 'after due consideration and discussion, it was resolved that…' was used. However, it is becoming more common for directors to want to record more detail.

Sample board meeting minutes are included in Appendix 3. The importance of the quality of the minutes prepared and signed off cannot be over emphasised. They are crucial evidence to support the argument that it is the directors (rather than anyone else, such as the beneficial owner) who has made each decision. Once again, you should refer to case law 16.1.

2. Record keeping

There are various reasons that directors (and trustees) are required to maintain a good standard of record keeping.

The Companies Act 2006 states that company records must be kept for at least 10 years from the date of the meeting. If a company fails to comply with this requirement, an offence is committed by every officer of the company who is in default.

The model articles provide that the directors must ensure that the company keeps a record of every unanimous or majority decision taken by the directors in writing. This must be kept for at least 10 years from the date of the decision recorded.

An offshore service provider may be required to maintain records in order to comply with their jurisdiction's codes of practice or other legislation, including AML legislation or guidance. A good standard of record keeping will enable a business to demonstrate compliance with such legislation, as well as assisting administrators to understand their clients' needs and to identify risks to (and opportunities for) their business.

3. General meetings

General meetings are meetings of the members, and are usually called by the directors. Annual general meetings are a special type of general meeting and these are discussed later in this chapter.

Prior to the introduction of the Companies Act 2006, the term 'extraordinary general meeting' was used to describe meetings of the shareholders that were not annual general meetings.

3.1 Notice of general meetings

The Companies Act 2006 provides that the directors may call a general meeting. Directors are required to call a general meeting in circumstances where the company has received requests to do so from members representing at least 5% of the paid-up capital with the right to vote at general meetings of the company or, where the company has no share capital, members who represent at least 5% of the total voting rights of all the members with a right to vote at general meetings.

3.2 Quorum

The quorum is the number of members that must be present in order for a meeting to be validly constituted.

The Companies Act 2006 provides that if a company has only one member, the quorum for general meetings is one. If the company has more than one member, the quorum shall be two qualifying persons unless the articles of association provide otherwise. Qualifying persons are individual shareholders, representatives of corporate shareholders or a proxy of a member (see below).

Meetings cannot take place if only one person is present, regardless of the capacity that they purport to attend in.

In determining attendance at a general meeting, it is immaterial whether any two or more members attending are in the same place.

Test yourself 16.2

What is meant by the term 'quorum' in relation to a meeting?

The period of notice required in order to call a general meeting is as follows under the Companies Act 2006, although a company's articles may specify a longer period.

- A general meeting of a private company must be called by notice of at least 14 days.
- A general meeting of a public company must be called by notice of at least 21 days for an annual general meeting and at least 14 days in all other cases.
- A general meeting may be called by shorter notice than that otherwise required if the members agree.

The shorter notice must be agreed to by a majority of the members with a right to attend and vote at the meeting, and who together hold not less than the requisite percentage in nominal value of the shares giving a right to attend and vote at the meeting (if the company has a share capital). The requisite percentage is:

- in the case of a private company, 90% or such higher percentage (not exceeding 95%) as may be specified in the company's articles; or
- in the case of a public company, 95%.

For companies that do not have a share capital, the members must together represent not less than the requisite percentage of the total voting rights at that meeting of all the members.

For the annual general meetings of public companies, an annual general meeting may be called by shorter notice if all the members entitled to attend and vote at the meeting agree to the shorter notice.

Test yourself 16.3

What notice period must be given under the Companies Act 2006 in respect of a general meeting of a private company?

The articles of association may indicate who is entitled to receive notice of the general meetings. In general, those who are entitled to receive notice of the general meetings include:

- auditors;
- directors; and
- shareholders with voting rights.

The following must be included in the notice of a general meeting:

- date of the meeting;
- time of the meeting;
- place of the meeting;
- whether it is an annual general meeting or other general meeting;
- the text of any special resolutions that are to be voted upon; and
- the members' right to appoint a proxy.

3.3 Chairing general meetings

If the directors have appointed a chairman, this person shall chair general meetings if they are present and willing to do so.

If the directors have not appointed a chairman, or if the chairman is unwilling to chair the meeting or is not present within 10 minutes of the time at which a meeting was due to start, the directors present (or if there are none, the meeting) must appoint a director or shareholder to chair the meeting.

3.4 Attendance and speaking by directors and non-shareholders

Directors may attend and speak at general meetings, whether or not they are shareholders.

The chairman of the meeting may permit other persons who are not shareholders of the company, or otherwise entitled to exercise the rights of shareholders in relation to general meetings, to attend and speak at a general meeting.

3.5 Annual general meeting

There are special rules surrounding the annual general meeting (AGM) of a company.

The Companies Act 2006 provides that private companies are not required to hold an AGM unless their articles state that they must. However, public companies are required to hold an AGM. The AGM of a public company must be held within six months of the financial year-end. If a company fails to hold an AGM, an offence is committed by every officer of the company.

The business of an AGM may include:

- receipt of the report and accounts laid before the meeting;
- declaration of the final dividend;
- election of the directors who have been appointed since the last AGM;
- the re-election of the directors who have retired by rotation; and
- the re-appointment of the auditors of the company.

Offshore companies may or may not be required to hold an AGM under their legislation. Some offshore centres provide that the AGM may be waived by the members, although there may be special provisions surrounding the waiver.

In Jersey, for example, all shareholders must agree to the waiver and any shareholder may change their mind and insist that an AGM is held.

3.6 Class meetings

Class meetings are meetings of the holders of a class of a company's shares. Class meetings are usually required to be held if the rights of the holder of the class of shares are to be varied.

4. Voting

The model articles provide that a resolution put to the vote of a general meeting must be decided by a show of hands unless a poll is duly demanded in accordance with the articles.

4.1 Poll votes

With a poll vote for a company that has a share capital, every member has one vote for each share that they own. The model articles provide that a poll on a resolution may be demanded in advance of the general meeting where it is to be put to the vote, or at a general meeting either before a show of hands on that resolution or immediately after the result of a show of hands on that resolution is declared.

A poll may be demanded by:

- the chairman of the meeting;
- the directors;
- two or more persons having the right to vote on the resolution; or
- a person or persons representing not less than one-tenth of the total voting rights of all the shareholders having the right to vote on the resolution.

A demand for a poll may be withdrawn if the poll has not yet been taken, and the chairman of the meeting consents to the withdrawal. Polls must be taken immediately and in such manner as the chairman of the meeting directs.

4.2 Proxies

Members of a company are entitled to appoint another person as their proxy (meaning their substitute or representative) to exercise all or any of their rights to attend and to speak and vote at a meeting of the company.

The member would complete a proxy form in the manner specified in the articles of association. The person who is appointed as the proxy must then act in accordance with the instructions of the member on whose behalf they are at the meeting. The articles may specify the form that the proxy document must take and the manner in which the proxy should be lodged with the company prior to the meeting.

Proxies can take different forms. The member may appoint a person but not direct them how to vote, they may appoint a person and direct them how to vote, or they may include an option for the shareholder to withhold their vote.

5. Resolutions

Resolutions are the way in which a decision is proposed and passed at a general meeting. There are various types of resolution, including ordinary resolutions, special resolutions and extraordinary resolutions.

5.1 Ordinary resolutions

An ordinary resolution must be passed by a simple majority of members. Most decisions require an ordinary resolution for the decision to be passed. An ordinary resolution is usually required for routine 'ordinary' business such as:

- approval of accounts;
- approval of a final dividend;
- appointment of a director;
- an increase in the authorised share capital; and
- the reappointment of auditors.

Special notice

Some resolutions require 'special notice' to be given of the intention to propose the resolution to the members. This is the case, for example, where a resolution at a general meeting of a company relates to the removal of an auditor or a director from office before the expiry of their period of office.

Where special notice is required, the members must be informed of the intention to propose the resolution at least 28 days before the meeting at which the resolution is to be proposed. Otherwise, the resolution is not effective.

Where that is not practicable to do so, the company must give its members notice at least 14 days before the meeting by advertisement in a newspaper having an appropriate circulation, or in any other manner allowed by the company's articles.

5.2 Special resolutions

A special resolution of the members or of a class of members of a company is a resolution that must be passed by a majority of not less than 75% of members who are entitled to vote. Special resolutions are generally required for important matters such as alterations to the articles of the company or changing the name of the company.

A resolution passed at a meeting is not a special resolution unless the notice of the meeting included the text of the resolution and specified the intention to propose it as a special resolution. If the notice of the meeting specified that the resolution was a special resolution then it may only be passed as such.

Once a special resolution has been passed, a printed and signed copy of the resolution must be delivered to Companies House within 15 days. The timeframe for delivery of a copy of a special resolution varies in offshore centres.

5.3 Extraordinary resolutions

The term 'extraordinary resolutions' is not used in the Companies Act 2006; however, it may still be found in the articles of many companies.

The term previously referred to resolutions that required a majority of 75% of members who are entitled to vote; however, the resolutions did not require any special notice to be given.

Test yourself 16.4

Give two examples of when a company would need to use a special resolution in general meeting.

6. Written resolutions of the members

Written resolutions may be proposed by the directors or by the members of private companies. However, they may not be used by public companies and they may not be used in all circumstances. For example, the following may not be passed as a written resolution:

- a resolution removing a director before the expiration of their period of office; or
- a resolution removing an auditor before the expiration of their term of office.

It is not necessary for all of the members of the company to sign the written resolution in order to pass it. The requirements to pass a written resolution are instead the same as they would be if the resolution were passed at a meeting.

For example, a written resolution is passed as an ordinary resolution if it is passed by members representing a simple majority of the total voting rights of members who are entitled to vote, and a written resolution is passed as a special resolution if it is passed by a majority of not less than 75% of the members who are entitled to vote. If a written resolution is to be passed as a special resolution, it must state that it was proposed as such. If the resolution stated that it was to be passed as a special resolution, then it might only be passed as such (i.e. 75% of the members must have signed the resolution).

Written resolutions are usually kept in the minute book. The requirements to file copies of certain resolutions (e.g. special resolutions) with the Registrar of Companies is the same for written resolutions as they are for those resolutions passed at meetings of the company.

Test yourself 16.5

What is a written resolution?

Chapter summary

- The articles of association usually set out how the directors shall conduct their meetings. There is no requirement in the legislation for board meetings to be held at any particular frequency.

- The chairman of the board (if there is one) usually acts as the chairman of the board meetings. It is the duty of the chairman to manage the meeting and ensure that all items on the agenda are discussed.
- An agenda may be required for board meetings. This may include items such as apologies for absence, approval of the minutes of the last meeting, matters arising from the last minutes, the business or transaction to be discussed and any other business.
- The quorum is the minimum number of persons necessary to be present at a meeting in order for the business of the meeting to be transacted. It is usually set out in the articles of association.
- The general rule is that directors' decisions are made by a majority of directors, either in a meeting or by written resolution. The articles of association govern the meetings of directors.
- Every company must keep minutes of all proceedings of its directors' meetings. Minutes are the official record of the company's activities and key decisions made. Minutes signed by the chairman are evidence of the proceedings of the meeting.
- The Companies Act 2006 states that company records must be kept for at least 10 years from the date of the meeting. The model articles require a copy of every decision recorded for at least 10 years after the date that the decision was made.
- General meetings are meetings of the members. The directors may call general meetings, or members with at least 5% of the voting rights of all of the members who have a right to vote at general meetings may require the directors to call a general meeting.
- The Companies Act 2006 requires that a general meeting of a private company must be called by notice of at least 14 days for a private company and at least 21 days for an AGM of a public company, and at least 14 days for any other public company general meetings. Shorter notice periods may be agreed upon.
- The shareholders with voting rights, the auditors and the directors are all entitled to receive notice of the general meetings.
- The Companies Act 2006 provides that private companies are not required to hold an AGM unless their articles state that they must. Public companies must hold an AGM within six months of the financial year-end.
- The model articles provide that a resolution put to the vote of a general meeting must be decided upon by a show of hands unless a poll is duly demanded in accordance with the articles.
- Members of a company are entitled to appoint another person as their proxy to exercise all or any of their rights to attend, speak at and vote at a meeting of the company.

- Resolutions are the way in which a decision is proposed and passed at a general meeting. Ordinary resolutions must be passed by a simple majority of the members. Special resolutions must be passed by a majority of not less than 75% of members who are entitled to vote.
- Written resolutions may be proposed by either the directors or the members of a private company. Written resolutions do not require a meeting to be held and instead, they are passed when the required majority of members sign the resolution (e.g. 75% for a special resolution or 50% for an ordinary resolution).

Test yourself answers

Test yourself 16.1

Items typically included on board meeting agendas include:

- approval of the minutes of the last minutes;
- matters arising from the last minutes; and
- review of action points arising from the last minutes.

Test yourself 16.2

The quorum is the minimum number of members that must be present at a meeting in order for the proceedings to be considered valid.

Test yourself 16.3

A general meeting of a private company must be called by notice of at least 14 days but may be called by shorter notice if the members agree.

Test yourself 16.4

A company would need to use a special resolution in a general meeting in the following circumstances:

- where alterations are made to the articles of the company; and
- where the name of the company is to be changed.

Test yourself 16.5

A written resolution is one that is proposed by the directors or by the members of private companies in writing (i.e. without the requirement for a meeting to be held). It is not necessary for all of the members of the company to sign the written resolution in order to pass it.

Chapter seventeen
Winding up

List of topics

1. Voluntary liquidation
2. Compulsory liquidation
3. Voluntary striking off

Introduction

This chapter explains the procedures involved in each of the various ways in which companies may be wound up (brought to an end or closed), including a members' voluntary liquidation, a creditors' voluntary liquidation, a compulsory liquidation and a voluntary striking off from the companies register.

1. Voluntary liquidation

A voluntary liquidation may be a members' voluntary liquidation or a creditors' voluntary liquidation.

1.1 Members' voluntary liquidation

The members of a company may decide to wind up the company when it is no longer required. The steps involved with a members' voluntary liquidation are as follows.

Gazette
The official newspaper record in the United Kingdom. The *London Gazette* is the gazette for the publication of notices relating to companies incorporated in England and Wales.

1. The directors make a statutory declaration of solvency.
2. The members pass a special resolution to commence a voluntary liquidation.
3. A copy of the special resolution is delivered to the ***Gazette*** and the Registrar of Companies.
4. A liquidator is appointed to wind up the affairs of the company.

Statutory declaration of solvency

The directors at a directors' meeting make a statutory declaration to the effect that they have made a full inquiry into the company's affairs and that, having done so, they have formed the opinion that the company will be able to pay its debts in full within 12 months from the commencement of the winding up, as may be specified in the declaration. This document will include a statement of the company's assets and liabilities as at the latest practicable date before the declaration.

The statutory declaration must be made by the directors within the five weeks immediately preceding the date of the passing of a resolution for winding up.

Special resolution of the members

The members pass a special resolution to commence a voluntary liquidation. The statutory declaration of solvency (discussed above) must be delivered to the Registrar of Companies within 15 days immediately following the date on which the resolution for winding up is passed.

Copy of the special resolution to be delivered to the Gazette

A copy of the special resolution must be delivered to the *Gazette* within 14 days of it being passed. The *Gazette* is the official newspaper record in the United Kingdom. The *London Gazette* is the gazette for companies incorporated in England and Wales. There are separate gazettes for companies that are incorporated within Scotland and Northern Island. The gazettes are published weekly.

Copy of the special resolution to be delivered to the registrar

A copy of the special resolution must be delivered to the registrar within 15 days of it being passed.

Appointment of a liquidator

A liquidator will need to be appointed. The appointment must be notified to the *Gazette* and the Registrar within 14 days, as well as advertised in a local newspaper. In a members' voluntary winding-up, the company in general meeting shall appoint one or more liquidators for the purpose of winding up the company's affairs and distributing its assets.

On the appointment of a liquidator, all the powers of the directors cease, except so far as the company in general meeting or the liquidator sanctions their continuance.

Test yourself 17.1

Outline the steps involved with a member's voluntary liquidation.

1.2 Creditors' voluntary liquidation

When a company cannot pay its debts, it should follow the procedures for a creditors' voluntary liquidation.

Special resolution of the members
A special resolution of the members is required. This must be advertised in the *Gazette* within 14 days and sent to the Registrar of Companies within 15 days.

A board meeting to resolve to convene a creditors' meeting is then held.

Meeting of the creditors
A creditors' meeting must be convened within 14 days of the shareholders' resolution being passed. At least seven days' notice of the meeting must be given to the creditors of the meeting. The meeting must also be notified to the *Gazette* and advertised in two local newspapers. The directors prepare a statement of affairs for review at the creditors' meeting.

Appointment of liquidator
The liquidator should be appointed and the appointment notified to the *Gazette*. The liquidator should be provided with the statement of affairs and is required to send it to the Registrar within seven days of the creditors' meeting.

Submission of documentation to the liquidator
Following the creditors' meeting, the liquidator is required to prepare accounts for delivery to the registrar of receipts and payments over the first 12 months in liquidation. After that, a liquidator's report must be sent every 12 months until the winding up is complete.

Test yourself 17.2

When is a creditors' voluntary liquidation commenced?

2. Compulsory liquidation

A compulsory liquidation of a company occurs when the company is ordered to wind up by the court.

Companies may be wound up by the court in various circumstances. Examples are as follows.

- A company registered as a public company has not been issued with a trading certificate more than a year after it was registered.
- A public company has fewer than two members.
- The company is unable to pay debts of over £750.
- The court is of the opinion that the company should be wound up on just and equitable grounds.

A petition to wind up the company, which must be advertised in the *Gazette*, is made to the court. If it is successful, a court order is granted. An official receiver is then appointed as the liquidator.

The official receiver has a duty to investigate the company's affairs and the causes of its failure. The official receiver may call a meeting of creditors to appoint a liquidator in the receiver's place. If they do not, they must notify the creditors and the court of their decision. If a liquidator is appointed in place of the receiver, the liquidator must notify the Registrar of Companies of their appointment as soon as reasonably practicable.

Upon receipt of a notice from the liquidator of the final meeting of the creditors or notice from the receiver that the winding-up is complete, the Registrar will register it and publish its receipt in the *Gazette*.

Test yourself 17.3

State three circumstances in which the court may order a compulsory liquidation.

3. Voluntary striking off

On application by a company, the Registrar of Companies may strike the company's name off the register.

The application must be made on the company's behalf by its directors or by a majority of them, and must contain the prescribed information. A copy of the application must be given to certain parties – such as every member, employee, creditor and director – within seven days from the day on which the application is made.

The Registrar publishes a notice in the *Gazette* stating that the registrar may exercise the power under this section in relation to the company, and inviting any person to show cause why that should not be done.

Three months after the publication in the *Gazette*, the Registrar must publish notice in the *Gazette* of the company's name having been struck off. On the publication of the notice in the *Gazette*, the company is dissolved. Companies House charge a fee of £10 for this service.

3.1 Striking off in offshore centres

In many offshore jurisdictions, there is no direct cost involved with striking off a company, and it requires no action on the part of the directors or members.

Company directors who wish for the company to be struck off could simply fail to pay the annual return of the company and the striking off would happen after a specified period. This is a popular method of dissolving a company in offshore centres in circumstances where the trust company's fees have not been settled or where contact with the beneficial owner is lost.

Company directors who allow companies to be struck off must bear in mind that the liability (if any) of every director, managing officer and member of the company continues and may be enforced as if the company had not been dissolved.

Once a company has been struck off, any assets that it owned become bona vacantia, meaning that they belong to the Crown or State because they are without a legal owner.

Some regulators are said to take a dim view of service providers and the directors of such companies that allow client companies to fail and to be struck off in this way.

Companies can be restored to the companies register by interested parties such as the directors or members. The effect of the restoration is as if the company had never been struck off in the first place.

Chapter summary

- A voluntary liquidation may be either a members' voluntary liquidation or a creditors' voluntary liquidation.
- With a members' voluntary liquidation, the directors make a statutory declaration of solvency following which the members pass a special resolution to commence a voluntary winding-up. Copies of the special resolution are published in the *Gazette* and delivered to the Registrar of Companies. A liquidator is then appointed.
- Upon appointment of a liquidator, all the powers of the directors cease.
- When a company cannot pay its debts, the procedures for a creditors' voluntary liquidation is required.
- A creditors' winding-up commenced when a special resolution of the members is passed. A board meeting is held to convene a meeting of the creditors.
- A creditors' meeting must be convened within 14 days of the shareholders' special resolution to commence a creditors' winding-up. A liquidator is then appointed.
- A compulsory liquidation occurs when the court orders a company to wind up in certain circumstances – for example, when the company is unable to pay debts of over £750 or the company is a public company with fewer than two members.
- The directors of a company may make a voluntary application to the Registrar of Companies for the company to be struck from the companies register.
- In offshore centres, it is possible for companies to be struck off the companies register for non-payment of their annual return. Company directors who allow a company to be struck off must bear in mind that the liability of every director and member continues and may be enforced as if the company had not been dissolved.

- Once a company has been struck off, its assets become bona vacantia, meaning that they belong to the Crown as they are without a legal owner.

Test yourself answers

Test yourself 17.1

The members of a company may decide to wind up the company when it is no longer required. The steps involved with a members' voluntary liquidation are as follows.

- The directors make a statutory declaration of solvency.
- The members pass a special resolution to commence a voluntary liquidation.
- A copy of the special resolution is delivered to the *Gazette* and the Registrar of Companies.
- A liquidator is appointed to wind up the affairs of the company.

Test yourself 17.2

A creditors' voluntary liquidation is commenced when a special resolution of the members is passed.

Test yourself 17.3

Examples of circumstances in which the court may order a compulsory liquidation include when:

- a company registered as a public company has not been issued with a trading certificate more than a year after it was registered;
- the company is unable to pay debts of over £750; and
- the court is of the opinion that the company should be wound up on just and equitable grounds.

Part eight

Chapter 18
Other vehicles

Chapter 19
Trust and company administration

Other vehicles and trust and company administration

After studying this part, students will have knowledge of the remaining range of entities that are available in offshore centres including foundations, partnerships (including those that are legal bodies and those that are not), special purpose vehicles and private trust companies.

Students will gain an understanding of some of the key terms used within the trust company business sector and an understanding of the various trust company business services that are provided by offshore service providers. They will learn about the risks of providing limited services and students will understand some key aspects of the role of the trust and company administrator and be able to describe some of the tasks undertaken by administrators.

Learning outcomes

At the end of this part, you will:

1. know the range of entities available in offshore centres;
2. understand the principles of trust and company administration; and
3. understand the role of the trust and company administrator.

Chapter eighteen
Other vehicles

List of topics

1. The range of entities available in offshore centres
2. Foundations
3. Partnerships
4. Special purpose vehicles
5. Private trust companies

Introduction

This chapter explains the range of entities available from offshore centres including foundations, partnerships (including general partnerships, limited liability partnerships, limited partnerships, incorporated partnerships and separate limited partnerships), special purpose vehicles and private trust companies.

1. The range of entities available in offshore centres

Offshore centres seek to be innovative in terms of the products that they offer and in terms of their legal environments. In order to remain competitive, offshore centres from common law jurisdictions have introduced legislation allowing for the formation of foundations, which appeal to clients from civil law countries where the concept of trusts is not widely recognised.

As a result, a wide range of entities is available from offshore centres. These include foundations, partnerships (including limited liability partnerships, separate limited partnerships and incorporated limited partnerships), special purpose vehicles and private trust companies. Such entities may be used together with or instead of the more traditional trusts and limited liability companies.

2. Foundations

Foundations have similar features to both trusts and companies. Foundations have a separate legal personality in the same way as companies. They can therefore contract in their own name. However, foundations do not have trustees, directors or shareholders.

founder
The person who requests for a foundation to be incorporated.

charter
A document which is usually available for public inspection and which sets out the name of the foundation, its duration, objects, and names and addresses of the first council members.

regulations (in relation to foundations)
A private document setting out the administration of the foundation.

The person who requests a foundation to be incorporated is known as the **founder**. A council administers the foundation and carries out its objects in accordance with the **charter** and **regulations that are specific to that foundation**. The council makes decisions in relation to the foundation; its functions are similar to that of a board of directors of a company or the trustees of a trust.

2.1 Restrictions on council members

As explained in Chapter 2, some offshore centres impose restrictions in respect of who can be appointed as a council member.

In some offshore centres, the provision of a member of the council of a foundation is a regulated activity, which must therefore be provided only by a licensed trust company business service provider.

For example, Jersey requires that each council must have a 'qualified' member and applications for foundations to be incorporated must be lodged by a 'qualified' person. Many offshore centres have introduced foundations legislation in the hope that it will be attractive to clients based in civil law jurisdictions in Europe and from emerging markets where the trust concept is less familiar than in common law countries.

2.2 Charter and regulations

A foundation is governed by its charter and regulations. The charter is usually available for public inspection and sets out the name of the foundation, its duration, objects, and names and addresses of the first council members.

The regulations are a private document setting out the administration of the foundation. The charter and regulations may provide for the founder to exercise certain rights, in the same way that a settlor of a trust is permitted to reserve certain powers.

The beneficiaries have no interest in the foundation's assets and are not owed a fiduciary duty by the foundation council unless this is expressly provided for by the charter or the regulations. This is very different to the duty owed by the trustee of a trust to the beneficiaries of that trust. This means the constitution of the foundation can be drafted more flexibly than would otherwise be possible. A foundation may exist with no beneficiaries, whereas a trust (unless it is a non-charitable or purpose trust) would fail for a lack of object and therefore cease to exist.

2.3 Guardians

The guardian's role is similar to that of an enforcer of a non-charitable purpose trust.

In offshore centres such as Panama, foundations may have a guardian. In others such as Jersey, a guardian must be appointed to oversee the administration of the foundation and ensure that the council carries on its functions properly.

2.4 Uses of foundations

The following are all uses of foundations.

- Foundations appeal to clients who are involved with jurisdictions where the concept of trusts is less well known.
- Foundations offer an enhanced level of confidentiality.
- Global charities may use foundations for making donations.
- Clients who wish to use foundations within commercial transactions, especially where an 'orphaned' special purpose vehicle is required. Special purpose vehicles are discussed in section 4.
- Foundations can be used for international structuring.

Test yourself 18.1

State three differences between a foundation and a company.

3. Partnerships

Various types of partnerships are offered in offshore centres. General partnerships have been available for many years; others such as the incorporated limited partnership and the separate limited partnership are relatively recent developments.

Partnerships avoid some of the risks that a sole trader may be exposed to as the responsibilities are shared between the partners. As well as sharing the responsibilities and liabilities of the partnership, each partner shares the profits and losses of the business.

Partnerships are simple arrangements that are cheaper to create than a company. They also do not involve the ongoing fees that companies are subject to – for example, annual return fees.

Partnerships do not generally have limited liability. However, they may be a preferred vehicle over a company because the business is not such that limited liability is required for the owners. In addition, the running costs and the administrative burden may be significantly lower.

3.1 General partnerships

General partnerships (also known as traditional partnerships) may come into existence with a verbal or written agreement between two or more parties who agree to carry out activities by way of business with a common objective to make a profit will then be referred to as the partners.

A partnership is not a body incorporated in accordance with the law. As a result, it does not have a separate personality in the same way that a company does. It is an arrangement between the partners who work together, for example, to make a profit.

The liability of partners of a general partnership (also known as a traditional partnership) is unlimited.

The partners themselves have to contract with third parties who wish to engage with the partnership. This is unlike transactions involving a company, where it is the company that is a party to a transaction rather than its directors or shareholders.

The partners of a general or traditional partnership are fully liable for the debts of a general partnership. This is markedly different from the position of a company where the directors and shareholders are not liable for its debts.

Partnerships cease to exist upon the death of a partner. This differs from the position with a company, which will continue to exist regardless of what may happen to its shareholders or directors (as companies have perpetual succession).

Test yourself 18.2

How may a general partnership come into existence?

3.2 Limited liability partnerships

The UK allows limited liability partnerships (LLPs) to be formed by incorporation under the Limited Liability Partnership Act.

In the UK, an LLP is a body corporate with a separate legal personality from that of its members, whose liability is limited. Two or more persons carrying on a lawful business with a view to profit must subscribe to an incorporation document that must then be delivered to the Registrar of Companies.

Upon incorporation of an LLP, its members are the persons who subscribed to the incorporation document. Others may become members in accordance with an agreement with the existing members. The incorporation document specifies members who are to be designated members. These people are responsible for carrying out certain duties – for example, filing the annual return with Companies House.

The LLP has the advantage of offering limited liability for its members while allowing them to structure their business as a partnership.

LLPs in offshore centres can differ from the UK model – for example, in Jersey, LLPs are not corporate bodies. Even so, Jersey LLPs do have a separate legal personality from that of the partners. It is the partnership itself that is responsible for any debts that it runs up, rather than the individual partners; this is the attraction of this vehicle for many accountancy firms and other businesses.

The liability of the partners (referred to as members in the UK) is limited to the amount that they have contributed to the capital of the LLP.

3.3 Limited partnerships

Limited partnerships (LPs) are not corporate bodies and have no separate legal personality. LPs must have at least two types of partners: a limited partner (whose liability is limited to the amount of its capital contribution provided it does not take part in the management of the partnership) and a general partner (whose liability is unlimited).

3.4 Incorporated limited partnerships

In some jurisdictions, including Jersey, it is possible to form incorporated limited partnerships (ILPs). These are the same as general partnerships, apart from the fact they are a body corporate. Therefore, an ILP has a separate legal personality from that of the partners and can hold assets and contract in its own name. The general partner is responsible for managing the assets of the partnership and owes fiduciary duties to the partnership in the same way that a director owes fiduciary duties to a company. As it is a body corporate, an ILP also offers the benefit of perpetual succession.

The general partner's liability remains unlimited for the debts of the ILP; however, the general partner acts as an agent of the partnership and is only liable for the debts that have not already been satisfied from the assets of the ILP. In practice, the liability of those persons managing the general partner can be limited by structuring the general partner as a limited company or limited partnership.

Test yourself 18.3

What is the limitation of the liability of a general partner in an incorporated limited partnership?

3.5 Separate limited partnerships

Separate limited partnerships (SLP) are similar to limited partnerships as they have a separate legal personality; however, they are not a body corporate. In all other respects, an SLP is the same as a traditional partnership.

The general partner's liability remains unlimited; however, they act as an agent of the partnership and are only liable for the debts that have not already been satisfied from the assets of the SLP. As with an incorporated limited partnership, it is usual for the general partner to be a limited liability company.

ILPs and SLPs offer a greater degree of operational flexibility than corporate structures – particularly where investment capital may be returned to investors – while retaining the additional protection and certainty that an LLP provides.

ILPs and SLPs lend themselves well to a variety of structures, including:

- all types of investment funds, including vehicles to be used for carried interests or performance fees;
- asset-holding structures;
- family office holding structures;
- structured finance transactions; and
- tax-transparent joint venture arrangements.

4. Special purpose vehicles

special purpose vehicle (SPV)
An entity that is established for a specific purpose or transaction.

A **special purpose vehicle (SPV)** is established for a specific purpose or transaction. Offshore SPVs are used in a variety of international finance arrangements.

SPVs are usually offshore companies; however, other vehicles such as LPs or PCCs may be used. The share capital of the SPV is typically owned by a trust with charitable beneficiaries. If this is the case, the SPV may make a small profit that can then be distributed to the charities.

Alternatively, the share capital of the SPV may be held by a non-charitable purpose trust without ascertainable beneficiaries but with an ascertainable purpose. The purpose may be to establish the underlying company and to enter into any agreements relating to a particular transaction.

The use of an SPV can isolate a purpose or transaction from other activities or parties involved with a transaction. An SPV can be used where it is necessary that the vehicle should not be treated as being controlled or owned by any party to a transaction. Such structures are usually owned by a charitable purpose trust and are referred to as 'orphaned structures', as they are said not to be beneficially owned by anyone.

SPVs may be used to enter into securitisation or debt defeasance (making debt null and void) transactions. Assets of all types are repackaged and securitised.

The SPV may issue debt instruments, can be used in off-balance-sheet investments and may be set up as a bankruptcy remote vehicle.

private trust company (PTC)
A company formed to act as a trustee of one particular trust or group of trusts (e.g. for one individual or family).

A purpose trust could be formed to incorporate and hold shares in a **private trust company**.

5. Private trust companies

A private trust company (PTC) is a company that is formed to act as a trustee dedicated to one particular trust or group of trusts – for example, for one individual or family. PTCs are permitted in many offshore jurisdictions including the British Virgin Islands, the Cayman Islands, Guernsey and Jersey.

The directors of a private trust company may be chosen by the settlor of the underlying trusts. Family members may be appointed to the board alongside trust company business professionals and other advisers. This allows the family members to be far more involved with the administration of the trust fund than would otherwise be possible if a professional trustee were appointed, and may allow the trust to hold investments that a professional trustee may otherwise not allow.

PTCs may enter into an agreement with a professional trust company to ensure that administrative matters such as record keeping requirements are adhered to and other important matters such as the preparation of financial statements are undertaken.

The legislation surrounding PTCs differs from jurisdiction to jurisdiction; however, in general they are not subject to the same level of regulation and supervision as other trust companies.

Test yourself 18.4

What is a private trust company?

Chapter summary

- Vehicles available from offshore centres include foundations, partnerships, special purpose vehicles and private trust companies.
- Foundations have similar features to both trusts and companies. They are incorporated by law and have a separate legal personality, but do not have shareholders.
- The council members of a foundation make decisions relating to the foundation.
- Foundations are governed by a charter and regulations. Unless the charter or regulations expressly provide, the beneficiaries have no interest in the assets of the foundation and are not owed a fiduciary duty by the foundation.
- A foundation may have a guardian to oversee its administration.
- General partnerships (also known as traditional partnerships) may come into existence with a verbal agreement. They are not an incorporated body and therefore have no separate legal personality.
- The liability of the partners of a general partnership is unlimited.
- Limited liability partnerships (LLPs) are formed by the process of incorporation and therefore have a separate legal personality. The liability of its members is limited.
- Limited partnerships (LPs) are not corporate bodies and have no separate legal personality.

- With a limited partnership, the limited partner's liability is limited to the amount of its capital contribution (provided it does not take part in the management of the partnership). The general partner's liability is unlimited.
- Incorporated limited partnerships (ILPs) are the same as general partnerships, except that they are corporate bodies and have separate legal personalities.
- Separate limited partnerships (SLPs) have a separate legal personality; however, they are not a body corporate. In all other respects, they are the same as a traditional partnership.
- A special purpose vehicle (SPV) is one that is established for a specific purpose or transaction. They are usually offshore companies.
- It is common for the share capital of a SPV to be owned by a charitable trust or a non-charitable purpose trust. They cannot therefore be said to be controlled or owned by any particular person, and are sometimes referred to as 'orphaned structures'.
- A private trust company (PTC) is a company formed to act as the trustee of one particular trust or group of trusts.

Test yourself answers

Test yourself 18.1

Differences between companies and foundations include:

- a foundation is governed by its charter and regulations whereas a company if governed by its articles of association;
- the council undertakes the objects of a company whereas the directors undertake the business of a company; and
- foundations do not have shareholders.

Test yourself 18.2

General partnerships may come into existence with a verbal agreement between two or more parties, who will then be referred to as the partners.

Test yourself 18.3

A general partner's liability remains unlimited for the debts of an ILP. However, the general partner acts as an agent of the partnership and is only liable for the debts that have not already been satisfied from the assets of the ILP. In practice, the liability of those persons managing the general partner can be limited by structuring the general partner as a limited company or limited partnership.

Test yourself 18.4

A private trust company is a company that is formed to act as a trustee of one particular trust or group of trusts – for example, for one individual or family.

Chapter nineteen
Trust and company administration

List of topics

1. Trust and company administration
2. The role of the trust and company administrator

Introduction

This chapter explains some of the main tasks that offshore administrators may undertake, including those that are specific to trust administration and those that are specific to the administration of companies. Finally, the chapter outlines the role of the trust and company administrator and some of the key aspects of the role.

Before reading this chapter, it is worth reminding yourself of some of the key terms used within the trust and company business industry that were explained in Chapter 2.

1. Trust and company administration

The term 'administration' is not always defined in the legislation of offshore centres. However, it may involve tasks such as:

- being appointed as the authorised signatory to a bank account;
- book-keeping;
- the preparation of accounts;
- the preparation of correspondence on behalf of entities under administration;
- the preparation of bank reconciliations; and
- the preparation of minutes and written resolutions.

In Guernsey, regulated administration activities are specified in the Regulation of Fiduciaries, Administration Businesses and Company Directors, etc. (Bailiwick of Guernsey) Law 2000 and comprise of:

a) The formation, management or administration of trusts and the provision of related advice, including:

  i) Acting as corporate or individual trustee or protector for trusts;

  ii) The provision to trusts of corporate or individual trustees or protectors;

b) Company or corporate administration including:

  i) The formation, management or administration of companies, partnerships or other unincorporated bodies and the provision of associated advice;

  ii) The provision to any such companies, partnerships or other unincorporated bodies of:

    A) Corporate or individual directors;

    B) Individuals or companies to act as company secretary or in any other capacity as officer of a company, partnership or other unincorporated body other than a director;

    C) Nominee services, including acting as or providing nominee shareholders;

    D) Registered offices or accommodation addresses (includes any postal, telecommunication or electronic address),

  iii) Acting as director of any company or unincorporated body, or as partner of any partnership, whether incorporated in Guernsey or elsewhere,

c) The provision of executorship services including acting as, or accepting an appointment made by will as, an executor of a will or administrator of an estate,

d) The formation, management or administration of foundations or the provision of associated advice, including

  i) Acting as corporate or individual foundation official;

  ii) The provision to foundations of corporate or individual foundation officials.

e) The formation, management or administration of pension schemes or gratuity schemes, and the provision of associated advice.

There are certain carve outs that apply to avoid unnecessary regulation, such as where the administration services are provided to a regulated financial services business, when a separate fiduciary licence is not required. Similarly, private arrangements and de minimis activities may be exempt from regulation – for example, a family company can be run by that family without a fiduciary licence and an individual may act as a director for up to six companies without requiring a personal fiduciary licence.

All of these tasks require careful thought and attention when undertaken on behalf of a trust or a company because administration services must be provided in accordance with all applicable laws and the service provider may incur a liability under a foreign company or trust law or AML laws as a consequence. It is therefore critical that service providers maintain comprehensive and current understanding of the laws and regulations, codes and regulatory guidance in place in all the jurisdictions connected to its own activities and indeed those of client entities.

For example, correspondence prepared when writing to a third party on behalf of a Jersey company must meet any requirements of the jurisdiction (in Jersey, the address of the registered office must appear on all business letters).

It is also very important that the person signing correspondence includes the capacity in which they are signing. If signing for and on behalf of a company, for example, they should state this fact.

1.1 Trust administration

Trust administration involves the administration of the trust assets in a manner that is in the best interest of the beneficiaries. Duties that are specific to the administration of trusts may include:

- liaising with the client and legal advisers in order to prepare initial trust documentation, such as the trust deed;
- making distributions to beneficiaries of the trust when due to life tenants or after the trustee has exercised a power of discretion. This task could involve preparing the relevant minutes of the trustee meeting at which the distribution was approved, preparing the instruction to the bank and presenting these documents to those with the authority to sign on behalf of the trustee. It is important to ensure that the trust cannot be considered to be a sham trust (i.e. that the settlor never really gave his assets away and continues to control them) and to ensure that there are no unintended taxation consequences. It is very important to keep income and capital entirely separate and show whether or not a distribution is capital or income, as each will be subject to different taxation treatment in the hands of the beneficiary. This is the reason that separate bank accounts for capital and income are maintained for offshore clients and that capital and income should not be mixed;
- making loans to beneficiaries and preparing any loan agreements, trustee minutes and payment;
- preparing documentation (such as deeds of addition or exclusion) when adding or removing beneficiaries to or from the trust;
- corresponding with beneficiaries or the settlor; and
- monitoring receipt of income due to the trust and ensuring that its liabilities, including its tax liabilities, are paid in a timely manner. As a trust is not a legal person, any tax liability is assessed on the trustees (rather than the trust itself) and is due to be paid by the trustees.

Trustees must ensure that the assets of the trust are properly vested in them and that they (rather than the client) remain in control of them. If an asset is given away (e.g. to an offshore trust) but an interest is kept in the asset (e.g. a settlor settles their house into the trust but continues to live in it rent-free), then this gift is known as a gift with reservation. Such a gift would still form a part of the person's estate upon their death.

1.2 Company administration

Company administration usually involves the management and control of the company's assets in a manner which is in the best interests of the company (and therefore ultimately in the best interests of all of the members).

A company administrator's tasks may include:

- the preparation and submission of company formation documentation to the Registrar of Companies. This may include making an application for the company name, preparing a statement of particulars detailing the identity of directors and the registered office, making an application for consent to issue shares, and preparing the memorandum and articles of the company;
- the preparation of statutory filings (annual returns) or the filing of special resolutions with the Registrar of Companies. In many jurisdictions, the directors are required to file an annual return with the Registrar, giving certain information about the company. The annual return is usually filed at the same time as an annual filing fee.
- the preparation of notices and draft minutes for ad-hoc meetings of the directors of the company or for meetings that are required by law – for example, the AGM;
- the preparation of documentation such as that required in order to waive an annual AGM;
- the maintenance of company statutory records (e.g. the register of members and the register of directors and secretaries); and
- the preparation of other documentation such as share certificates and declarations of trust.

Test yourself 19.1

State three tasks that a company administrator may undertake.

2. The role of the trust and company administrator

The role of a trust and company administrator will vary between jurisdictions and from firm to firm, as the role will be dependent upon the organisation's business, its size and its structure.

Larger companies, for example, may have more prescriptive procedures. Some functions (such as the preparation of minutes, book-keeping or reviews) may be centralised, meaning that specialist teams of administrators undertake the work.

2.1 Trust and company administrator competence

Many individuals who work in the trust and company administration sector belong to a professional body such as ICSA.

The demand for professionals to be members of such bodies is driven by Codes of Practice issued by some offshore centres' regulators. These impose a requirement for trust companies to have minimum levels of qualified staff.

2.2 Regard for the rationale of the structure

Administrators must understand the economic or commercial rationale for the structures under their administration. Understanding what the client is aiming to achieve by having an offshore structure is key to administering it in the correct manner and in identifying any deviations from what was expected to happen. This is also vital in aiding the identification of illegal or potentially illegal activity such as money laundering or terrorist financing.

Very often, professional intermediaries have been involved in the structure's establishment and there will be documented legal and or taxation advice. Where this is the case, administrators must ensure that:

- it is appropriate and covers all of the relevant circumstances;
- the advice and strategy remains effective – for example, where legislation changes; and
- the entity is administered in accordance with the advice.

For example, if it is imperative that no UK assets are acquired in order for the structure to avoid a taxation liability in the UK, the administrator will need to have a system in place to ensure that it does not inadvertently acquire such assets. A simple failure to inform a discretionary investment manager of this requirement may result in the structure failing in its aims.

2.3 Advice

It is not generally the role of the trust and company administrator to provide tax or legal advice to clients. Even so, the administrator should consider the taxation and legal consequences of their actions or inactions and remain apprised of developments in legislation in order to protect the integrity and legitimacy of the structures under administration.

The administrator's role will include liaising with other professional advisers such as tax or legal advisers or accountants. Trust companies will strive to build good relationships with such intermediaries – partly to ensure that the client's affairs are managed to a high standard and partly because they are a good source of new business opportunities. As such, professionals will often assist their clients to choose offshore services providers.

An administrator should ensure that advice (e.g. tax or legal advice) is sought where necessary. It is equally important that where advice has been obtained, it is appropriate (i.e. it covers all of the relevant circumstances) and that the entity is administered in accordance with that advice.

2.4 Fiduciary duties

As explained in Chapters 12 and 14, both trustees and directors have fiduciary duties. It is important that administrators bear these duties in mind when administering offshore entities. A trustee must always act in accordance with the trust deed and in the best interests of the trust beneficiaries (which is not necessarily what they might request or 'demand'); similarly, directors must act in accordance with the articles of association and in the best interests of the company.

A trust and company administrator should be familiar with the legislation governing trusts and companies and other entities in their jurisdiction.

However, administrators will not only administer entities created or incorporated from within their own jurisdiction in an international finance centre. It is more likely that they will also be required to administer entities incorporated in other offshore jurisdictions and, less frequently, entities incorporated in mainland jurisdictions. It is therefore important that they consider all relevant legislation when performing their day-to-day role.

2.5 Regard for constitutional documentation

While an administrator is unlikely to be familiar with the constitutional documents of all entities under their administration, they should understand the need to refer to this documentation whenever they are acting on behalf of an entity. Administrators must ensure that their actions are in accordance with the constitutional documentation concerning the entities under their administration – for example, the trust deed and any supplemental deeds relating to the trust and any memorandum and articles of a company.

It should be noted that a letter of wishes from a settlor can provide only informal guidance to a trustee or trustees. It is not a constitutional document of a trust and must not be regarded as a set of instructions.

A breach of a trustee's duty resulting from a failure to take the trust documentation into account may result in the trustee being liable to account to the beneficiaries for the breach.

2.6 Policies and procedures

At times, policies and procedures can appear to delay or complicate needlessly the provision of services to clients. The policies and procedures of an organisation usually exist to protect the organisation or its employees against a risk that more junior employees may not understand. For this reason, policies and procedures should always be followed.

The organisation may be required to maintain some procedures (e.g. those covering AML/CFT) by law. Others may exist in order to ensure that the trust company does not act outside the scope of its licence to conduct financial services business. An administrator who seeks to understand the reason for the existence of such policies and procedures will enhance their technical knowledge, and will be in a position to add value to their organisation by giving feedback to management on the effectiveness and efficiency of its policies and procedures.

2.7 Record keeping

A high standard of record keeping is essential in order to demonstrate compliance with the laws, orders and codes of the jurisdiction. It also ensures that client records are as useful as possible to the organisation, allowing it to service the client better and to ensure that the history of the entity is preserved.

A trustee cannot predict when it may need to rely on those records. For example, it may need to refer to them when dealing with future beneficiaries or when defending past actions when memories fade. Administrators should seek to protect the reputation of their organisation, their industry and their jurisdiction.

They must also bear in mind their personal obligations under AML legislation.

Test yourself 19.2

Why is it important that trust and company administrators always follow the procedures adopted by their organisation?

2.8 Customer due diligence

'Knowing' a client is a key part of trust and company administration. Administrators will often be required to ask clients for customer due diligence information and should be in a position to explain the requirements of their organisation to the clients.

The information obtained when CDD has been conducted must be considered and updated throughout the business relationship so that administrators are in a position to understand any transaction that they are involved with. This will allow the administrator to identify both opportunities and the risks involved in a transaction.

Administrators and managers and indeed directors must be vigilant in attempting to identify illegal or potentially illegal activity and reporting the same to their firm's MLRO.

A failure to report a suspicion or knowledge of illegal activity where there are reasonable grounds for a person to have acquired knowledge or to have possessed a suspicion may result in a criminal prosecution in some jurisdictions for having committed the offence of 'failure to report'.

2.9 Risk awareness

Administrators should be able to manage their client's expectations and should understand that they may not be able to fulfil their client's wishes at times – for example, where to do so would expose the trust company to an unacceptable level of risk.

Similarly, if the creation of a trust is to provide for vulnerable beneficiaries or those who cannot manage their finances, the trustee must strive to manage these relationships. Acting in the best interests of a beneficiary or beneficiaries is not always the same as acceding to their requests.

Administrators should seek to protect the reputation of their organisation, their industry and their jurisdiction, and must bear in mind their personal obligations under the AML legislation.

Chapter summary

- Trust and company administrators are individuals who are employed in the trust and company administration sector. They are sometimes referred to as 'trust officers'.
- Trust administration involves the administration of the trust assets in a manner that is in the best interest of the beneficiaries. Tasks that are specific to the administration of trusts include liaising with other professionals to prepare initial trust documentation and other tasks, making distributions to beneficiaries and ensuring that the assets are properly vested with the trustee.
- Company administration usually involves the management and control of the company's assets in a manner that is in the best interests of the company (and therefore ultimately in the best interests of all of the shareholders).
- Tasks specific to the administration of companies include the preparation of company formation documentation, the preparation of statutory filings, and the preparation of notices and minutes of meetings.
- The role of the trust and company administrator is varied. Administrators should always have regard for the rationale of the structures under their administration, the fiduciary duties of the trustee and directors, the constitutional documentation, the policies and procedures of the organisation, any customer due diligence requirements and risk. It cannot be stressed too highly that the need to be vigilant in identifying illegal or potentially illegal activity must be 'part and parcel' of a professional administrator's role.

Test yourself answers

Test yourself 19.1

Three tasks that a company administrator may undertake include the following:

- The preparation and submission of company formation documentation to the Registrar of Companies. This may include making an application for the company name, preparing a statement of particulars detailing the identity of directors and the registered office, making an application for consent to issue shares, and preparing the memorandum and articles of the company.

- The preparation of statutory filings (such as annual returns) or the filing of special resolutions with the companies register. In many jurisdictions, the directors are required to file an annual return with the registrar, giving certain information about the company. The annual return is usually filed at the same time as an annual filing fee.
- The preparation of notices and draft minutes for ad-hoc meetings of the directors of the company or for meetings that are required by law – for example, the AGM.

Test yourself 19.2

Trust and company administrators should always follow their organisation's procedures because those policies and procedures usually exist to protect the organisation or its employees against a risk that more junior employees may not understand.

The organisation may be required to maintain some procedures (e.g. those covering AML/CFT) by law. Others may exist in order to ensure that the trust company does not act outside the scope of its licence to conduct financial services business. An administrator who seeks to understand the reason for the existence of such policies and procedures will enhance their technical knowledge, and will be in a position to add value to their organisation by giving feedback to management on the effectiveness and efficiency of its policies and procedures.

Appendix one
Sample trust deed

INDEX

Clause

4. Power to Make Loans to Beneficiaries
5. Power to Borrow Money
6. Power to Permit Occupation of Property by Beneficiaries
7. Power to Pay Duties and Taxes
8. Power to Apportion between Income and Capital
9. Power to Appropriate
10. Power to Engage in Trade
11. Power to Take Advice
12. Power to Guarantee Debts
13. Power to Give Receipts
14. Power to Effect Compromises
15. Power to Give Indemnities
16. Protection of Property
17. Companies
18. Trustees may act Notwithstanding Personal Interest
19. Transactions with other Trusts
20. Contracts with Individual Trustees

SECOND SCHEDULE
Initial Property

THIRD SCHEDULE
The Beneficiaries

FOURTH SCHEDULE
Excluded Persons

FIFTH SCHEDULE

Appointment of New or Additional Trustees

THIS SETTLEMENT known or referred to as the ' **Trust**' is made the day of [**insert year in full**] BETWEEN of (hereinafter called 'the Settlor') of the one part AND of (hereinafter called 'the Original Trustee') of the other part.

WHEREAS: the Settlor being desirous of making such irrevocable Settlement as is hereinafter contained has had transferred or delivered to the Original Trustee or otherwise placed under the control of the Original Trustee the property specified in the Second Schedule hereto.

NOW THIS DEED WITNESSETH as follows:

1. INTERPRETATION

In this Deed wherever the context permits:

(1) The following words shall have the following meanings:

a) 'Beneficiaries' means:

i) all and any of the persons specified in the Third Schedule hereto;

ii) such other persons as are added to the class of Beneficiaries in exercise of the power conferred upon the Trustees by Clause 10 hereof;

and who (in either case) remain as Beneficiaries from time to time;

b) 'charity' shall mean any trust foundation or company established exclusively for purposes recognised as charitable by the laws of the island of Jersey and the word 'charitable' shall be construed accordingly;

c) 'company' means any body of persons corporate or unincorporate (of whatsoever kind) incorporated or otherwise brought into existence in any part of the world;

d) 'deed' means an instrument in writing;

e) 'Excluded Persons' means:

i) all and any of the persons specified in the Fourth Schedule hereto;

ii) any person constituted an Excluded Person pursuant to Clause 9 hereof;

f) 'infant' means any individual who has not attained the age of eighteen notwithstanding that such individual may by and in accordance with the law of his or her domicile be of full age, and the expressions 'minority' and 'full age' shall be construed accordingly;

g) 'person' means any individual or any company;

h) 'the Proper Law' means the law to the exclusive jurisdiction of which the rights of all parties and the construction and effect of each and every provision of this Settlement shall from time to time be subject and by which such rights construction and effect shall be construed and regulated;

i) 'the Regulations' means the regulations contained in the First Schedule hereto;

j) 'Settlement' means the settlement created by these presents;

k) 'the Trustees' means the Original Trustee or other the trustee or trustees for the time being hereof and for the avoidance of doubt any person may be appointed or remain as a sole trustee of this Settlement;

l) 'the Trust Fund' means:

i) the property specified in the Second Schedule hereto;

ii) all money investments or other property hereafter paid or transferred by any person or persons to or so as to be under the control of and (in either case) accepted by the Trustees as additions to the Trust Fund;

iii) all accumulations (if any) of income held as an accretion to capital;

iv) the money investments and property from time to time representing the said money property and additions;

m) 'the Trust Law' means the Trusts (Jersey) Law 1984 and any statutory amendments or re-enactments thereof;

n) 'the Trust Period' means such period as commences on the date hereof and continues for the duration of this Settlement PROVIDED always that nothing in this definition shall affect or prevent:

i) the exercise by the Trustees of their power pursuant to Clause 5(7) hereof to specify a particular date or event as the date or event upon which the Trust Period will terminate;

ii) the possibility of this Settlement terminating upon there ceasing to be any property or assets to constitute the Trust Fund or otherwise by operation of law; or

iii) the exercise of the power contained at Clause 12(3) hereof to amend this definition upon the occasion of any change in the Proper Law so as to ensure that this Settlement shall be valid enforceable and effective under the new Proper Law;

but save as aforesaid references in this Settlement to the 'Trust Period' shall not be construed as implying that this Settlement has or is required to have any finite or fixed period of existence.

(2) In the interpretation and construction of each and every provision hereof:

a) references to the children and issue of any person shall include legitimate legitimated illegitimate and adopted children and issue of such person and in the case of the issue of any person shall include the children and remoter issue of such person through all degrees PROVIDED THAT:

i) any legitimated person shall be treated as the child of his legitimative mother and father and of no other person;

ii) where a man's sperm is used for the purposes of medical, surgical or obstetric services provided for the purpose of assisting a child's mother to carry the child, that man shall not be regarded as the father of that child unless that man and the child's mother received those services together; and

iii) where a woman's ova are used for the purposes of medical, surgical or obstetric services provided for the purpose of assisting another woman to carry a child the woman who carried the child and not the woman who provided the ova shall be regarded as the mother of the child;

AND PROVIDED FURTHER THAT notwithstanding the provisions of sub-paragraphs (i) (ii) and (iii) hereof any adopted person shall be treated as the child of his adoptive parents and of no other person;

b) words in the singular shall include the plural and words in the plural shall include the singular;

c) words denoting any gender shall include all genders;

d) subject to any change in the Proper Law and as otherwise herein provided the words used herein shall bear the meaning ascribed to them by the Trust Law and the Interpretation (Jersey) Law 1954;

e) the headings and sub-headings to this Deed are inserted only for reference to the provisions hereof and shall not affect the construction of such provisions;

f) unless the context otherwise requires where this Settlement refers to any enactment the reference is a reference to that enactment as amended and includes a reference to that enactment as extended or applied by or under any other enactment including any other provision of that enactment.

2. PROPER LAW

This Settlement is established under the laws of the island of Jersey and subject and without prejudice to any transfer of the administration of the trusts hereof to any change in the Proper Law and to any change in the law of interpretation of this Settlement duly made according to the powers and provisions hereinafter declared the Proper Law shall be the law of the island of Jersey which said island shall be the forum for the administration hereof.

3. DECLARATION OF TRUST OF ORIGINAL AND ADDITIONAL PROPERTY

(1) The Trustees shall stand possessed of the Trust Fund upon with and subject to the trusts powers and provisions herein declared and contained of and concerning the same and the Trustees shall be at liberty at any time during the Trust Period to accept any money investments or property of whatsoever nature and wheresoever situate from any person or by will or by the provisions of any other trust or otherwise to the intent that the same shall be held by or on behalf of the Trustees as an accretion to the Trust Fund and from and after the date of such acceptance the Trustees shall hold the same accordingly.

(2) This Settlement shall be known or referred to under the name or reference first above stated or by such other name or reference as the Trustees in their absolute discretion shall from time to time think fit.

For trusts with no fixed maximum duration only:

(3) Subject to Clause 5(7) and Clause 12(3) hereof it is intended that this Settlement shall be capable of continuing for an unlimited period.

4. TRUSTS OF INCOME AND CAPITAL

The Trustees shall stand possessed of the Trust Fund and the income thereof upon the trusts and with and subject to the powers following, that is to say:

(1) During the Trust Period the Trustees may pay appropriate or apply the whole or any part of the income of the Trust Fund to or for the maintenance or otherwise for the benefit of all or such one or more exclusive of the other or others of the Beneficiaries in such shares and proportions if more than one and generally in such manner as the Trustees shall from time to time in their absolute discretion think fit.

(2) The Trustees shall hold any income appropriated to any of the Beneficiaries under the provisions of the preceding sub-clause to pay or apply the same to or for the benefit of such beneficiary with power to declare in respect of the same such other trusts (not exceeding the Trust Period) for the benefit of such beneficiary as the Trustees may in their absolute discretion determine including, but without prejudice to the generality of the foregoing, provisions for maintenance education or advancement or for accumulation of income whether during minority or otherwise, and with such discretionary trusts and powers exercisable by such persons as the Trustees shall in their like discretion determine.

(3) Subject to the foregoing powers the Trustees shall during the Trust Period accumulate the income of the Trust Fund and add the accumulations to the capital of the Trust Fund.

(4) At the end of the Trust Period the Trustees shall hold the Trust Fund UPON TRUST as to both capital and income for all or such one or more exclusive of the other or others of the Beneficiaries in such shares and proportions if more than one and generally in such manner as the Trustees shall prior to or at the end of the Trust Period in their absolute discretion determine and in default of and subject to such determination UPON TRUST for such of the Beneficiaries as shall then be living in equal shares absolutely.

(5) Subject as aforesaid the Trustees shall hold the Trust Fund UPON TRUST as to both capital and income for such charitable purposes as the Trustees shall determine and in default of and subject to such determination for charitable purposes generally.

5. POWERS OF APPOINTMENT AND ADVANCEMENT

Notwithstanding the trusts and powers hereinbefore declared and contained the Trustees may at any time during the Trust Period if in their absolute discretion they shall so think fit:

(1) By any deed revocable during the Trust Period or irrevocable appoint such new or other trusts powers and provisions governed by the law of any part of the world of and concerning the Trust Fund or the income thereof or any part thereof for the benefit of the Beneficiaries or any one or more of them exclusive of the other or others at such age or time or respective ages or times and in such shares and proportions and subject to such powers of appointment vested in any person and such provisions for maintenance education or advancement or for

accumulation of income or forfeiture in the event of bankruptcy and otherwise at the discretion of any person and with such discretionary trusts and powers exercisable by such person and generally in such manner as the Trustees may think fit for the benefit of such Beneficiaries or any one or more of them as aforesaid and for the purpose of giving effect to any such appointment by the same deed revoke all or any of the trusts powers and provisions herein contained with respect to the Trust Fund or the part thereof to which such appointment relates and so that in the event of any such appointment the Trustees shall thenceforward hold the Trust Fund or the part thereof to which such appointment relates upon and subject to the trusts powers and provisions so appointed in substitution for any of the trusts powers and provisions hereof so revoked as aforesaid and in priority to the other trusts powers and provisions herein declared and contained and in any appointment under the foregoing power the Trustees may delegate to any person all or any of the powers and discretions by this Settlement or by law vested in the Trustees.

(2) Raise the whole or any part of the capital of the Trust Fund and apply the same to or for the benefit of all or any one or more exclusive of the other or others of the Beneficiaries generally in such manner as the Trustees shall in their like discretion think fit.

(3) Pay or transfer the whole or any part of the capital or income of the Trust Fund to the trustees for the time being of any other trust wheresoever established or existing (whether governed by the law of the island of Jersey or by the law of any other state or territory) under which any one or more of the Beneficiaries are interested notwithstanding that such other trust may also contain trusts powers and provisions (discretionary or otherwise) in favour of some other person or objects if the Trustees shall in their absolute discretion consider such payment to be for the benefit of such one or more of the Beneficiaries.

(4) Settle capital on all or any one or more of the Beneficiaries and any settlement made by the Trustees under this present power upon or for the benefit of any one or more of the Beneficiaries as aforesaid may be created in and under the law of any part of the world (being a part of the world the local law whereof recognises settlements of the kind proposed to be made) and may contain such trusts powers and provisions whatsoever (including trusts powers and provisions to be exercised at the discretion of any person) as the Trustees shall think proper for the benefit of such Beneficiaries.

(5) Apply the whole or any part of the capital or income of the Trust Fund in or towards the payment or discharge of any tax duty or fiscal imposition whatsoever levied or imposed in any part of the world upon the trustees of or otherwise in respect of any other trust in which the Beneficiaries or any one or more of them shall be interested wherever such trustees shall be resident and wherever such trust is established or

existing and whether governed by the law of the island of Jersey or by the law of any other state or territory.

(6) Form companies in any part of the world and may at their discretion transfer to those companies all or any part of the capital and income of the Trust Fund whether by way of subscription, loan (at or free of interest and whether secured or unsecured) or otherwise and the cost and expenses of forming such a company and transferring all or any part of the capital and income of the Trust Fund shall be a charge on the Trust Fund.

(7) Appoint by deed that a specified future date or event shall be the date or event upon which the Trust Period shall terminate and any such deed may be revocable prior to the date or event specified therein or irrevocable but no such deed shall purport to cause the Trust Period to end after a date or event upon which it must already end by virtue of this Settlement or any deed supplemental hereto or by operation of law.

6. PROVISIONS RELEVANT TO CLAUSE 5

(1) For the purposes of Clause 5 hereof the word 'trust' shall mean any trust foundation anstalt or other similar juridical entity (whether or not having a separate legal personality) created by any settlement declaration of trust will codicil or other instrument or document under the law in force in any part of the world and a person shall be deemed to be interested under a trust if any capital or income comprised in the trust is or may become liable to be transferred paid applied or appointed to him or for his benefit either pursuant to the terms of the trust or in consequence of an exercise of any power or discretion thereby conferred on any person.

(2) No power conferred by Clause 5 hereof shall authorise any payment or transfer or advance to the trustees of another trust if any of the Excluded Persons would or might be or become beneficiaries or able to benefit under or by virtue of such other trust in any circumstances.

(3) Upon the payment or transfer pursuant to Clause 5 hereof of any money or property to the trustees of any other trust the Trustees hereof shall not be bound to see to the further application of such money or property.

7. PAYMENTS TO CHARITY

In exercise of the trusts and powers hereinbefore contained the Trustees may at the request of any Beneficiary if they in their absolute discretion shall so think fit pay or apply any part of the capital or income of the Trust Fund to or for the benefit of any charity or other charitable purposes approved by such Beneficiary and any such payment or application shall be deemed to be for the benefit of such Beneficiary and the Trustees shall not be restricted by any rule of law as to the amount or manner of such payment or application and the receipt in writing of the treasurer or other officer of any such charity shall be a sufficient discharge to the Trustees for any capital or income paid to such institution hereunder.

8. PAYMENTS TO INFANTS

Where the Trustees are authorised or required to pay or apply any income or capital of the Trust Fund to or for the benefit of any infant the Trustees may without seeing to the application thereof in their absolute discretion either pay the same to him as his absolute property notwithstanding that he is an infant and the receipt of any such infant Beneficiary shall be a good discharge to the Trustees therefor or pay the same to any parent or guardian of such infant or apply the same in such manner as may be directed in writing by such parent or guardian and the receipt of such parent or guardian in either case shall be a sufficient discharge to the Trustees for any income or capital so paid or applied.

9. POWERS OF EXCLUSION AND DISCLAIMERS

(1) The Trustees may at any time during the Trust Period by deed declare either irrevocably or revocably that a person or member of a class (whether or not ascertained) named or specified in such declaration and who is would or might but for this clause be or become a Beneficiary or otherwise be able to benefit hereunder as the case may be:

a) shall be wholly or partially excluded from future benefit hereunder; and/or

b) shall cease to be a Beneficiary; and/or

c) shall be an Excluded Person;

and any such declaration shall have effect accordingly PROVIDED THAT any such declaration that a person or member of a class shall be an Excluded Person shall be irrevocable and PROVIDED FURTHER that this power shall not be capable of being exercised so as to affect any transmissible interest to which any Beneficiary has previously become indefeasibly entitled (whether in possession or in reversion) under any irrevocable exercise of the Trustees' powers.

(2) Any person of full age to whom or for whose benefit any capital or income of the Trust Fund may be liable whether directly or indirectly to be appointed transferred or applied in any manner whatsoever by or in consequence of the exercise of any trust power or discretion vested in the Trustees or in any other person may by declaration in writing effective upon receipt by the Trustees during the Trust Period:

a) irrevocably declare that he shall be an Excluded Person; or

b) revocably during the Trust Period or irrevocably and either for no specified time or for such period as may be specified in such declaration:

i) disclaim his interest as an object of such trust power or discretion with respect to the whole or any specified part or share of the capital or income of the Trust Fund; or

(ii) declare that he shall cease to be a Beneficiary.

(3) A Beneficiary who by declaration pursuant to paragraph (b) of sub-clause (2) above disclaims his whole interest in the capital and income of the Trust Fund or declares that he shall cease to be a Beneficiary shall for all the purposes of this Settlement be deemed not to be a Beneficiary for as long as such declaration remains in effect notwithstanding that it is stated to be revocable or made to have effect only for a specified period.

10. POWER OF ADDITION

(1) The Trustees shall have power at any time during the Trust Period to add to the class of Beneficiaries such one or more persons (not being or none of them being an Excluded Person) as the Trustees shall in their absolute discretion determine.

(2) Any such addition shall be made by deed signed by the Trustees and:

a) naming or describing the person or persons to be thereby added to the class of Beneficiaries; and

b) specifying the date (not being earlier than the date of the declaration but during the Trust Period) from which such person or persons shall be so added.

11. POWER TO IGNORE INTERESTS

The Trustees in exercising any of the powers hereby conferred in favour of any particular person are hereby expressly authorised to ignore entirely the interests of any other person interested or who may become interested under these presents and in particular (but without prejudice to the generality of the foregoing) no appointment or advancement made in exercise of any power hereinbefore contained shall be invalid on the grounds that:

(1) an insubstantial illusory or nominal share is appointed to any one or more objects of such power or left unappointed; or

(2) any object of such power is thereby altogether excluded;
but every such appointment or advancement shall be valid notwithstanding that any one or more objects of the power is or are not thereby or in default of appointment to take any share in the Trust Fund.

12. POWER TO CHANGE PROPER LAW

(1) The Trustees may at any time during the Trust Period by deed declare that:

a) this Settlement shall from the date of such declaration take effect in accordance with the law of some other state or territory in any part of the world (being a place under the law of which trusts are recognised and enforced); and

b) the forum for the administration thereof shall thenceforth be the courts of that state or territory.

(2) As from the date of any such declaration the law of the state or territory named therein shall be the law applicable to this Settlement and the courts thereof shall be the forum for the administration thereof but subject to any further exercise by the Trustees of the power contained in sub-clause (1) hereof.

(3) So often as any such declaration shall be made the Trustees shall be at liberty to make such consequential alterations or additions in or to the trusts powers and provisions of this Settlement as the Trustees may consider necessary or desirable to ensure that the trusts powers and provisions of this Settlement shall (mutatis mutandis) be as valid enforceable and effective as they are under the laws of Jersey.

(4) Notwithstanding anything in this clause hereinbefore contained the provisions hereof shall not authorise any such declaration which would or might directly or indirectly result in an Excluded Person obtaining any benefit.

13. ADDITIONAL POWERS OF THE TRUSTEES

The Trustees shall have the additional powers discretions rights and immunities set out in the Regulations.

14. EXERCISE OF POWERS

(1) The Trustees shall exercise the powers and discretions vested in them as they shall think most expedient for the benefit of all or any of the persons actually or prospectively interested under this Settlement and may exercise (or refrain from exercising) any power or discretion for the benefit of any one or more of them without being obliged to consider the interests of the others or other.

(2) Subject to sub-clause (1) hereof every discretion vested in the Trustees shall be absolute and uncontrolled and every power vested in them shall be exercisable at their absolute and uncontrolled discretion and the Trustees shall have the same discretion in deciding whether or not to exercise any such power.

15. DELEGATION OF TRUSTS AND POWERS

(1) The Trustees shall have power at any time by deed revocable during the Trust Period or irrevocable to delegate to any person (including in cases where there is more than one Trustee to any one of the Trustees) the execution or exercise of all or any trusts and powers (both

administrative and dispositive) hereby or by law conferred on such Trustee.

(2) Without prejudice to the generality of the foregoing the Trustees shall have power at any time by deed revocable during the Trust Period or irrevocable to appoint an investment manager whom the Trustees reasonably consider competent and qualified to manage the investment of the Trust Fund.

(3) In any delegation pursuant to sub-clauses (1) or (2) hereof the Trustees shall have the benefit of the indemnities contained in the Trust Law in respect of any such delegation.

16. RESTRICTION AND RELEASE OF POWERS

The Trustees shall have power at any time by deed revocable during the Trust Period or irrevocable to release or to any extent restrict the future exercise of any powers hereby or by law conferred on them notwithstanding the fiduciary nature of any such power provided that the power conferred upon the Trustees by Clause 10 hereof shall not be capable of being released or restricted unless at the date of any such release or restriction there are at least two Beneficiaries.

17. RESTRICTION ON EXERCISE OF POWERS

Despite anything contained elsewhere in this Settlement no discretion or power conferred on the Trustees or on any other person shall be exercisable after the expiration of the Trust Period or in such a way as to infringe any rule against perpetuities or excessive accumulations applicable hereto.

18. POWER OF APPOINTMENT OF NEW OR ADDITIONAL TRUSTEES

(1) If any trustee hereof whether original additional or substituted shall die or being a corporation shall be dissolved or shall give notice of his or its desire to withdraw and be discharged from the trusts hereof under the provisions of sub-clause (2) of this clause or shall refuse or become unfit to act or be removed as a trustee hereof (any such trustee being hereinafter referred to as an 'Outgoing Trustee') then the persons specified in the Fifth Schedule hereto in order of priority may by deed appoint one or more other persons (whether resident within or without the island of Jersey) but subject to any exclusions or provisions (if any) specified in the said Fifth Schedule to be a trustee hereof in place of such Outgoing Trustee.

(2) If any trustee hereof shall at any time desire to withdraw and be discharged from the trusts hereof he or it may (subject to any exclusions or provisions, if any, specified in the said Fifth Schedule) so do by notice in writing signed by himself or in the case of a corporate trustee by any of its officers given to the person having for the time being power to appoint new or additional trustees hereof and upon the posting or personal delivery of such notice the trustee so doing

shall cease to be a trustee hereof to all intents and purposes except as to acts and deeds necessary for the proper vesting of the Trust Fund in the continuing or new trustee or otherwise as the case may require PROVIDED that it shall not be possible if there shall ever be more than one trustee of this Settlement in office for the time being for all such trustees to resign by simultaneously giving notice pursuant to this sub-clause.

(3) The person for the time being having the power to appoint new trustees hereof shall (subject always to any exclusions, if any, specified in the said Fifth Schedule) have power to appoint one or more other persons (whether resident within or without the island of Jersey) to be an additional trustee hereof.

(4) Acts and deeds to be done or executed for the proper vesting of the Trust Fund in continuing new or additional trustees shall be done and executed by the Outgoing Trustee and the continuing trustees (if any) at the expense of the income or capital of the Trust Fund PROVIDED THAT an Outgoing Trustee who is or may be liable as a trustee hereof or who may at the death of any person be liable as a trustee or former trustee hereof for any liabilities whether existing future contingent or otherwise shall not be bound to transfer the Trust Fund unless reasonable security is provided for indemnifying such Outgoing Trustee against such liabilities.

(5) Any new or additional trustee appointed under the provisions hereof or by a court of competent jurisdiction shall have such powers rights and benefits as to remuneration or otherwise as may be agreed in writing at or prior to his or its appointment (in case of a trustee appointed as hereinbefore provided) between such new or additional trustee and the person making such appointment or (in the case of a trustee appointed by a court) as the order appointing such trustee may direct.

(6) Any trustee for the time being of this Settlement being a corporation shall have power to act by its proper officers.

19. INDEMNITY OF OUTGOING TRUSTEE

An Outgoing Trustee shall be released from liability in respect of all claims demands actions proceedings and accounts of any kind brought or made by any Beneficiary or other person (whether in existence or not) actually or prospectively interested under this Settlement or any trustee of this Settlement for or in respect of any act or omission in relation to the Trust Fund or the income thereof or the trusts of this Settlement or any of the Outgoing Trustee's duties hereunder except only liability:

(1) arising from any breach of trust to which such trustee (or in the case of a corporate trustee any of its officers or employees) was a party or to which he was privy; or

(2) in respect of actions to recover from such trustee (or in the case of a corporate trustee any of its officers or employees) trust property or the

proceeds of trust property in the possession of such trustee officers or employees.

20. TRUSTEE INDEMNITY

In the execution of the trusts and powers hereof no trustee shall be liable for any loss to the Trust Fund arising in consequence of the failure depreciation or loss of any investments made in good faith or by reason of any act or omission made in good faith or of any other matter or thing except liability for breach of trust arising from the fraud wilful misconduct or gross negligence of the trustee who is sought to be made liable.

21. TRUSTEES REMUNERATION

(1) Any trustee for the time being hereof being an advocate solicitor accountant or other individual engaged in any profession or business or any person associated or in any way connected with the Trustees (including in the case of a corporate trustee any person associated with or beneficially interested in the shares of or in any way connected with such corporate trustee) shall be entitled to charge and be paid all usual professional or other charges for business done and time spent and services rendered by him or his firm and expenses incurred by him or his firm in the execution of the trusts and powers hereof whether in the ordinary course of his profession or business or not and although not of a nature requiring the employment of an advocate solicitor accountant or other professional person and any such person shall be entitled to retain any commission which would or may become payable to him notwithstanding that such commission is payable as a direct or indirect result of any dealing with property which is or may become subject to the trusts hereof.

(2) Any trustee for the time being hereof who shall be a company authorised to undertake trust business shall be entitled in addition to reimbursement of its proper expenses to remuneration for its services in accordance with such company's usual or published terms and conditions for trust business in force from time to time.

(3) No trustee hereof or director or other officer of any corporation which is a trustee hereof shall be liable to account for any remuneration or other profit received by him in consequence of his acting as or being appointed to be a director or other officer or servant of any company even though his appointment was procured by an exercise by him or by the Trustees of voting rights attached to securities in the Trust Fund or by any abstention from exercising such voting rights.

(4) Any trustee for the time being hereof or any person associated or in any way connected with such trustee (including in the case of a corporate trustee any person connected with or beneficially interested in the shares of or in any way connected with such trustee) who carries on the business of banking may act as banker for this Settlement on

the same terms as those made with an ordinary customer without being liable to account to the Trust Fund for any profits earned thereby except for interest payable on any sums placed with such trustee or associate on an interest bearing account as an investment of any part of the Trust Fund.

22. PROVISIONS AS TO EXCLUDED PERSONS

Subject only to Clause 21 hereof no Excluded Person shall be capable of taking any benefit of any kind by virtue or in consequence of this Settlement and in particular but without prejudice to the generality of the foregoing provisions of this clause:

(1) the Trust Fund and the income thereof shall be possessed and enjoyed to the entire exclusion of any such Excluded Person and of any benefit to him by contract or otherwise; and

(2) no part of the capital or income of the Trust Fund shall be paid or lent or applied for the benefit either directly or indirectly of any such Excluded Person in any manner or in any circumstances whatsoever; and

(3) no power or discretion hereby or by any appointment made hereunder or by law conferred upon the Trustees or any of them shall be capable of being exercised in such manner that any such Excluded Person will or may become entitled either directly or indirectly to any benefit in any manner or in any circumstances whatsoever.

23. VARIATION OF TERMS OF SETTLEMENT

The Trustees may at any time during the Trust Period by deed vary amend add to or delete any or all of the provisions of this Settlement including the trusts powers and discretions and the administrative powers herein and in the Schedules declared and contained PROVIDED ALWAYS that:

(1) they shall be satisfied that such variations amendments additions or deletions are for the benefit of all or any one or more of the Beneficiaries; and

(2) they shall have obtained a prior written opinion approving any such variations amendments additions or deletions from a lawyer qualified for at least five years in the jurisdiction of the Proper Law; and

(3) no such variation amendment addition or deletion shall infringe the Proper Law or permit any Excluded Person to benefit in any way under or by virtue of the trusts or powers contained in this Settlement; and

(4) no such variation amendment or addition shall be made to the provisions of this clause but it shall be permissible to delete this clause in its entirety.

24. CONFIDENTIALITY

Subject to the provisions of the Trust Law and to any order of a court of the jurisdiction of the Proper Law the Trustees shall not be obliged to disclose to any Beneficiary or any other person having any interest in this Settlement or any other person whatsoever:

(1) any accounts or document forming part of any accounts of this Settlement or the accounts of any company in which the Trustees shall have any interest PROVIDED THAT this shall not enable the Trustees to withhold production of the accounts of the Settlement from a Beneficiary who requests that a copy of such accounts be made available to him within a reasonable period after the expiry of the relevant accounting period; or

(2) any document disclosing the deliberations of the Trustees as to the manner in which they exercised a power or discretion or performed a duty conferred or imposed upon them; or

(3) any document disclosing the reason for any particular exercise of a power or discretion or performance of a duty or the material upon which such reason shall or might have been based; or

(4) any document relating to the exercise or proposed exercise of any power or discretion or the performance or proposed performance of any duty.

25. IRREVOCABILITY

This Settlement shall be irrevocable.

26. PRELIMINARY EXPENSES

The Trustees shall have power to pay out of the Trust Fund all expenses of whatever nature of and incidental to the creation of this Settlement.

THE FIRST SCHEDULE hereinbefore referred to: Regulations

1. GENERAL POWER

The Trustees shall have all powers of investment management sale exchange partition hypothecation mortgage pledge assignment leasing insurance repair building development protection improvement equipment dealing and disposition and all other powers of a natural person acting as absolute beneficial owner of the Trust Fund and their powers shall not be restricted by any principle of construction (or rule or requirement of the Proper Law save to the extent that such is obligatory) but shall operate according to the widest generality of which the foregoing words are capable notwithstanding that certain powers are hereinafter more particularly set forth.

2. POWERS OF INVESTMENT

(1) Trust moneys may be invested or laid out in the purchase of (or at interest upon the security of) such stocks funds shares securities or other investments or property of whatsoever nature and wheresoever situate and whether involving liability or not and whether producing income or not or upon such personal credit with or without security as the Trustees shall in their absolute discretion think fit including the purchase erection and improvement of any property as a residence for any person who is a Beneficiary hereunder and the purchase and improvement of chattels for the use of such person to the intent that the Trustees shall have the same full and unrestricted powers of investing and transposing investments and laying out moneys in all respects as if they were absolutely entitled thereto beneficially and without regard to the requirements of the Proper Law (save to the extent that these are obligatory) and in the professed exercise of this power the Trustees shall not be liable for any loss to the Trust Fund arising from any investment or purchase made in good faith.

(2) Without prejudice to the generality of the preceding paragraph hereof:

a) the acquisition of any investment although of a speculative nature shall be deemed to be an authorised investment of trust moneys and the Trustees shall not be under any obligation or be liable for any loss occasioned by any failure to diversify investments notwithstanding that the whole or a substantial part of the Trust Fund may consist of a single asset or the stocks shares or debentures of a single company;

b) the acquisition of any reversionary interest in property or any policy or securities or other investments not producing income or in respect of which no dividend interest or rent is payable shall be deemed to be an authorised investment of trust moneys;

c) the acquisition of any limited interest in property including any limited equitable interest under a settlement or trust or any annuity or policy or securities or other investments being of a wasting nature shall be deemed to be an authorised investment of trust moneys;

d) the Trustees shall have power to make any such investment as is mentioned in paragraphs (b) and (c) of this sub-regulation notwithstanding that the making thereof may affect or alter the interests of the persons respectively interested in capital and income hereunder;

e) the Trustees shall have power to apply any moneys forming part of the capital or income of the Trust Fund in the purchase or subscription of partly paid shares and shall have power to pay up such shares at such times and in such manner as they shall in their absolute discretion determine;

f) the Trustees shall have power pending the investment thereof for any period to place any moneys forming part of the Trust Fund on current or deposit account with any bank or any other company or corporation conducting the business of banking or accepting moneys on deposit in any part of the world and may open and maintain banking accounts in their joint names or in the name of any one of them or the name of this Settlement;

g) the Trustees may invest the whole or any part of the capital or income of the Trust Fund in effecting purchasing or otherwise acquiring and paying premiums on any policy of assurance upon the life of any person whether such policies be whole life or endowment or policies to cover death within any term (howsoever short) or policies restricted to death by accident and generally upon any terms and conditions as the Trustees shall think fit and the Trustees shall have all the powers of an absolute beneficial owner as respects any policy forming part of the Trust Fund including the power to exercise any option afforded by such policy or to sell or realise any such policy or to convert the same into a fully paid up policy or into any other form of assurance;

h) the Trustees shall have power to leave any assets subject to any of the trusts of this Settlement in the state of investment in which they may be from time to time;

i) the Trustees shall have power at any time to sell or call in any investments or property for the time being comprised in the Trust Fund or transpose or convert the same into any other investments or property the acquisition of which with moneys subject hereto is hereby authorised.

3. TRUSTEES NOT BOUND TO INTERFERE IN BUSINESS OF COMPANY IN WHICH TRUST INTERESTED

The Trustees shall not be bound or required to interfere in the management or conduct of the business of any company wherever resident or incorporated in which the Settlement shall be interested although holding the whole or a majority of the shares carrying the control of the company but so long as the Trustees shall have no actual notice of any act of dishonesty or misappropriation of moneys on the part of the directors having the management of such company the Trustees shall be at liberty to leave the conduct of its business (including the payment or non-payment of dividends) wholly to such directors without requiring to be supplied with any information concerning the company or its affairs beyond that to which every shareholder would be entitled and no Beneficiary hereunder shall be entitled to require the distribution of any dividend by any company wherever incorporated or resident in which the Settlement may be interested or require the Trustees to exercise any powers they may have of compelling any such distribution.

4. POWER TO MAKE LOANS TO BENEFICIARIES

The Trustees shall have power to lend the whole or any part of the Trust Fund:

(1) on reasonably prudent commercial terms to any person whatsoever; and

(2) on such terms as to repayment and interest or interest free and whether with or without security to any Beneficiary (or to any company in which a Beneficiary may have an interest notwithstanding that others may also be interested in that company);

as the Trustees may in their absolute discretion think fit but so that no such loan shall be made on terms that repayment shall be postponed beyond the Trust Period.

5. POWER TO BORROW MONEY

The Trustees may at any time and from time to time borrow money or other property on the security of the Trust Fund with power to charge any part of the capital or income (including any future income) of the Trust Fund with the repayment of any moneys or property so borrowed and may pay or apply the money or property so raised in any manner in which money or other property forming part of the capital of the Trust Fund may be paid or applied and so that the Trustees shall have power to enter into any joint borrowing arrangements with any person and whether or not involving joint or several liability and no purchaser lender or other person paying or advancing money or other property on a sale mortgage charge or other transaction purporting to be made by the Trustees under or for any of the purposes of this Settlement shall be concerned to see that the money or property is wanted or that no more than is wanted is raised or otherwise as to the propriety of the transaction or the application of the money or other property.

6. POWER TO PERMIT OCCUPATION OF PROPERTY BY BENEFICIARIES

The Trustees shall have power to permit any Beneficiary to reside in any dwelling occupy any land or have the custody and use of any chattels which may for the time being be held subject to the trusts hereof upon such conditions as to payment of rent rates taxes and other expenses and outgoings and as to insurance repair and decoration and for such period and generally upon such terms as the Trustees in their absolute discretion shall think fit and it shall be no bar to the exercise of such power that some person or persons in addition to the Beneficiary shall also thereby incidentally have the use or enjoyment of such dwelling house land or chattels.

7. POWER TO PAY DUTIES AND TAXES

In the event of any tax duty or fiscal imposition whatsoever becoming payable in the island of Jersey or elsewhere in respect of the Trust Fund or any part thereof in any circumstances whatsoever the Trustees shall have power to pay all such taxes duties or fiscal impositions out of the Trust Fund or the income thereof and shall have entire discretion as to the time and manner in which the said taxes duties or fiscal impositions shall be paid and the Trustees may pay such taxes duties or fiscal impositions notwithstanding that the same shall not be recoverable from the Trustees or the Beneficiaries or other persons entitled hereunder or that the payment shall not be to the advantage of any Beneficiary or other person entitled hereunder.

8. POWER TO APPORTION BETWEEN INCOME AND CAPITAL

The Trustees shall have power to treat as income or as capital any dividends stock dividends rights interests rents or profits derived from any property at any time constituting the whole or any part of the Trust Fund and generally to determine what part of the receipts of this Settlement is income and what is capital whether or not such property is wasting hazardous or unproductive or was purchased at a premium or discount and notwithstanding the time when such dividends stock dividends rights interest rents or profits were earned accrued declared or paid to make such reserves out of income or capital as the Trustees deem proper for expenses taxes and other liabilities of this Settlement to pay from income or from capital or to apportion between income and capital any expenses of making or changing investments and of selling exchanging or leasing including brokers commissions and charges and generally to determine what part of the expenses of this Settlement shall be charged to capital and what part to income and to determine as between separate funds and separate parts or shares the allocation of income gains profits losses and distributions. Any decisions of the Trustees under this Regulation whether made in writing or implied from their acts shall so far as the law may permit be conclusive and binding on the Beneficiaries and all persons actually or prospectively interested under this Settlement.

9. POWER TO APPROPRIATE

The Trustees shall have power to appropriate the Trust Fund or any part thereof in such manner and in accordance with such valuation as they in their absolute discretion think fit and without the consent of any Beneficiary hereunder being required for any such appropriation.

10. POWER TO ENGAGE IN TRADE

The Trustees shall have power to engage in any trade or venture in the nature of trade whether solely or jointly with any other person and whether or not by way of partnership under the jurisdiction of the Proper Law or elsewhere and make such arrangements in connection therewith as they think fit and may delegate any exercise of this power to any one or more of their number or to a company or partnership formed for this purpose PROVIDED THAT the persons carrying on any trade or venture in the nature of trade authorised by this Regulation shall have power to determine what are the distributable profits thereof and so much of the distributable profits as accrue to the Trustees (and no more) shall be income of the Trust Fund for the purposes of this Settlement. Any power vested in the Trustees under this Settlement shall (where applicable) extend to any arrangements in connection with any such company or partnership as aforesaid and in particular but without prejudice to the generality of the foregoing the Trustees' powers of borrowing and charging shall extend to any borrowing arrangements made in connection with such company or partnership as aforesaid and whether made severally or jointly with others or with unequal liability.

11. POWER TO TAKE ADVICE

The Trustees shall have power to take the opinion of legal counsel locally or where necessary or appropriate elsewhere concerning any matter in any way relating to this Settlement or to their duties in connection with the trusts hereof and in all matters to act in accordance with the opinion of such counsel AND in addition the Trustees shall have power to employ and take advice from any of the professional advisers or agents referred to in the Trust Law and shall have the benefit of the indemnity in respect thereof contained in the Trust Law. The professional fees commissions and disbursements of all such advisers or agents including legal counsel shall be payable out of the income or capital of the Trust Fund as the Trustees shall think fit.

12. POWER TO GUARANTEE DEBTS

The Trustees shall have power at any time in their absolute discretion and on such terms as they deem fit to appropriate or to apply the capital or income of the Trust Fund or any part thereof in securing the payment of money owed by any Beneficiary or the performance of any obligations of any Beneficiary and to give any guarantee or to become surety for any Beneficiary (or in any of the aforesaid cases in respect of any company in which a Beneficiary shall have an interest notwithstanding that others may also be so interested) and for these purposes to hypothecate mortgage or charge any investments or property for the time being forming part of the Trust Fund or to deposit or transfer any such investments or property with or to any person firm or company on trust or by way of security.

13. POWER TO GIVE RECEIPTS

The Trustees shall have power to give receipts for any money securities or other property or effects and so that any receipt so given shall be a sufficient discharge to the person paying transferring or delivering the same and shall effectively exonerate him from seeing to the application thereof or being answerable for any loss or misapplication thereof.

14. POWER TO EFFECT COMPROMISES

The Trustees shall have power to:

(1) accept any property whether movable or immovable before the time at which it is transferable or payable;

(2) pay or allow any debt or claim on any evidence which they may think sufficient;

(3) accept any composition or any security movable or immovable for any debt or any property due to or claimed by the Trustees;

(4) allow any time for payment of any debt;

(5) compromise compound abandon submit to arbitration or otherwise settle any debt account claim or thing relating to the Trust Fund without being liable for any loss to the Trust Fund thereby occurring.

15. POWER TO GIVE INDEMNITIES

The Trustees shall have power to enter into any indemnity in favour of any former trustee or any other person in respect of any tax duty or fiscal imposition or other liability of any nature prospectively payable in respect of the Trust Fund or otherwise in connection with this Settlement and to charge or deposit the whole or any part of the Trust Fund as security for such indemnity in such manner in all respects as they shall think fit.

16. PROTECTION OF PROPERTY

The Trustees shall not be liable for any loss damage or depreciation that may happen at any time or from any cause to any property forming part of the Trust Fund and they shall not be bound to see nor be liable or accountable for omitting or neglecting to see to the upkeep repair or insurance of any such property but may repair alter renew improve maintain store replace and insure any such property in such manner and to such extent as they shall think fit the cost thereof to be borne by the income or capital of the Trust Fund as the Trustees shall in their absolute discretion think fit.

17. COMPANIES

(1) The Trustees may at any time at the expense of the income or capital of the Trust Fund arrange or join or concur in arranging for the incorporation or registration of any company in any part of the world (whether or not with limited liability) for all or any of the following purposes (with or without other purposes) that is to say:

a) to purchase take on lease or otherwise acquire and to hold or employ in any business or otherwise turn to account or dispose of all or any of the property for the time being subject to the trusts hereof or any rights of any kind over the same either with or without any other assets and so that the Trustees may accept from any such company such consideration for any such purchase lease or other acquisition as the Trustees shall in their discretion think fit (whether in the form of cash stocks shares or securities of the same or any other company rents options or in any other form whatsoever);

b) to manage cultivate or otherwise administer all or any of the property for the time being subject to the trusts hereof either with or without any other assets or to act as nominee agent or attorney (whether sole or joint) for the Trustees and so that the Trustees may pay or allow to any such company such fees share of profits or other remuneration for such management cultivation or other work of administration or for acting as such nominee agent or attorney as they may in their discretion think fit and may permit any such company to act as nominee agent or attorney (whether sole or joint) for any other person approved of by the Trustees;

c) to be one of the trustees or sole trustee hereof or of any appointment or appointments made hereunder with respect to any part or parts of the Trust Fund held on trusts distinct from those relating to any other part or parts and so that the Trustees may permit any such company to be one of the trustees or sole trustee of any other trust approved of by the Trustees.

(2) The Trustees shall have power:

a) to agree to any reconstruction amalgamation or other arrangement or scheme concerning any company whose shares comprise or form part of the Trust Fund (and in this and the two following sub-clauses of this clause the word 'shares' includes stock funds debentures debenture stock mortgage or any other securities);

b) to accept in addition to or in lieu of those already held other shares in any company whose shares comprise or form part of the Trust Fund in connection with or as part of any such reconstruction amalgamation arrangement or scheme as aforesaid;

c) to agree to the winding up of any company whose shares comprise or form part of the Trust Fund.

18. TRUSTEES MAY ACT NOTWITHSTANDING PERSONAL INTEREST

Subject as herein otherwise expressly provided any of the Trustees may exercise or join or concur in exercising any or all of the powers and discretions hereby or by law given to the Trustees notwithstanding that he may have a personal interest in the mode or result of exercising any such power or discretion but any of the Trustees may abstain from acting except as a merely formal party in any matter in which he may be personally interested as aforesaid and may allow a co-trustee to act alone in the exercise of the powers and discretions aforesaid in relation to such matter.

19. TRANSACTIONS WITH OTHER TRUSTS

The Trustees may in the execution of any of the trusts hereof or in exercise of any of the powers hereby or by law given to them sell property or lend money to or buy property or borrow money from or carry out any other transaction with the trustees of any other trust or the executors or administrators of any estate (not being a trust or estate under which any Excluded Person shall have any beneficial or prospective interest whatsoever) notwithstanding that the Trustees or any of them are or is the same persons or person as those trustees executors or administrators or any of them and where the Trustees are the same persons as those trustees executors or administrators the transaction shall be binding on all persons then or thereafter interested hereunder though effected and evidenced only by an entry in the accounts of the Trustees.

20. CONTRACTS WITH INDIVIDUAL TRUSTEES

(1) Any of the Trustees may contract with the Trustees as vendor or purchaser or otherwise in a matter in which he is personally interested provided that there is at least one trustee who has no personal interest in such contract.

(2) This provision is additional and without prejudice to the provisions of the last preceding regulation (relating to transactions in which one or more of the Trustees are interested in different fiduciary capacities).

THE SECOND SCHEDULE hereinbefore referred to: Initial Property

THE THIRD SCHEDULE hereinbefore referred to: The Beneficiaries

THE FOURTH SCHEDULE hereinbefore referred to: Excluded Persons

THE FIFTH SCHEDULE hereinbefore referred to: Appointment of New or Additional Trustees

IN WITNESS WHEREOF this Deed has been executed on the date first above written.

[SIGNED by **[ ]**)

in the presence of:)**]**

[THE COMMON SEAL of **[ ]**)

LIMITED was hereunto affixed in)

the presence of:)**]**

Director

Director/Secretary

Appendix two
Model articles for private companies limited by shares

INDEX TO THE ARTICLES

PART 3
SHARES AND DISTRIBUTIONS
SHARES

21. All shares to be fully paid up
22. Powers to issue different classes of share
23. Company not bound by less than absolute interests
24. Share certificates
25. Replacement share certificates
26. Share transfers
27. Transmission of shares
28. Exercise of transmittees' rights
29. Transmittees bound by prior notices

DIVIDENDS AND OTHER DISTRIBUTIONS

30. Procedure for declaring dividends
31. Payment of dividends and other distributions
32. No interest on distributions
33. Unclaimed distributions
34. Non-cash distributions
35. Waiver of distributions

CAPITALISATION OF PROFITS

36. Authority to capitalise and appropriation of capitalised sums

PART 4
DECISION-MAKING BY SHAREHOLDERS
ORGANISATION OF GENERAL MEETINGS

37. Attendance and speaking at general meetings
38. Quorum for general meetings
39. Chairing general meetings
40. Attendance and speaking by directors and non-shareholders
41. Adjournment

VOTING AT GENERAL MEETINGS

42. Voting: general
43. Errors and disputes
44. Poll votes
45. Content of proxy notices
46. Delivery of proxy notices
47. Amendments to resolutions

PART 5
ADMINISTRATIVE ARRANGEMENTS

48. Means of communication to be used
49. Company seals
50. No right to inspect accounts and other records
51. Provision for employees on cessation of business

PART 1 INTERPRETATION AND LIMITATION OF LIABILITY

Defined terms

1. In the articles, unless the context requires otherwise:

'articles' means the company's articles of association;
'bankruptcy' includes individual insolvency proceedings in a jurisdiction other than England and Wales or Northern Ireland which have an effect similar to that of bankruptcy;
'chairman' has the meaning given in article 12;
'chairman of the meeting' has the meaning given in article 39;
'Companies Acts' means the Companies Acts (as defined in section 2 of the Companies Act 2006), in so far as they apply to the company;
'director' means a director of the company, and includes any person occupying the position of director, by whatever name called;
'distribution recipient' has the meaning given in article 31;
'document' includes, unless otherwise specified, any document sent or supplied in electronic form;
'electronic form' has the meaning given in section 1168 of the Companies Act 2006;
'fully paid' in relation to a share, means that the nominal value and any premium to be paid to the company in respect of that share have been paid to the company;
'hard copy form' has the meaning given in section 1168 of the Companies Act 2006;
'holder' in relation to shares means the person whose name is entered in the register of members as the holder of the shares;
'instrument' means a document in hard copy form;
'ordinary resolution' has the meaning given in section 282 of the Companies Act 2006;
'paid' means paid or credited as paid;
'participate', in relation to a directors' meeting, has the meaning given in article 10;
'proxy notice' has the meaning given in article 45;
'shareholder' means a person who is the holder of a share;
'shares' means shares in the company;
'special resolution' has the meaning given in section 283 of the Companies Act 2006;
'subsidiary' has the meaning given in section 1159 of the Companies Act 2006;
'transmittee' means a person entitled to a share by reason of the death or bankruptcy of a shareholder or otherwise by operation of law; and
'writing' means the representation or reproduction of words, symbols or other information in a visible form by any method or combination of methods, whether sent or supplied in electronic form or otherwise.

Unless the context otherwise requires, other words or expressions contained in these articles bear the same meaning as in the Companies Act 2006 as in force on the date when these articles become binding on the company.

Liability of members

2. The liability of the members is limited to the amount, if any, unpaid on the shares held by them.

PART 2 DIRECTORS

DIRECTORS' POWERS AND RESPONSIBILITIES

Directors' general authority

3. Subject to the articles, the directors are responsible for the management of the company's business, for which purpose they may exercise all the powers of the company.

Shareholders' reserve power

4. (1) The shareholders may, by special resolution, direct the directors to take, or refrain from taking, specified action.

   (2) No such special resolution invalidates anything which the directors have done before the passing of the resolution.

Directors may delegate

5. (1) Subject to the articles, the directors may delegate any of the powers which are conferred on them under the articles:

   a) to such person or committee;

   b) by such means (including by power of attorney);

   c) to such an extent;

   d) in relation to such matters or territories; and

   e) on such terms and conditions;

   as they think fit.

   (2) If the directors so specify, any such delegation may authorise further delegation of the directors' powers by any person to whom they are delegated.

   (3) The directors may revoke any delegation in whole or part, or alter its terms and conditions.

Committees

6. (1) Committees to which the directors delegate any of their powers must follow procedures which are based as far as they are applicable on those provisions of the articles which govern the taking of decisions by directors.

(2) The directors may make rules of procedure for all or any committees, which prevail over rules derived from the articles if they are not consistent with them.

DECISION-MAKING BY DIRECTORS

Directors to take decisions collectively

7. (1) The general rule about decision-making by directors is that any decision of the directors must be either a majority decision at a meeting or a decision taken in accordance with article 8.

(2) If:

a) the company only has one director, and

b) no provision of the articles requires it to have more than one director,

the general rule does not apply, and the director may take decisions without regard to any of the provisions of the articles relating to directors' decision-making.

Unanimous decisions

8. (1) A decision of the directors is taken in accordance with this article when all eligible directors indicate to each other by any means that they share a common view on a matter.

(2) Such a decision may take the form of a resolution in writing, copies of which have been signed by each eligible director or to which each eligible director has otherwise indicated agreement in writing.

(3) References in this article to eligible directors are to directors who would have been entitled to vote on the matter had it been proposed as a resolution at a directors' meeting.

(4) A decision may not be taken in accordance with this article if the eligible directors would not have formed a quorum at such a meeting.

Calling a directors' meeting

9. (1) Any director may call a directors' meeting by giving notice of the meeting to the directors or by authorising the company secretary (if any) to give such notice.

(2) Notice of any directors' meeting must indicate—

a) its proposed date and time;

b) where it is to take place; and

c) if it is anticipated that directors participating in the meeting will not be in the same place, how it is proposed that they should communicate with each other during the meeting.

(3) Notice of a directors' meeting must be given to each director, but need not be in writing.

(4) Notice of a directors' meeting need not be given to directors who waive their entitlement to notice of that meeting, by giving notice to that effect to the company not more than seven days after the date on which the meeting is held. Where such notice is given after the meeting has been held, that does not affect the validity of the meeting, or of any business conducted at it.

Participation in directors' meetings

10. (1) Subject to the articles, directors participate in a directors' meeting, or part of a directors' meeting, when:

a) the meeting has been called and takes place in accordance with the articles, and

b) they can each communicate to the others any information or opinions they have on any particular item of the business of the meeting.

(2) In determining whether directors are participating in a directors' meeting, it is irrelevant where any director is or how they communicate with each other.

(3) If all the directors participating in a meeting are not in the same place, they may decide that the meeting is to be treated as taking place wherever any of them is.

Quorum for directors' meetings

11. (1) At a directors' meeting, unless a quorum is participating, no proposal is to be voted on, except a proposal to call another meeting.

(2) The quorum for directors' meetings may be fixed from time to time by a decision of the directors, but it must never be less than two, and unless otherwise fixed it is two.

(3) If the total number of directors for the time being is less than the quorum required, the directors must not take any decision other than a decision:

a) to appoint further directors, or

b) to call a general meeting so as to enable the shareholders to appoint further directors.

Chairing of directors' meetings

12. (1) The directors may appoint a director to chair their meetings.

(2) The person so appointed for the time being is known as the chairman.

(3) The directors may terminate the chairman's appointment at any time.

(4) If the chairman is not participating in a directors' meeting within ten minutes of the time at which it was to start, the participating directors must appoint one of themselves to chair it.

Casting vote

13\. (1) If the numbers of votes for and against a proposal are equal, the chairman or other director chairing the meeting has a casting vote.

(2) But this does not apply if, in accordance with the articles, the chairman or other director is not to be counted as participating in the decision-making process for quorum or voting purposes.

Conflicts of interest

14 (1) If a proposed decision of the directors is concerned with an actual or proposed transaction or arrangement with the company in which a director is interested, that director is not to be counted as participating in the decision-making process for quorum or voting purposes.

(2) But if paragraph (3) applies, a director who is interested in an actual or proposed transaction or arrangement with the company is to be counted as participating in the decision-making process for quorum and voting purposes.

(3) This paragraph applies when:

a) the company by ordinary resolution disapplies the provision of the articles which would otherwise prevent a director from being counted as participating in the decision-making process;

b) the director's interest cannot reasonably be regarded as likely to give rise to a conflict of interest; or

c) the director's conflict of interest arises from a permitted cause.

(4) For the purposes of this article, the following are permitted causes:

a) a guarantee given, or to be given, by or to a director in respect of an obligation incurred by or on behalf of the company or any of its subsidiaries;

b) subscription, or an agreement to subscribe, for shares or other securities of the company or any of its subsidiaries, or to underwrite, sub-underwrite, or guarantee subscription for any such shares or securities; and

c) arrangements pursuant to which benefits are made available to employees and directors or former employees and directors of the company or any of its subsidiaries which do not provide special benefits for directors or former directors.

(5) For the purposes of this article, references to proposed decisions and decision-making processes include any directors' meeting or part of a directors' meeting.

(6) Subject to paragraph (7), if a question arises at a meeting of directors or of a committee of directors as to the right of a director to participate in the meeting (or part of the meeting) for voting or quorum purposes, the question may, before the conclusion of the meeting, be referred to the chairman whose ruling in relation to any director other than the chairman is to be final and conclusive.

(7) If any question as to the right to participate in the meeting (or part of the meeting) should arise in respect of the chairman, the question is to be decided by a decision of the directors at that meeting, for which purpose the chairman is not to be counted as participating in the meeting (or that part of the meeting) for voting or quorum purposes.

Records of decisions to be kept

15. The directors must ensure that the company keeps a record, in writing, for at least 10 years from the date of the decision recorded, of every unanimous or majority decision taken by the directors.

Directors' discretion to make further rules

16. Subject to the articles, the directors may make any rule which they think fit about how they take decisions, and about how such rules are to be recorded or communicated to directors.

APPOINTMENT OF DIRECTORS

Methods of appointing directors

17. (1) Any person who is willing to act as a director, and is permitted by law to do so, may be appointed to be a director:

a) by ordinary resolution, or

b) by a decision of the directors.

(2) In any case where, as a result of death, the company has no shareholders and no directors, the personal representatives of the last shareholder to have died have the right, by notice in writing, to appoint a person to be a director.

(3) For the purposes of paragraph (2), where 2 or more shareholders die in circumstances rendering it uncertain who was the last to die, a younger shareholder is deemed to have survived an older shareholder.

Termination of director's appointment

18. A person ceases to be a director as soon as:

a) that person ceases to be a director by virtue of any provision of the Companies Act 2006 or is prohibited from being a director by law;

b) a bankruptcy order is made against that person;

c) a composition is made with that person's creditors generally in satisfaction of that person's debts;

d) a registered medical practitioner who is treating that person gives a written opinion to the company stating that that person has become physically or mentally incapable of acting as a director and may remain so for more than three months;

e) by reason of that person's mental health, a court makes an order which wholly or partly prevents that person from personally exercising any powers or rights which that person would otherwise have;

f) notification is received by the company from the director that the director is resigning from office, and such resignation has taken effect in accordance with its terms.

Directors' remuneration

19. (1) Directors may undertake any services for the company that the directors decide.

(2) Directors are entitled to such remuneration as the directors determine:

a) for their services to the company as directors, and

b) for any other service which they undertake for the company.

(3) Subject to the articles, a director's remuneration may:

a) take any form, and

b) include any arrangements in connection with the payment of a pension, allowance or gratuity, or any death, sickness or disability benefits, to or in respect of that director.

(4) Unless the directors decide otherwise, directors' remuneration accrues from day to day.

(5) Unless the directors decide otherwise, directors are not accountable to the company for any remuneration which they receive as directors or other officers or employees of the company's subsidiaries or of any other body corporate in which the company is interested.

Directors' expenses

20. The company may pay any reasonable expenses which the directors properly incur in connection with their attendance at:

a) meetings of directors or committees of directors,

b) general meetings, or

c) separate meetings of the holders of any class of shares or of debentures of the company, or otherwise in connection with the exercise of their powers and the discharge of their responsibilities in relation to the company.

PART 3 SHARES AND DISTRIBUTIONS

SHARES

All shares to be fully paid up

21. (1) No share is to be issued for less than the aggregate of its nominal value and any premium to be paid to the company in consideration for its issue.

(2) This does not apply to shares taken on the formation of the company by the subscribers to the company's memorandum.

Powers to issue different classes of share

22. (1) Subject to the articles, but without prejudice to the rights attached to any existing share, the company may issue shares with such rights or restrictions as may be determined by ordinary resolution.

(2) The company may issue shares which are to be redeemed, or are liable to be redeemed at the option of the company or the holder, and the directors may determine the terms, conditions and manner of redemption of any such shares.

Company not bound by less than absolute interests

23. Except as required by law, no person is to be recognised by the company as holding any share upon any trust, and except as otherwise required by law or the articles, the company is not in any way to be bound by or recognise any interest in a share other than the holder's absolute ownership of it and all the rights attaching to it.

Share certificates

24. (1) The company must issue each shareholder, free of charge, with one or more certificates in respect of the shares which that shareholder holds.

(2) Every certificate must specify:

a) in respect of how many shares, of what class, it is issued;

(b) the nominal value of those shares;

(c) that the shares are fully paid; and

(d) any distinguishing numbers assigned to them.

(3) No certificate may be issued in respect of shares of more than one class.

(4) If more than one person holds a share, only one certificate may be issued in respect of it.

(5) Certificates must:

a) have affixed to them the company's common seal, or

b) be otherwise executed in accordance with the Companies Acts.

Replacement share certificates

25\. (1) If a certificate issued in respect of a shareholder's shares is:

a) damaged or defaced, or

b) said to be lost, stolen or destroyed,

that shareholder is entitled to be issued with a replacement certificate in respect of the same shares.

(2) A shareholder exercising the right to be issued with such a replacement certificate:

a) may at the same time exercise the right to be issued with a single certificate or separate certificates;

b) must return the certificate which is to be replaced to the company if it is damaged or defaced; and

c) must comply with such conditions as to evidence, indemnity and the payment of a reasonable fee as the directors decide.

Share transfers

26\. (1) Shares may be transferred by means of an instrument of transfer in any usual form or any other form approved by the directors, which is executed by or on behalf of the transferor.

(2) No fee may be charged for registering any instrument of transfer or other document relating to or affecting the title to any share.

(3) The company may retain any instrument of transfer which is registered.

(4) The transferor remains the holder of a share until the transferee's name is entered in the register of members as holder of it.

(5) The directors may refuse to register the transfer of a share, and if they do so, the instrument of transfer must be returned to the transferee with the notice of refusal unless they suspect that the proposed transfer may be fraudulent.

Transmission of shares

27\. (1) If title to a share passes to a transmittee, the company may only recognise the transmittee as having any title to that share.

(2) A transmittee who produces such evidence of entitlement to shares as the directors may properly require:

a) may, subject to the articles, choose either to become the holder of those shares or to have them transferred to another person, and

b) subject to the articles, and pending any transfer of the shares to another person, has the same rights as the holder had.

(3) But transmittees do not have the right to attend or vote at a general meeting, or agree to a proposed written resolution, in respect of shares

to which they are entitled, by reason of the holder's death or bankruptcy or otherwise, unless they become the holders of those shares.

Exercise of transmittees' rights

28. (1) Transmittees who wish to become the holders of shares to which they have become entitled must notify the company in writing of that wish.

(2) If the transmittee wishes to have a share transferred to another person, the transmittee must execute an instrument of transfer in respect of it.

(3) Any transfer made or executed under this article is to be treated as if it were made or executed by the person from whom the transmittee has derived rights in respect of the share, and as if the event which gave rise to the transmission had not occurred.

Transmittees bound by prior notices

29. If a notice is given to a shareholder in respect of shares and a transmittee is entitled to those shares, the transmittee is bound by the notice if it was given to the shareholder before the transmittee's name has been entered in the register of members.

DIVIDENDS AND OTHER DISTRIBUTIONS

Procedure for declaring dividends

30. (1) The company may by ordinary resolution declare dividends, and the directors may decide to pay interim dividends.

(2) A dividend must not be declared unless the directors have made a recommendation as to its amount. Such a dividend must not exceed the amount recommended by the directors.

(3) No dividend may be declared or paid unless it is in accordance with shareholders' respective rights.

(4) Unless the shareholders' resolution to declare or directors' decision to pay a dividend, or the terms on which shares are issued, specify otherwise, it must be paid by reference to each shareholder's holding of shares on the date of the resolution or decision to declare or pay it.

(5) If the company's share capital is divided into different classes, no interim dividend may be paid on shares carrying deferred or non-preferred rights if, at the time of payment, any preferential dividend is in arrears.

(6) The directors may pay at intervals any dividend payable at a fixed rate if it appears to them that the profits available for distribution justify the payment.

(7) If the directors act in good faith, they do not incur any liability to the holders of shares conferring preferred rights for any loss they may suffer by the lawful payment of an interim dividend on shares with deferred or non-preferred rights.

Payment of dividends and other distributions

31. (1) Where a dividend or other sum which is a distribution is payable in respect of a share, it must be paid by one or more of the following means:

a) transfer to a bank or building society account specified by the distribution recipient either in writing or as the directors may otherwise decide;

b) sending a cheque made payable to the distribution recipient by post to the distribution recipient at the distribution recipient's registered address (if the distribution recipient is a holder of the share), or (in any other case) to an address specified by the distribution recipient either in writing or as the directors may otherwise decide;

c) sending a cheque made payable to such person by post to such person at such address as the distribution recipient has specified either in writing or as the directors may otherwise decide; or

d) any other means of payment as the directors agree with the distribution recipient either in writing or by such other means as the directors decide.

(2) In the articles, 'the distribution recipient' means, in respect of a share in respect of which a dividend or other sum is payable:

a) the holder of the share; or

b) if the share has two or more joint holders, whichever of them is named first in the register of members; or

c) if the holder is no longer entitled to the share by reason of death or bankruptcy, or otherwise by operation of law, the transmittee.

No interest on distributions

32. The company may not pay interest on any dividend or other sum payable in respect of a share unless otherwise provided by:

a) the terms on which the share was issued, or

b) the provisions of another agreement between the holder of that share and the company.

Unclaimed distributions

33. (1) All dividends or other sums which are:

a) payable in respect of shares, and

b) unclaimed after having been declared or become payable, may be invested or otherwise made use of by the directors for the benefit of the company until claimed.

(2) The payment of any such dividend or other sum into a separate account does not make the company a trustee in respect of it.

(3) If:

a) 12 years have passed from the date on which a dividend or other sum became due for payment, and

b) the distribution recipient has not claimed it, the distribution recipient is no longer entitled to that dividend or other sum and it ceases to remain owing by the company.

Non-cash distributions

34. (1) Subject to the terms of issue of the share in question, the company may, by ordinary resolution on the recommendation of the directors, decide to pay all or part of a dividend or other distribution payable in respect of a share by transferring non-cash assets of equivalent value (including, without limitation, shares or other securities in any company).

(2) For the purposes of paying a non-cash distribution, the directors may make whatever arrangements they think fit, including, where any difficulty arises regarding the distribution:

a) fixing the value of any assets;

b) paying cash to any distribution recipient on the basis of that value in order to adjust the rights of recipients; and

c) vesting any assets in trustees.

Waiver of distributions

35. Distribution recipients may waive their entitlement to a dividend or other distribution payable in respect of a share by giving the company notice in writing to that effect, but if:

a) the share has more than one holder, or

b) more than one person is entitled to the share, whether by reason of the death or bankruptcy of one or more joint holders, or otherwise, the notice is not effective unless it is expressed to be given, and signed, by all the holders or persons otherwise entitled to the share.

CAPITALISATION OF PROFITS

Authority to capitalise and appropriation of capitalised sums

36. (1) Subject to the articles, the directors may, if they are so authorised by an ordinary resolution:

a) decide to capitalise any profits of the company (whether or not they are available for distribution) which are not required for paying a preferential dividend, or any sum standing to the credit of the company's share premium account or capital redemption reserve; and

b) appropriate any sum which they so decide to capitalise (a 'capitalised sum') to the persons who would have been entitled to it if it were distributed by way of dividend (the 'persons entitled') and in the same proportions.

(2) Capitalised sums must be applied:

a) on behalf of the persons entitled, and

b) in the same proportions as a dividend would have been distributed to them.

(3) Any capitalised sum may be applied in paying up new shares of a nominal amount equal to the capitalised sum which are then allotted credited as fully paid to the persons entitled or as they may direct.

(4) A capitalised sum which was appropriated from profits available for distribution may be applied in paying up new debentures of the company which are then allotted credited as fully paid to the persons entitled or as they may direct.

(5) Subject to the articles the directors may:

a) apply capitalised sums in accordance with paragraphs (3) and (4) partly in one way and partly in another;

b) make such arrangements as they think fit to deal with shares or debentures becoming distributable in fractions under this article (including the issuing of fractional certificates or the making of cash payments); and

c) authorise any person to enter into an agreement with the company on behalf of all the persons entitled which is binding on them in respect of the allotment of shares and debentures to them under this article.

PART 4 DECISION-MAKING BY SHAREHOLDERS

ORGANISATION OF GENERAL MEETINGS

Attendance and speaking at general meetings

37. (1) A person is able to exercise the right to speak at a general meeting when that person is in a position to communicate to all those attending the meeting, during the meeting, any information or opinions which that person has on the business of the meeting.

(2) A person is able to exercise the right to vote at a general meeting when:

a) that person is able to vote, during the meeting, on resolutions put to the vote at the meeting, and

b) that person's vote can be taken into account in determining whether or not such resolutions are passed at the same time as the votes of all the other persons attending the meeting.

(3) The directors may make whatever arrangements they consider appropriate to enable those attending a general meeting to exercise their rights to speak or vote at it.

(4) In determining attendance at a general meeting, it is immaterial whether any two or more members attending it are in the same place as each other.

(5) Two or more persons who are not in the same place as each other attend a general meeting if their circumstances are such that if they have (or were to have) rights to speak and vote at that meeting, they are (or would be) able to exercise them.

Quorum for general meetings

38. No business other than the appointment of the chairman of the meeting is to be transacted at a general meeting if the persons attending it do not constitute a quorum.

Chairing general meetings

39. (1) If the directors have appointed a chairman, the chairman shall chair general meetings if present and willing to do so.

(2) If the directors have not appointed a chairman, or if the chairman is unwilling to chair the meeting or is not present within ten minutes of the time at which a meeting was due to start:

a) the directors present, or

b) (if no directors are present), the meeting, must appoint a director or shareholder to chair the meeting, and the appointment of the chairman of the meeting must be the first business of the meeting.

(3) The person chairing a meeting in accordance with this article is referred to as 'the chairman of the meeting'.

Attendance and speaking by directors and non-shareholders

40. (1) Directors may attend and speak at general meetings, whether or not they are shareholders.

(2) The chairman of the meeting may permit other persons who are not—

a) shareholders of the company, or

b) otherwise entitled to exercise the rights of shareholders in relation to general meetings, to attend and speak at a general meeting.

Adjournment

41. (1) If the persons attending a general meeting within half an hour of the time at which the meeting was due to start do not constitute a quorum, or if during a meeting a quorum ceases to be present, the chairman of the meeting must adjourn it.

(2) The chairman of the meeting may adjourn a general meeting at which a quorum is present if:

a) the meeting consents to an adjournment, or

b) it appears to the chairman of the meeting that an adjournment is necessary to protect the safety of any person attending the meeting or ensure that the business of the meeting is conducted in an orderly manner.

(3) The chairman of the meeting must adjourn a general meeting if directed to do so by the meeting.

(4) When adjourning a general meeting, the chairman of the meeting must:

a) either specify the time and place to which it is adjourned or state that it is to continue at a time and place to be fixed by the directors, and

b) have regard to any directions as to the time and place of any adjournment which have been given by the meeting.

(5) If the continuation of an adjourned meeting is to take place more than 14 days after it was adjourned, the company must give at least 7 clear days' notice of it (that is, excluding the day of the adjourned meeting and the day on which the notice is given):

a) to the same persons to whom notice of the company's general meetings is required to be given, and

b) containing the same information which such notice is required to contain.

(6) No business may be transacted at an adjourned general meeting which could not properly have been transacted at the meeting if the adjournment had not taken place.

VOTING AT GENERAL MEETINGS

Voting: general

42. A resolution put to the vote of a general meeting must be decided on a show of hands unless a poll is duly demanded in accordance with the articles.

Errors and disputes

43. (1) No objection may be raised to the qualification of any person voting at a general meeting except at the meeting or adjourned meeting at which the vote objected to is tendered, and every vote not disallowed at the meeting is valid.

(2) Any such objection must be referred to the chairman of the meeting, whose decision is final.

Poll votes

44. (1) A poll on a resolution may be demanded:

a) in advance of the general meeting where it is to be put to the vote, or

b) at a general meeting, either before a show of hands on that resolution or immediately after the result of a show of hands on that resolution is declared.

(2) A poll may be demanded by:

a) the chairman of the meeting;

b) the directors;

c) two or more persons having the right to vote on the resolution; or

d) a person or persons representing not less than one tenth of the total voting rights of all the shareholders having the right to vote on the resolution.

(3) A demand for a poll may be withdrawn if:

a) the poll has not yet been taken, and

b) the chairman of the meeting consents to the withdrawal.

(4) Polls must be taken immediately and in such manner as the chairman of the meeting directs.

Content of proxy notices

45. (1) Proxies may only validly be appointed by a notice in writing (a 'proxy notice') which:

a) states the name and address of the shareholder appointing the proxy;

b) identifies the person appointed to be that shareholder's proxy and the general meeting in relation to which that person is appointed;

c) is signed by or on behalf of the shareholder appointing the proxy, or is authenticated in such manner as the directors may determine; and

d) is delivered to the company in accordance with the articles and any instructions contained in the notice of the general meeting to which they relate.

(2) The company may require proxy notices to be delivered in a particular form, and may specify different forms for different purposes.

(3) Proxy notices may specify how the proxy appointed under them is to vote (or that the proxy is to abstain from voting) on one or more resolutions.

(4) Unless a proxy notice indicates otherwise, it must be treated as—

a) allowing the person appointed under it as a proxy discretion as to how to vote on any ancillary or procedural resolutions put to the meeting, and

b) appointing that person as a proxy in relation to any adjournment of the general meeting to which it relates as well as the meeting itself.

Delivery of proxy notices

46. (1) A person who is entitled to attend, speak or vote (either on a show of hands or on a poll) at a general meeting remains so entitled in respect of that meeting or any adjournment of it, even though a valid proxy notice has been delivered to the company by or on behalf of that person.

(2) An appointment under a proxy notice may be revoked by delivering to the company a notice in writing given by or on behalf of the person by whom or on whose behalf the proxy notice was given.

(3) A notice revoking a proxy appointment only takes effect if it is delivered before the start of the meeting or adjourned meeting to which it relates.

(4) If a proxy notice is not executed by the person appointing the proxy, it must be accompanied by written evidence of the authority of the person who executed it to execute it on the appointor's behalf.

Amendments to resolutions

47. (1) An ordinary resolution to be proposed at a general meeting may be amended by ordinary resolution if:

a) notice of the proposed amendment is given to the company in writing by a person entitled to vote at the general meeting at which it is to be proposed not less than 48 hours before the meeting is to take place (or such later time as the chairman of the meeting may determine), and

b) the proposed amendment does not, in the reasonable opinion of the chairman of the meeting, materially alter the scope of the resolution.

(2) A special resolution to be proposed at a general meeting may be amended by ordinary resolution, if:

a) the chairman of the meeting proposes the amendment at the general meeting at which the resolution is to be proposed, and

b) the amendment does not go beyond what is necessary to correct a grammatical or other non-substantive error in the resolution.

(3) If the chairman of the meeting, acting in good faith, wrongly decides that an amendment to a resolution is out of order, the chairman's error does not invalidate the vote on that resolution.

PART 5 ADMINISTRATIVE ARRANGEMENTS

Means of communication to be used

48. (1) Subject to the articles, anything sent or supplied by or to the company under the articles may be sent or supplied in any way in which the Companies Act 2006 provides for documents or information which are authorised or required by any provision of that Act to be sent or supplied by or to the company.

(2) Subject to the articles, any notice or document to be sent or supplied to a director in connection with the taking of decisions by directors may also be sent or supplied by the means by which that director has asked to be sent or supplied with such notices or documents for the time being.

(3) A director may agree with the company that notices or documents sent to that director in a particular way are to be deemed to have been received within a specified time of their being sent, and for the specified time to be less than 48 hours.

Company seals

49. (1) Any common seal may only be used by the authority of the directors.

(2) The directors may decide by what means and in what form any common seal is to be used.

(3) Unless otherwise decided by the directors, if the company has a common seal and it is affixed to a document, the document must also be signed by at least one authorised person in the presence of a witness who attests the signature.

(4) For the purposes of this article, an authorised person is—

a) any director of the company;

b) the company secretary (if any); or

c) any person authorised by the directors for the purpose of signing documents to which the common seal is applied.

No right to inspect accounts and other records

50. Except as provided by law or authorised by the directors or an ordinary resolution of the company, no person is entitled to inspect any of the company's accounting or other records or documents merely by virtue of being a shareholder.

Provision for employees on cessation of business

51. The directors may decide to make provision for the benefit of persons employed or formerly employed by the company or any of its subsidiaries (other than a director or former director or shadow director) in connection with the cessation or transfer to any person of the whole or part of the undertaking of the company or that subsidiary.

DIRECTORS' INDEMNITY AND INSURANCE

Indemnity

52. (1) Subject to paragraph (2), a relevant director of the company or an associated company may be indemnified out of the company's assets against:

    a) any liability incurred by that director in connection with any negligence, default, breach of duty or breach of trust in relation to the company or an associated company,

    b) any liability incurred by that director in connection with the activities of the company or an associated company in its capacity as a trustee of an occupational pension scheme (as defined in section 235(6) of the Companies Act 2006),

    c) any other liability incurred by that director as an officer of the company or an associated company.

    (2) This article does not authorise any indemnity which would be prohibited or rendered void by any provision of the Companies Acts or by any other provision of law.

    (3) In this article:

    a) companies are associated if one is a subsidiary of the other or both are subsidiaries of the same body corporate, and

    b) a 'relevant director' means any director or former director of the company or an associated company.

Insurance

53. (1) The directors may decide to purchase and maintain insurance, at the expense of the company, for the benefit of any relevant director in respect of any relevant loss.

    (2) In this article:

a) a 'relevant director' means any director or former director of the company or an associated company,

b) a 'relevant loss' means any loss or liability which has been or may be incurred by a relevant director in connection with that director's duties or powers in relation to the company, any associated company or any pension fund or employees' share scheme of the company or associated company, and

c) companies are associated if one is a subsidiary of the other or both are subsidiaries of the same body corporate.

Appendix three
Sample company board meeting minutes

ANY COMPANY LIMITED 182 (1)

MINUTES of a BOARD MEETING held on 30th March [year]

At [address] at 10.00 a.m.

Present: XYZ (in the chair)

ABC

DEF

GHI

In attendance : JKL (company secretary)

(Mr. TSS, auditor was in attendance for items covered by Minute 3 i and ii) (2)

An apology for absence due to illness was received from UVW and this was accepted. Those present signed the attendance book. (3)

The board reminded themselves of the seven duties of directors set out in the Companies Act 2006 and confirmed that in taking all decisions they would continue to take account of these duties and bear in mind the disparate interests of the company's stakeholders. (4)

1 MINUTES

The minutes of the board meeting held on 29th February [year] previously distributed were taken as read, approved and signed. (5)

2 DIRECTORS INTERESTS

The register recording interests of board members as advised to the company was laid on the table. (6)

3 RISK CONTROL

The Secretary tabled an updated statement of risk control which would form part of the forthcoming Annual Report, as a result of an investigation and report recently completed by the Risk Control sub-committee of the Board. This was ratified. It was noted that an updated Delegated Authority chart had been issued to all employees and agents, drawing attention to the instruction that on no account should bribes be offered or taken. (7)

4 SHAREHOLDER MATTERS

It was resolved that a share transfer covering 500 Ordinary shares in the company from Mrs MNO to Mr PQR be and it hereby is approved and that a share certificate in the name of Mr PQR be issued and the required entries be made in the Register of Members. The secretary was asked to write to Mr PQR welcoming him as a shareholder. Action: JKL (8)

A report from the company secretary recommending that responsibility for the share registration work of the company be placed with Share Registrars Ltd. was accepted and the terms of the contract approved. The company secretary was requested to make the necessary arrangements in liaison with the chairman. Action: JKL

(Mr DEF, having previously notified the company that he had a consultancy agreement with Share Registrars Ltd did not take any part in this discussion or decision.) (9)

5 FINANCE

i) Management accounts.

The accounts for the month of February and the cumulative 11 months were tabled and discussed in detail. The favourable comparison with budget was welcomed, as was the managing director's opinion that the trading and financial situation would continue to show improvement, both in real terms and against budget. It was noted that the situation regarding discounts and promotional payments was still being clarified and additional controls would be introduced from the commencement of the new financial year.

A number of estimated provisions were listed for possible incorporation in the year end accounts. Action: ABC

ii) Depreciation. It was agreed to change the company's accounting policies so that depreciation would be charged on vehicles, office equipment and computers at 33.3 per cent p.a. straightline. It was noted that this change would have to be recorded in the published Accounting Policies.

iii) Capital expenditure.

a) It was agreed that a further five production units at a cost of around £4,000 each could be purchased in stages over the remainder of 2XXX to allow the sale of [detail]. Mr UVW (whom failing, the company secretary) would authorise each item bearing in mind the effect on cash flow. Action: UVW/JKL (10)

b) The chairman referred to Capital Expenditure Project form number 13/2XXX for the investment in [detail] which projected a first year return of 14 per cent rising to 17 per cent in year 2 on a fully absorbed basis. The project was approved for implementation no earlier than 31st December [year] Action: ABC

iv) Cash flow. The latest projection for the period ending 31st December [year] was tabled, discussed and approved

v) Investigations for the replacement of the company vehicles allocated to six area managers would be carried out. The guidance of the auditors as to the company's and individual's tax situation would be sought. Action: GHI

vi) Bank Mandate. The secretary reported that the company's bankers had requested that a new mandate on the main drawing account be completed. It was resolved that the company operate the No 1 Main Drawing account in its name with the Finance Bank Plc on the terms and subject to the restrictions set out in a new mandate a copy of which initialled by the chairman for the purposes of identification is attached to these minutes, and that the secretary be and he hereby is empowered to take such actions as might be necessary to give effect to this resolution Action: JKL (11)

vii) Borrowings. The secretary reported that in the absence of Mr UVW he had negotiated an additional £100,000 overdraft facility with the Finance Bank on the same terms as the existing facility. This additional borrowing was available for the eight weeks until end August [year]. Although he had expected to receive documentation requiring board approval to evidence this borrowing this had not arrived before the meeting.

It was resolved that the chairman, ABC and UVW (whom failing the company secretary) be and they hereby are empowered to sign such documents and take such actions to provide the company's bankers with the documentation they required in order to facilitate the advance of this additional borrowing requirement.

The secretary was instructed to let each board member have copies of the relevant items and documentation when these were to hand.

The secretary confirmed that even with this additional borrowing the limits in the Articles had not been breached. Action: XYZ, ABC, UVW, JKL (12)

6 CURRENT TRADING

The managing director reported that [synopsis of report.........]. An analysis showing the deterioration over a five-year period of sales of the main product was tabled and it was agreed that the deadline for delivery of supplies of Project X needed to be brought forward to compensate for the expected shortfall in sales in the latter part of the calendar year.
Action: ABC

DEF requested that his dissent from this course of action be noted in the minutes with the note that in his opinion not enough was being done to incentivise the sales force and he had serious doubts concerning the effectiveness of the recently appointed sales manager. (13)

7 PERSONNEL

A report from the divisional director (Personnel) had been sent to all members and the contents were accepted. It was agreed that negotiations should commence with employee representatives to try to agree the wage increase with effect from 1st July [year] along the lines outlined in the report.

It was noted that all employees and agents had been reminded of their obligations in compliance with the Bribery Act.

8 PROPERTY

The following items were noted: (14)

[Facility address]: Little progress had been made on any of the pending rent reviews which would update the list accompanying the agenda for the meeting other than the following:

[Facility]: Approval was granted to a letter of response to the landlords requesting that an extension to the user be agreed.

[Facility]: Evidence thought to be misleading had been submitted by the landlord's agents.

[Facility]: The landlord's agents had reduced their figure for the reviewed rent to £13,500. Negotiations continued.

The sale of [facility] was proceeding with exchange of contracts expected for mid-July and completion by 1st August. It was noted that receipt of the sale monies had not been built into the cash flow forecast and that if this sale completed as anticipated the additional overdraft facility would not be needed.

The possibility of selling the business and licensing or underletting the lease at [facility] was being pursued urgently.

Insurance: The secretary would draft a letter to be sent to all landlords of leased premises requesting that the interest of the company be noted on the insurance policies to ensure any liability in the event of loss was minimised. Action: JKL

(Mr DEF apologised and with the permission of the chairman left the meeting) (15)

9 SAFETY MATTERS

i) The monthly report was accepted, no actions being required.

ii) The secretary reported:

a) that he had investigated the requirements of the current health and safety legislation regarding fire precautions in the workplace and tabled a brief synopsis of the action he felt it was necessary for the company to take in order to comply with the requirements. The board requested him to obtain detailed cost estimates for the various requirements with, in each case, an indication of the proposed timetable for implementation of the recommendations.

b) that he had commissioned reports to determine whether there were any asbestos containing materials in the company's properties
Action: JKL (16)

10 SEALING

The secretary produced the Register of Sealing (and documents signed as deeds) to the board and approval was granted to the affixing of the company seal to items numbered 345 to 357 and 359 to 361, and approval granted to the signing as a deed of item 358. The chairman was authorised to sign the register in evidence of this approval. (17)

11 BOARD MEETING TIMETABLE

The dates of future meetings of the board were confirmed as 28th April, 30th May, 30th June, 28th July, 31st August, 29th September, 25th October, 23rd November, and 21st December.

The secretary was requested to inform Messrs DEF and UVW of these dates as soon as possible. (18)

Chairman .... 28th April [year] (19)

Action points: (20)

Welcoming shareholder	JKL	[Completion date]
New Share Registrars	JKL	[Completion date]
Provisions in accounts	ABC	[Completion date]
Capex products purchase	UVW(JKL)	[Ongoing]

Explanatory notes

1 Ideally minute pages should be consecutively numbered to try to prevent fraudulent alterations. The subject of each minute (where applicable) should be indexed and a degree of cross-referencing provided. Some companies use the financial year to delineate minutes (e.g. 2011/X etc. – changing to 2012/X for the first board meeting in the new financial year).

2 Stating the exact period of attendance of advisors, and even of members if not present for the whole meeting, is advisable.

3 It is arguable that only if an apology for absence is accepted that the absence is acceptable. In some boards if no apology is made, that fact is stated in the minutes (i.e. *'No apology was received from....'* which underlines the implied obligation for directors to be present). Under Regulation 81 of Table A of CA85, if a director does not attend board meetings for six months or more without permission of the board, he can be removed from the board.

It may also be advisable for directors to sign an attendance book – although it would not normally be necessary to minute this if done as a routine. Some charities require this.

4 CA06 places explicit duties on directors and to be able to demonstrate that they were aware of these duties wording such as this could be inserted in the minutes once a year as a reminder (and in the minutes of any board which a director is attending for the first time so that newcomers have the point brought to their attention).

5 Ideally the chairman should initial each page of the minutes except for the last which should be signed. See 19 below.

6 Listed PLCs, and companies with shareholders not on the board, should consider incorporating in their ANNUAL REPORT a statement of risk and control mechanisms devised as well as the fact that these are regularly assessed by the board. Being able to use the defence (e.g. for an allegation of bribery) that *'reasonable steps have been taken'* would seem to indicate that it needs a constant a constant reassessment of the possibility and a repeated reminder that it must not occur. Board attention in this way may be of assistance in meeting this aim.

7 Under CA06 there is an implied requirement to record items in which directors have an interest – e.g. indemnities, loans, potential and/or actual conflicts of interest etc. It may be prudent to maintain a 'Register of Directors' Interests' into which details of such items are entered and to have this available at each board meeting so that all members are aware of each of their interests. This may also assist the secretary should an item of business require a 'disinterested quorum'. This register can be updated regularly if the concept of requiring directors to complete a statement of their interests each year is adopted. (See form in DIRECTORS – APPOINTMENT)

8 Directors of many LTDs have the right to refuse to allow transfer of shares to a person of whom they do not approve. It is probably unlikely that an LTD would need to retain external registrars to deal with its share registration work as is suggested here – although this is often used by listed PLCs.

In addition placing the initials of the person due to deal with the item enables the minutes (already a document of record and reference) to act also as a means of encouraging prompt action.

9 Depending on the Articles' requirements, it is important that any director with an interest in the subject matter should declare that interest and that the point be noted. DEF's interest with Share Registrars should have been entered in the Register of Directors' Interests – see 7 above.

10 Framing a decision in this way leaves some leeway for delay should the circumstances at the time warrant such delay and also covers the situation should UVW not return.

11 Where a lengthy document is required to be approved, rather than repeating the whole item in the minutes, it could be copied and attached to the minutes. It should then be numbered either consecutively after the last page number for that meeting's minutes, or take the number of the past page and 'a', 'b', 'c' etc., added with a designatory letter for each page of the item. Banks may wish to have a set form of resolution adopted for the approval of their mandate and similar forms.

12 Reference should be made to the Articles to ensure the board are acting in accordance with them. They often set out the requirements and restrictions on board activities, particularly constraints on the maximum the board can borrow on behalf of the company. If such pre-set figures need to be exceeded the Articles should be changed otherwise the directors will be acting *ultra vires* and could be held personally liable to repay the excess borrowed.

13 In the event that any director wishes to exercise his common law right to have his dissent recorded, this must occur.

14 To save the time of the meeting, it may be possible to distribute a report (as here) with the agenda and simply report on any update since the date of the agenda.

15 Ideally all directors should be present for the whole meeting – and there is a presumption that this is the case. If it is not possible, the time that a director left (or arrived, if late) should be noted in the minutes.

16 The Health and Safety Executive has recommended that safety should be a regular item for discussion by the board. This is sound advice not least since it may be valuable evidence that the company took and takes safety considerations seriously. It might be best if there were a regular safety report – at the very least the board could review the results of the regular 'Responsible Persons' inspections regarding fire safety required to be carried out at every place of work.

17 Although not a statutory requirement, the use of a Register of Seals (and/or of documents signed as deeds) and subsequent board approval of all entries provides board authority for the items. It also enables details to be noted of items signed as deeds where the use of the seal has been dispensed with. The chairman should sign under the last number authorised at the meeting and should add the date. Ideally the number of each seal entry in the Register should appear on the item sealed as a further cross-reference of authority.

18 Meetings arranged in the absence of a colleague can clash with other commitments already entered into, hence early advice of meeting dates is essential. The dates of board meetings may best be arranged on a rolling 18 month basis, with the immediate six months dates fixed, the following six months subject to some leeway and the third six months indicative only. Progressively each six month section becomes firmer with additional outline indications tacked on.

19 Inserting a place for the chairman to sign and adding the date (of the next planned meeting) emphasises the importance of signing as well as improving the presentation of the minutes themselves

20 Some companies that utilise the actions points concept (see 8 above), additionally list these at the end of the minutes and insert a required 'completion date' for each.

[Source: *One Stop Company Secretary*, 7th edition, ICSA Publishing, 2011]

Glossary

additional settled funds The funds that are settled into the trust after its creation.

administrative provisions Provisions within a trust instrument relating to administrative matters such as the manner in which trustees may be appointed.

alternate director A person who has been appointed to attend and vote at a meeting of the directors on someone's behalf.

anti-avoidance legislation Legislation that has been introduced in order to restrict or eliminate the opportunities to minimise taxation via the use of offshore centres, particularly where the transaction has no purpose other than the minimisation or avoidance of taxation.

arising basis of taxation Under the arising basis of taxation, a person will pay UK tax on all of their income as it arises and on the gains as they accrue, wherever that income and those gains are in the world.

articles of association The internal regulations of a company that set out how the company shall be managed.

asset Something that is owned or from which a benefit can arise and having an economic value.

authorised share capital The amount of share capital that the company is authorised by its memorandum to issue.

bearer shares Shares that are considered to be owned by 'the bearer' (i.e. whoever has them in their possession). Cash is an example of a bearer instrument.

beneficial owner The individual(s) or company that retains a direct or indirect ownership interest in the assets of an entity.

beneficiary A person who is entitled by the terms of a trust to benefit from the trust property or in whose favour a discretion to distribute the trust property may be exercised.

blind trust This may refer to trusts where a charity is the only named beneficiary. The term is also used to describe trusts where the settlor is not aware of the investments that are held by the trustee or where the contributor of funds is not known to the beneficiary.

called-up share capital The value of the issued shares that remain unpaid and whose holders have been called upon to pay for the shares.

capacity A party to a contract must have legal capacity (the power legally to enter into it) for it to be enforceable. Vulnerable people such as children do not have capacity.

certainty of intent The requirement that the settlor must have intended to create a trust.

certainty of object The requirement to have ascertainable beneficiaries.

certainty of subject The requirement to have identifiable trust property.

certificate of incorporation A document issued by the Registrar of Companies that is conclusive evidence that a company is duly registered.

chargeable asset An asset that may be subject to capital gains tax when it is disposed of (i.e. sold or given away).

chargeable gain A gain made on the sale of an asset that is liable to capital gains tax.

charitable trust A trust that has been established for charitable purposes.

charter A document which is usually available for public inspection and which sets out the name of the foundation, its duration, objects, and names and addresses of the first council members.

common law A system of law under which the judges are guided by previous decisions of the courts under the doctrine of judicial precedent.

completely constituted For a trust to be completely constituted, the settlor must have properly vested legal ownership of the assets with the trustee.

consideration For a contract to exist and be binding, there must be the reciprocal exchange between the parties of a promise in return for a financial or non-financial value or benefit, which is referred to as the 'consideration'. Consideration must be given by both parties to a contract and is defined as 'some right, interest, profit or benefit accruing to one party, or some forbearance, detriment, loss or responsibility given, suffered or undertaken by the other' (Currie v Misa [1875]).

constructive trust A trust that arises by operation of the law.

corporate veil This refers to the separation of the legal personality of the company from that of its owners and controllers.

corruption Transparency International defines corruption as 'the misuse of entrusted power for private gain'. Public sector corruption involves, for example, the diversion of state funds for the benefit of politicians' own families.

CRS The international standard for the reciprocal exchange of tax information relating to non-resident customers

cy-près doctrine This provides that if a charitable trust finds itself without beneficiaries, the court can make an order that the trust property be applied for similar charitable purposes.

data controller An organisation that processes personal data.

de facto director A director who has not formally been appointed as a director but nevertheless fulfils the role of a director.

de jure director A director who has formally been appointed as a director and whose name should be included on the register of directors of the company.

declaration of trust (in relation to a nominee shareholding) A short document within which the trustee admits and declares that the shares are held upon trust absolutely for the beneficial owner and in which the trustee undertakes to deal with the shares as instructed by the beneficial owner.

declaration of trust (in relation to a settlement) A declaration of the trustee which sets out the terms upon which the trust assets are held and to which the settlor of the trust is not a party.

deed of settlement A document that is executed when a settlor creates an express trust. Also referred to as a settlement deed or trust instrument.

deemed domiciled A person becomes deemed domiciled for IHT purposes if they have been present in the UK for any part of the last 17 out of 20 years including the tax year in question.

direct taxes Taxes on income (e.g. income tax).

director A person appointed by the shareholders to be responsible for the management and control of a company, as, defined by the Companies Act 2006 as 'any person occupying the position of a director, by whatever name called'.

dispositive provisions The provisions within a trust deed that set out the terms upon which the trustees hold and may distribute the trust property.

dissolution The legal process by which a company or a firm ceases to exist.

dividend A share of the after-tax profits of a company distributed to its shareholders after a director's decision to pay a class of shareholders.

doctrine of judicial precedent Under the doctrine of judicial precedent, a judge is bound to follow decisions that have been reached in earlier court cases.

dummy settlor A person whose name is recorded within a trust instrument as the settlor of a trust but who is not the provider of the funds used to create the trust.

earned income Income that is earned (e.g. salary or bonuses from employment or income from a trade or profession or from a pension).

enforcer A person appointed to a non-charitable purpose trust whose duty it is to enforce the trust.

entities Used to describe both legal persons (such as companies) and legal arrangements (such as trusts).

equity A system of law administered by the Court of Chancery that developed alongside the common law in instances where justice could not be delivered from common law remedies.

exchange control regulations Regulations or other controls that are imposed by the governments of some countries that fear or are experiencing scarcity of foreign currency (and often, precious metals). Such controls may limit or ban the amount of foreign or local currency that can be traded or purchased, or may involve controls which restrict residents from removing currency from the jurisdiction.

excluded persons Persons who are specifically named as being excluded from benefit in a trust deed or a person who has been excluded following the exercise of a power by the trustee.

excluded property trust Excluded property trusts are those created by non-UK domiciled individuals (who have not yet been deemed domiciled in the UK) with non-UK situs assets. Such trusts receive favourable IHT treatment.

express trust A trust created intentionally by the settlor during their lifetime or one that may come into existence upon their death as a result of their will.

FATCA The US standard for the reciprocal exchange of tax information relating to non-resident customers.

fiduciary duty A person with a fiduciary duty has a duty to act in the best interests of another person.

fiduciary relationship A relationship founded on trust. A person with a fiduciary duty has a duty to act in the best interests of another person.

Financial Intelligence Unit (FIU) Used to describe the authority in a jurisdiction that has responsibility for receiving and dealing with suspicious activity reports from financial institutions.

financial services business Used to describe the carrying on of funds services business investment business, general insurance mediation business money services business or trust company business.

fiscal policies Policies that relate to the public revenues (i.e. income from taxation).

forced heirship In some countries, the laws require the assets held in a person's estate to pass to stated heirs (usually the person's spouse and children). This is known as forced heirship and such heirs are known as 'forced heirs' (or sometimes 'fixed heirs').

foundation A type of legal entity which does not have a share capital or shareholders, and which has a separate legal personality.

founder The person who requests for a foundation to be incorporated.

Gazette The official newspaper record in the United Kingdom. The *London Gazette* is the gazette for the publication of notices relating to companies incorporated in England and Wales.

gift with reservation A gift whereby the donor retains an interest in the asset (this could involve retaining a benefit or control of the asset).

inaugural meeting The first meeting of the directors.

incorporation The legal process by which a company and other legal bodies are created by law.

indirect taxes Taxes on expenditure (e.g. VAT).

inheritance tax (IHT) A tax charged upon the death of a person, based upon the value of their estate.

initial settled funds The assets that are used to create the trust.

injunction A judicial order that restrains a person from doing something or orders someone do to something.

inside information Information that relates to particular securities, is specific or precise, has not been made public and if it were made public, would be likely to have a significant effect on the price of any securities.

integration A stage of the money laundering process that involves reintroducing the criminal property into the economy so it appears to have originated from a legitimate source.

inter vivos A transfer that is made during the lifetime of the settlor.

invitation to treat An invitation to another person to make an offer.

issued share capital The nominal value of shares that have actually been issued to members of the company.

jurisdiction A territory over which authority is exercised by laws which are under the control of a system of courts different to that of its neighbouring areas.

layering A stage of the money laundering process which is designed to hide the source and ownership of criminal property (e.g. by using a complex system of transactions).

legal arrangements Legal arrangements include fiduciary arrangements such as trusts.

legal persons Those persons that are incorporated by law (e.g. companies).

letter of wishes A private document written by the settlor of a trust to the trustee, setting out their wishes in relation to the trust fund.

liability A legal obligation to another person.

life interest trust A trust where an individual (known as the life tenant) has an absolute right to enjoy the trust property or income arising from the trust property during their lifetime.

life tenant A person who is entitled to benefit from the income of a fixed income trust during their lifetime.

Mareva injunction An order of the court which prevents a defendant to an action from disposing of the assets or transferring them from the jurisdiction.

member A person who subscribed to the memorandum of association of a company or a person who has who has been allotted or acquired one or more shares in a company and whose name has been entered on to the register of members or shareholders.

memorandum of association A short document that evidences the subscribers' intention to form a company under the legislation and that they agree to become members of the company.

model articles Articles of association created by the Companies Act 2006; these apply unless a company excludes them in place of other articles.

money laundering Money laundering occurs whenever there is an arrangement involving the proceeds of crime.

nominal value This is the amount shown on a share certificate and is also the par value of the shares.

nominee shareholder A person who is the legal owner of a share and who holds the share absolutely for and on behalf of the beneficial owner.

non-cooperating countries and territories (NCCT) One of the FATF's AML/CFT Initiatives which enabled a classification of centres or jurisdictions so that international pressure could be brought to bear on them to implement changes in their anti-money laundering regimes.

non-executive director A director who is not involved with the day-to-day activities of the company and who can bring an independent view to the board of directors.

obiter dicta The obiter dicta of a case are words that are said 'by the way' and do not form a part of the ratio decidendi.

objects (in relation to a trust) The trust's beneficiaries.

objects clause A clause within the memorandum of a company that, prior to the introduction of the Companies Act 2006, restricted the activities of a company to those contained within the clause.

offshore centre A jurisdiction which seeks to create a competitive advantage through its laws and which provides financial services primarily to non-residents.

ordinary resolution A resolution that must be passed by a simple majority of members.

ordinary shares A share of equity ownership in a company that entitles the holder to vote and receive a dividend (if one is paid), after a dividend has been paid to preference shareholders.

paid-up share capital The amount of the issued share capital of a company that has actually been paid for.

par value The nominal value of a share.

par value company A company registered with a share capital and shares that are expressed as having a nominal value.

partnership An agreement whereby two or more people run a business and share any profit and loss that they make.

perpetual succession This refers to the fact that incorporated bodies such as companies remain unaffected by the existence of their owners or controllers and will continue to exist until formally dissolved by law.

perpetuity period The time period within which future interests in the trust property must vest with one or more of the beneficiaries.

personal data Data that relates to a living individual (the data subject) who can be identified from that data.

placement A stage of the money laundering process which involves placing the proceeds of crime into the financial system (e.g. by depositing the proceeds of crime into a bank account).

precedent A previous court decision, which should guide the court in future cases.

pre-emption right The right of existing members to be offered the shares in the company for sale whenever a member wishes to sell their shares, before they are offered to non-members.

preference shares A share that does not usually have value rights and receives a dividend prioritised over ordinary shareholders and usually at a fixed percentage.

prima facie evidence 'On the face of it' evidence.

private trust company (PTC) A company formed to act as a trustee of one particular trust or group of trusts (e.g. for one individual or family).

purpose trust A trust in which the trustee holds the property in order to carry out a specific purpose.

quantum meruit This term means 'as much as he deserved'.

quorum The number of members that must be present in order for a meeting to be validly constituted.

ratio decidendi The ratio decidendi of a case is any rule of law or legal principle that is treated by the judge as necessary for the basis of the decision made.

redeemable shares A type of share that may be repurchased by the company at a future date.

register of directors A register which is required to be maintained by law and which contains the name and other particulars of a company's directors. source of wealth Activities which have generated the total net worth of a person.

register of members A register which is required to be maintained by law and which contains the name and other particulars of a company's members.

registered office The address of a company which has been notified to the authorities (as required by law) as the address to which legal notices can be sent.

registered office The address of a company that has been notified to the authorities (as required by law) as the address to which legal notices can be sent.

regulations (in relation to foundations) A private document setting out the administration of the foundation.

remittance basis of taxation Individuals who are non-domiciled in the UK (or those who are not resident in the UK) pay UK tax only on the amount of their foreign income and gains that they remit to the UK.

rescission The revocation or cancellation of a contract. The effect is to bring the parties to the contract back to the position that they were in before the contract was effected.

reserved companies A company that is incorporated by service providers and the Registrar of Companies is advised that the company will be transferred to a client within the next six months.

resulting trust This arises in circumstances where the trust that was intended has failed.

revocation An offer may terminated by revocation. This means that the offeror cancels the offer and it is no longer open for acceptance.

Serious Organised Crime Agency (SOCA) The FIU in the UK.

service provider Organisations or individuals who provide financial services business offshore may simply be referred to as service providers.

settlor The person who provides trust property whether during their lifetime or by their will.

shadow director One who has not been formally appointed but who is deemed in law to be a director due to the function that they are fulfilling.

sham trust An arrangement that purports to be something that it is not. Such trusts may be set aside as invalid.

share capital The money provided by a company's members in return for shares in the company.

share certificate A document evidencing a person's title to their shares in the company.

shareholder A person who holds legal title to one or more shares in a company.

shelf company A company that has been incorporated by a service provider and therefore is instantly available for use.

sole trader An individual who is the sole owner of their business.

source of funds Activities that generate funds for a relationship.

special purpose vehicle (SPV) An entity that is established for a specific purpose or transaction.

special resolution A resolution of the members that must be passed by a majority of not less than 75% of members who are entitled to vote.

specific performance An equitable remedy that a court may make which orders the parties to the contract to fulfil their obligations under it.

stare decisis A Latin term for 'let the decision stand'.

structure Used to describe a group of trusts and companies that are connected by their ownership or their assets and are aimed at meeting the needs of a particular client or group of clients.

subscribers The persons who subscribe to the memorandum of a company and who are deemed to be the first members of the company.

suis juris Of legal capacity and in agreement.

three certainties The three conditions that are required in order to create a valid trust: certainty of object, certainty of subject and certainty of intent.

tipping off The committing of an offence under Article 333 of the PoCA.

transfer pricing Agreeing a price between two connected parties for the sale of goods or services.

trust instrument The document which creates a legally binding trust arrangement and which sets out the terms of the trust.

trust property The property which is held by the trustee on trust for the benefit of the beneficiaries.

trustee The person who holds the trust property for the benefit of the beneficiaries and who has a fiduciary duty to act in their best interests.

ultimate beneficial owner The individual(s) that retains a direct or indirect ownership in the assets of a financial product, service, structure or entity, howsoever the legal title is constructed.

ultra vires The doctrine of ultra vires meant that the activity of a company would be void if the company was not authorised to undertake the activity if it was not specified within the objects clause.

unearned income Unearned income includes income that is received from sources other than from employment (or a trade or profession).

veil of incorporation See 'corporate veil'.

wasting asset An asset that has a limited life and therefore decreases in value over time (e.g. a car or a factory machine).

Directory of web resources

Basel Committee on Banking Supervision
www.bis.org/bcbs

British Virgin Islands Financial Services Commission
www.bvifsc.vg

The Cheque and Credit Clearing Company Limited
www.chequeandcredit.co.uk

Companies House
www.companieshouse.gov.uk

The Financial Action Task Force (FATF)
www.fatf-gafi.org

The Group of International Finance Centre Supervisors
www.gifcs.org

Guernsey Financial Services Commission
www.gfsc.gg

HM Revenue & Customs
www.hmrc.gov.uk

Institute of Chartered Secretaries and Administrators
www.icsa.org.uk

International Association of Insurance Supervisors (IAIS)
www.iaisweb.org

International Monetary Fund (IMF)
www.imf.org

International Organization of Securities Commissions (IOSCO)
www.iosco.org

Jersey Finance Limited
www.jerseyfinance.je

Jersey Financial Services Commission
www.jerseyfsc.org

Jersey Legal Information Board
www.jerseylaw.je

The Judicial Committee of the Privy Council
www.jcpc.gov.uk

The National Archives
www.legislation.gov.uk

Organisation for Economic Co-operation and Development (OECD)
www.oecd.org

The Payments Council
www.paymentscouncil.org.uk

UK Payments Administration Limited
www.ukpayments.org.uk

Index

www.ingramcontent.com/pod-product-compliance
Ingram Content Group UK Ltd.
Pitfield, Milton Keynes, MK11 3LW, UK
UKHW051928100926
8556IPUK00022B/1439